"Egan's harrowing, meticulously reported book reveals how, for half a century, one of our most respected, most beloved entertainers got away with brazenly drugging and raping more than sixty women, abetted by prominent figures in law enforcement, the news media, and Hollywood. Although Cosby seemed to believe he was untouchable, Egan documents how he was eventually brought to justice by dogged prosecutors, some very courageous women, and the #MeToo movement."

—**Jon Krakauer**, *New York Times* bestselling author of *Into the Wild, Into Thin Air, Under the Banner of Heaven,* and *Where Men Win Glory*

"Veteran crime writer Nicki Weisensee Egan takes apart one of the first great cases of the #MeToo era with finesse and ace reporting. She brings years of up-close reportage on the Cosby case, plus dozens of new interviews with accusers and back room accounts of the endless court battles, to expose the secret life of America's Dad, a premeditated sex predator and the trail of private wreckage he inflicted for decades."

—**Nina Burleigh**, national politics correspondent at *Newsweek* and *New York Times* bestselling author of *Golden Handcuffs: The Secret History of Trump's Women*

"*Chasing Cosby* is the definitive account of a case that is a turning point in the law of sexual assault. It reads like a novel—but its lessons are very real."

—**Susan Estrich**, professor of law at the University of Southern California, nationally syndicated op-ed columnist, and bestselling author of *Sex and Power*

"Nicole Weisensee Egan's powerful, personal account of the Cosby case is a perfect cautionary tale for our time. In the middle of the #MeToo movement, this riveting look at the shattered nice-guy facade of a man once dubbed 'America's Dad' unearths a greater truth: that the celebrities and leaders we exalt on TV (and elsewhere) are not always the people we want them to be; and sometimes the truth one finds behind the curtain of a public persona is much darker than we ever want to believe."

—**Mark Dagostino**, *New York Times* bestselling co-author of *Accused: My Fight for Truth, Justice, and the Strength to Forgive*

"The power of *Chasing Cosby* flows from Nicole Weisensee Egan's steadfast resolve to ascertain the truth. Her dogged reporting and deft storytelling paints a worthy portrait of those who suffered at the hands of 'America's Dad.' Egan's work reminds us of the great price our society pays when fame protects the mighty, and what it means to not be believed."

—**Chelsia Rose Marcius**, author of *Wild Escape: The Prison Break from Dannemora* and *The Manhunt that Captured America*

"You might think you know the story of Bill Cosby's downfall. But until you've read investigative journalist Nicole Weisensee Egan's book, you don't know the whole story. Reporting on the case for more than a decade, Egan takes readers on a riveting journey documenting how numerous women came forward with horrific accounts of abuse leading to Cosby's arrest and ultimate conviction. The book is incredibly researched, compellingly written, and a must-read for anyone who followed the Cosby case or who wants to know the insider account of the unbelievable true story."

—**Shanna Hogan**, *New York Times* bestselling author of *Picture Perfect*

CHASING COSBY

CHASING COSBY

THE DOWNFALL OF AMERICA'S DAD

NICOLE WEISENSEE EGAN

SEAL PRESS

FOR THE COSBY SURVIVORS

Seal Press
1700 Fourth Street
Berkeley, California
sealpress.com

Printed in the United States of America

Published by Seal Press, an imprint of Perseus Books, LLC, a subsidiary of
Hachette Book Group, Inc. The Seal Press name and logo is a trademark
of the Hachette Book Group.

The Hachette Speakers Bureau provides a wide range of authors for speaking events.
To find out more, go to www.hachettespeakersbureau.com or call (866) 376-6591.

The publisher is not responsible for websites (or their content) that are not owned
by the publisher.

Editorial production by Christine Marra, Marrathon Production Services.
www.marrathoneditorial.org

Book design by Jane Raese
Set in 9.5 point Parable

Library of Congress Control Number: 2018968042

ISBN 978-1-58005-896-4 (hardcover); ISBN 978-1-58005-897-1 (e-book)

LSC-C

10 9 8 7 6 5 4 3 2 1

CONTENTS

PART THREE
(June 2017–September 2018)

NOTE FROM THE AUTHOR

I first began covering this story on January 20, 2005, when news of Andrea Constand's drugging and sexual assault allegations against Bill Cosby first broke in Philadelphia. After Andrea settled her civil lawsuit with Bill Cosby in November 2006, I thought the story was over. She had signed a confidentiality agreement, so she couldn't speak; there were no new accusers; and the criminal case against him had been closed long ago.

Yet for some reason I couldn't throw away my voluminous Cosby files—the notes I'd made while reporting on the case for the *Philadelphia Daily News*. One day I gathered the thousands of pages of documents, interviews, and research I'd accumulated, packed them up in a waterproof box, and carried it down to my basement. And that's where they stayed for another eight years.

When the case resurfaced in late 2014 and the number of new accusers kept climbing, I walked down to my basement, opened that waterproof box, lugged all of those files back up to my home office, and dug back into the story. Those notes and emails were so helpful when it came to recreating what happened in 2005, when I was the lone reporter investigating the allegations against Cosby. Anything I use in this book from 2005 that is in quotations is from those notes, my published stories, or from conversations in which I was a participant, except where I explain otherwise in my notes section at the end of the book, where I cite the sources I used, including ones I don't mention in the text.

In some instances, like with the details of what happened to Andrea in the first chapter, I've woven in details about the case I learned more than a decade later from court documents, courtroom testimony, official court transcripts, victim impact statements, depositions in her civil lawsuit, police reports, police interviews, and my own interviews. For my *People* coverage I used the reporting that is publicly available in stories in the magazine and online. For the rest of the book I relied on my own reporting from the court proceedings I attended, documents in the criminal and civil cases, articles from other journalists whose work I respect, interviews I conducted myself with more than seventy people, and, when necessary, videos of the impromptu press conferences held by Cosby's spokespeople outside the courthouse during both trials.

I struggled with how to refer to people on second reference. In some cases, just using their last name seemed too formal. In the end, we decided that we'd use last names for everyone except the victims and their families and Cosby's immediate family.

Some who helped me can't be named, but I am deeply grateful to them for helping to ensure this book is accurate. Andrea and her family could not speak to me due to the confidentiality agreement they signed with Cosby when she settled her lawsuit with him. Cosby; his attorney at the time, Marty Singer; and America Media, Inc., which owns the *National Enquirer*, were similarly barred from speaking about the case due to the same confidentiality agreement. I still reached out to them and everyone else I could for fact checking or comment. Cosby, through his spokesman, declined to participate. Others simply never responded. If they did get back to me, I included their response or mentioned them in my notes section.

This has been a thorough investigation over the years. The full extent of the material sourced here is at the end of my book, in the List of Sources and Notes sections. I encourage the reader to read everything listed in the sources as well as the notes for each chapter at the end of the book.

Although I have included allegations from many different women in this book, only Andrea's has resulted in a criminal case and conviction. However, their accounts are in statements to law enforcement, court filings and/or testimony related to civil and criminal court proceedings or have appeared in other media.

Cosby has denied Andrea's drugging and sexual assault allegations as well as similar allegations against him from more than sixty other women, including those whose stories are told in this book, except where noted in the text. Cosby is currently incarcerated while appealing his conviction and his prison sentence.

INTRODUCTION:
COSBY'S GIFT

One Friday night not long ago I was flipping through channels on my television when I came across a rerun of *The Cosby Show*. There on my screen was the loveable, sweater-clad Dr. Cliff Huxtable, sitting between his son, Theo, and his wife, Claire, in a learning specialist's office. Theo had done poorly on a Greek mythology test that week, even though he knew the material, so all three were meeting with the specialist, who thought Theo should be tested for dyslexia. If Theo does indeed have it, she assured the Huxtables, he could get help to overcome the learning disorder.

"Dyslexia!" Cliff says with a relieved smile on his face, gratified to know why his son was struggling in school. "Now fix it!" he quips, jubilant. Cue the laugh track.

Like millions of other Americans who helped make the comedy one of the most popular shows in the history of television, I became a fan of *The Cosby Show* when it first aired in the 1980s. It debuted my senior year of high school, the same year my older brother died, and watching the show gave me an escape out of my own, fraught home and into the cozy normalcy of a family not traumatized by death. For me the Huxtables were a thirty-minute visit to a warm and stable world, where the kids would borrow each other's clothes without permission and sneak out to concerts, all while the parents lovingly guided them with witty life lessons. My own mother was nearly paralyzed with grief over the loss of her only son, and my father had all he could do to hold her together while juggling the demands of a job that took him out of town two or three nights a week. *The Cosby Show* was steady. *The Cosby Show* made me feel safe.

Watching the show again brought me back for a moment to that time in my life, and I mean that in a good way. Cliff Huxtable's tough-love parenting style, sprinkled with humor, also reminded me of my own father. And this episode was particularly tender—it revealed a dad who worried for his son while at the same time acknowledging his own flaws as a parent. When Theo tells his parents he is indeed dyslexic, Cliff and Claire erupt in cheers.

What I also appreciated, though I didn't know it when I was a teenager, was that the show was never overly saccharine—funny, yes, but not hyper-sentimentalized. In this episode Vanessa chastises Cliff for calling Theo "lazy" all those years when it was really dyslexia holding him back, and Cliff doesn't laugh her off; he knows she's right. Then, when Theo later proudly reveals he got a B-plus on his next test, Cliff couldn't be prouder. "I think he should probably finish undergraduate school in two years because there's no sense in holding him back in going to medical school and becoming what? Dr. Huxtable Jr.!"

"Theo's Gift" had heart, intelligence, and humor, a recipe that was the show's hallmark. It was real and familiar. I'd watched my own father and brother engage in similar battles throughout my childhood—although, unlike Cliff and Theo, they were never able to resolve their issues before my brother's death. When Bill Cosby's son died young too, I couldn't help but feel an emotional connection to him—his love for his family, the grief he must have felt. I mourned with him.

That night, watching the rerun while my husband, used to my fascination with Cosby by now, read a book, I found myself mesmerized, laughing along with the jokes, smiling at the warm-hearted moments. And horrified too. Because now, all these years later, I knew that the Bill Cosby on my screen—with his dad jokes and self-deprecating style of imparting wisdom to his kids, the man who left an entire generation wishing he was their father—was also a monster.

A monster who preyed on women, manipulating them into a false sense of security, drugging them, and assaulting them. And masquerading as Cliff Huxtable—the personification of the family-oriented, warm comedy he'd been performing for decades—was the perfect disguise.

For nearly half a century, enabled by a cadre of paid handlers and silencers who did their jobs protecting his carefully honed image, Bill Cosby drugged and sexually assaulted women who thought he was their mentor. He slowly and carefully coaxed each one into feeling safe and cared for and then left them to pick up the pieces of their lives.

I WAS STILL A believer in the Bill Cosby/Cliff Huxtable myth in 2005, when Andrea Constand first told the police what Cosby had done to her. I was working as a reporter for the *Philadelphia Daily News*, a tabloid-style daily that was part of the Knight-Ridder newspaper chain, when I first heard that a woman had accused Cosby of drugging and sexually assaulting her. Along with the rest of America, I was shocked. And itching to disbelieve. *Not the Cos!* I thought. But then my boss assigned me the story, and I began reporting.

I made calls. I asked questions. I read files.

I grew more and more astounded.

With every conversation, every interview, every new source, the validity of the charges came to light. The women who spoke out were credible. Crimes had been committed, and it didn't matter that the perpetrator was one of America's most beloved cultural icons. The truth had to be revealed.

So I wrote about the case. I wrote and wrote—about Andrea Constand, the court filings, the evidence, the other accusers. The more I wrote about the case, the more the story spread and other news outlets picked it up and broadcast the details I'd reported.

I was thrilled to see my stories go out on Knight-Ridder's wire service. But Cosby, obviously, was not. It wasn't long before Cosby's attorney, Marty Singer, threatened to sue my newspaper. Then the prosecutor on the case made veiled threats to have me arrested.

Meanwhile other media outlets were stepping away from the scandal. Maybe they were too skeptical, I surmised at the time. Or maybe they were too afraid. Cosby had always had an uneasy, often adversarial relationship with the press, and few were eager to take him on. "Newspaper columnists have been . . . reluctant to join the fray," wrote Tony Norman, a columnist for the *Pittsburgh Post-Gazette*. "Who can blame us? Nobody wants to incur the wrath of Cos over what may turn out to be a frivolous charge."

But I couldn't give it up. I believed Andrea. And the lies that I believed Cosby's attorneys were telling about her infuriated me. Cosby's power and influence may have swayed other reporters and editors, but my editors supported me as I dug deeper into the research and the slowly unfolding truth: while Cosby was enjoying the adoration of a public who loved his down-to-earth, no-profanity comedy routines, television shows, and Jell-O pudding pop commercials, cementing his image as America's Dad, he was also leading a dark, secret life cultivating friendships with young women by promising them mentorship and connections and then waiting until they felt secure to drug and violate them.

BILL COSBY CHOSE his victims carefully, with the instincts of a predator. He chose young, vulnerable, star-struck women, many of them budding actresses, models, and singers, all of them in less powerful positions than him, blinded by his squeaky-clean reputation, and whom, he knew, would not be believed should they come forward with their tales of mentorship and betrayal run amok.

He used the same technique, over and over again.

First, he'd befriend a young woman he'd met either through their agent or by chance. She might be an aspiring model or actress or just a pretty young woman dazzled by his attention and confident he was who he seemed to be. His status as a beloved celebrity created instant trust.

He'd ask them about their lives and offer advice, auditions, and help with their careers. He might even meet their mom, flattering her with praise for her children or inviting her to a performance at which he'd roll out the red carpet with backstage passes and premium seats and pose for a picture or two. Perhaps he'd come to a family dinner, praising the home-cooked meals of a hardworking grandmother and bringing ice cream to offer the children. And Jell-O pudding pops.

Then, when the time was right, he'd entice them into an environment he controlled—a hotel room, his dressing room, his own house, or even a friend's home that he was borrowing—and he'd slip a drug into a drink or offer "cold medicine." Several hours, a day, or even two days later the woman would wake up, bruised and disoriented, with her clothes off and a strange sense that violence had been done.

Andrea Constand was the first to publicly accuse Cosby of both drugging and sexually assaulting her, but soon after, thirteen other women came forward with similar stories. They were drugged and then assaulted or he tried to drug or assault them. All of them said

Bill Cosby—that lovable, wholesome father figure—was a not who we thought he was. They were the original #MeToo women, long before there was a movement, speaking out to support Andrea by calling out their own truth against a powerful, wealthy, influential man.

These years of reporting on Bill Cosby's crimes have taught me the dangers of deifying celebrities. We don't know who they truly are; we see only what they allow us to see. Their images are carefully managed. The peeks and glimpses we get through interviews they give are so well orchestrated that we never realize there is a man (or woman) behind the curtain, pulling the strings.

It's not just celebrities, though. We assume someone is a good person just because they excel in one area, a cognitive bias called the "halo effect." We thought O. J. Simpson was a good person because he was a football star, refusing to believe he was capable of the type of violence his wife, Nicole, reported. We assumed former Penn State defensive coach Jerry Sandusky was a saint because he adopted foster children and founded a charity for at-risk boys, never suspecting it was merely a façade he created and cultivated to cover up his sexual abuse of young boys. The same goes for Catholic priests, Boy Scout leaders, gymnastics team doctors, and others who used their positions of trust in the community to get away with unspeakable crimes for years on end.

And for Bill Cosby.

WHEN ANDREA FIRST spoke out, Cosby was one of the most famous and powerful entertainers in the country, if not the world. His long, seemingly happy marriage to Camille, the mother of their five children, only added luster to his picture-perfect image as a devoted husband and father. He counted South African president Nelson Mandela and civil rights pioneers Jesse Jackson and Al Sharpton among his friends. He cherished his role as a humanitarian and educational philanthropist, donating millions to charities and colleges alike while chalking up numerous awards, including the Kennedy Center Honors for lifetime achievement in the performing arts and the Presidential Medal of Freedom. Nearly sixty colleges and universities across the country had showered him with honorary degrees. (Many of these awards and more than half of these degrees would later be stripped from him, one by one.)

He broke cultural and racial barriers, becoming the first African American to costar in a TV show with his first role in *I Spy*, for which he won three Emmys. He'd written best-selling books about parenthood, and he based much of his Grammy Award–winning comedy routine—later used to develop *The Cosby Show*—on his folksy, relatable experiences as a father and husband. His fame—and wealth—continued to grow as he became the pitchman for products such as Jell-O and Coca-Cola. "The three most believable personalities are God, Walter Cronkite, and Bill Cosby," Anthony Tortorici, Coke's PR chief, told *Black Enterprise* magazine in 1981.

And Andrea's allegations in 2005 did little to tarnish the public perception of him. He was inducted into the NAACP Image Awards Hall of Fame in 2006 and, in 2010, awarded the National Football Foundation's gold medal, which each year recognizes "outstanding Americans" for their "honesty and integrity." He was honored with the Mark Twain Prize for American Humor in 2009 and the Johnny Carson Award for Comedic Excellence in 2014 and was made an honorary chief petty officer by the US Navy, which he'd served in from 1956 to 1960, in 2011.

He had amassed a mountain of accolades.

Maybe that's why the rest of the media didn't seem to want to believe the drugging and sexual assault accusations.

Honestly, at first, neither did I.

But I saw there was another truth.

I became as determined as ever to find out new information or get interviews no one else had. The crime itself was just so chilling, the method so diabolical. These women were powerless. They couldn't fend him off, let alone walk away—the drugs he gave them made that impossible. And no one seemed to realize how dangerous it is to give someone a drug without their knowledge or consent. What if they were allergic to it or it interacted badly with another intoxicant or drug in their system? What if they got into a car and drove after being drugged and got into an accident? Someone could have died.

During my journey I have wrestled with so many questions about Bill Cosby, and I still do: Who is he as a human being, really? How could someone who's done so much good in this world do so much evil at the same time?

As a journalist, I wanted the details. I wanted facts and answers. Instead of seducing women, the way most "casting couch" Hollywood stars might, why did Cosby drug them? Could he be a somnophiliac—someone who can only have sex with an unconscious person?

How many people in Hollywood knew what Cosby was doing and stayed quiet? And why? Are there other victims who have not yet come forward? How many—six more? Sixty? Why did this scandal take hold in 2014 but not in 2005?

And as a woman in America, I also have questions about the culture we live in. Why is there a visceral distrust of sexual assault claims—from the public, the media, and the criminal justice system—unlike any other violent crime?

I explore all these questions in *Chasing Cosby* and offer my reflections as well on how fear, bullying, and intimidation helped silence these women, as we've seen play out in countless other examples of powerful men who were able to keep their sexual misconduct secret for decades.

The Cosby story is a lens through which we can look inward at our own beliefs and prejudices and how it influences who we choose to believe and why, who we choose to idolize and why.

Ultimately, though, this is a David-and-Goliath–like tale of courage; of one woman who stood up to her attacker; of her mother, whose fierce love for her daughter transcended her fear of confronting a beloved national icon; of her attorneys, whose two-woman firm proved to be more than a match for some of the biggest sharks in the legal world; and of the prosecutors, who finally listened to what all of them had to say and arrested America's Dad.

But first let me take you back to January 2005, when it all began.

PART ONE

(JANUARY 2005–OCTOBER 2014)

You took a little drop, and you put it in a drink . . .
the girl would drink it . . . and hello, America!

—Bill Cosby to Larry King, 1991

CHAPTER ONE

POUND CAKE AND POLICE REPORTS

On the morning of January 13, 2005, thirty-one-year-old Andrea Constand woke up sobbing from a nightmare. Horrifying, violent dreams had plagued her for the past year, and they were growing worse. Sometimes they made her scream out so loudly that her parents could hear her from their bedroom. Other times she woke up sweating, shaken. This time her dream was so frightening that she phoned her mother, Gianna.

Gianna was on her way to work when her cell phone rang, and she answered it right away. She had been worried about her youngest daughter since she had moved back home from Philadelphia the previous April to enroll in massage school and become a massage therapist, like her father. She'd returned home a different person. "I knew something was wrong, but I could not put my finger on it," Gianna said.

That morning, though, Andrea was finally ready to tell her mom what had been tormenting her. She'd been learning about physical boundaries in massage school, and the lessons had triggered something in her subconscious that she could no longer avoid. In her dreams she watched a woman being sexually assaulted in front of her, and it was all her fault. She was consumed with guilt that spilled over into her waking hours, terrified that other women were being similarly violated because she hadn't spoken out.

Until that day Andrea had told no one about the night when a friend of hers—an older man who had become a father figure and, really, a mentor—had betrayed her in the most horrific way possible.

But now it was time. Lying in bed with her tears still wet on her face, she picked up the phone and called her mother, who was driving to the doctor's office where she worked as a medical secretary.

"Mom, I think I have PTSD," she burst out. Then she went on to say Bill Cosby drugged and raped her.

Gianna froze, then began to shake. She knew the famous entertainer had mentored Andrea when she was working as the director of operations for the women's basketball team at Temple University. He sat on the board of trustees and was one of its most famous alumni, and Andrea had met him on campus. Cosby had taken her under his wing, inviting her to dinners with high-powered educators and out to concerts and other events, making her feel at home in a strange city, far away from her family and friends.

Gianna had met Cosby too. A couple of years before, Cosby had gotten tickets for Gianna and her older daughter, Diana, to see him perform in Toronto. They all took photos after the show, grinning for the camera. Cosby had been charming and avuncular to both as Gianna and Diana thanked him for the tickets.

But Gianna knew her daughter was telling the truth. She was so distraught about what Andrea was saying that she feared she'd get in a car accident if they kept talking while she was driving, so she asked Andrea if she could call her back once she got to work.

Andrea was insistent. It was as if she'd waited this long to tell the truth, and now that she had, she couldn't stop. "Mom, you've got to hear me out," she said. Then she said it again: Bill Cosby drugged and raped me.

THAT SENTENCE SET OFF a chain reaction of events that would change her life, her family's lives, and, most irrevocably, that of the man she had just accused.

Cosby, then sixty-seven, was a beloved national father figure. He was one of the most powerful men in Hollywood and in his native Philadelphia, which reveled in being able to claim America's Dad as one of their own. Andrea was terrified at the thought of reporting the crime to police, but she knew she had to. She didn't want what had happened to her to happen to anyone else.

That day Andrea started calling lawyers.

"I was really scared, and I wanted to protect myself," she said. "I didn't know where to turn. I had a lot of questions. And then I thought that Mr. Cosby"—she always called him Mr. Cosby—"would retaliate against me, that he would try to hurt my family."

After Gianna got home that evening, together they called the Durham Regional Police Department near Toronto, Ontario, where they lived. The following day the case was referred to the Philadelphia Police Department, erroneously believing that's where Cosby lived. Four days later the case was assigned to Detective Richard Schaffer of the Cheltenham Township Police Department, which covered Elkins Park, just outside of Philadelphia, where Cosby owned a mansion—and where Andrea's sexual assault had occurred.

That week was a surreal one for Andrea. While she was conferring with lawyers and making phone calls to law enforcement, a police source tipped off Harry Hairston, an investigative reporter for Philadelphia's Channel 10, the NBC affiliate. The allegations against the entertainer broke on Channel 10's five o'clock evening newscast on Thursday, January 20, and soon the world learned that a Temple University employee had accused Bill Cosby of groping her. The details were sketchy at first—the drugging part not so clear in that first story.

I was just starting to wrap up for the day at the *Philadelphia Daily News* when the news hit the airwaves and my boss assigned me the story. I'd been a crime investigative reporter for fourteen years and had a good head start on some of the angles I'd need to probe: in 2002, I'd written an exposé on the resurgence of drug-facilitated sexual assaults at some of the nightclubs in Philadelphia and had been horrified by what I'd discovered. Not only is it premeditated rape, in my opinion, it's also the perfect crime. The drugs predators use wipe out the victim's resistance and memory and move swiftly through their systems so that by the time they regain consciousness, it might already be too late to go to a hospital to get their blood and urine tested.

The story hit home in another way as well. Not long ago I'd been one of those women dancing the night away at a club on Philadelphia's Delaware Avenue, never suspecting that someone could easily slip a drug into my drink that would leave me helpless to defend myself.

I couldn't believe I was now looking into similar allegations about America's Dad. Few details about the case were being released, including the alleged victim's name, which is the norm in such cases. I needed to somehow find out all I could about her to figure out if she was credible. No one in law enforcement was talking, but thankfully I had sources at Temple who were able to fill in some blanks, including supplying me with her name, though I didn't publish it until we had her permission, which is the usual media policy with sexual assault victims—though that would quickly change with this case.

Andrea had a stellar reputation at Temple, where she'd worked as the director of operations for the women's basketball team from late 2001 through March 2004. "She's straight up, stable, smart, and hard-working," a former colleague said. "She's very level headed, very professional."

With her long, curly, reddish-brown hair and statuesque physique, standing six feet tall, Andrea was strikingly attractive. A former high school and college basketball star who'd once dreamed of playing for the pros, Andrea had been recruited for the job by Dawn Staley, the Temple women's coach, who was also a close friend of Cosby.

Staley had a huge, framed photo of her and Cosby on the Temple basketball court, signed by Cosby himself, hanging in the waiting room of her office, and Cosby had dedicated the screening of his movie *Fat Albert* to Staley at its world premiere. Inside the back cover of Temple's women's basketball media guide is a photo of a laughing Cosby sitting next to a beaming Staley. "Staley has 'Cos' to laugh" is the caption. There is also a photo of Cosby with an owl, the school's mascot, and the caption, "Temple's most famous alum, Bill Cosby, is a frequent visitor to the Liacouras Center," where the women's basketball games were played.

Cosby had generously made commercials for Comcast Cable to promote the women's team, and he would regularly show up unannounced at women's games. Part of Andrea's job was building the team's profile in the media, and who better to help with that than the Cos himself?

ANDREA HAD NO criminal record of any kind, and the only news clippings I found about her were of her illustrious basketball career. In fact, she was one of the top female basketball players in Canada while she was in high school.

"You see players who have savvy, can shoot, or play defense. She's got it all and is the most complete player we've ever had," said Bryan Pardo, her high school coach.

Her stellar performance at basketball training camps and tournaments caught the eye of fifty or so coaches in America who actively recruited her, including the University of Connecticut, Michigan, Cincinnati, and UNC-Charlotte. U-Conn, which was ranked seventeenth preseason at the time after making it to the NCAA Final Four the previous March, really wanted her.

"Everyone in the United States knew about her," Joan Bonvicini, the head coach for Arizona's women's basketball team, told me. "We recruited her pretty hard."

After many sleepless nights weighing the pros and cons of each of the schools, Andrea chose Arizona, which offered her a full scholarship worth about $80,000. Arizona had an abysmal 6–25 record, but she hit it off with the coach and liked the players, who made her feel at home.

Andrea was excited to begin her new life in Arizona. "The school is beautiful, and you can't go wrong with the climate," she told reporters at the time. "I like the intensity down there. . . . I have a big desire to win and the intense basketball [in the United States] is where I want to be. I'm mentally and physically prepared."

Andrea, a guard forward, was popular both on and off the court, Bonvicini said. She didn't want to comment on Andrea's allegations but did tell the Associated Press, "She's always been honest and upstanding. . . . I've never known her to lie." Andrea had the same reputation at Temple. "She was serious about her career and serious about her sport," the former colleague told me. "She was always trying to do what was best for the team."

Andrea and Cosby's friendship began about a year after she arrived at Temple in December 2001. After a donor introduced them at a women's basketball game, they struck up an amiable rapport. While she viewed him as a grandfather figure—he was more than double her age—he would later say he had his eye on a romantic relationship with her from the start. But Andrea, who was involved with a woman at the time, was clueless. To her, Cosby was a genial, generous mentor, a gentle adviser who encouraged her to pursue a career in sports broadcasting, even suggesting she straighten her hair and paying for her to get a professional headshot done.

Over the next fourteen months their friendship deepened, and one day, while pondering a life change, Andrea reached out to Cosby. She wanted to quit her job and enroll in massage school to become a massage therapist like her father, Andy, but she was nervous about how to tell her boss. So she went to her friend and mentor for advice. At first they spoke on the phone, and then he invited her to his home to talk more that evening. A few hours later Andrea headed over, relieved. Cosby was someone she could confide in as she began heading toward yet another crossroads in her professional life.

There was nothing unusual about his invitation to his mansion in January 2004 to discuss her career. Except for how it ended.

COSBY WAS IN the middle of a crossroads of his own when Andrea went to police a year later. He'd recently embarked on an ambitious series of town halls, hosting and financing gatherings in inner cities across the nation to talk about the problems in poor, black communities. He was committed to the cause, but he had managed to stir up a controversy and was dealing with a backlash against some of his messages about race and poverty.

Yet he had good reason to believe he was the perfect messenger for this particular message. Cosby was a self-made man who had risen from the humblest of beginnings in Philadelphia. His mother worked twelve hours a day as a cleaning lady to support the family, while his father, an alcoholic, flitted from job to job before finally enrolling in the Navy when Cosby was young. From then on, his father was a rare presence in his family's life, coming home only for brief periods of time while serving three tours of duty.

His father's transgressions left a heavy imprint on Cosby's life, imbuing in him a lifelong aversion to alcohol. He claims he tried it just once: when he was a teen a friend offered him a beer, and he took three sips, then refused to drink the rest, unnerved by the slight loss of control he felt. Drugs were something he said he avoided altogether, saying he was offered a hit of marijuana at a party when he was a teen but declined, turned off by the "weird odor."

Cosby spent part of his childhood in a North Philadelphia housing project, with the roar of nearby trains rattling the floors of their two-bedroom apartment day and night. Still, with hot water and a bathroom with a tub, it was among the nicer places his family lived while he was growing up. Though short on money, Anna Cosby wanted the best for her four sons, trying to instill in them a passion for education. Yet throughout his young life Cosby struggled in school, more comfortable being the class clown than the class valedictorian, more likely to play sports and chase girls in his free time instead of doing his homework.

For all of his emphasis on education in his later years, Cosby was never a star student himself. He dropped out of high school his junior year and got a job working at a shoe repair store before finally enlisting in the Navy to try to figure out what to do with the rest of his life. By the time his tour of duty was up, he was twenty-three years old and ready to apply himself. He'd earned his high school equivalency degree while in the Navy, so now he just had to figure out how to pay for college. He ended up getting a track scholarship to Temple University and began bartending on the side for spending money. It was there his ability to weave a funny tale finally began to pay off.

Cosby began honing his skills as a comic, trying out his new routines on his customers. He was so good at it that his boss offered him an extra five dollars a night to sit at the end of the bar and tell jokes to the entire room. From there it was onward and upward, with a summer stint at the Gaslight Café in New York City's Greenwich Village, where he caught the attention of a prominent agent who signed him as a client.

He quickly learned to avoid any racial discussion in his routines, stung by a review in the *New York Times* in June 1962 with the headline "Philadelphia Negro Aims His Barbs at Race Relations" that opened with a line saying he was "hurling verbal spears at the relations between whites and Negroes."

It was the beginning of his long, often hostile relationship with the press.

In the end it was too hard to juggle college and a burgeoning career as a stand-up comic, so Cosby dropped out of Temple and began his meteoric rise to fame, performing all over the country while turning those same routines into best-selling albums and books. On a two-week stint in Washington, DC, he met and fell in love with Camille

Hanks, marrying her in January 1964. As he seamlessly transitioned to television stardom and success as a product pitchman, there was never a hint of anything unseemly in his personal life.

Perhaps there were clues along the way that we missed, though. It seems clear that being in control was important to Cosby. After all, he didn't like even the smallest loss of control he felt from just three sips of beer, a miniscule amount by anyone's standards. One of his most famous routines involves a childhood quest to find the "Spanish Fly," an aphrodisiac that would render a woman helpless with just a couple of drugs slipped into her drink. He spoke of it in a best-selling album in 1969 and a best-selling book in 1991. But nobody thought much of it then; certainly nobody thought it should keep him from becoming an antidrug crusader in the early 1970s with an album for kids warning about the dangers of doing drugs.

But it all helps to explain why at first it was so hard to believe Andrea's accusations. She was accusing him of not only sexually assaulting her but also drugging her beforehand. Sure, Cosby's life wasn't entirely free of scandal—it was widely acknowledged that he'd had an affair and a possible love child. But when those particular secrets erupted, they came on the heels of the 1997 murder of Cosby's only son, Ennis, and the scandal didn't leave a mark on him.

So there was certainly no reason to question Cosby's seemingly earnest intentions for embarking on his crusade for accountability within the black community. He began hosting the inner-city town halls after a now-infamous speech he gave in Washington, DC, in May 2004. Cosby was in the capital for a joint event by the NAACP and Howard University to celebrate the fiftieth anniversary of the *Brown vs. Board of Education* US Supreme Court decision, which ended segregation in America's schools, where he would receive an award for educational philanthropy.

As he waited to take the stage, he couldn't get out of his head that the "heroes of the landmark decision" would be horrified at what was currently happening in parts of black America. So he decided to speak up that very evening.

After graciously accepting the award, Cosby compared the youth of the day getting arrested for minor infractions, like "stealing a pound cake," to the civil rights heroes of the 1950s and 1960s, who went to jail for a cause: "Ladies and gentlemen, these people, they opened the doors, they gave us the right, and today, in our cities and public schools we have fifty percent dropout rates," he told the audience. "In our own neighborhoods, we have men in prison." He continued,

> No longer is a person embarrassed because they're pregnant without a husband. No longer is a boy considered an embarrassment if he tries to run away from being the father of a child. . . . In the neighborhoods that most of us grew up in, parenting is not going on. . . . Those of us sitting out here who have gone on to some college or whatever we've done, we still fear our parents. And these people are not parenting. They're buying things for the kid: Five-hundred-dollar sneakers—for what? They won't buy or spend two hundred fifty dollars on Hooked on Phonics! Looking at the incarcerated—these are not political criminals! These are people going around stealing Coca-Cola! People getting shot in the head over a piece of pound cake! Then we all run out and are outraged, "The cops shouldn't have shot him!" What the hell was he doing with the pound cake in his hand? I wanted a piece of pound cake just as bad as anybody else. And I looked at it, and I had no money! And something called parenting said, *If you get caught with it, you're going to embarrass your mother.* Not *you're going to get your butt kicked.* No. *You're going to embarrass your mother.*

He railed and fumed at the way black youth dressed—with their "hat on backwards, pants down around the crack"—and spoke, mocking them for having names like "Shaniqua, Shaligua, Mohammed, and all that crap." As stories of his speech made their rounds, this quickly became known as the "pound cake speech," and the outrage from the African American community came fast and hard. Cosby was accused of blaming the poor, prompting him to clarify his remarks. He released a public statement a couple of weeks later explaining that he wanted his comments to be a call to action for African Americans to "turn the mirror around on ourselves."

Instead, he found that mirror shining on him. And by the most unlikely of people.

CHAPTER TWO

A WONDERFUL SENSE OF HUMOR

While Cosby was doing his best to live down the pound cake speech, Andrea was hiring lawyers.

After talking to a couple of attorneys, Andrea hired Dolores Troiani and Bebe Kivitz, former prosecutors and now partners in a four-year-old, two-person law firm in Devon, on the outskirts of Philadelphia's tony Main Line. Troiani and Kivitz were not high-profile power brokers or even particularly media savvy. But Andrea trusted them, and they took the case for one simple reason.

"We believed her," Troiani said. "From the very beginning we knew she was going to be such a powerful witness."

Troiani and Kivitz were good at their jobs. More than twenty years as prosecutors meant that, between them, they'd seen it all—from white-collar crimes to gritty street murders. Kivitz was five-foot-six, with shoulder-length auburn hair and friendly green eyes. Soft spoken and diplomatic, it was easy to see why a client would feel safe in her counsel. Troiani was five-foot-one, with short, closely cropped, dark brown hair and was both outspoken and fearless, exactly who you want in your corner when you are taking on one of the country's most powerful men. Troiani had a reputation for rarely negotiating plea deals when she was a prosecutor, and I believed it. The two women had become friends while working at the Philadelphia district attorney's office and decided it was time to go out on their own when they partnered up in 2001.

They were a small firm going up against some of the most powerful legal giants in the country, all of them male. But they were both tough. They had been going after criminals of all kinds for decades and were not at all intimidated by a Hollywood funnyman and snack salesman.

Troiani dealt with the media for the most part, while Kivitz was the liaison with the Montgomery County district attorney's office, which was overseeing the investigation, working in tandem with the Cheltenham township police.

Cosby turned to an equally low-key but well-respected lawyer to represent him. Philadelphia attorney Walter Phillips Jr., a former city prosecutor and state special prosecutor, had been appointed by Governor Ed Rendell to chair the state's Commission on Crime and Delinquency. Phillips battled mobsters and corrupt politicians throughout his career, building his reputation as an "anticorruption scourge," as the *Philadelphia Inquirer* called him.

Phillips was rarely on the defense side of things, but as Cosby's lawyer, he came out of the gate firing hard, and he went straight for Andrea. "The allegation as I understand it is utterly preposterous and bizarre, coming one year after it was supposed to take place," he told reporters.

The Associated Press's first story was dismissive too: "The attorney hired to defend comedian Bill Cosby from allegations he fondled a female acquaintance questioned Friday why the woman took a year to come forward."

Even the School District of Philadelphia weighed in with a supportive statement, saying Cosby "is a hero to our many students and communities. Dr. Cosby regularly donates, free of charge, his time and talent to develop programming for PSTV, the District's cable television station, that educates, entertains and inspires . . . we are immensely grateful."

Cosby's family, unsurprisingly, was indignant on his behalf. Cosby's uncle, Thornhill Cosby, who once headed the Philadelphia NAACP, passionately supported his nephew. "I don't believe any of it," he said. "Why does that woman wait for a whole year to come forward?"

Despite the support that came from within and outside his hometown, Cosby postponed some upcoming town halls he had scheduled while the case continued to unfold.

"He just didn't feel right about appearing on a public stage these days when these allegations are out there, and there's been so much media coverage of it," Phillips said of the postponements when I called him to ask. But Cosby, he assured me, was holding up well. "He's got such a wonderful sense of humor that it still comes through when you talk to him," he observed. Then he added, "but he's obviously very much down and upset by what has transpired over the last few days."

That may have been true, but it was nothing like what Andrea was going through.

WHILE COSBY HAD an entire cadre of paid handlers to deal with every aspect of this crisis and enhanced security at each of his homes—some even had gates—Andrea was on her own and quickly found herself besieged. Reporters staked out her home, ambushing her and her parents. A *National Enquirer* reporter, posing as a flower deliveryman, arrived on her doorstep, drew a few comments out of Andrea, and then trumpeted it as an exclusive interview on the cover. "I know what he did. He knows what he did," she said, according to the paper, which did not use her name. "But everything will come to light and the truth will be known."

Andrea's parents were the victims of media trickery as well. They were on their way out the door when a man approached them outside their home, chatting with them about Andrea as if he was a friend. They were shocked when they saw their comments in their local newspaper, the *Toronto Sun*, the following day explaining that Cosby had for a long time been "a great friend and mentor." Gianna said that Andrea had "enjoyed his friendship, his humor and his spirit . . . She shared her thoughts with him and he guided her ideas and gave her words of wisdom." Her father described Andrea as truthful and honest, saying she wasn't one to lie.

Though the comments they made did little damage, they quickly learned their lesson, and it was the one and only "interview" they gave. Both told the reporter they noticed a change in Andrea after she moved back home from Philadelphia in April 2004. "We knew something was going on, but we didn't know what it was," her father, Andy, said.

Criticism of Andrea had already begun to surface, with one celebrity journalist openly speculating on CNN about whether her allegations were motivated by money—a claim often directed at women who accuse wealthy men of sexual misconduct and one Marty Singer would shortly be making to the media.

Andrea's father was outraged at the insinuations. "We live a good life. I have a nice house. I have four cars," he said. "We're not in it for the money. Justice has to be served."

And then came the turning point, though no one recognized it at the time. Nine days after Andrea first spoke to police, the *Sun* ran the "interview" with Andrea's parents about the case, accompanied by a photo of Andrea and including her name, even though Andrea had not given her permission and had not even spoken with them, and her parents had not knowingly granted an interview with a reporter.

Until this moment she had been anonymous, her role in the Cosby scandal relatively private. Now there was no stopping the chain reaction, and it wasn't long before other news organizations began doing the same.

This in itself was more than an egregious error; it was a transgression that should never happen. Sexual assault victims are given this anonymity, this extra level of protection that other crime victims don't have, for a reason: they are less likely to be believed and more likely to be the targets of retaliation and backlash, especially in high-profile cases.

And, of course, when the accused is a beloved national icon. Kristen Houser, spokesperson for the National Sexual Violence Resource Center, said, "Personal safety becomes a huge factor," she said. "We've seen people harassed at home, on social media. Some even receive death threats."

Andrea was now the one being attacked, instead of the man she accused. And she couldn't say a word in her own defense.

CHAPTER THREE

WE DON'T PUNISH PEOPLE
FOR MAKING MISTAKES

Bruce L. Castor Jr., as he insisted on being referred to in the media to differentiate himself from his powerful Philadelphia attorney father bearing the same moniker, had been Montgomery County's district attorney for five years when Andrea's case reached his desk. Because the county included Philadelphia's wealthy Main Line, he'd had a number of high-profile cases, so he was a familiar figure to local reporters, including me.

Over the years Castor had successfully prosecuted Caleb Fairley, a troubled twenty-one-year-old who killed a young mother and her son after they wandered into his parents' Collegeville, Pennsylvania, children's clothing store, as well as Ponzi schemer Craig Rabinowitz, who murdered his wife and tried to make it look like an accidental bathtub drowning to collect on her life insurance policy and use it to pay off the pyramid scheme he'd created to finance his affair with a stripper named Summer.

Castor had even managed to get a conviction in the General Wayne Inn murder, a case he built on circumstantial evidence. Investigators never found the actual murder weapon, instead using the imprint of a gun in the suspect's holster to prove he once owned a gun that matched the bullet found in the victim's head.

All of these crimes became gripping books or television shows, featuring Castor as the hard-hitting DA. An aggressive, telegenic, confident prosecutor who thrived on publicity even as he developed a reputation for being arrogant and aloof, Castor cultivated media coverage, holding press conferences at the drop of a hat.

When the Cosby investigation began, Castor had just lost a bid to become the Republican nominee for attorney general in a contentious primary, in which his opponent raised questions about $600,000 in campaign donations from former US Transportation secretary

Drew Lewis and his wife. There was nothing illegal about the contribution, but Lewis was Castor's friend and neighbor and had been prosecuted by Castor's office for a second DUI in 2001 and landed in a cushy rehab center instead of prison. Castor also came under attack for not referring the case to the state attorney general's office because Lewis was a friend. Castor insisted he'd done nothing wrong, but was beaten by his opponent, Tom Corbett, who later went on to become governor. Despite this crushing loss and his battles with the leadership of his party, he hadn't yet abandoned his hopes of one day holding a higher office.

No one could deny, however, that Castor was a tough, law-and-order prosecutor unafraid to take on difficult cases. Just five years prior his office had arrested Pennsylvania state trooper Michael Evans for preying on teenage girls and women he met on duty, using the power of his badge to force them to perform sexual favors or watch him fondle himself.

"He used his uniform as a disguise . . . to operate as a predator," said Risa Vetri Ferman, Castor's first assistant, who handled the case. "All of these women were in vulnerable situations. All of them called for help and he was the person who came in response."

Evans, then thirty-three, agreed to a plea bargain that landed him a five- to ten-year prison sentence. Afterward Castor told reporters it was the right resolution, saying it was a "difficult case" and would have been a difficult trial. Ferman agreed, noting the victims would have been subject to personal attacks had they testified, a common defense tactic in cases like this and something Evans's attorney confirmed he'd planned to do.

The Evans case set off the biggest scandal in the history of the state police and spawned a slew of civil suits, which revealed a long-standing toleration of sexual misconduct among its members. I'd spent the last couple of years investigating the agency, so it was on my mind. So was the 2001 case of a nineteen-year-old woman who said she'd been drugged and sexually assaulted by a Villanova University student, a case Castor handled. "If in fact a drug was used to incapacitate her, I find it extremely nefarious," he said at the time. "This is at the same level as putting a knife or a gun on a woman to have your way with her."

The Cosby case seemed like a natural one for Castor to latch onto for headlines—another feather in his cap to prove that when it came to prosecuting criminals, he was fearless, no matter how powerful or high profile they were and no matter how flimsy or nonexistent the evidence was, much like in the Evans case, where there was no physical evidence and the victims did not immediately report the crimes to police.

Instead, Castor was uncharacteristically silent.

Then, four days after the story broke, he finally confirmed the investigation publicly in a terse, four-paragraph press release given to only three reporters who worked out of the Norristown courthouse where his office was located. He confirmed the basics of Andrea's complaint, saying authorities had asked Phillips for permission to interview Cosby. The contents of the press release were pretty standard—except for the last line:

> After detectives complete the investigation, District Attorney Castor will decide if criminal charges against Cosby, or anyone else, are warranted.

The language surprised me. *What does* or anyone else *mean?* I wondered. *Was he threatening to arrest the victim?*

When Castor held a news conference about the case on January 26, his comments made it clear how skeptical he was of Andrea's story. "I think that factors such as failure to disclose in a timely manner and contacts with the alleged perpetrator after the event are factors that weigh toward Mr. Cosby," he said, referring to reports Andrea had taken her parents to a performance of Cosby's in Canada the previous August. "Usually in large time gaps, it involves frightened children victims," he said. With adults, "jurors tend to frown upon lengthy delays between the conduct and the reporting unless they are given a good explanation."

He said investigators had interviewed Cosby earlier that day: "I'm not going to say what he told us, but I can say that he and his lawyer have been fully cooperative with us, without delay or hesitation," he said. "And that helps us move forward more quickly than you might otherwise have thought we would. The alleged victim was cooperative as well but I won't make any decision concerning anyone's credibility until all of the statements are taken and the evidence is in."

The key issue in his decision about whether to prosecute this case would be whether the accused acted with criminal intent. "We punish people for intentional or reckless criminal conduct," he said. "We don't punish people for making mistakes and doing stupid things. The dividing line between intentional or reckless criminal conduct and making a stupid or foolish mistake is one of the more difficult decisions a prosecutor has to make." He said he hoped to make his decision about whether to prosecute in a couple of weeks, after detectives determined whether there was any violation of the law.

I shouldn't have been so surprised by Castor's reaction. Time and again studies have shown that many in law enforcement are just as skeptical of sexual assault victims' claim as the general public, if not more so, especially when the accused is someone the women knew; that there is a second victimization when an investigator questions victims and implies they are somehow to blame or clearly doesn't believe them. Still, Castor's handling of the Evans case showed he knew better—after all, many of those victims were adults who had delayed reporting their assaults to law enforcement as well.

His comments infuriated Troiani, who was horrified Castor was maligning Andrea, prompting her to make her first public comments about the case. Troiani knew her client's experience was typical of most sexual assault victims.

"What's bizarre and preposterous is for someone to think it was unusual to have a delay like this," she said. "There's many reasons victims of sexual assault do not come forward immediately. Fear. Shame. There's betrayal. There's celebrity. This was a man she thought was a friend, a mentor. It's perfectly understandable to see why she would have difficulty coming forward."

MORE AND MORE, Andrea was struggling emotionally. In addition to the nightmares, she was having flashbacks to the night of the assault. During the day she had problems with her attention span. She started therapy to help her deal with the trauma of the assault and now with the media blitz she'd been subjected to since going to police.

She'd wanted Cosby to be put on trial; instead, she found herself in the crosshairs.

Troiani's fury was boiling over at the way her client was targeted. She'd been a prosecutor in the 1970s and 1980s and had witnessed decades of rape cases, and she knew it was common to put the rape victim on trial. But that didn't make it any better.

This idea—that the victim gets put on trial in sexual assault cases, unlike in any other crime—is one of the many reasons sexual assault is the most underreported violent crime. Less than one-third of sexual assault victims report the offense to police, and "here's the perfect example of why," said Delilah Rumburg, executive director of the National Sexual Violence Resource Center. "They're not going to be believed. The criminal justice system is questioning them in the media. It takes a very brave person to come forward, especially when the accused is famous."

She also found it difficult to swallow Castor's other comments about Andrea. "I would assume [he] knows that it's not unusual for [sexual assault] victims to wait to come forward," she said. "We still see this all the time. That's just unconscionable to say that you would cast doubt on a victim because they waited a year to come forward."

Phillips, who was also chairman of the Pennsylvania Commission on Crime and Delinquency, a group that administers millions of dollars to aid victims of violent crime, should know better too, she said. After reading or hearing news reports of his comments calling Andrea's claims "bizarre and preposterous," victims' advocates had been contacting Rumburg with their concerns.

On January 28, State Senate majority whip Jeffrey Piccola, a Republican, issued a press release calling on Phillips to either step down as Cosby's lawyer or to resign from the commission. "I think he needs to decide whether he's going to represent criminal defendants or be an advocate for victims of crime," he said.

Rumburg thought Phillips should resign from the commission. "I need to listen to what the advocates in the field are saying, and they clearly feel that he cannot represent Mr. Cosby and still represent the best interests of victims in his position as chair," said Rumburg, who also served as chair of the commission's victim services' advisory group. "There's a real cry of alarm going up across the field."

Yet the outcry had little if any impact. Phillips wouldn't comment on the controversy, and Governor Rendell remained committed to him as well, saying there was no conflict of interest.

"Wally Phillips is a renowned attorney and if there were a conflict of interest or a challenge to him performing his duties as chair and him defending any client, then he would recuse himself from any situation that would be in conflict," said Kate Philips, Rendell's spokeswoman.

So FAR, NONE of the major newspapers were covering the case at all, which I thought was strange, especially given that Cosby had been making so much news with his town halls. The Associated Press and other wire services weren't saying much either. The silence was eerie.

Meanwhile I was hearing whispers that Cosby's supporters were suggesting liberals created Andrea's allegations in retaliation for his tirades against poor black people, a theory columnist Tony Norman addressed in the *Pittsburgh Post-Gazette*.

"At Free Republic, a conservative Web forum, opinions range from skeptical of Constand's charges against Cosby to speculation about a plot to slime the comedian for leaving 'the liberal plantation' last year," he wrote. "With the left and the right openly voicing the opinion that Cosby is being set up, he may yet win the war for public opinion."

If he did win, it may have been because when the press finally did cover the case, journalistic rules were broken, violating Andrea's privacy and diminishing her story. On January 27, a copy of a Philadelphia police report, which included Andrea's name, appeared on the website of the TV show *Celebrity Justice* under the headline "CJ Obtains Confidential Document in Cosby Case."

Harvey Levin, *Celebrity Justice*'s executive producer who later founded celebrity gossip website TMZ, said it was an accident that Andrea's name was not blacked out on the air and pointed out that the error was fixed within ten minutes. The event prompted a Philadelphia Police Department Internal Affairs investigation into how the show got the internal police document, which are called "white papers." They were not public record in Philadelphia, so either someone in law enforcement or an attorney connected to the case had leaked it. But Levin wouldn't say how he got the document, only that he didn't pay for it.

Now that two outlets had broken the code of not revealing the identity of a sexual assault victim, other news agencies soon began using Andrea's name and photo.

The pro-Cosby leaks also continued. That same day ABC, citing a "source close to the investigation," reported that law enforcement had concluded there was "sexual contact" between Cosby and Andrea and that they were now trying to determine whether or not it was consensual.

I was ready to break a story too, though. In my next piece I revealed that Andrea's attorneys had turned over tapes that proved she was telling the truth about what happened that night. Andrea's mother, Gianna, had taped a phone conversation with Cosby that took place after Andrea went to police, and it was the first evidence Andrea had to support her claims.

The revelations caused barely a ripple; no other news media picked up on the story. Instead, the Cosby people responded with a counterattack. No doubt frustrated because they couldn't find any skeletons in Andrea's closet and determined to shatter her credibility, they went to *Celebrity Justice* with false claims. On February 7, *Celebrity Justice* posted a story that reported "sources connected with Bill Cosby" told them that before Andrea went to police, her mother, Gianna, "asked the comedian to make things right with money."

"We're told she asked Cosby to help pay for her daughter's education and to generally help her out financially, and this conversation occurred before the accuser ever contacted police," the story said, adding that it appeared at least one conversation was taped by the accuser and her mom. "A Cosby rep called this a classic shakedown."

Other media outlets picked up the story, treating it as truth even though all the details in the story were wrong, including simple technicalities, like the timing of Gianna's call, which was after Andrea went to police, not before. I did what I could to set the record straight with my own follow-up story, sharing accurate details about the taped call and saying it was Cosby who had offered financial compensation to Andrea's mother—not she who asked him for money—and that she had not taken him up on the offer.

Still, *Celebrity Justice* ran yet another story the next day, this one headlined, "Cosby's Attorney Claims Accuser After Cash" and said Cosby's attorney was "firing back big time" against the sexual assault allegations against his client.

Marty Singer, Cosby's attorney, was quoted saying, "These people contacted Mr. Cosby with the intention of requesting money from Mr. Cosby. It is very obvious."

I felt good about the coverage I was contributing to the public debate, but I was also more than a little unnerved: my exclusives about the taped phone calls had landed me on some prime-time cable news shows—and in hot water with the DA, Bruce Castor. One morning I was talking about my story on the radio when Castor called in, hinting that Andrea's attorneys could be arrested if they were the ones who told me about the tapes and that I could be arrested for speaking or writing about them.

"A person may not disclose the existence or the contents of a legally obtained electronic interception unless it is a law enforcement officer doing it in the course of his or her duties and then it becomes public," Castor said. "And no person at all may disclose the existence of an inadmissible or illegally obtained interception. To do so," he warned, "is a felony punishable by up to seven years in prison."

Castor was telling other members of the local media I could be arrested and put in jail if I spoke about this taped conversation, a point I made to Rita Cosby (no relation) on her Fox News Channel show one evening as we discussed the players in the case. "I find his behavior, frankly, as intimidating as anything I've ever seen . . . the DA's behavior throughout this entire case [is] puzzling. He's almost been an apologist for the other side."

As for me, I had my editors on my side, and I wasn't going to back down. It was clear to me by now that Cosby had the rest of the media under his thumb. If I didn't keep reporting the truth, who would? And besides, I was already close to publishing another explosive story.

CHAPTER FOUR

COLD MEDICINE

Thousands of miles away from where the scandal was unfolding in and around Philadelphia, Tamara Green was standing in her kitchen, drinking her morning cup of coffee, and watching the morning news on CNN when she saw a story saying a woman had accused Bill Cosby of drugging and sexually assaulting her at his home in Pennsylvania.

A trial lawyer for nearly twenty years and now fifty-seven, Tamara was semiretired, handling appeals while spending her days enjoying the view from her beach house in southern California. That morning, watching CNN, Tamara thought, *Really? At his age, he's still doing that? Well, now they'll get him.*

On her screen, Cosby's defense attorney was calling Andrea's claims "preposterous." *My eye*, Tamara thought. *He did the same thing to me thirty years ago.*

Though she had never gone to the police or gone public with what she said happened to her, over the years she had told a few friends and her estranged second husband about when Cosby assaulted her in a similar way around 1970. So her ears perked, and she followed the news closely for the next few days, expecting to hear he'd been arrested. Instead, "I heard a press release from the district attorney saying he thought the case was 'weak' and why did she wait so long to come forward?" she said. "I worked in a DA's office, and that's DA-speak for, 'We're not filing charges.' I felt compelled to come forward after I heard that."

She called Castor's office, police in Philadelphia and Cheltenham township, and, really, anyone she could think of in law enforcement. When no one got back to her, she called Kivitz and Troiani, whom she'd read were representing Andrea. "What can I do to help you? They're going to destroy Andrea," she told them. She then found her way to me, hoping going public would make law enforcement believe Andrea was telling the truth.

"I realize that him doing it to me thirty years ago doesn't prove he did it to this girl today, but I don't think it's right that they're going to disregard this woman and her allegations," she said. "I really felt this woman who had the courage to come forward against the great Bill Cosby had been disrespected."

Indeed, she believed it was already clear that Castor didn't believe Andrea. Most of the public probably didn't believe her either, buying into a widely held false belief that most sexual assault victims lie about being raped, despite statistics showing that false reports of sexual assault are rare—as little as between 2 and 10 percent.

All the more reason I was excited about the opportunity to tell her story. If there was more than one accuser, it took the Cosby case to a different level. But first I had to check her out to confirm her credibility. I learned that Tamara had made the news a handful of times when speaking on behalf of her clients. Her most famous case involved Liza Minnelli and her ninety-five-year-old stepmother, Lee. Tamara had represented Lee when she sued Liza after Liza sold the Beverly Hills home where she'd lived for forty years.

About a week after our initial chat, Tamara called and told me she'd spoken with a detective on the case and with Ferman, Castor's first assistant. To truly help Andrea, though, she felt her story needed to be told in the media so that the public was aware of what she had to say. She still had little faith that Castor would prosecute Cosby.

A colorful, sharp-witted, former fashion model, Tamara had strong features—flashing blue eyes and chin-length reddish-brown hair—and was clearly not lacking in confidence. She told me she wanted to talk on the record and use her photo, "because if I duck and run or hide and become an unnamed source, then people will not believe it. And I also think that because I'm a person of good reputation, a career lawyer and a mother, I think it will get other women to come out and say it happened to them. But, like I said to the detective I spoke with, 'If it's only me and this girl, it's two too many.'"

Though she insisted she knew what she was getting herself into, to this day I'm not sure she truly understood the kind of scrutiny her life would be subjected to. Tamara's voice was strong and clear as she told me what happened to her.

BACK IN THE late 1960s and early 1970s Tamara was a model and aspiring singer doing television commercials for Coca-Cola, Pontiac, and Maybelline when she met Cosby through Dr. Leroy Amar, a mutual friend and the same doctor who prescribed Cosby Quaaludes for his back pain throughout the seventies, though Tamara knew none of this at the time.

"I ran in the Hollywood crowd," she said. "I wanted to audition to get a record contract. I was originally introduced to Bill as a singer for his production company." Instead, she began helping him and Amar open a club on La Cienega Boulevard in Los Angeles.

"My job was to call Amar and Cosby's friends and sell memberships to raise capital to open the club," Tamara said.

She'd had the job only about a week when she felt sick one day and called Café Figaro, a hot-spot restaurant in Los Angeles frequented by Amar and Cosby, to tell Amar she was going home. Instead, Cosby took the call and suggested she join him at Figaro's and have lunch. "Maybe you'll feel better," he told her.

So Tamara drove over and sat at a table with Cosby and six or eight others, including actress Cicely Tyson, who had appeared in a couple of episodes of *I Spy* and in 1981 married jazz great Miles Davis at Cosby's Massachusetts home. Cosby was his best man.

But Tamara was still feeling unwell. "I really feel sick," she admitted to Cosby.

"Would you like some Contac?" he asked.

Thinking the over-the-counter cold medicine couldn't hurt, she nodded. Cosby left the table for a few minutes and returned with two gray-and-red capsules, which she took. He didn't bring them in a sealed packet, and it didn't occur to her that they weren't exactly what he said they were.

Twenty minutes later she felt much better.

Hooray for Contac, Tamara thought. But the pleasant sensation didn't last.

"About ten minutes after that I'm almost face down in my salad. I was really just stoned, I mean, smashed."

Cosby told Tamara she must be sicker than she thought and offered to drive her home in his car. By this time she felt "loaded," with no motor control, so she agreed that he should take her home.

Not long after that, they pulled up in front of her apartment complex, a series of ten bungalows in a horseshoe shape on El Centro Boulevard. Each had a small front porch. Cosby half-carried Tamara, who could barely walk, up the two stairs of her porch, fumbled through her pocketbook for her keys, then ushered her through her living room and back into her bedroom.

"Let's put you to bed," Cosby said, trying to pull her dress over her head.

Tamara felt stoned but clear-minded enough to be angry: something wasn't right. She'd taken Contac before, and she'd had the flu before, but she'd never felt anything like this.

You son of a bitch. You drugged me, she thought.

"I started fighting him, and he's kissing on me, peeling off my clothes, wants to put me on my bed," she said. "I'm starting to freak out, and I'm telling him, 'You're going to have to kill me.'"

She picked up a lamp and threw it at her bedroom window, hoping it would shatter the glass and get somebody's attention. The window cracked but didn't break.

"I was just going to make noise. I was ready to do anything I could to get him off me and out of my apartment. He's got most of my clothes off, and he's prepared to have his way with me."

A few minutes later she passed out.

When she woke up many hours later, she saw he'd left two hundred-dollar bills on her coffee table in the living room.

"That did it for me," she said. "I put my clothes back on, and I reeled out of my apartment and fell off my own front porch. I was all cut up and beat up, and I staggered out into the street and stopped a car. I got into a car with a little Mexican man wearing one of those field laborer hats with the pompom on the back. I said, 'Take me to Figaro's' because I thought Bill had gone back there."

All she found was her car in the parking lot where she'd left it.

"So I got into my car, drove out of the parking lot, hit a parked car on the opposite side of the street, headed into the intersection, smashed into an old person's car. He got out, looked at our cars, then he drove away. I parked my car at a club called The Climax—all-night movies and food. I parked it near the brightest lit place, then I went to the restroom." All she had with her were the two hundred-dollar bills Cosby had left, but it was more than enough to pay the club's entrance fee. "I slept it off there. They had these back rooms that played movies, full of pillows and stuff like that. They threw me out of there at 8 A.M."

She felt horrible. "I was hungover, and I'm all beaten up from falling off my porch. I'm sick because I'd been sick to begin with."

WHEN SHE'D RECOVERED enough, Tamara went to Los Angeles Children's Hospital to see her sixteen-year-old brother. She hadn't made sense of the Cosby thing yet, but in the meantime she had other things on her mind: her brother was dying from cystic fibrosis. She wanted to see him and decided she'd go visit him. When she arrived, she found out her brother had just had a famous visitor.

"When I got there my mother was there and I found out Bill had been there," she said. "My brother was the hero of the children's ward. He got a new portable radio, and Bill visited all of the children there."

After that, she didn't have the heart to go to law enforcement about what Cosby did to her. "Him making such a big fuss over my brother. . . . I just couldn't take that away from him. My brother was very, very ill. He was terminal. And my brother thought that it was just the bee's knees that the great Bill Cosby was my friend and had come to the hospital to see him and made him a hero and made the other terminal kids happy. He gave autographs and attaboys, and I just couldn't take that away from him."

She never returned to her job, but she saw him about a week later. "You're lucky you went to see my brother," she told him. "I'm not going to make a fuss about this, but I'm going to tell everyone I know what you did to me for the rest of my natural life."

Which is exactly what she did. "Somebody would say, 'Bill Cosby. What a wonderful guy.' I never missed an opportunity to say, 'He tried to rape me.'" Still, she had never even thought about going public until she heard what happened to Andrea. She knew she would be attacked for waiting so long to come forward but says she had to support Andrea.

"Even though she took a long time to do it, she still had to muster up the courage to take on the great Bill Cosby," Tamara says. "I never came forward. It doesn't mean it didn't happen. It just means he went and bought me off—by going to the children's terminal ward."

By the time her brother died about a year later, Tamara's life was full, and she didn't want to go to the cops. Her first marriage failed, and she spent three or four years caring for her young son while going to law school. "I never dreamed about practicing law, but in the end I'm the mouth that roared," she joked.

Tamara knew there would be consequences for speaking out against a powerful man like Cosby but wasn't worried about her past being used against her in an effort to tarnish her image. "I'm not a perfect person, but I'm a great person," she said. "I've kicked a few asses in my time, and I've made a few enemies. I don't have the kind of past I need to be ashamed of. . . . I had a DUI once. I've never been a junkie, never been an addict, never been in rehab. I've been in therapy for severe depression."

I spoke to people Tamara talked with through the years to corroborate that she hadn't made up the allegations against Cosby after hearing about Andrea. I went back to them more recently. All of them said they believed her. "She was so upset I thought it had just occurred," said her cousin, Lauren Scott, who recalls Tamara telling her about it in the early 1970s. "It was the truth. There was no way she could fake that emotion and anger."

Castor and Ferman wouldn't respond to my phone calls requesting a comment about Tamara's story, but Troiani said she found her credible. "She's an attorney, and she seemed to be still angry after all these years, which is only an indication of how much an attack like this affects somebody's life," she said. "When you talk to that woman, you know that this happened to her and these feelings are still not fully resolved for her."

All Phillips had to say was this: "Mr. Cosby does not recognize [Tamara's name]. In any event, the incident you described did not happen in any way, shape, or form." And then his team did their best to keep our story from running by threatening to sue us if we ran the piece.

But the paper's lawyers went over the story and deemed it publishable. We put it on the front page on February 8 with the headline, "My Cosby Story." By the time I got in to work that morning, my phone was ringing off the hook with other reporters trying to reach her. One of them was a producer for the *Today* show, asking if I could connect her with Tamara. I gave Tamara her message, and her interview aired on the *Today* show two days later.

I'd also heard from a few nighttime cable news talk shows, and when a booker for the MSNBC show *The Abrams Report* asked me to come on that evening, I agreed. Like it or not, the conflict-heavy, issue-oriented shows on the Fox News Channel, MSNBC, and CNN were becoming a key source of information for millions of viewers, who were tuning in to them more frequently than traditional network news. The shows were becoming powerful weapons for shaping public opinion.

That night Dan Abrams, the host, did not bother to hide his skepticism. He mentioned the *Celebrity Justice* story saying Andrea's mother had tried to extort money from Cosby, something the "experts" he had on the show took as the truth, one of whom was a defense attorney and considered herself a friend of Cosby.

Abrams also read from a statement released by Cosby's attorney that morning after my story came out: "As we informed the *Daily News* before they printed today's story, Ms. Green's allegations are absolutely false," said the statement on behalf of Phillips but emailed by David Walk, another Cosby attorney. "The incident she describes did not happen. Not a single detail in the article has been corroborated by anyone. The fact that she may have repeated this story to others is not corroboration. It is irresponsible of the *Daily News* to publish an uncorroborated story of an incident that is alleged to have happened thirty years ago."

Noting that the Cosby team "seems to be chastising the paper for going forward with the story even after they denied it," Abrams asked me for my response.

"Typical strong-handed tactics," I replied. "They want to try to clamp down on anything that might possibly put . . . the person that they work for in a bad light. I mean, there was a lot of intimidation going on, frankly."

And Tamara faced the same hostile questioning on the *Today* show.

"This is a tough story to cover, but these allegations seem serious enough," cohost Matt Lauer said in the introduction to the segment. Although years later Lauer would be fired following allegations of inappropriate sexual behavior, in 2005 his reputation was still stellar. Crowds of fans gathered outside the *Today* show studio each morning, calling his name and hoping for a glimpse of him. Each summer he'd take viewers on a five-day, globe-spanning adventure called "Where in the World Is Matt Lauer?" The audience loved it—and him—and his ratings showed it.

"Bill Cosby is an icon known for his support of education, his generosity, his outspoken belief of personal responsibility. . . . I spoke with Green and asked why she waited thirty years to come forward," he said. The interview went downhill from there.

I was already noticing how differently the national male TV hosts were reacting to the story. They weren't even trying to be impartial. I'd always found Lauer smug and condescending, but his lack of professionalism surprised me. Twelve years later, when Lauer was fired for "inappropriate sexual behavior in the workplace," CNN cited this interview as one of five worth rewatching for his callous treatment of Tamara.

COSBY'S PEOPLE JUMPED all over Tamara. Her past was sifted through, and they uprooted every damaging piece of information they could find about her. Attorney David Walk emailed reporters and producers—including me—a copy of a February 9 *New York Post* story that discussed a thirteen-count state bar complaint filed against Tamara the previous March. He also provided phone numbers of two attorneys who he said had negative information about Tamara. Greta Van Susteren actually spoke to one of them, but the worst the attorney could say was that she was annoying. I tried not to laugh when she revealed this on her show when I was a guest. I'd tried to reach them, too, but seriously? This was the damaging information they had about her? That she was annoying?

My boss defended our story, but most media outlets simply focused on the thirty-year lag and the bar complaint. The Associated Press waited more than a day, a lifetime in their news cycle, to write about Tamara, and when they did, they led with the details of the complaint. When I caught up with Tamara she told me her law license was currently active. A spokeswoman for the bar confirmed this, saying there had been no guilt or innocence determination yet and that they were just at the beginning of the process. In the meantime Tamara had voluntarily enrolled herself in the bar's disciplinary program in October 2004, which she was in the process of completing.

"It's the equivalent of lawyer traffic school," she said. "Once a week I go to sit in a room and talk to other lawyers."

I was struggling with how to deal with these revelations in my own coverage. Other media outlets had used the information to attack Tamara's credibility. But was it relevant to what Tamara was saying? Did it really tarnish her trustworthiness? If she'd had a history of making false allegations about being sexually assaulted, certainly that would have been relevant. But was this? I soul searched, uneasy with what I'd learned but unsure where to draw the line of reliability. I was also mad. Cosby's attorneys clearly had this information when I asked them for comment but didn't give it to me, instead saving it for after we published to try to discredit Tamara and me at the same time.

I went to Rumburg again to get her thoughts. I thought the heavy-handed tactics were unconscionable and wanted to write about it, but I needed an outsider to weigh in.

Rumburg was clear in her view. She said any state bar complaint is "totally irrelevant" to Tamara's claims about Cosby drugging and groping her. "It has absolutely nothing to do with this case. She has nothing to gain. So why would she come forward if it's not a true story?" she said. What's even worse is that this kind of attack discourages other victims from coming forward, especially if they are accusing someone who is a celebrity or high profile. "We cannot have open season on any victim who comes forward with a claim of sexual assault."

I included Rumburg's comments in my story about the bar complaint; I also used the opportunity to call out the Cosby people for their slimy tactics. "It didn't take long," I wrote. "The day after California attorney Tamara Green went public with allegations Bill Cosby drugged and groped her 30 years ago, Cosby's people began circulating dirt on Green."

And so on. Tamara didn't let the intimidation tactics slow her down either. She went on show after show on CBS, MSNBC, and Fox News as Cosby's team dug further, hoping to find more to discredit her. Andrea and her parents were watching some of her interviews, silently cheering her on, grateful for the support. Tamara somehow kept her composure—and her sense of humor—as she openly admitted to her past mistakes.

"I think it's hilarious they're trying to smear me," she cheerfully told me at one point when we caught up with each other. "If that's all the dirt they have, then I can run for president." She said she'd expected them to do this and didn't regret going public. "They can dig up all they want. I've never drugged and raped anybody, though."

Yes, she told anyone who asked, she had been arrested for battery in 1989. "That is absolutely true," she said. "And I am here to tell you that if I find you in bed with my boyfriend after you ate dinner at my house and sucked down my wine, I will punch you in the nose. Because that's what happened. A longtime friend slept with my boyfriend."

She clarified it was a misdemeanor charge that was expunged—which is why it didn't show up in my background check—after she paid the woman's medical bills. She was also put on probation, she said, which she served.

Cosby's media army had even called Tamara's mental health into question so she opened up about the counseling she sought after her "otherwise fabulous husband" ran off with a topless dancer with a coke habit in the mid- to early 1990s.

"That depressed me so bad that I went down to my friendly community health center and checked myself in," she said. "I took myself some mental health the way I would have taken myself to the emergency room if I had a broken arm."

Tamara was grilled on *The Abrams Report* that same night. As Abrams rattled off various incidents the Cosby people clearly provided to him, she decided to come clean about one more past transgression, one that hadn't yet been reported: a DUI, though she'd told me about it before my story ran.

"I blew a .08 in the mid-nineties coming home from a dinner party," she admitted. "I pled up. I didn't fight it, and I did forty-eight hours in jail, which I want to tell you is a life-changing experience. You become very polite after that. And I want to tell you that the search that was performed on me before I went into jail was less intrusive than what Bill Cosby did to me."

After that, Tamara's one-woman media blitz was nearly over. She was battered but still standing proud behind her story—and it was clear she'd had an impact. After her TV appearances more women began emerging with terrifyingly similar stories.

CHAPTER FIVE

IT SMACKS OF SENSATIONALISM

Obviously, past mistakes like Tamara's don't bolster the public's perception of a woman making shocking claims against a powerful man, but this is exactly why rape-shield laws were created—to protect sexual assault victims from being smeared by defendants. It's hard enough coming forward to talk to strangers about your own sexual violation without having your life story examined as a testament to your character.

"The crime is the crime. It has nothing to do with who I am, what I do, how I dress, where I was," Rumburg said. "The courts of law have recognized that someone who's in the sex trade can be sexually assaulted. I just shudder because it's going to be less and less safe for victims to come forward in the criminal justice system."

I thought about this a lot after the revelations about Tamara's past. For me the important takeaway was that she had told other people what happened to her along the way, proving that she didn't just make it up after hearing about Andrea's case on TV. She had nothing to gain by coming forward. Everything Cosby's people cited in her past happened decades after her encounter with Cosby happened. Do you need to be perfect in order to be believed as a sexual assault victim? Andrea actually was, and she still wasn't believed. Though she had no skeletons in her closet, Cosby's people still found a way to sling dirt at her by flat-out lying.

And with what other crime do we bring up a person's other transgressions to decide whether they're telling the truth?

Defense attorneys are not allowed to use these tactics in court unless they can show it's relevant to the sexual assault accusation, so they've learned to leak it to the media instead. And it's another reason sexual assault victims do not want their names revealed publicly and why so few report the crimes to police, Rumburg said.

"We continue to attack and place blame on the victim," she said. "You know what happens when we do this? We're emboldening the rapist. They know if they say the right thing, the media will take hold of it, and we'll get into the whole victim-blaming thing. Why as a society do we cast suspicion on a victim like this?"

It was a question I kept coming back to myself. Psychologist David Lisak says it's a viewpoint that goes back hundreds of years. "For centuries, it has been asserted and assumed that women 'cry rape,' that a large proportion of rape allegations are maliciously concocted for purposes of revenge or other motives," he wrote in a 2010 paper analyzing ten years of false sexual assault reports. "Most famously, Sir Matthew Hale, a chief justice of the court of the King's bench of England, expressed this view in a form that became the basis for special jury instructions that would be used late into the 20th century," he wrote, which warned jurors that rape is "an accusation easily to be made and hard to be proved."

Kristen Houser believes the attitude is rooted in the "ancient, historical battle between genders" and protecting the ruling class. For thousands of years women have been viewed as property, she points out. "We didn't even make it possible to rape your spouse until fifteen, twenty years ago," she said. "This is part of the structure of the patriarchy, that you don't recognize or validate the experiences of women when they implicate bad behavior or human rights violations by the ruling class, which in this case is men."

And Cosby had certainly been a part of that ruling class for many years. By the time Tamara met up with him in 1969 or 1970, he had already won three Emmys in a row for his role on *I Spy*. Ironically, he was also about to record an album called *Bill Cosby Talks to Kids About Drugs*, which received widespread accolades.

Though he had never finished high school or college, education was becoming his passion. Temple University awarded him a bachelor's degree, and he went on to get a master's and PhD from the University of Massachusetts at Amherst. He had just started venturing into educational television for children, starting with *Sesame Street* and *The Electric Company*. Even *Fat Albert and the Kids*, based on his life growing up in the Philadelphia projects, was created to be more than entertainment, showing how the kids dealt with day-to-day problems, which is why Cosby used the cartoon, one of the first to feature African American children, for his PhD thesis.

"Fat Albert is two things: He is a modern superhero and he is a teacher," Cosby wrote. "He is a sympathetic hero that children, especially Black children, can empathize with as he struggles with value conflicts and the peer group problems that confront children today."

After Cosby's son, Ennis, died in 1997, Cosby started to publish a series of books about the adventures of five-year-old Little Bill, using the escapades he got into to help children learn how to solve problems in their own lives. He developed the books into a series for Nick Jr. His interactions with children in his show and book *Kids Say the Darndest Things* or as Cliff Huxtable on *The Cosby Show* only enhanced his wholesome reputation.

This was the man Tamara and Andrea were both saying had done unspeakable things to them. And most people simply found it hard to believe. Or they just didn't want to believe it. Maybe it was easier to believe these women were liars than to accept that a wolf who had been hiding in sheep's clothing for forty years had bamboozled us all.

But Tamara was determined to keep telling the world what happened to her, and she took advantage of every opportunity she was offered to make a public statement. The only one of the three networks that didn't have her on its morning show was ABC, which made me wonder if they had made a deal with Cosby to back off the story in exchange for a future interview, which I learned was called "trading up"—turning down one story to get another, better one—in the national TV world.

During Tamara's flurry of television appearances she began getting calls from other women with similar stories about Cosby. They came from all over—California, Colorado, Texas. The women told her what they'd never been able to tell anyone in law enforcement: that Cosby had done to them what he'd done to Tamara.

Tamara told them to contact Andrea's attorneys and the DA's office. These women later became some of the twelve Jane Does in Andrea's lawsuit.

"I'm not going to be alone when this is all said and done," she predicted.

And she wasn't.

Andrea's attorneys were getting a steady stream of calls from other accusers as well, all of them saying they came forward because they saw Tamara on TV. They were willing to go to the police and to testify in court, but they had no civil lawsuits of their own, no other motives besides using their own stories to show that both Tamara and Andrea were telling the truth.

"I'm not suing anybody," said one of the women, who became Jane Doe Number Two and had been introduced to Cosby by her modeling agent. "I just wanted to stick up for [Andrea] and for Tamara Green. I don't want people to think they're crazy. I believe them 100 percent."

She had reason to believe them. At the time she told me her whole story but did not want me to write about her, as she was still deeply confused and ashamed about what had happened to her. It took her another decade before she finally worked up the courage to tell her story publicly and allow her name and photo to be used. By the time she did, her agent had died.

Jane Doe Number Two, or Jennifer "Kaya" Thompson, was one of many models whose agents connected them with Cosby, saying he wanted to mentor them, help them with their careers. Cosby would later say in a deposition that every Thursday Sue Charney's modeling agency would send him five or six teen models to the studio where he filmed *The Cosby Show*. Jennifer was one of them.

"The girls, young women, were from out of state many of them, and many of them were financially not doing well, and so we agreed that it might be nice if they would come on the Thursday and see the show and have dinner between shows," he said. "We performed, then there's a break where food is in my dressing room. The girls, women eat. It's a very, very good meal, probably better than anything they'd had the time that they're in New York. And then they would—some of them came for the first show, some came for the second. Anyway, they went home after the first and the second show with just one dinner meal between shows."

Troiani asked him what type of models were chosen for this. "The ones that she felt had come to New York and weren't doing as well as they thought they would," he replied. "And some that she felt, if I'm correct, some that she felt might—that she felt had potential to be very good, but hadn't yet. And for the time and the work and some money that she put into them, this was sort of like a present."

Troiani asked him why he asked for that particular type of model. "Because they are out of and away from home. Modeling is a business of being selected and I wanted to—I love Sue and I love what Sue was doing, and Sue is at a level where quite a few of the models she started with or brought in and nurtured and spent money on left her or the other agencies or the girl would go to another agency, so I was trying."

He said sometimes the girls came to these dinners more than once and that he gave some of them jobs as extras on the show. Charney died in 2011. In 2015, her sister, Alice Opell, told the *Washington Post* she didn't think her sister knew anything untoward was going on.

But Jennifer knew none of this at the time. She was just seventeen years old in 1988 when she hopped on a train to New York City from her suburban Washington, DC, home, a spur-of-the-moment decision. A beautiful mixed-race woman with café-au-lait skin and curly black hair, she walked right into Charney's office, and Charney hired her on the spot. Then Charney sent her to meet Cosby.

Jennifer's father is African American, she said, and his first name was Bill, like Cosby's, so she instantly felt comfortable with him. Together they even called Jennifer's mother, and Cosby assured her he would watch out for her daughter if they allowed her to move to New York City. He said she'd be safe sharing an apartment with other models. When her parents eventually agreed, he had them over for dinner with Jennifer, reassuring them he would watch out for their daughter.

At first Jennifer's relationship with Cosby was platonic. They established an easy fellowship, and he even got her a small walk-on role on *The Cosby Show*. But she noticed as time went on that he was touching her quite a lot—inviting her to his townhouse, for instance, and offering her a glass of amaretto while massaging her shoulders. She had a feeling he wanted more—much more—and she slowly withdrew from him, abandoning her hopes of becoming a model and returning home to her parents.

In the summer of 1989 she mailed one of her poems to Cosby:

Receive a phone call from the Big Man
Who Says He Has a Plan
He is a thief, a hypocrite and a whore
Who Only Wants More . . . than life offers

But she was also hurt and wanted closure. So she went to New York to meet with Cosby. First, they had lunch with Dr. Alvin Pouissant, a psychiatrist who was also a consultant for *The Cosby Show*. Afterward she went to Cosby's townhome. This time Cosby openly pushed her to participate in sexual acts, and she finally gave in, masturbating him with lotion until he was satisfied. When it was over, he handed her seven crisp hundred-dollar bills, and she fled. Cosby confirmed that something sexual happened between he and Jennifer in his deposition for Andrea's case, though he took issue with calling it "masturbation," insisting on characterizing what happened between them as "She performed a sexual act with her hand and I had an orgasm."

Later Cosby contacted her and offered to pay her way to Spelman College and to buy her a car. She declined.

"I hated him," she said. "And I knew he was trying to bribe me to keep me quiet."

The encounters with the man she viewed as a father figure had her in and out of therapy for years. She told no one except her mother—until she clicked on the television one day and saw Tamara talking about what happened to her.

Oh my God, she thought. *I have to do something.*

TROIANI AND KIVITZ watched as Tamara faced pointed questions and brutal attacks wherever she went. Both had spent years putting sex offenders in jail, so the aggressive treatment didn't surprise them.

Troiani, in fact, was the first female prosecutor to try a rape case in Chester County, which is in the Philadelphia suburbs. She appeared in court, professional and prepared, only to find that the judge didn't want her to use the word "penis" during the proceedings. He also determined it was worthwhile to ask whether the victim had had an orgasm during her rape and what clothing she'd been wearing when she was assaulted.

Troiani's most famous case had also been in Chester County, when she was an assistant district attorney. She helped convict the Johnston brothers, who had famously murdered their family members in a multi-million-dollar theft and burglary ring. The brothers were sentenced to life in prison without parole, and their exploits were the basis for the movie *At Close Range*, starring Sean Penn.

With cases like those on Troiani's record, taking on a case against America's Dad didn't faze her, and she found Cosby's legal team and Castor's comments reminiscent of the attitudes she'd encountered as a sex crimes prosecutor in the 1970s. She hardly blinked when Cosby's people released another statement about Tamara claiming she was "peddling a highly defamatory, fictional story about something she claims occurred with Mr. Cosby three decades ago." The statement went on to say that "her claims are false, fabricated and defamatory. Mr. Cosby denies her assertions."

Tamara also kept her sense of perspective. "Well, what do you expect him to say?" she told host Rita Cosby (no relation) during an interview on Fox News. "He really has no choice but to say that."

Meanwhile I had been getting increasingly irate phone calls from Marty Singer, Cosby's attorney. He had made a career out of libel cases—not so much for actually suing news organizations for libel but instead preventing damaging stories about his clients from running by threatening to sue. He had tried to keep Tamara's story out of the papers and was especially mad because I kept appearing on national shows to talk about my stories. Many were also going out on the Knight-Ridder wire service.

"You're really enjoying all the attention, aren't you?" he said, his voice dripping with contempt, in one of those calls.

"Oh sure, Marty, I just love it," I replied, keeping it light. I wasn't going to take the bait.

By then I was fed up. I was working long hours, sticking around the newsroom late at night to appear via satellite in Philadelphia on live national news talk shows, and then driving nearly an hour back to my home. I was exhausted, but I was also committed. Whatever part of America watched these shows to learn about what was happening was enough motivation to keep me going. The more people who heard the truth, the more likely it would maybe someday be accepted. Maybe it would even prompt more victims to come forward.

And besides, the national print media had retreated from the story. These prime-time cable news programs were the only way to get the message spread nationwide. For instance, Van Susteren's show aired on Fox News, which was beating all the other cable outlets in ratings. How could I ignore an opportunity to represent the truth?

Still, I had a small taste of what it felt like to be under public fire, and it wasn't fun. It was anxiety inducing, and tensions only mounted when an article attacking me and my newspaper appeared in the *Philadelphia Weekly*, one of the local alternative newspapers, chastising me for not including Tamara's bar complaint in my initial story about Tamara, even though I didn't know about it before we published. The headline was "Media Watchers Wonder Whether the *Daily News* Has It in for Cosby." Journalism experts spoke out too, questioning my paper's decision to publish Tamara's story on the cover. Keith Woods, dean of faculty at the Poynter Institute journalism school, said that one witness isn't enough to substantiate the story.

"If you have an allegation between two people in one room, witnessed by no one but the two," Woods said, "until you have more information, I don't know if you can make it a lead story or a front-page story." According to Woods's criteria, then, a rape—by nature rarely having witnesses—can never make the front page.

Temple University journalism department chair Bonnie Brennen also weighed in. "It smacks of sensationalism more than news," she told Kia Gregory, the author of the story.

Gregory also quoted Cosby's criminal defense attorney, Walter Phillips Jr.: "We are very disappointed in the coverage of the *Daily News*," he told her. "It's not responsible journalism."

The editor of my paper, Michael Days, defended the decision. "It was told by a veteran reporter," he said. "We didn't move too fast. We fully vetted the story. I don't think any of that goes against Green's credibility. What does she have to gain [from] coming forward, other than being attacked?"

I suspected someone from Cosby's team initiated the article, but I couldn't prove it and wasn't going to waste my time reacting to their tactics. It was the same kind of smear campaign they were using against Andrea, her mother, and Tamara, and the journalism experts played right into their hands.

Still, I was irritated. And frustrated by the narrow thinking of academics who were dismissing the horrible implications of their rulebook-style analysis. With crimes like sexual assault, which are inherently "he said, she said," with no witnesses, a story can only be told by relying on the people in the room. And if a news outlet decides that's not good enough, the story never gets told. Conversely, if a news agency engages in victim blaming or shaming in its coverage of sexual assaults, it not only impacts how the public views the crime, it influences how vigorously law enforcement investigates them. And the perpetrators get away with their crimes. Putting Tamara's story on the front page told the world we believed her.

Every day, news outlets make difficult decisions about how to report on sexual crimes, deciding when to put a story forward or hold it back in hopes of finding some corroborative evidence—which almost never comes in cases like this. And if we do decide to publish it, the debate begins about how much space to give it and whether it deserves to be on the cover. Some papers are more cautious, and that's their choice. But my newspaper was known as the "people paper," and it was part of our ethos to not be afraid to stand up for the underdog, to take on those in power. As a tabloid, we were used to being called "sensationalistic." But I knew we were ethical, and I liked that we were gutsy. And yes, sometimes we were even brave. What we were not was the newspaper of record, like our sister paper, the *Inquirer*, a broadsheet. So we had the latitude to devote our resources to the stories we thought were important, to follow our own rules at times, not just documenting whatever was happening in the city that particular day or toeing the establishment line.

We also had a different circulation structure from most newspapers. We had very few home subscribers, so we relied heavily on street sales of the paper. In other words, we had to convince our readers to shell out their hard-earned cash for our paper each day. And that meant making sure the stories on our cover would make someone want to buy it. Tamara's story certainly qualified. She allowed us to use her name and photo, an unusual choice for an alleged sexual assault victim. Had she stayed anonymous, I doubt we would have put it on the cover.

In the end, it came down to this: if the big-establishment papers weren't going to give sexual assault victims a voice against a powerful person, we would. And then we'd let the nighttime talk shows continue the conversation, spreading the story over the airwaves to cities across the country.

Except then the TV shows started retreating too.

Cosby's people were pressuring the bookers to stay away from the story and to keep me off their shows. They'd call the producers and make threats, or they'd offer promises of future favors. This kind of "trading up" is shifty at best, and yet it plagues the national media, particularly in television.

Here's how it works. A negative story about a powerful person is about to released. The powerful person offers the media organization something enticing, like an exclusive interview or an invitation to events otherwise closed to the press, like Cosby's town halls—but only if they drop the negative story. I'd never heard of such tactics before I covered this case. It was disillusioning to say the least.

And there were still more reasons why journalists avoided the story. Tony Norman, the African American columnist for the *Pittsburgh Post-Gazette*, explained to readers that it was an especially tricky subject to tackle for African American journalists. "There is concern in the African-American community that the scrutiny into Cosby's life will dampen his activism," he wrote. "Charges like those leveled at Cosby can't help but curb his outspokenness on a host of hot-button issues of particular concern to black folks. Will Cosby withdraw from participating in the great debates in the civil rights community because of embarrassment?"

So the story was quiet. But it was too late for Bill Cosby. The allegations of drugging and sexually assaulting trusting young women had been broadcast around the country, and suddenly women from California to Florida were saying Cosby had assaulted them too. One by one, each had a story to tell.

One met him at Clemson University in South Carolina when he came to perform.

Another was a flight attendant he invited to come by the studio where he was filming *I Spy*.

Others, like Jennifer Thompson, were models who met him through their agents, accepting his offer to mentor them.

Bruce Castor remained silent as a steady parade of new female accusers gave statements to Andrea's attorneys, who then turned their contact information over to his detectives. Each one shared details of her story, and with each story Cosby's pattern of premeditated sexual assault became more clarified. I knew very little about what they had to say back then. That knowledge came later. All I could do was report that "a steady stream" of new accusers were emerging. I was getting many tips via email and letters as well. Some were about other women being molested and/or drugged by Cosby, while others were more general anecdotes about being treated poorly by him. I was doing my best to follow up on each and every one when, suddenly, on the evening of February 17, 2005, Castor announced he was closing the case, just four weeks after he'd opened it.

I put down my pen.

The women didn't matter. Their accounts didn't matter. The case was closed.

CHAPTER SIX

BLINDSIDED

Bruce Castor announced his decision not to charge Cosby in a carefully worded page-and-a-half press release with a time stamp of 5:45 P.M., long after his support staff and his assistant, who usually dealt with such things, had left for the day.

Castor not only wrote and typed the release up himself but also signed it and sent it to the media himself, all of which was unusual. So was his decision not to hold a news conference, something he routinely did with big moments in his cases. None of the investigators on the case were aware of his plan. In fact, detectives were still in the middle of their investigation and had just that morning met to draw up a list of investigative leads. The sudden pronouncement stunned them:

The District Attorney has reviewed the statements of the parties involved, those of all witnesses who might have firsthand knowledge of the alleged incident, including family, friends and co-workers of the complainant, and professional acquaintances and employees of Mr. Cosby.

Detectives searched Mr. Cosby's home for potential evidence. Investigators further provided District Attorney Castor with phone records and other items that might have evidentiary value. Lastly, the District Attorney reviewed statements from other persons claiming that Mr. Cosby behaved inappropriately with them on prior occasions. However, the detectives could find no instance in Mr. Cosby's past where anyone complained to law enforcement of conduct, which would constitute a criminal offense . . .

The District Attorney finds insufficient credible and admissible evidence exists upon which any charge against Mr. Cosby could be sustained beyond a reasonable doubt.

Castor, who continued to refer to the allegations as "inappropriate touching" even though Andrea had told detectives it was digital penetration, said he couldn't find any criminal intent on Cosby's behalf. He was dismissive of Gianna's taped phone call, calling it "illegally obtained"—even though Ferman, his own assistant, had researched the issue for him and told him the recording was legal—and of the new accusers' statements, which he called "too remote in time to be considered legally relevant."

As I read his release, my amazement grew. How could the case be over before it was fully investigated? Even more shocking was what he had to say about Andrea, the alleged victim in the case:

> Because a civil action with a much lower standard of proof is possible, the District Attorney renders no opinion concerning the credibility of any party involved so as not to contribute to the publicity, and taint prospective jurors. The District Attorney does not intend to expound publicly on the details of his decision for fear that his opinions and analysis might be given undue weight by jurors in any contemplated civil action. District Attorney Castor cautions all parties to this matter that he will reconsider this decision should the need arise. Much exists in this investigation that could be used (by others) to portray persons on both sides of the issue in a less than flattering light.

I honestly can't recall any case I have covered before or since where a prosecutor disparaged a sexual assault victim in this way. As harsh as his words were, an earlier draft of the release had even stronger language, which he omitted after consulting with Ferman. Still, what he had to say back then was enough to upset Troiani and Kivitz, who were both former sex crimes prosecutors; they were stunned by the venom he directed toward Andrea. "I have never seen a DA come out and trash a victim like this," Troiani fumed when I spoke with her that evening.

Nor could they believe no one had bothered to call them to let them know. Ferman, in fact, asked Castor if she should call Troiani and Kivitz to tell them about the decision, which was their standard procedure, but Castor told her not to and said he would fax over the press release himself. Instead, they found out when a local reporter from ABC's Channel 6 showed up at their office for a reaction.

Troiani was furious. The fact that she wasn't notified in advance spoke volumes to her about the manner in which the investigation was conducted. "This is inexplicable," she raged. "Why would he not give us the courtesy of telling us this would happen?"

Kivitz and Troiani were not just angry, though. They were deeply disappointed. Initially, they'd thought it was unlikely Castor would charge Cosby, especially because Castor had political aspirations at the time and wouldn't want to alienate Cosby fans, a large percentage of voters. But after so many accusers emerged, they had started to hope: just six days earlier, Kivitz had called his office with names of other accusers who had contacted them. Maybe he would change his mind. Maybe he would see there was a truth that couldn't be avoided. Maybe he would feel something—a spark of regret, a pang of compassion— for the women who had been tricked, violated, molested. Maybe there would be a prosecution. Instead, they were blindsided.

Andrea was in town running errands with her sister when her mother finally reached her at 7:30 that night and gently broke the news to her. Not only was she not at home and surrounded by the love and support of friends and family, but she couldn't go home either— the press had surrounded her house, hoping for a glimpse, a photo, a comment. Andrea waited until she couldn't anymore and finally gave up and snuck home.

Tamara was furious too. As outspoken as ever, she called for a new district attorney to protect its citizens because the DA was supposed to be the people's lawyer, "not Bill Cosby's." She was understandably angry—and emotionally exhausted too: for the last weeks she'd been inundated with women in television studios, supermarkets, and doctor's offices telling her how they'd been sexually assaulted. How they never told anyone about it. "I have been asked in the course of being interviewed whether I think women's rights have progressed since the early 1970s when this happened to me," she said. "All I can say is a woman came forward in Montgomery County in 2005 and complained of a sexual assault, and how's it working for her?"

Phillips, though, said his client was "gratified" by Castor's decision. "Mr. Cosby looks forward to moving on with his life."

But all was not lost. Andrea's next step was to file a civil suit, where Tamara's and the other women's testimony could be pivotal.

PUBLIC OPINION OF Cosby was as glowing as ever. While Andrea was still reeling over the decision, my newspaper and the *Pittsburgh Post-Gazette* sent reporters out into the streets of Philadelphia to see if the case had shattered his squeaky clean, Dr. Huxtable image, and the reporters came up all but empty handed. Hardly anyone thought Cosby was guilty.

The *Post-Gazette* reporter even came across a group of women who'd grown up with Cosby in the Richard Allen projects during the 1940s and 1950s. They were hanging out at a local Wendy's in North Philadelphia, not far from the projects, when they told the reporter their support for Cosby was unwavering.

"He's a good guy," Edith Duffan insisted. "He's done well for the poor. He's also helping a lot of the children." She praised Cosby's loyalty, saying he had never lost touch with his friends from the old neighborhood and that he'd even treated Duffan and her family members to dinner and a show when they went to Las Vegas. They all saw Frank Sinatra perform at Caesar's Palace, a night she'd never forget. She scoffed at Tamara's story, saying it was ridiculous to try to make a fuss so long after something happened.

Her friend, Evelyn Jubillue, agreed: "It wouldn't take me no thirty years to know I was groped."

The temperature on campus at Temple University, where Cosby was a donor and frequent visitor, was no different. The students loved "Dr. Huxtable," and David Adamany, the university's president at the time, stood firmly behind the Cos as well.

"As far as we're concerned, nothing has happened," he said. "Some allegations have been made. They remain unproven and every celebrity in America can be singled out for this sort of thing. So, until there is some conclusion to these allegations, that's all they are. And there's been no change in the relationship between Temple and Bill Cosby."

John Chaney, Temple's legendary men's basketball coach, was equally defiant on Cosby's behalf. "I've known him when he didn't have a dime in his pocket," he said. "He's done nothing but contribute to others. He's sent youngsters to college, saved programs. He's just been an enormous gift to life here at the university."

The support from the upper echelons of the university was not surprising. Not only was Cosby an alumni and had sported a Temple sweatshirt on *The Cosby Show* more than once, but he'd also spoken at commencements, dispensing homespun comedy and life advice to thousands of graduates since the early 1990s. In 2003 he'd begun hosting Cosby 101, an orientation and pep talk for fall freshmen, transfer students, and their parents. In the mid-1980s a local campaign to improve Temple's image included commercials in which Cosby was quoted as saying, "I could have gone anywhere, but I chose Temple."

He'd spearheaded the Cosby Academic Posse Program, or CAPP, to encourage academic achievement among underperforming schoolchildren by providing tutoring services. Several academic scholarships in the family's name were given to Temple students, including the Camille and Bill Cosby Scholarship in Science. The university's Cosby Scholarship Committee of the provost's office also determined recipients of other awards.

Even those who were not fans of Cosby's town halls didn't think the allegations would impact his legacy. Syndicated columnist Clarence Page, who compared Cosby's plight to that of Michael Jackson and his child molestation case, said Cosby's forty-year history as a wholesome family man made him an American icon who appeals to both blacks and whites. "The preponderance of the evidence we've been allowed to see makes it look very bad for Michael," Page said. "I don't see that with Cosby at all."

And so the news media engines geared down. The Associated Press's story on the case closing was just five hundred words, and the *New York Times* and the *Washington Post* each ran a paragraph about the decision two days later. They must have felt there wasn't much more to say.

ONE OF THE most puzzling aspects of the criminal case had been Castor's aversion from the very beginning to prosecuting it. This made me suspicious, and I wondered whether Castor had some kind of a prior relationship with Cosby. One day, I came across some intriguing information.

In 1983 Castor's father, a prominent Philadelphia attorney, had represented millionaire philanthropist F. Eugene Dixon when he sold his home on New Second Street in Elkins Park. The house—a sixteen-room, nearly six-thousand-square-foot stone mansion—was sold to Bill Cosby. Castor Senior had Dixon's power of attorney. This was the same house where Andrea said she'd been drugged and sexually assaulted.

It would not have been that interesting—except that Castor Junior never revealed his father's relationship with Cosby to Andrea's lawyers. Phillips, Cosby's attorney, was the one person who did know, and he said he only found out because Castor Junior casually mentioned it one day. "Just in the course of a conversation, he happened to say it," Phillips told me, unbothered. He said that to his knowledge Castor Junior had never met Cosby, not before the investigation or during it, and that was good enough for him.

Joseph F. Lawless, author of the book *Prosecutorial Misconduct* and an expert on criminal procedures, had another opinion. He didn't mince words, saying Castor Junior should have told both sides about the house sale right up front. "When you don't disclose [prior relationships], or only disclose it to one side, it looks as if you're trying to hide something or keep information from one side or the other. That is what can create an appearance of impropriety."

I decided to write a story that revealed Castor Junior's past connection to Cosby. Maybe it wasn't earth-shattering news, but it demonstrated favoritism toward Cosby and a general unprofessionalism. I also hoped the story might prompt people to contact me with more information about the relationship between Castor Junior and Cosby. Neither Castor nor his father returned my phone calls requesting comment, but in 2016, Castor Junior insisted he wasn't aware of his father's role at the time. He explained to the website Billy Penn that his father later told him the attorney who was supposed to handle the transaction was sick the day of the sale, so he filled in, and that Cosby wasn't even present.

My story ran that Saturday with the headline "DA's Dad Aided Cosby's Mansion Buy." Below that it said, "Comedian's lawyers advised of link, but accusers were never notified, they say."

But no other media picked up on the story, not even the *Philadelphia Inquirer*. What little media attention there had been quickly fizzled away. Another dead end.

The one story to arise in the following days would come from the *Washington Post*, which ran a nearly five-thousand-word story in the

Style section with the headline, "Cos and Effect: Bill Cosby Has Always Been One to Speak Out. Now He's Really Hearing It." It was a story exploring what impact the criminal case might have on Cosby's now-stalled town hall crusade, one that was clearly already in the works when the case erupted.

Cosby himself was quiet. Other than an occasional speech and comedy performance or two, Cosby kept to himself, declining to make any public comments about the case.

I soon learned why. He'd granted an exclusive interview to his long-time nemesis, the *National Enquirer.*

CHAPTER SEVEN

A DEAL WITH HIS DEVIL

Cosby's decision to grant the *National Enquirer* an interview—let alone give them an exclusive—was shocking. He had the power and influence to take his pick of interview requests from papers with far more respectable reputations. He'd made a deal with his own devil, and I couldn't figure out why.

Cosby had had a long, tempestuous relationship with the *Enquirer*. The enmity was understandable. In 1997 the *Enquirer* had reported on Cosby's affair with Shawn Upshaw, the former Shawn Berkes, a scandal that erupted just two days after the murder of his only son. The *Enquirer* lumped both together on the cover with the headline blaring "COSBY MURDER SECRETS" with the subhead "The Mistress, Her Shocking Story of Love, Lies and Money."

They interviewed Shawn, who told them Cosby had promised to leave his wife for her and had been paying her $3,000 a month since the mid-1970s. Their affair exploded into the headlines just when her daughter, Autumn Jackson, was arrested and charged with extortion for threatening to tell the tabloids she was his out-of-wedlock daughter if he didn't give her $24 million. Cosby acknowledged he'd had an affair with Upshaw but denied being Autumn's father.

Shawn was a twenty-year-old college student when she first met Cosby at a grand opening for a nightclub at the Marriott Hotel on Century Boulevard near the Los Angeles airport in September 1973. Cosby was thirty-six. "I wasn't supposed to be in there because I was underage, but Carol Denmark, a friend of my mother's, was the headliner," she told me.

Carol was singing when Cosby came in. He went around the room, picked up a couple of ladies to dance with, then, maybe because she was sitting at Carol's table, asked Shawn to dance. While they were dancing to a Gladys Knight song he was very touchy feely.

"He was whispering in my ear, 'I want to take you out for breakfast. When the show is over will you please come to breakfast with me?' He was hitting on me. And I thought, 'Okay. That'd be fun.'"

They talked throughout the dance, and then he escorted her back to her table. She looked up and saw a girlfriend of hers walk in. The friend said, "'Shawn, I've got to go. Take me home now. I'm going to get in trouble. It's past my curfew.' I said, 'Okay.'" She paused to write a note for Cosby, who was now off dancing with different "little old ladies." The note read, "Bill, I'm so sorry. I had to leave. I can't have breakfast with you. If you're ever back in town, I'd be happy to have breakfast with you, or lunch or dinner. Nice meeting you." She ended it with her phone number.

She left it on the table, asking Carol's husband to give it to Cosby, then left to take her friend home. By the time she got to her own home around 3 A.M. her mother was up getting ready for work. "She said, 'Your phone has been ringing off the hook, but you locked your bedroom door, so I can't answer it.'"

She walked into her room, and it rang again. Cosby was on the other end of the line. And he was angry. "What are you doing turning me down?" she said he asked her.

After that he called her every day for the next month. She knew he was married, but she was open to having a relationship with him.

"I don't want to say I didn't have morals. I guess I just didn't think there was anything wrong with it. I wasn't an actress or a model. I worked at a carpet company and went to the West LA junior college."

Both say their affair lasted just a few months. But here's where their stories diverge: she says it ended after she realized she was pregnant and that he conspired with her to put another man's name on the birth certificate, an ex-boyfriend who was incarcerated. He says he knew nothing of the pregnancy until he invited her to his suite at the Las Vegas Hilton and she pulled out a photo of a fourteen-month-old baby girl with curly hair and olive skin named Autumn and said, "This is your daughter."

Whether Autumn is or isn't his daughter, Cosby financially supported her for years. But after she dropped out of college, he cut her off, so she blackmailed him. When she and her friends arrived in New York City to collect the payoff, FBI agents arrested them.

And there was one more Cosby scandal the tabloid covered.

In March 2000 the *Enquirer* revealed that a twenty-year-old actress who'd had a bit role as a waitress on *The Cosby Show*, had accused the comedian of sexual assault. The *Enquirer* spoke to an unidentified high-ranking police official, her father, and grandfather, all of whom told them Cosby had invited her to his home for a business meeting, grabbed her breasts, tried to put his hand down her pants, and exposed himself before she fled on January 28. Three days later she reported it to the police. Although Cosby's name wasn't in the police report—"out of deference to his celebrity status," the police source told the tabloid—the *Enquirer* reporter saw that the address where it happened was Cosby's Manhattan townhome.

However, the woman's twin sister told the *New York Post* her sister was not molested. The complaint itself simply said she was subject to "sexual contact."

Cosby's spokesman confirmed that the woman had dinner at Cosby's home but vehemently denied anything untoward had happened between them. Cops forwarded the complaint to the Manhattan district attorney's office without ever interviewing Cosby. What little media interest there was quickly died down after the Manhattan district attorney's office announced it was not going to file charges against Cosby. She has never spoken publicly about what happened. But Cosby was asked about her during his deposition, and the ensuing discussion was lengthy. He said he developed a romantic interest in her, and that one day he offered her a ride to the train station in the car that took him home from *The Cosby Show*. Later, he called and spoke with her about her family—her twin sister and her brother—and their education.

Eventually, he invited her to his house to talk about her career, and what she might have to do in order to become an actress. She visited Cosby's home, she stayed for about three hours, and they reviewed "how to walk, how to think in terms of acting."

The second time she went to his house, it was the night in question—the night she addressed when she went to the police. Cosby said he fed her dinner, gave her three drinks—wine and Frangelico—then reviewed some basic acting techniques with her. After that, he said, "We then went to the sofa. We laid down together. I was behind her," he said.

He went on to say he massaged her back but he never lowered his pants and tried to get her to perform oral sex on him.

Troiani, reading from the police report, pressed him on the issue, and Cosby retorted: "You are reading something that was reported, yet no policeman called me, no police station called me. And had it not been for someone slipping this information to the media, it would have never gone anywhere."

He said he spoke to her once more after that but could not remember who initiated the call. "We were talking, and she asked me what happened," he said. "And I told her . . . exactly what I told you." The woman also asked if she was still going to get the part in a movie they'd talked about. "I just told her, 'No.'"

That was the last time they spoke.

Cosby was so angry at the *Enquirer* that he threatened to file a $250 million lawsuit against the tabloid if it didn't apologize and retract the story, but the tabloid stood by its reporting. The scenario was so familiar to me by this point that I wondered whether the twenty-year-old actress was offered an "educational trust," like Cosby would later do with Andrea and had tried to do with Jennifer Thompson.

Cosby never filed a lawsuit.

PERHAPS THE TABLOID'S splashiest Cosby story—and its most egregious conduct—was in the wake of the murder of Bill Cosby's son, Ennis. A twenty-seven-year-old PhD student on break from college, Ennis was driving north on the 405 in Los Angeles on his way to see a friend when he got a flat in the left front tire of his mother's car, a Mercedes 600SL convertible. He stopped to fix it and a man later identified as Mikhail Markashev, an eighteen-year-old Ukrainian-born immigrant who'd had frequent brushes with the law, shot him in the head. Markashev saw Ennis as an opportunity to rob the unsuspecting Cosby son for cash, but the attack went awry.

It was tragedy upon tragedy. Camille was both grief stricken and struggling with her own guilt, justified or not. She had just spoken to

Ennis the night before and had warned him to be careful driving a flashy car while he was in the city because of a rash of recent car jackings. She also worried he'd be hassled by cops suspicious of a young black man driving a luxury vehicle. She'd even gone so far as to rent him a more modest car for a while so he wouldn't drive hers. It was like she had a premonition, as though she could have—should have—stopped him.

She emerged from her grief just long enough to tell her husband that she wanted to hire a private investigator to find her son's killer. "The only thing I could think about was catching this guy," she said. "I wanted that murderer more than anything else in the world."

Cosby himself was silent at first, uttering nothing more than "He was my hero" to reporters gathered outside his Manhattan townhome. But after burying his only son on their two-hundred-acre estate in Shelburne Falls, Massachusetts, where the family had moved in September 1971, he was ready to talk. He wanted people to know it was okay to laugh again.

In yet another sign of his sway with the media, all Cosby had to do was pick up the phone and call Andrew Heyward, the president of CBS News, and ask if anchor Dan Rather wanted to come speak with him about Ennis. Rather, of course, agreed. But Rather also used it as an opportunity to ask about that *other* Cosby story that had been making news for the past two weeks: Autumn Jackson.

Cosby's spokesman at first insisted Cosby barely knew Jackson, saying she was just one of the hundreds of young people he'd help put through school, but Cosby admitted to Rather that he'd had a brief affair with her mother in the early 1970s and that it was possible he was her father.

"I mean, if you said, 'Did you make love to the woman?' The answer is yes. 'Are you the father?' No, the father's name [is on the birth certificate]. I had nothing to do with it. I didn't call her and say, 'Put that man's name down.'"

Although Rather had asked Cosby about Ennis, when CBS released excerpts of the interview the next day on its morning show and Rather's evening broadcast, the focus of the segment was the affair. Camille was so enraged that she released a statement chastising the media. "All personal negative issues between Bill and me were resolved years ago," she said. "We are a united couple."

During this time the *Enquirer* had been relentless in its reporting about Ennis's murder. In one cover story it said Camille had hired "gunmen" to "hunt" their son's killer. The week after Cosby's CBS interview it published a cover story saying Camille was sedated and on the verge of a nervous breakdown. By that time Camille had had it.

The normally reticent Camille was so angry that she wrote an opinion piece for *USA Today* headlined "Don't Believe the Tabs," saying she had been "emotionally abused" by the "lies" in the *Star*, the *Globe*, and the *National Enquirer* during the coverage of their son's death.

"I am outraged about the tabloids' immorality, and inhumaneness," she wrote. "I was depicted as being out of control, emotionally and psychologically unstable and on the verge of a nervous breakdown." She called on the *Enquirer* to retract the story. (They didn't.)

Even when the paper offered a $100,000 reward to help catch the killer, Cosby was still cool to the paper. The reward did lead to the killer's capture and conviction, but Cosby refused to thank them or even acknowledge their contribution.

The *Enquirer* was unrepentant. Editor Steve Coz said Cosby himself had said Camille was "not handling it well at all" and "It is a fact that Camille is on medication. . . . We stand by all of our stories about the Cosby family tragedy."

What I didn't know then was that sometimes he did cooperate with the *Enquirer*, like when they wrote about his daughter Erinn's stint in a drug-rehab program. He wasn't happy about it, but he did it. As he told *USA Today* in 1998, referring to the *Enquirer*, "if you know that this is a demon, you might as well deal with it straight on—better than a demon that pretends to be an angel." The latter was a reference to the mainstream media.

He made it seem as though he was protecting his daughter, but twenty-six years later the *New York Post* reported a different motivation. According to the *Post*, Cosby had given the story about his daughter's drug addiction to the *Enquirer* to keep them from printing a worse one—they had planned to write about Cosby "swinging" with some showgirls with singer Sammy Davis Jr. When Cosby agreed to an exclusive about his daughter, they dropped the other piece, the *Post* reported.

Bill Cosby was trading up.

THE *ENQUIRER* MADE the most of their big get, splashing the headline and Cosby's photo across the cover of its March 14, 2005, edition, which hit newsstands March 3: "WORLD EXCLUSIVE INTERVIEW—COSBY TELLS ALL! SEX CHARGES, THE LIES, THE TRUTH."

In the four-page article Cosby was given free rein to defend himself. Asked about the civil suit Andrea was planning to file against him, a "furious Cosby" told the *Enquirer*, "I am not going to give in to people who try to exploit me because of my celebrity status. . . . Sometimes you try to help people and it backfires on you and then they try to take advantage of you.'"

He also had choice words about Tamara, complaining that the press showed her too much respect. "My problem is with some media and how it appeared that Miss Green was allowed to be a wrecking ball," he said. "When Miss Green spoke, they pointed out that she was a lawyer. This gives her credibility."

Something about the interview still felt off to me. I couldn't understand why he would choose the *Enquirer* to speak with, not when their animosity reached so far back. I called his spokesman to be sure it was a real interview, given the *Enquirer*'s history on this case. He confirmed it was. My suspicions only grew when I saw the full-page sidebar they did with Cosby belatedly thanking them for helping solve his son's murder.

"At the time, I had tabloid-itis," Cosby said, as an explanation of his delayed expression of gratitude. "I was also juggling an extortion case. And it was a difficult time, and at that time, I didn't feel like I owed you a 'thank you.' But today, I can look back on it, and there should be accountability. And I say, 'Thank you' because I realize now that even though I challenged the *Enquirer* back then to put up a reward, the *Enquirer* did not have to do that."

The headline over that particular story was "BILL COSBY: THANKS, ENQUIRER." Editor Barry Levine used much of the space detailing how the *Enquirer* helped solve the case but also got Cosby to open up about his grief, saying it was still too painful for him to visit the New York City school where Ennis taught. The "thoughtful performer," as Levine described Cosby, had this advice for people "rocked by tragedy in their own lives," saying there's lots of evil in this world, but "You can't blame God."

The sidebar ended with a celebration of the comedian's kindness and generosity: "Happily, Cosby—a humanitarian who's given millions to charity—told the *Enquirer* his health is good." It followed with a cheerful quote from the comedian:

> I'm at the top of my game, and I'm telling *Enquirer* readers that when they see Bill Cosby, they're seeing today a better Bill Cosby—a stronger Bill Cosby.

While inwardly I grimaced about writing a story about a *National Enquirer* story, after I verified that the interview was legitimate, I had to do one. Like it or not, Cosby talking about the scandal was news, no matter who he chose to speak with.

Because Tamara was castigated in the *Enquirer* story, I needed to get a reaction from her as well. It was classic Tamara. She said she was amused that Cosby called her a "wrecking ball" in the interview. "I've been called a lot of things in my life, but this is my absolute favorite," she told me, laughing. "I'm going to find a way to get it on my license plate. I swear to God."

In the end I was glad I did do the story about the *Enquirer*'s interview with Cosby because it led me to a much better one.

It also led me to my worst confrontation yet with Marty Singer.

CHAPTER EIGHT

THE JOKE

A little over a week after he learned he would not be criminally charged with drugging and sexually assaulting Andrea Constand, Cosby appeared on stage at the State Theater in New Brunswick, New Jersey. The audience of eighteen hundred was upbeat and enjoying the Cos's signature patter of comic observations when he cracked a joke about slipping drugs into a woman's drink. He invited a woman from the audience onto the stage and called out to her.

"Before I get started," he said, smiling wryly, "let me ask you: Did I put anything into your drink?"

"No," she replied, laughing.

The audience thought it was hysterical.

I found out about the joke through sheer serendipity. I was interviewing Stuart Zakim, the *Enquirer*'s spokesperson, about the tabloid's Cosby interview when he let it slip about Cosby's joke, which he believed was referring to Andrea's allegations. Zakim happened to be in the audience for the February 26 performance. I was incredulous that Cosby would be that cavalier about the case, and I called Cosby's people for a reaction. They insisted he was not joking about Andrea. "Mr. Cosby's saying that he did not refer to anything involving Miss Constand," David Brokaw, Cosby's spokesman, said. "This was a reference to Shawn Upshaw."

Apparently, in February Shawn Upshaw told the *Enquirer* that Cosby gave her a drink back in 1973 that "looked strange" to her; that she realized she'd been drugged after she drank it, and that she woke the next morning knowing they'd had sex but not having a specific memory of it. But her story basically ended there. After Andrea's case made the news, the *Enquirer* called her to see if he'd ever done anything like that to her. I wasn't sure I believed the joke was about Shawn and not Andrea, but I hunted down a copy of the paper so I could read it myself.

"SHOCKING CHARGES: Cosby Drugged TWO Women for Sex" blared the front page. Exclusive interviews with both Shawn and Andrea flashed across the cover of the tabloid. The headline for Shawn's story was "Cosby Drugged Me, Too!—Says the Mom of His 'Love Child.'" The piece ran alongside the tabloid's "exclusive" with Andrea—that is, the story written by the reporter who had posed as a flower deliveryman.

What wasn't shocking was that Cosby was unhappy with the articles I'd been writing since that very first one about the taped phone call between Gianna and Cosby, especially because they landed me on national TV and went out on the Knight-Ridder wire service. I'd started hearing from Cosby's lawyer, Marty Singer, pretty regularly, so I wasn't surprised when he was soon calling me regarding the story about Cosby's joke I was working on. I'd called Shawn to verify it was a real interview and ended up doing a lengthy one with her about her affair with Cosby. His joke, she told me, was "in poor taste." Singer was not happy. Just her name seemed to send Cosby's team into a tizzy.

He chastised me for my previous stories, said I'd created a news story where no news story existed, and told me Shawn's story was not true. We had a heated back and forth: "Are you saying she is lying and therefore it's okay for Mr. Cosby to joke about it?" I asked.

"Her story is a complete fabrication and lie. Correct. Her story about my client allegedly doing something to her is a complete false and defamatory story."

If you feel it's false and defamatory, "do you intend to sue the *Enquirer*?" I volleyed back. Of course, the *Enquirer* had just gotten an exclusive interview with Cosby, so a lawsuit would have dramatically upset that alliance, and Singer knew it.

"What we do with the *National Enquirer* is irrelevant because the *National Enquirer* has not done what you have done," Singer snapped. "Anyone who has said anything negative about my client, you run. And now we believe you've gone too far and, in the past, have gone too far."

Then I asked him whether they'd sue my paper if I did a story about the joke Cosby had told onstage.

"If you repeat the version of what [Shawn] told the *National Enquirer*, my client has had it. . . . My client will sue. You repeat defamatory stories. . . . All of your columns have constantly been on the attack of Mr. Cosby. And that, therefore, is malice."

I WAS GLAD I'D held my ground with Singer, but his threats had me unsettled. It wasn't the first time he'd threatened to sue me and my paper, but this time his anger was more palpable than ever, and he made no pretense of hiding it. A longtime celebrity attorney, his client list featured celebrities involved in some of the biggest Hollywood scandals in the past couple of decades—Charlie Sheen, John Travolta, Britney Spears, and Arnold Schwarzenegger—and his "'cease and desist' and proceed 'at your peril' letters to media outlets and accusers [were] legendary," the *Los Angeles Times* noted in a profile of the famed litigator.

All I knew was that he was threatening to sue my paper and trying to kill my stories. I found the whole experience nerve wracking. Brokaw was always pleasant and professional to me, a true gentleman, and Phillips was courteous and respectful too. But Singer was on the attack from the minute we started talking. It was his MO, and I believed his threats were more than bluster.

He wanted the story killed, and if my career went with it, all the better.

His barrage of threats exhausted me mentally, but I refused to let it affect my coverage. I wouldn't be scared away from writing tough stories, important stories. So I told my editor about the menacing messages from Singer, which he passed along to his bosses, and then I wrote about the joke. Like my other Cosby stories, our attorneys reviewed it before it ran. I also interviewed Karen Baker, director of the National Sexual Violence Resource Center, and Troiani to get their reactions.

"I'm really disappointed that he would find any humor in sexual assault," Baker said. "Sexual assault and drug-facilitated sexual assault are reprehensible. I would hope he would use his celebrity status to help people understand that."

Troiani wasn't happy either. "This provides insight into this man's character, that he would believe that it is acceptable and even funny to drug a woman in order to have sexual contact with her."

Singer was irate. He had sent threatening letters to my paper that I never saw but I'm sure were similar to others he'd sent, littered with the buzzwords for libel: "the height of recklessness" and "extreme recklessness" and stating that such conduct amounts to "constitutional malice."

My editor kept me insulated from all of the bullying missives so I could focus on doing my job. Still, the multipage letters were aggressive and threatening, even though they never claimed at any point that the stories were wrong. The lawyers reviewed most of the stories but my editors let me carry on. Papers get libel threats all the time, and they weren't going to suddenly fold under pressure, no matter how famous and powerful his client was.

My story ran on March 8.

There was little reaction from other media. UPI did a 128-word story about it with the headline "Cosby Jokes About Doping Woman's Drink," citing my story.

We didn't get sued.

But Bill Cosby was about to.

CHAPTER NINE

CAREER ADVICE

On the same day my story about the joke ran, Andrea's attorneys filed their long-awaited civil suit against Cosby. It didn't come as a surprise to anyone, least of all the comedian himself. He'd even said in his *Enquirer* interview he was expecting it.

The suit included claims of battery, assault, invasion of privacy, defamation, and intentional infliction of emotional distress. Troiani and Kivitz asked for sums in excess of $150,000 plus attorney's fees and punitive damages.

Filing the suit was the first step toward closure for Andrea, they said in a statement. "Our client is seeking the justice due her in a forum where she can expect to be treated with the dignity and respect she deserves," they said. Since the alleged assault, Andrea had "suffered serious and debilitating injuries, mental anguish, humiliation, embarrassment, physical and emotional upset, including, but not limited to, post-traumatic stress disorder, depression, sleeplessness, isolation, flashbacks, and anxiety," the suit also noted.

The lawsuit confirmed what I had already reported—that Cosby had offered Andrea financial compensation after she went to police, an offer she did not accept. And that she'd volunteered to take a lie detector test, an offer detectives said wasn't necessary. It also fleshed out some of the details on the case I'd been wondering about, most of them about the night in question.

In January 2004 Cosby invited Andrea to his mansion to give her career advice. Andrea had told Cosby that she was quitting her job at Temple to become a massage therapist, and he offered to help; she agreed to meet him at his home around 9 P.M.

As they sat and talked, Andrea admitted to Cosby that she was worried about her future and feeling anxious about her career. Cosby offered her three blue pills, which he said were an herbal medication that would help her to relax.

"Should I take all three pills?" Andrea asked. Yes, Cosby assured her, all three pills were necessary for the medication to work. She took the pills with bottled water.

Within a short period of time Andrea's knees began to shake. Her arms and legs felt immobile, and she began to feel dizzy and weak.

"I don't feel well," she told Cosby.

Feigning concern, he led her to a sofa and laid her down. It wasn't long before she was rendered semiconscious. That was when Cosby moved in. He touched her body, fondling her breasts and vaginal area and sexually assaulted her. He took his penis out of his pants and rubbed it against her hand. Then he left, and she slipped into a drugged sleep.

She woke around 4 A.M. Her clothes and underwear were strewn about, and her vagina felt raw. Confused and dismayed, Andrea looked for Cosby. He greeted her in his bathrobe. Neither one said a word.

Andrea left his home, betrayed and ashamed. Cosby was a celebrity and a man of great stature at Temple University, where she worked. He was friends with her boss, Dawn Staley. How could she report what had happened? The outcome seemed as unbearable as the act itself.

She did not go to police for several reasons, Troiani told me. Her feelings of betrayal and shame, Cosby's celebrity status, and Cosby's stature at Temple all kept her from telling anyone the truth of what happened. A year later, though, she went to the police in Canada, and told the officials that Bill Cosby had sexually violated her.

By this point, we still hadn't revealed Andrea's identity, though many other media organizations had without her permission. On one of my TV appearances I'd even commented on how all the journalistic rules were being broken in this case.

Now that the lawsuit was filed, I went to Troiani and asked her if we could use her name and photos. She said yes. They could have filed the lawsuit as a Jane Doe and they didn't. They'd used her actual name.

That was one reason. The other was obvious.

It was already everywhere.

WITH SEXUAL ASSAULT cases a great deal of attention is paid to the character of the two people involved. Their lives are exhumed, their motivations studied, their trustworthiness analyzed. When the accused is a well-known celebrity like Cosby, the focus is usually on the person accusing him.

Knowing the case would inevitably dig deep into the crevices of Andrea's life, I had been working on a portrait of her that was respectful of her privacy but also offered an authentic profile of a woman and a life upended by a cruel act of violation. So I reached out to people in Andrea's life, asking questions and outlining a profile of her youth, coming-of-age years, and adulthood. I've also woven in details I learned many years later.

I discovered she came from a tight-knit family. Her father, Andy, had moved from Greece to Canada when he was five years old, and it was in Canada where he eventually shortened his last name from "Constantinople" to Constand and became a massage therapist. Her mother, Gianna, emigrated from Italy to Canada when she was ten years old. She was a medical secretary and the niece of a World War II hero who was being considered for sainthood. She and Andy married at age nineteen, and Andrea had an older sister, Diana, who was married to a Toronto police detective.

"Andy and I raised our daughters to be respectful, kind, honest, loyal, and loving human beings," said Gianna. "Although we were young, we invested all our time and energy into making sure they would choose the right path in life."

Though the sisters were very different, they were also very close, Diana said.

"Andrea loved anything that had a ball attached to it," Diana said, "and was not remotely interested in my dolls and Barbies."

Friends, former teammates, and coaches described her as outgoing and energetic, a health and fitness buff who loved the outdoors and was as tough and aggressive on the court as she was warm and compassionate off the court. "It's not in her character to say something happened that didn't happen," said Anthony Simms, a friend for more than fifteen years. "People can go into her history and dig and dig and dig, but . . . I'm pretty sure it's the cleanest slate you'll ever find. She's a good person."

Andrea had dreamed of being a professional basketball player from the time she was a child. Her parents moved to Scarborough, a suburb of Toronto, so she could attend Albert Campbell Collegiate and play for its extremely competitive basketball team. There she excelled on the court, becoming one of Canada's top female high school basketball players, once scoring fifty-one points in a single game. The *Toronto Star* even named her to its high school seniors' basketball all-star team.

In 1992 Andrea enrolled at the University of Arizona, where she had been recruited to play basketball. She loved the school, but her performance on the court lagged. Her freshman year she averaged just 1.8 points per game. She started only five games and hit just 18 percent of her three-point shots. Her sophomore year wasn't much better—she averaged only 1.7 points per game. In her junior year she improved, but only slightly, making an average of 3.1 shots on the court.

She realized she was homesick, and it was also affecting her studies and her training, so her father came up with the idea of having his parents move to Tucson from Canada. They were retired from the restaurant business and thought the warm climate would suit them.

"I had always enjoyed a special relationship with my grandparents," Andrea said. "Not only had I grown up in their home, but I spoke Greek before I spoke English."

They moved there in late 1994, during Andrea's junior year in college. "They got an apartment close to mine, and I was there most days, talking and laughing over my favorite home-cooked meals," she said. "The homesickness quickly evaporated."

That's when she began to turn around her college experience. "It was an amazing time in my life," she said. "I learned a lot, developed a circle of really good friends, many of them teammates, and traveled around the United States to compete."

Andrea wanted to leave a greater legacy as a player. So during the off season she worked one on one with assistant coach Traci Waites to improve her footwork, perimeter shooting, and ball handling. She worked hard; kept a positive, can-do attitude; and committed herself to improving her skills and game play.

The hard work paid off. During her senior year Andrea raised her scoring average ten points. She scored fourteen points when the Wildcats won the National Invitational Tournament in March 1996 and was one of the NCAA leaders in three-point percentages.

Andrea was deeply grateful to Waites. "I owe so much of my success to Coach Waites," she said. "She wanted me to succeed, and her commitment allowed me to succeed."

Waites refused to take the credit. "She was just determined," she said. "She really wanted to do well, and she always worked hard. She always had a positive attitude."

Andrea's improvement was significant enough to bolster her dreams of playing for the WNBA. In 1996 she left the University of Arizona to train. She flew on her own dime to Detroit, Salt Lake City, Phoenix, Los Angeles, and Sacramento, but she didn't get chosen for any of the teams in those cities.

Then, in August 1997, she was named to Canada's squad for the World University Games in Sicily. It wasn't the WNBA, but it was a top-tier competition and an opportunity to showcase what she could do. "I'm on a mission," Andrea said. "First to help Canada do well, then to play basketball in Italy, and to finally crack a spot on a team in the WNBA."

While in Sicily she signed a $30,000 pro contract with one of the top teams in Europe, viewing it as yet another stepping stone to her ultimate goal. Although scouts had approached her before she left Canada, she hadn't received an offer to play for a US team yet. The European circuit seemed like a good alternative, and she had a sense that her dream was finally within reach. Thrilled, she imagined becoming the first Canadian woman to play in the WNBA. The decision, which made headlines back in her home country, surprised Michele Belanger, her coach for the World University Games. "Most people wouldn't do it like that," she told me. "Most people would go to an agent, check the whole situation out, because you want to make sure you get paid."

After playing professionally in Europe for a year and a half, Andrea was ready to try again with the WNBA. She returned home to Toronto, where she'd be closer to scouts, and took a job at a Nike store while still training in her off hours. She took a few college courses, which the University of Arizona paid for, and finished earning her degree. She also took a job coaching for a teen basketball program, Blue Chip Basketball. The kids loved her. But Andrea wanted more.

In 2001 Andrea set aside her professional basketball dreams for good. She loved the game, but if she was going to be recruited for a pro team, it would have already happened. She had to accept her reality, move on, and pursue another goal. That's when a mutual friend introduced Andrea to Dawn Staley, the women's basketball coach at Temple.

Staley and Andrea hit it off, and Staley offered her a job as director of operations. She also offered her a place to live. Staley owned a thousand-square-foot loft condo in a building at Thirteenth and Callowhill Streets, just a couple of miles south of Temple and a short subway ride away. The apartment Andrea moved into was beautiful, with thirteen-foot ceilings, hardwood floors, and a fireplace.

Andrea quickly became close with R. M. Stineman and Purna Rodman Conare, the couple who lived across the hall from her. They still remember the first time they saw her step off the elevator with her then-girlfriend. They were both six feet tall, red haired, and thin.

They look like models, they thought.

They struck up an instant friendship. When she'd come home, she'd look to see if they were up, and if a light was on, she'd knock on the door. "We probably ate together at least once a week," Conare said. "If one of us was cooking, we'd say, 'Do you want to come over?'" Andrea took to the job and infused it with a newfound excitement for the game. She was innovative—trying new techniques and keeping the team motivated with her upbeat encouragement. The team returned the affection, appreciating her devotion to their success and her ever-present smile. "She was real upbeat, real outgoing," a former player said. "I never really saw her have a bad day."

Andrea was a natural beauty who never wore makeup or paid much attention to her hair or her appearance. So when Cosby invited Andrea to a blues club in New York City and asked her to wear makeup, she went to Stineman for help.

"I bought her some stuff at CVS and showed her how to do it. I took pictures at each step to show her how."

They both remembered when she became friends with Cosby. She was aware of his fame but had never watched *The Cosby Show* or seen his Jell-O commercials. She didn't even know who Fat Albert was, so she wasn't "bowled over by his celebrity," Stineman said. "She felt completely safe with him," he said. "He was mentoring her. He was in some ways a father figure. She trusted him."

Still, she soon grew restless. She liked her job, but it wasn't how she wanted to spend her life. And she knew what she wanted to do: become a massage therapist like her father. "I wanted to pursue a career in the healing arts," she said. "I also wanted to work closer to home, where I would be reunited with my large, extended family and many friends." She was excited to begin the next phase of her life.

But everything changed for Andrea after that night at Cosby's house. Andrea became despondent. Her smile faded; her spark extinguished. She withdrew into herself.

MY PROFILE OF Andrea ran in the *Daily News* on March 9, 2005. It was a nuanced portrait, and I was happy with how it portrayed both Andrea and the unfolding of the case. There was one key detail about Andrea, however, that I had left out of the story: during one of my interviews a former teammate told me Andrea was gay.

I was surprised. Cosby's defense, according to an ABC report, was that what happened between he and Andrea was consensual. I called Troiani, who confirmed Andrea was gay. But she didn't want me to write about it, saying Andrea wanted her sexuality to remain private. When I pointed out that the fact that Andrea was gay could undermine Cosby's pretense that Andrea was a willing participant in what happened between them, Troiani was skeptical. "Cosby's people will just find some guy she dated in college to say that she's not *really* gay."

Given the smear tactics Cosby's people were already using, I had to admit that Troiani was likely right. I made no mention of it in my story, and Andrea kept her secret for many years to come until *she* was ready to reveal it to the world.

Meanwhile the filing of the civil lawsuit itself got even less coverage than the decision not to prosecute Cosby. The mainstream papers barely made note. *The Abrams Report* was on the story, however, and invited Troiani to appear on the air the night she filed the suit. Troiani was thoroughly grilled—it was clear where Abrams stood on the matter. He wasted no time and drilled into the time lapse between the assault and Andrea's decision to come forward to the police.

"Why didn't she just go and complain about it right away?" he asked.

It was a question Troiani had answered many times and would be compelled to answer again and again in the coming weeks—and years. She repeated what had become rote to her by now.

"There are many reasons why women who are put in this situation do not come forward immediately," she replied. "They feel they can no longer trust anyone. They feel shame. They feel fear, and this case was certainly compounded by the fact that the person who was accused is Bill Cosby, an icon in this area and certainly an icon at Temple where she worked."

So why did she come forward? he wanted to know.

"She had to find some closure. And it was haunting her, as it does haunt every victim of a sexual assault."

Abrams then read a statement Cosby's attorneys sent him, which asserted a tone of moral superiority: "Mr. Cosby will address this matter through the judicial process and not through the media."

Abrams also read quotes from Cosby's *Enquirer* interview, in which he claimed Andrea's suit was an attempt to exploit him due to his celebrity status.

"You know," Abrams said after reading the quotations, "it sure sounds like what he's saying is that this woman is trying to exploit him and effectively get money from him because he's a celebrity,"

"That's why he's being sued for defamation," Troiani shot back.

By now Abrams's open skepticism didn't surprise me. It is what so many sexual assault victims encounter when they finally muster up their courage and go to police, especially when the accused is popular and powerful. They get criticized for delaying reporting, then when they finally do muster up the courage to go to authorities, their personal lives are subjected to the type of scrutiny I'm not sure many of us could survive. If by some miracle the victim has nothing in her past that can be used to question her credibility, the defendant will simply make up lies. And the media will run with it.

It was no different for Andrea. Cosby's attorneys had used the tactic to discredit her, and it looked like it was working.

Then came the Jane Does.

CHAPTER TEN

FASHION WEEK

As negotiations during the civil suit against Cosby quietly got under- way, starting with who would be deposed and when, new information came to light about the other women who Cosby had assaulted. In addition to Tamara, there were twelve more accusers who had stories similar to Andrea's and were willing to testify.

The women were identified in court documents as Jane Does One through Twelve. Like Tamara, they didn't have lawsuits of their own nor did they intend to file suits; they just wanted to buttress Andrea's extraordinary tale with their own.

One of the most shocking revelations was buried in a footnote of the court papers. Though Troiani and Kivitz had provided law enforcement with the names and contact information of all the women who had contacted them, police never interviewed the majority of them. No one in law enforcement called; no one asked questions that might demonstrate a pattern in Cosby's behavior and lend credence to Andrea's case. It was yet more confirmation to them that Bruce Castor made his decision without doing a thorough investigation.

Cosby, meanwhile, filed his response to the allegation in the suit that May. He denied drugging and sexually assaulting Andrea, saying he only gave her Benadryl and all she did was sleep over.

But now, with the civil suit gaining traction, the Jane Does had another opportunity to support Andrea. I wanted to talk to them, but their identities were kept secret from the public. So I told Kivitz and Troiani I was interested in speaking with anyone who decided they wanted to talk, and a couple of months later one of them called me.

Forty-six-year-old Beth Ferrier had been known simply as Jane Doe Number Five until we spoke on June 17, 2005. Her call came just as a national Father's Day poll revealed that Bill Cosby's Cliff Huxtable was TV's "Number 1 Dad" and the television father that adults would most like to have had while they were growing up. The poll also revealed that Cliff Huxtable wasn't just a role model for a new generation; he took the number-one spot for all age groups, beating out beloved father figures such as Charles Ingalls of *Little House on the Prairie*, Howard Cunningham of *Happy Days*, Tim Taylor of *Home Improvement*, and even Ward Cleaver of *Leave It to Beaver*.

I shouldn't have been surprised the drugging and sexual assault scandal hadn't left a mark, that he was still America's favorite dad. He'd spent decades nurturing that perception of him, even writing a best-selling book about fatherhood. But we now knew that fourteen women total said he'd done unspeakable things to them. Shouldn't that resonate with the public? How could all of these women be lying? More importantly, why would they lie? They had nothing to gain. It was discouraging. Could nothing affect his Teflon image?

Perhaps Beth could.

Like Andrea, Beth was a jock while growing up. She played basketball, ran track, and swam on the swim team in school. One of three children and the only girl, Beth was raised in the Midwest, then moved to Denver the summer before her sophomore year in high school. They had a solidly middle-class life. Her father was in banking and land development, and her mother was an oral surgeon's assistant and held old-fashioned, traditional values. She loved to bake brownies and insisted on sewing her daughter's clothes—it was a labor of love. They went to church, Episcopalian, every Sunday.

Like many of her peers in high school, Beth wanted to be a cheerleader, but she didn't make the squad. Tall and pretty with olive skin, long dark brown hair, and an infectious smile that lit up her hazel eyes, she decided to try modeling, and the summer before her junior year in high school she and her mom went to see Jo Farrell, the owner of JF Images in Denver, the top agency in the city. Though she was five-feet-eleven and 125 pounds, slim by anyone else's standards, she was told she wasn't fit for modeling.

"Let's face it, honey, you're not that pretty. You'll never model," Jo said.

Beth was stung but didn't want to give up. She had a spark for fashion and style and believed it was a job she could do and do well. Still, she put modeling aside for the time being, finished high school, and then enrolled at the University of Northern Colorado in Greeley to study special education, still planning to give modeling a try when the time was right. She was only in school for a year before her father fell ill with bone cancer, and Beth went home to help care for him. Though she began taking classes at a local community college, her father insisted she go back to Greeley, which she did after he died in June of 1981.

It was a sad time in Beth's life, but it was also, in other ways, a joyous one. Soon after her father's death Beth met a young man, and after a whirlwind courtship they married in February 1982. She also reinvigorated her dreams of being a model and signed with Steven Vannoy of Vannoy Talent, Denver's number-two modeling agency, even though he too told her she needed to lose weight. He got her a gig or two, and her career was looking like it was off to a promising start when fate intervened.

One day, while driving to Greeley to see her husband play in an alumni football game, Beth was in a car accident that would change the course of her life. An elderly farmer plowed through a stop sign, and she slammed her brand-new black BMW 320i, a wedding gift from her husband, into him, totaling the vehicle.

"I was hospitalized and had head injuries, damaged teeth, and facial injuries," she said. "I nearly died."

Beth was still in the hospital when one of her first modeling photos, for a New York City clothing designer, appeared in the *Rocky Mountain News*. The full-page ad made a splash.

"Everyone started calling around, trying to figure out who I was," she said.

But she was still in the hospital, with broken bones and several jaw surgeries looming, surgeries that were necessary to repair the damage to her teeth. It would take some time for Beth to get back on her feet.

And when she did, she was more in demand than ever. The jaw surgeries required a special diet, and by the time she had recovered, she had lost forty pounds, making her body shape ideal for the modeling industry, which in the 1970s had come to favor Twiggy-like angles. The jobs came in, and Beth kept busy. It wasn't long before she signed with Elite in Chicago, an edgy, top-tier agency that also represented Cindy Crawford and many other famous models. They flew her all over the country for shoots for clients like Nordstrom, landing her on the pages of *GQ* and *Vogue*. Her career soared even after she gave birth to her son in January 1984, with her body snapping back into shape in a matter of weeks.

Vannoy was still her "mother agency," as she called it, which every model had, but it was struggling financially, so in the summer of 1984 Beth gritted her teeth and went back to Farrell, the same woman who told her she was too fat and not pretty enough for JF Images to represent her.

This time she got a much different response from the modeling maven.

"I go to see this woman, and she's like, 'Oh my God. I've got to have you. You are *it*,'" Beth said. "I signed with her, and then she signed me up to go to New York City to be a part of Fashion Week."

This was a big deal. Fashion Week is the kind of break every model dreams of—a week-long, high-profile event where top fashion brands reveal their new designs for buyers, the media, and the public. It's an event where modeling stars are launched, and Beth was thrilled. She was twenty-four years old and on the cusp of seeing her dream become reality.

In September 1984, Beth flew to New York with another model, Tony, and the agency's fashion director, Denise. Farrell had arranged for them to stay at an employee's apartment in New York City. Before they left, she had some more good news for Beth and Tony: she had set up a meeting for them with none other than comedy star Bill Cosby.

It was the first season of *The Cosby Show*, which was already getting rave reviews. Producers Marcy Carsey and Tom Werner, developers of the hit comedies *Taxi*, *Mork and Mindy*, and *Soap*, had formed a production company and approached Cosby about creating a new comedy, even though the prevailing opinion in Hollywood was that the sitcom was dead. The show debuted on September 20 and was a fast hit—that year it ranked third in the Nielson ratings and would go on to spend five consecutive seasons as the number-one show.

But before the world met Dr. Huxtable, Cosby had developed an unusual relationship with modeling agencies across the country. He would come to them saying he wanted to mentor a particular model and help them become an actress, and the agents would send the women his way.

Although Beth was no teenager, she was naïve. She was blissfully unaware of any ulterior motives, taking Farrell at her word about why she was going to meet the legendary comedian.

"He was going to help us with our careers," Beth told me. Farrell told Beth and Tony that Cosby would critique their look and their runway skills and then arrange for them to meet with other agencies and TV commercial people.

Like the Huxtables, Bill Cosby lived in a stately brownstone, but instead of in Brooklyn, Cosby's was in the tony Upper East Side of Manhattan. It was at the brownstone that he welcomed them into his home, all smiles. He was a warm and gracious host, Beth said, and he peppered her with friendly questions. "How are you? Do you like to work out? Do you like to run? You're an athlete. Cool," he said.

Beth noticed that he seemed to be paying more attention to her than the others but didn't think much of it. Even if he was more focused on her, he was genial with everyone throughout the week, taking them all to dinner at Mr. Chow and arranging for them to attend a taping of *The Cosby Show*. Then, one night later in the week, Beth and Denise were enjoying drinks in Cosby's brownstone when Denise became ill. Tony came to pick her up, but Cosby convinced Beth to stay.

"Denise will be okay," he assured her. "We should really talk about your career and your dad," he added, showing concern for her recent loss of her father.

"He was kind, saying, 'You poor thing. Your dad was so important to you . . .'" she said. And then she marveled, "He knew everything about me before I got there."

THEIR FRIENDSHIP GREW quickly, and by the end of the visit, though they were both married, they had begun an affair. Soon, Beth said, she fell in love, and although they lived in different cities, they stayed in touch. He would fly to Chicago to take her to a show or to dinner. She hobnobbed with him and his celebrity friends, meeting Richard Gere and Whoopi Goldberg, among others.

"I was completely enamored of him," she said. "I just enjoyed his company so much. He gave me all the attention anyone could give you. Here's your favorite wine. Here's your favorite champagne."

Several months later he bought her a plane ticket to New York. When she arrived she went straight to his brownstone, where they were supposed to share a romantic few days together. The next morning, he gave her a $100 bill and sent her to the local deli for bagels and cream cheese. When she returned to his home, laden with bagels, his demeanor had changed. With no explanation he told her to pack her bags and move into a nearby hotel. Puzzled and upset, she checked into the hotel, doubting herself for having an affair. She quickly checked out and flew back to Chicago, mystified, without saying goodbye to Cosby.

It wasn't long before he called her, telling her he was not happy with her for leaving town without telling him. "I disobeyed him, so he didn't trust me anymore," she said.

Yet she couldn't end their relationship. It was another several months before she mustered the strength to tell him she was done. This time she meant it.

Several weeks later he called to tell her he was coming to Denver and asked her to meet him at the now-defunct nightclub where he was performing. He wouldn't stop calling her, so she agreed to meet him in his dressing room backstage, where he waited with a cup of coffee for her. "My intent was to tell him in front of his bodyguards and everyone and say, 'I'm done. Leave me alone,'" she said. That's not what happened.

"Here's your favorite coffee, something I made to relax you," he said.

Still guarded, she drank the coffee and quickly began to feel woozy.

The next thing she knew, she was waking up in the back of her car, alone. She had no idea what had happened to her.

"My clothes were a mess. My bra was undone. My top was untucked. And I'm sitting there going, 'Oh my God. Where am I? What's going on?' I was so out of it. It was just awful."

After gathering her senses, she said she decided to confront Cosby and went to his hotel. Although it was the middle of the night, he let her into his room. She quickly lost her courage. They sat on the bed, saying nothing.

The following day she said Farrell told her, "Cosby forgives you. You had too much to drink." But Farrell was angry at Beth for "drinking too much" and fired her. Her career with JF Images was over. Farrell wouldn't talk to me for my story but in 2006 she denied any culpability, telling the *Denver Post*, "I am just floored by this. I don't know the truth of it. Bill has been a good friend over the years, and I have never seen him be anything but a gentleman. I know these girls, and I am not going to comment on them. But these women never said anything to me about this. And their innuendo is that I kind of put [her] in there with Bill. It's mind-boggling. I don't set up interviews in bars. Here I am pulled in on this, and it makes me sad because my reputation has always been golden in this city."

THAT NIGHT HAUNTED Beth for the next twenty years, but she spoke of it to no one.

"I felt very threatened by Cosby," she said. "He knew everything about me. There wasn't anything to hide about me, but [Cosby] is a very powerful person that everyone believes, that everyone loves and admires. I did."

It wasn't until February 2005 that she knew she had a story to tell. She was in line at an Albertsons grocery store in Denver when she saw the front page of the *National Enquirer*: "BILL COSBY SEX ACCUSER'S STORY: WHAT REALLY HAPPENED," the headline screamed.

Though she never read the *Enquirer* and knew it wasn't always a reliable source of information, she snatched it up and bought it. It was her a-ha moment. She took the paper home, locked herself in her bedroom, and read it.

Beth was incredulous. The details of Andrea's allegations about Cosby drugging and sexually assaulting her were chilling—and all too familiar. "It just reminded me of exactly what he did to me, the drugging," she said. "I thought, *Finally. Oh my God. That has to have been what he did to me.*"

She called the *Enquirer*, hoping they could connect her with Andrea. She ended up agreeing to tell her story to the tabloid for $7,500, but first the paper told her she had to pass a lie detector test, which she did. Still, her story was never published; instead, the paper ran a front-page interview with Cosby—the story Cosby had traded up for.

So Beth called me.

CHAPTER ELEVEN

I COULDN'T CARE LESS
WHAT YOU THINK OF ME

Beth was ready to talk, and she told me everything she remembered about her time with Cosby. As she described exactly what had happened to her, I took notes, typing madly and interrupting once in a while to ask a question or clarify a detail.

When she was done she seemed relieved. "I've suffered in silence," she said. "I hope by going through this process and also getting some counseling now that I've talked about it, I'll be able to put it to rest."

I reached out to the *Enquirer*, Farrell, and Cosby's spokesperson for a comment I could include in my story about Beth, but none of them would talk to me, so we moved ahead and prepared the text for publication. The story ran on Thursday, June 23, 2005, just as the battle over revealing the identities of the twelve Jane Doe witnesses in the civil lawsuit was heating up.

Cosby's attorneys wanted their names revealed. Andrea's attorneys were vehemently opposed. They argued that Cosby's team already knew who the women were because they had been sent a confidential list of the names and addresses, so it wasn't necessary to rob the women of their privacy. As they battled over privacy issues, Cosby was going public.

Cosby had stayed away from the press as much as he could, but now he granted ABC's *Nightline* an exclusive interview—his first TV interview since Andrea's allegations first surfaced in January. ABC was the only network that didn't interview Tamara, and I wondered once again whether Cosby had traded up—offered ABC an exclusive interview with him and even access to his town halls in exchange for soft pedaling the story. On the air, reporter Michel Martin never mentioned Andrea's name.

She did, however, mention that Cosby had been accused of "inappropriate conduct with women" and asked him whether he believed his "personal issues" disqualified him from speaking about the "moral issues" he was discussing at his town halls.

Cosby's reply was murky and unclear.

She pressed further, with a question about whether his affair with Shawn Upshaw also disqualified him from lecturing anybody about their morals.

Cosby replied with a vague "Mm hmm."

Finally, Martin pushed hard enough on the question of morality that Cosby offered a strange but edifying reply: "I couldn't care less what you think of me as long as you begin to execute that which will save your children." News outlets turned this into headlines such as "Cosby Says Allegations Won't Stop Activism."

Cosby was still performing, though he was also clearly fuming over the media coverage of Andrea's case. The Smoking Gun website obtained an internal Cosby document showing that he had ordered promoters not to advertise his concert appearances with papers that had covered the case in a manner he didn't like, including Philadelphia's *Inquirer* and *Daily News*. The document was a recently revised rider to his contract that listed his specific demands on everything from toilet paper preferences ("high quality . . . Cottonelle or equivalent") to luxury travel accommodations ("Presidential Suite quality"), and it made clear which newspapers were to be left out of any promotions.

Cosby was doing his best to reclaim the life he'd had before the allegations made news. He later set aside his ire at my former newspaper and did an unexpected interview with the *Philadelphia Daily News*'s Elmer Smith, an African American columnist who had written a recent column about Cosby's "cross-country crusade," praising the way he'd refined his message and gotten rid of his "condescending tone."

Cosby called him after reading the column, Smith wrote, and the two spoke for about ninety minutes.

"To his credit, and my relief, he wasn't calling to rebut the column," Smith wrote. "He was calling to say he had a right and a responsibility to speak out and that he would continue to do that no matter how many of us tick birds land on his back."

Cosby also delighted his fans when he made a surprise visit to Hatch Middle School—a low-income, predominantly African American school in Camden, New Jersey—for its awards ceremony in late June 2006. He had been invited by NAACP president Bruce Gordon, a Hatch alumnus who was speaking at the school's afternoon commencement. Cosby told the students they'd be "a nobody living amongst nobodies" if they didn't work hard to use their brains and "become geniuses," Lettice Campbell, a parent, told the *Philadelphia Inquirer*. "He's good," she went on. "He talks to them on their level, so they can understand. It's the best ceremony I've been to."

Cosby's efforts to resolidify his reputation as America's Dad were paying off.

ANDREA'S CIVIL SUIT was getting heated. The lawyers for both sides were constantly arguing over issues large and small.

At first the conflicts were over logistical matters, like where and when the depositions would be held. But soon they became more contentious, like when Troiani and Kivitz asked Cosby if he gave the *Enquirer* an interview so they wouldn't run Beth's story. Cosby's lawyers objected to the question, but the judge overruled, and he had to answer. That reply revealed an astonishing level of cooperation between Cosby and the tabloid: not only did he get to read and comment on the story about him before it ran—which is taboo in the news business— he got to read and comment on Beth's interview as well.

Cosby's deposition was so contentious that at one point in the proceedings he stormed out of the room. Andrea's attorneys had to get the judge to intervene to force him to finish answering their questions.

Finally, the two parties reached a détente.

On November 8, 2006, Andrea settled with Cosby for an undisclosed amount of money, and the suits were dismissed. Andrea made peace with the decision: already traumatized by having to relive the horrifying details of her assault in front of Cosby at her deposition while he made jokes and belittled her and his attorney disparaged and sneered at her, this spared her from having to endure it all over again and in public.

The two-sentence release from Andrea's attorneys said simply that Andrea and Cosby had "resolved their differences, and, therefore, the litigation has been dismissed pursuant to local court rule."

Andrea's lawsuit against the *Enquirer* and Singer, which were filed after Troiani and Kivitz learned the *Enquirer* had given Cosby control over their story, were settled as well. All included confidentiality agreements; details of their settlements were tightly locked up, and none of the parties were permitted to speak about the case. Andrea's confidentiality requirement was expanded to include her parents' silence as well.

Still, she could finally move ahead with her life.

And I was moving on too. By then I was working full time at *People* magazine. The editors at *People* had seen my coverage of Cosby and asked me to freelance for them, and when my paper suddenly announced it was going through yet another massive staff reduction and was looking for volunteers to take a buyout, I took it and was later hired by *People*. It was not an easy decision. I loved my job at the *Daily News*, but I had no idea what it would look like after this latest round of cutbacks or if my newspaper would even exist. It was always threatened with extinction because we were both owned by the same company. Surely the magazine industry was more stable than newspapers these days. I worried I'd miss investigative journalism if I left, but after months of tangling with Cosby's emissaries, I was feeling pretty bruised and battered, and a change of pace seemed like a good idea.

At *People* I'd still be covering crime, but I'd have a healthy mix of human interest and other topics to write about, and I'd get to work from home instead of commuting. I'd even get to write about ordinary people doing extraordinary things, one of the magazine's mantras, *before* they died, instead of writing about them after they were the victim of some terrible tragedy.

It sounded divine.

Now, nearly a year later, the case was over. I sent news of the settlement to my boss at *People* and asked the editors there if we could now run a story about the accusers. If these women were brave enough to allow us to use their names and photos shouldn't we be brave enough to publish it? In the interim, Jane Doe Number Seven had revealed her identity to *Philadelphia* magazine, becoming the third accuser, along with Beth and Tamara, to use her own name on the record.

Jane Doe Number Seven was ex-model Barbara Bowman, who'd worked for the same Denver modeling agency as Beth. Like Beth, Barbara said she'd been introduced to Cosby through her agent, Jo Farrell, in 1985, when she was just eighteen years old.

A blonde-haired, blue-eyed, all-American beauty, Cosby befriended Barbara, and soon Farrell arranged for her to move to New York City. Once there, he continued to mentor her and introduced her to costars Phylicia Rashad and Lisa Bonet. Barbara trusted Cosby; he was generous with his time and connections, and he'd even been kind to her mother and grandparents.

Cosby first sexually assaulted Barbara at a hotel in Reno in 1986, she said. She told no one and continued as his protégé. "Who's gonna believe this?" she told *People*. "He was a powerful man." She did her best to keep him at a careful distance, but not long afterward she found herself alone with Cosby in his Manhattan townhouse. He gave her a glass of red wine, and she soon felt sick.

"The next thing I know, I'm sick and I'm nauseated and I'm delusional and I'm limp," she said. "I can't think straight." And then she was unconscious.

When she came to, she was wearing a man's T-shirt that wasn't hers, and Cosby was in a white robe. She was also confused: How could one glass of wine make her pass out?

There was a third incident with him in Atlantic City a month or two later. She had her own room, on a separate floor from Cosby. Again Cosby gave her a glass of red wine, and after sipping it, Barbara felt "completely doped up again." She somehow made it back to her room and passed out. The next day, when she went to his room to get her missing luggage, which had just arrived, Cosby threw her on the bed and began trying to take her pants off. But Barbara resisted, trying to keep them on, and Cosby grew angry. He sent her to the airport for her flight back to Denver.

Barbara didn't tell authorities what happened, though she did approach an attorney. But the lawyer wouldn't take her story seriously, Barbara said, so she dropped it. Until she heard about Andrea's lawsuit. When Barbara learned of Andrea's case, she contacted Montgomery County authorities as well as Andrea's lawyers. Through his lawyer,

Cosby told *Philadelphia* magazine that Barbara's story was "absolutely untrue." He declined comment for our story.

WE RAN THE story about the accusers in our December 18, 2006, issue of *People* magazine. There was no reference to it on the cover or mention of it in the press release generated each week to highlight the biggest and exclusive stories.

The low-key media strategy worked. Cosby, who was still hosting his town halls, ignored the story, and the record of the women's experiences was made public. They had been able to tell their story to a national audience, a testimony that would be read and not forgotten.

And that was that. The civil suit was settled; the case was closed.

And it stayed that way for the next eight years—until a relatively unknown comedian performed in Philadelphia, changing everything.

PART TWO

(OCTOBER 2014–JUNE 2017)

They're never in the mood for us.

They need chemicals.

—Bill Cosby, from his memoir *Childhood*

CHAPTER TWELVE

THEN CAME HANNIBAL

In October 2014 Bill Cosby was in the middle of a career resurgence. His biography by former *Newsweek* editor Mark Whitaker had just come out to rave reviews and was climbing the bestseller list. He had a comedy special coming up on Netflix and was in development with NBC to star in a family sitcom. He was about to embark on another comedy tour based on a special that had aired on Comedy Central the year before. The special, *Far from Finished*, was Cosby's first stand-up TV special in three decades, and it attracted two million viewers.

It was as if the scandal in 2005 had never happened, as if fourteen women hadn't accused him of heinous offenses. The book didn't even mention Andrea's allegations, let alone her civil suit or any of the other accusers. And no one in the media was asking Whitaker or Cosby why.

The situation was clear: Cosby had successfully repaired what little damage there was to his reputation after Andrea's case made the news. He slipped right back into his revered status as public moralist and children's advocate, chalking up even more awards and honors, including his entrée into the NAACP's Image Awards Hall of Fame in 2006 for being a "true humanitarian and role model."

He'd written *Come On, People: On the Path from Victims to Victors* with Alvin Pouissant, a book that took a "hard look" at the state of black America while offering advice on how to overcome the "deep-rooted" challenges of the poor, embodying the message of those controversial town halls.

He was also the recipient of Philadelphia's prestigious Marian Anderson Award in 2010, given to prominent artists who achieved distinction through their humanitarian work. Prior recipients included Harry Belafonte, Oprah Winfrey, Quincy Jones, and Danny Glover. In announcing the award, then-Philadelphia mayor Michael Nutter called Cosby "a comedian whose gentle humor . . . pioneered a path forward for African American artists."

Andrea, meanwhile, was all but forgotten. She finished massage school, purchased a loft in downtown Toronto, and began her career as a massage therapist. Tamara sold her seaside home and hid herself away on a little fruit farm she purchased in the hills outside San Diego, with just her dog and cat for company. Beth began competing in triathlons and finally became a teacher, and Barbara went on to star in thirty TV commercials, including ones for McDonald's and Holiday Inn.

Troiani and Kivitz had moved on to other cases as well and had also ended their legal partnership in 2011 when Kivitz and her husband decided to move back into Philadelphia. Kivitz went back to work for her old firm, while Troiani found someone else to partner up with. Though she was glad their case had a successful outcome for Andrea, Troiani was astounded by how little impact the case had on Cosby's life.

"That was the most disappointing part of it," she confessed to me later. "People didn't seem to care at all. It certainly made me regret leaving the DA's office because I always felt I could have convicted him, even back then."

But then came Hannibal Buress.

Buress was a comedian on the rise, and in October of 2014 he was on tour with a new national stand-up comedy show. After more than a dozen years as a comedian, he was finally starting to make it big. The thirty-one-year-old Chicago native started his career in New York City in 2006 with just $200 in his pocket, walking right into an open-mic night at a comedy club. He was so strapped for money that he was actually homeless for a while, sleeping on park benches and subways in between performing gigs after he wore out his welcome at his sister's home.

But now he was performing in actual theaters, and although he hadn't yet been booked in any large arenas, he'd come a long way in eight years. And comedy wasn't his only gig; he was also a regular on Comedy Central's *Broad City* and Adult Swim's *The Eric Andre Show*. For a short time he wrote for blockbuster shows like *Saturday Night Live* and *30 Rock* and played the memorable Officer Watkins alongside Seth Rogan and Zac Efron in the hit movie *Neighbors*. His laid back, cerebral routines earned him raves from *GQ* to the *New York Times*.

In 2014 Buress appeared in the Trocadero Theatre in Philadelphia and performed a routine he'd been doing off and on for months. In it he referenced Cosby's controversial town halls, criticizing him for lecturing people about how to dress and behave when he had skeletons in his own closet.

"It's even worse because Bill Cosby has the fuckin' smuggest old-black-man persona that I hate," Buress said. He went on:

> He gets on TV, "Pull your pants up, black people. I was on TV in the eighties! I can talk down to you because I had a successful sitcom." Yeah, but you rape women, Bill Cosby, so turn the crazy down a couple of notches . . .
>
> I don't know what I'm doing by telling you. I guess I want to just at least make it weird for you to watch *Cosby Show* reruns. Dude's image is a public Teflon image. I've done this bit on stage, and people think I'm making it up. . . . When you leave here, Google "Bill Cosby rape." That shit has more results than "Hannibal Buress."

Unbeknownst to Buress, sitting in the audience that evening was Dan McQuade, a contributing editor for *Philadelphia* magazine, who wrote blog posts for the magazine's website. McQuade only went to the show that night because a friend had an extra ticket and offered it to him at the last minute. McQuade doesn't quite remember why he decided to videotape Hannibal's Cosby diatribe but thought he might have realized in the moment that anything said about Cosby in Philadelphia was worth a mention in his column.

"I just pulled my phone out and immediately hit record," he later told the website *Billy Penn*. When Buress finished his Cosby bit, McQuade knew he had something. He wrote the piece, and it was posted online the following afternoon, a Friday, with the video he shot with his iPhone.

The headline: "Hannibal Buress on Bill Cosby: You're a Rapist."

McQuade's story might easily have faded away, but *Buzzfeed* reporter Ariane Lange saw a post about it on Facebook.

"I noticed [*Philadelphia* magazine] hadn't mentioned reaching out to Cosby or Buress, and I hadn't seen the story anywhere, so it seemed worth aggregating with a request for comment," she said. When she didn't hear back from either camp, she posted her own story with a straightforward headline, similar to the one Phillymag.com used, that Monday.

Less than an hour later *Gawker* picked it up and posted a story.

The gossip website was in its heyday and was particularly interested in the angle on Cosby because it had just resurfaced the 2005 allegations in a piece they ran in February; that story also covered Dylan Farrow's letter in the *Times* accusing her father, Woody Allen, of molesting her.

The February 2014 *Gawker* article ran under the headline, "Who Wants to Remember Bill Cosby's Multiple Sex-Assault Accusations?" *Gawker* had speculated that there had been no public outcry about Cosby, even after it got national coverage in *People* in 2006, because "nobody wanted to live in a world where Bill Cosby was a sexual predator. It was too much to handle."

Then *Newsweek* followed up, publishing interviews with Cosby accusers Tamara Green and Barbara Bowman. *Slate* jumped in with a piece pondering why no one cared. More likely, it said, it was because the allegations were a relic of the past, like Cosby himself.

Whatever the reason, the story didn't pick up and take hold in February, just eight months earlier.

This time it did.

The online coverage spread so rapidly that even Buress himself was stunned.

"Boy, that escalated quickly," he wrote on his Twitter feed less than four days after McQuade's story and video were posted. "I mean, that really got out of hand fast."

That same morning Howard Stern interviewed Buress on his radio show, and the shock jock made the most of the controversy to promote Hannibal's appearance. "The Comedian Who Toppled Cosby Stops by to Talk Fame, Jokes and the Future," was the headline on Stern's website.

All the attention bemused Buress. He wasn't trying to take down Cosby or start a discussion about rape, he said. "If I was going to do it, I would have did it on my own," he said. "It was just something that I was doing at that venue right there. . . . I just read some stuff and researched . . . anybody can get that information."

The scandal was about to get bigger—and an unlikely party fueled it. The British tabloid the *Daily Mail*—with one of the biggest readerships in the world—posted a story online around the same time Buress was wrapping up his interview with Stern, and it traveled the globe.

Buress mentioned the Cosby brouhaha again at the top of a performance in St. Louis on October 25. "I don't know if you heard . . ." he told the crowd ironically.

He said there'd been some backlash with people asking how he could say such a thing about a pioneer like Cosby. "You can't be a pioneer and a rapist?" he joked.

He added that he'd been accused of attacking Cosby to help his own career. "That's not how you help your career," he deadpanned.

Buress said he even texted his longtime buddy and fellow comedian Dave Chappelle to ask him for advice on how to handle the situation. "He said Chappelle first told him it would be best to have a conversation with Cosby and squash it," the *St. Louis Post-Dispatch* story said. "Then he said Chappelle watched the video and quickly told him not to call Cosby." The video spoke for itself.

After that, Buress pretty much stopped talking about Cosby. He'd gotten hate mail and death threats—not everyone was happy with what he'd done. "It was just weird to see people talk shit about you," he said. "I saw people I thought I was cool with bashing me online. People were writing me. It was a weird thing."

Like it or not, what he'd unwittingly started couldn't be stopped.

The *Daily Mail* took its coverage a step further and interviewed Barbara Bowman, who had just spoken to *Newsweek* in February after being out of the spotlight for years. This time she hoped people would listen to her. "I was drugged and raped by that man," she told the tabloid. "He is a monster. . . . My hope is that others who have experienced sexual abuse will not be intimidated into silence by the famous, rich and powerful. If I can help one victim, then I've done my job."

She told the same tale she'd told us in 2006, saying she feared that Cosby would soon be hitting the airwaves again in his new comedy, once again playing the quintessential family man. "Maybe he should also teach his fictitious TV family how to escape the talons of sexual predators," she told the *Daily Mail*. "Bill used to tell me that he was my father figure and that I needed to trust him as a father, 100 percent. Then he'd drug me and attack me."

Cosby was more than aware that momentum was gathering in the media and that his past was becoming present again. He postponed an appearance on *The Queen Latifa Show*, which the *Washington Post* noted in a story titled, "Is the World Starting to Turn Against Bill Cosby?"

The writer also made an interesting observation, noting that the allegations were nothing new. "Without intending to, Buress became a perfect example of the conundrum of male allyship: it wasn't enough 13 different women accused Cosby of drugging, raping and violently assaulting them. It was only after a famous man, Buress, called him out that the possibility of Cosby becoming a television pariah became real."

Barbara made the same point in an op-ed she penned for the *Post* a couple of weeks later titled, "Bill Cosby Raped Me. Why Did It Take 30 Years for People to Believe My Story?" In the essay she railed against all of those who refused to believe her. "As a teenager, I tried to convince myself I had imagined it," she wrote. "I even tried to rationalize it: Bill Cosby was going to make me a star and this was part of the deal." She told her agent, who did nothing, as well as an attorney, who accused her of making it up. She tried again when she granted interviews in 2006 with *Philadelphia* magazine, *People*, and, in February 2014, *Newsweek*. And still there was no public outcry.

Until Buress.

"While I am grateful for the new attention to Cosby's crimes, I must ask my own questions: Why wasn't I believed? Why didn't I get the same reaction of shock and revulsion when I originally reported it? Why was I, a victim of sexual assault, further wronged by victim blaming when I came forward? The women victimized by Bill Cosby have been talking about his crimes for more than a decade. Why didn't our stories go viral?"

I was wondering the same thing as I watched in astonishment as coverage unfolded and the tale exploded. I was pleased but confounded: it was a "déjà vu all over again" situation because there was absolutely nothing new to any of these claims. Our 2006 story was even available online. At the time I was wrapped up in another major story that was emotionally exhausting, and without something new to report, I had nothing new to add. But I still watched for new developments in the case.

And I thought about the industry in which I'd made my career. What puzzled me most was how the media would jump on a story one minute while having ignored it the previous one. What kind of profession was I immersed in when stories had no logical reasoning for unfolding?

It was one thing for the media to ignore Barbara's story in 2006, but she had just done a *Newsweek* interview in February that was ignored as well. Now, just eight months later, she was a media darling.

In the end I had to agree with *Slate* writer Amanda Hess, who had speculated that the phenomenon was a combination of three factors. One was the timing of the story, which coincided with Cosby's new biography, a Netflix special, and an NBC deal. Another was that there was a video of Buress's routine, which had quickly spread across social media. And the third was that Buress was a comedian.

As a comedian Buress could just flat-out call Cosby a rapist instead of hedging and using protective language like journalists did, Hess said. "And as depressing as it is, a person in Buress' position is not saddled with the same rape myths that victims are," she told the website Billy Penn. "There's a widespread belief that when a woman accuses a man of rape, she just might be lying for some sort of personal gain. It's a totally irrational conclusion, but it's a sadly prevalent one. It's harder to argue that Buress has anything to gain by taking on Cosby."

I believe it's also because Buress spoke about Cosby being a rapist so matter-of-factly—urging people to Google "Bill Cosby" and "rape"— that the allegations took on a new ring of truth for those in the audience and anyone viewing the video.

As for why the scandal fizzled in 2005 and exploded in 2014, chalk it up to social media and the internet for spreading the word and inciting a response. In 2005, when Facebook was still for college students; Twitter, Snapchat, and Instagram did not yet exist; and most news websites were in their infancy, Cosby's people were able to control the media. But they couldn't control social media. And once the public has access to information themselves, they can quickly come to their own conclusions.

Troiani agreed that social media made trading up, a term she'd become familiar with in 2005 as well, almost impossible. "If some [news] organization kills a story, some other one will pick it up, and they don't have to be an organization," she said. "They just have to have a computer."

It was also an entire new, younger generation controlling the dialogue. They'd grown up learning about the signs of child sexual abuse in public schools. And they weren't clinging to their image of Cosby as Dr. Huxtable because they had no idea who Dr. Huxtable was.

Many were also now working for the online news organizations that had sprung up since 2005 and were now driving the coverage, finally forcing the mainstream press to weigh in, whether they wanted to or not.

COSBY LEARNED THIS for himself when his handlers tried to quell the growing scandal with a meme contest. Instead, they made it worse. The hashtag #CosbyMeme was launched on November 10, when Cosby posted a tweet inviting fans to meme him. The link led to a meme generator loaded with photos of Cosby mugging in various poses and sweaters on BillCosby.com—all wholesome, charming, dad-like visuals reminiscent of Cosby's untarnished reputation.

Twitter followers responded with memes mocking him, focusing on the drugging and sexual assault allegations, including, "America's Favorite Dad by Day, Serial Rapist by Night"; "My Two Favorite Things, Jello Pudding and Rape"; and "I Like My Women the Way I Like My Puddin' Pops, Passed Out Cold."

There were also followers who saw the contest as an opportunity to educate people about rape culture. One described it as evidence of "a culture in which rape is pervasive and normalized due to societal attitudes about gender and sexuality." In his Twitter thread, he gave examples of behaviors associated with rape culture like "victim blaming, sexual objectification, trivializing rape, denial or widespread rape. Or refusing to acknowledge the harm of certain forms of sexual violence that do not conform to certain stereotypes of stranger or violent rape."

A few hours after its launch Twitter users realized that Cosby's social media team was removing the word "rape" from the memes. Not long afterward they deleted the original #CosbyMeme tweet and took down the meme generator, with the link now redirecting users to Cosby's homepage.

CHAPTER THIRTEEN

CALL US BY NAME

The meme debacle did Cosby no favors, and after his team squelched the contest, he quickly canceled an upcoming appearance on *The Late Show with David Letterman.*

He didn't cancel a previously scheduled interview with NPR's *Weekend Edition,* however. It was to be a joint appearance with his wife, Camille, to discuss sixty-two pieces of African American art that Cosby and Camille had donated to an exhibit in Washington, DC. The Cosbys had built an impressive collection since they'd visited the Heritage Gallery in Los Angeles in 1967 and discovered the work of Charles White, an African American artist from Chicago, and they had agreed to loan some of that impressive collection to the Smithsonian's National Museum of African Art on its fiftieth anniversary. It was widely viewed as one of the most valuable private collections of its kind in the world, and now the Cosbys were allowing the public to enjoy some of it as well.

But instead of focusing on the art, reporter Scott Simon asked Cosby about the various charges.

Cosby refused to answer.

The piece was so controversial that NPR's ombudsman Scott Schumacher-Matos wrote a column a few days later about whether listeners thought it was unfair of Simon to ask Cosby about the allegations when the interview was supposed to be about the artwork. The number of responses he got was "overwhelming," he wrote, revealing an interesting pattern that suggested a "generational divide" on the issue.

"Emailers, who presumably trend older, were mostly critical of Simon," he wrote. "Some 400 Facebook posts were equally divided. All ages use Facebook, though its audience is growing grayer. The online commenters at the bottom of the web story sided mostly with Simon, but, meanwhile, what might be most telling is that so did the traffic on Twitter, which appears to have the youngest audience."

With these news developments, it was time for us to join in the coverage. We started by covering the backlash and the canceled appearances, with stories both online and in print. I knew Andrea couldn't talk about the case, but I tracked down Tamara, who had been silent since her February interview with *Newsweek*.

It had been nearly ten years since we'd last spoken, but it felt like no time had passed as soon as I heard her voice. I felt this kinship with her. We had both been ridiculed in 2005 for trying to tell this story, and public thrashings, I discovered, can have a bonding effect. Only she could understand the incredulity I was feeling over how this case was exploding in the media. I couldn't help but think, *Where were all of you nine years ago?* At the same time, though, I was glad the allegations were now getting the type of attention they deserved. And I was determined to claim the story once again from all of these Johnny-come-latelies.

Tamara hadn't changed at all in the intervening years. Though I found out later she'd been diagnosed with Parkinson's disease, a progressive nervous system disorder, she was as feisty and quick witted as ever, the colorful phrases rolling off her tongue.

"He is in fact a sexual predator," she said. "I don't dispute the fact the man has done much good, but he is a flawed man. He's not the fictional Dr. Huxtable or the Jell-O salesman. This is Bill Cosby who for years felt entitled because of his status as a celebrity and because for years he was above the law. And he'll always be a small man because a great man would embrace his faults as well as his talents."

She said she thought the scandal might go away for good if he would just admit what he did and apologize. "I keep thinking of two words—he needs to *own it*," she said. "He needs to say, 'I am a flawed character. I let stardom go to my head. I am an older and wiser man, and I want to apologize to the people that I have hurt.' How hard can that be?"

Cosby said nothing.

But Joan Tarshis did.

Joan became the next woman to accuse Cosby and the first new accuser. Now sixty-six years old, Joan saw the stories in the news and came forward to say that Bill Cosby had drugged and assaulted her on two occasions in 1970, when she was in her early twenties, and trying to make it as a comedy writer.

She had flown from New York to Los Angeles to work on a mono-
logue with Godfrey Cambridge, another famous comedian, and was
staying with two women, one of whom knew Cosby. She invited her
to lunch with him at Universal Studios, where he was filming *The Bill
Cosby Show*, a sitcom in which he played a high-school gym teacher in
Los Angeles. They hit it off, and Cosby invited her back to lunch a few
times.

One day after they finished eating, Cosby asked her to stay and work
on some material with him. He invited her to his bungalow on the set,
made her a drink called a red eye—a bloody mary topped off with beer,
a drink she'd enjoyed at their lunches together. This time she passed
out on the couch. She woke to find him removing her underwear. She
quickly told him she had a yeast infection so he wouldn't rape her because then Camille would find out, so he grabbed her by the hair and
forced her to perform oral sex on him instead, which was even worse.

Joan went back home to New York, too shaken to tell anyone what
happened. And when Cosby himself called her at home to invite her to
the Westbury Music Fair, where he was performing, she was afraid to
say no. He'd spoken to her mother first, charming her in his usual way.
Cosby sent a limo to pick her up, and when she got to his hotel, once
again he gave her a red eye before they headed out to the show. She
had another glass of wine or soda in the limo. By the time she and the
chauffeur got inside the theater, she was feeling drugged. She asked
the chauffeur to take her back to the limo, where she passed out. The
next thing she remembers is waking to find herself naked in bed with
Cosby in his hotel room. He was naked, too.

She could have sold her story to the tabloids, she said—they'd even
approached her at one point. Instead, she stayed silent. Until now.

"As more and more of his rape victims have come forward, all telling similar stories, the time is right to join them," she told the website
Hollywood Elsewhere, a site she chose for her first stunning interview
because a longtime friend owned it.

Between Tamara and Joan, not to mention Barbara Bowman, Cosby's people could ignore the story no longer. They posted a statement
on his website to respond to their claims.

"Over the last several weeks, decade-old, discredited allegations
against Mr. Cosby have surfaced," the statement from Cosby attorney

John Schmitt said. "The fact that they are being repeated does not make them true. Mr. Cosby does not intend to dignify these allegations with any comment. He would like to thank his fans for the outpouring of support and assure them that, at age 77, he is doing his best work. There will be no further statement from Mr. Cosby or any of his representatives."

Troiani was irate. She'd been watching everything unfold but had no intention of weighing in until she saw that statement. It violated Cosby's settlement agreement with Andrea. He wasn't supposed to disparage Andrea or any of the thirteen other women. She dashed off a letter to Schmitt on Monday:

> We consider your statement that the allegations against your client William Cosby were "discredited" to be a violation of the confidentiality provisions of the Settlement Agreement. It was agreed that neither Cosby nor his undersigned counsel would disclose any defenses or make any public appearances or interviews about the information . . . which includes not only Ms. Constand's allegations but also the allegations made by others.

Noting that despite Andrea turning down all interview requests, Troiani wrote, "Every time the allegations are mentioned, Ms. Constand's name is mentioned." As a result, "all of the news reports about your statement link it to my client."

Troiani demanded a retraction. "We believe we are entitled to issue a statement in fair response which clarifies that Ms. Constand's allegations were not discredited but rather were resolved to her satisfaction."

Later that same day the statement on Cosby's website was amended, and it became a joint one with Troiani:

> The statement released by Mr. Cosby's attorney over the weekend was not intended to refer in any way to Andrea Constand. As previously reported, differences between Mr. Cosby and Ms. Constand were resolved to the mutual satisfaction of Mr. Cosby and Ms. Constand years ago.

AS I WAS arranging to interview Joan, yet another accuser emerged.

Linda Joy Traitz, a former waitress at Café Figaro—the same spot Tamara alleged her drugging took place—said Cosby tried to drug her in the early 1970s. She said the incident occurred when Cosby, who came in from time to time, offered her a ride home one night.

"He drove out to the beach and opened a briefcase filled with assorted drugs and kept offering me pills 'to relax,' which I declined," she wrote on her Facebook page. "He began to get sexually aggressive and wouldn't take 'No' for an answer. I freaked out and demanded to be taken home."

Almost immediately Marty Singer resurfaced, launching a fierce attack on Linda Joy. Cosby's team had clearly been busy digging into her background to see if there was anything negative about her that they could use to discredit her. He then released this statement to the media on November 20, which included details he said were from her "long criminal record":

> Ms. Traitz is the latest example of people coming out of the woodwork with fabricated or unsubstantiated stories about my client. Linda Joy Traitz is making ridiculous claims and suddenly seems to have a lot to say about a fleeting incident she says happened with my client more than 40 years ago, but she hasn't mentioned either her 3½ year incarceration or her extensive criminal record. . . . For the first time, she is claiming that in 1970, my client drove her to the beach and had a briefcase full of drugs and offered her pills to relax, which she says she turned down and demanded to be taken home after Mr. Cosby came on to her. There was no briefcase of drugs, and this is an absurd fabrication. . . . As the old saying goes, "consider the source."

It was an old, tried-and-true tactic to try to discredit Cosby's accuser, one that had worked remarkably well with the mainstream media for decades and one Singer would continue to use in the coming days as more accusers emerged, but I had to smile when I read an analysis by *Buzzfeed*'s Kate Aurthur who wasn't sure what Singer's point was other than that sometimes women who may have been sexually assaulted can go on to have sad lives afterward.

Exactly.

This time, though, the allegations were coming fast and furious, and Singer's statements were powerless to stop them. Their stories spread like wildfire online quicker than he could stamp them out. First Joan, then Linda Joy.

And then model Janice Dickinson.

On the very day we ran my interview with Joan, Janice Dickinson told *Entertainment Tonight* that Cosby drugged and raped her in 1982.

She had written about it in her 2002 memoir, *No Lifeguard on Duty*, and then told Howard Stern in 2006 that HarperCollins, her publisher, asked her to take the incident out of her book, fearing Cosby would sue. "The guy's a bad guy, let me say that," she told Stern. "He preys on women who've just come out of rehab."

Singer immediately issued a harsh statement, calling it an "outrageous defamatory lie" and saying Janice's publisher "could confirm that no attorney representing Mr. Cosby tried to kill the alleged rape story (since there was no such story) or tried to prevent her from saying whatever she wanted about Bill Cosby in her book." Janice later sued him and Cosby for defamation for these remarks.

Meanwhile Joan was already creating new news. She had talked to CNN's Don Lemon. He asked her why she didn't do more to avoid being forced to perform oral sex on Cosby.

"You know, there are ways not to perform oral sex if you didn't want to do it," he told her. His questioning caused a stir, with people accusing him of blaming the victim, and he later issued an apology.

THE FLOOD OF fresh reports from the newest accusers were impossible to ignore, and soon there was a fallout for Cosby. Netflix announced it was shelving its Cosby comedy special, which had been scheduled to air Thanksgiving week, while NBC announced it had scrapped the family sitcom it was developing with Cosby. And the TVLand channel pulled all *The Cosby Show* reruns from the air.

Apparently sensing this scandal wasn't going away, the Associated Press finally released footage from an interview it had conducted with Cosby weeks before. On November 6, during an interview that was also supposed to be about the artwork Cosby and Camille were lending to the Smithsonian Institution and just before NPR's Simon began his interview, Cosby was asked about the allegations. Cosby declined to comment, saying, "I don't talk about it."

But as the interview was winding down—and while the camera was still running and Cosby was still wearing a microphone on his lapel—Cosby asked the Associated Press reporter not to use the "no comment" comments he had made earlier and asked the reporter for an assurance none of what he said would be used.

"Of what value will it have?" he said. "I would appreciate it if it was scuttled," he went on. "I think if you want to consider yourself to be serious, that it will not appear anywhere. . . . And we thought, by the way, because it was the AP, it wouldn't be necessary to go over that question with you. . . . We thought the AP had the integrity to not ask."

I HAD BEEN TRYING to reach Beth Ferrier, but my phone numbers for her no longer worked. When we finally connected, Beth acknowledged that she'd been difficult to reach and described the backlash she'd experienced after speaking out in 2005 and 2006. "I've had to change my number several times because people were threatening me. It was horrific," she said. "I lost everything."

Members of her family stopped speaking to her, and so did some of her friends. "Anytime I brought it up, they shook their head in shame, like, 'How dare you?'" she said. She slowly rebuilt her life and was working as a special education teacher until May 2011, when she broke her neck in a triathlon.

She had no TV, so she didn't even realize the case was making news again until a member of the media tracked down a friend of hers. *I'm not going to say a word,* she thought at first, but soon she decided she couldn't stay silent. "I just hope something positive comes out of it this time. He was a father figure. We believed him. We felt safe with him. But there needs to be an outcry, and it needs to be huge."

Like Tamara, she wasn't looking for revenge, just an acknowledgment that it happened.

And an apology.

"This time use your energy, your wealth, and your intelligence to tell the world the truth," she said, imagining she was speaking to Cosby. "Call us by name. You know us."

Bruce Castor had also reemerged. But this time he was singing a different tune, telling reporters he wanted to arrest Cosby in 2005 and thought he was guilty but didn't think he could prove it. "I think he did it," he said, saying Cosby was "evasive" in questioning. "I thought the victim was credible, but she waited a year and didn't have a cogent recollection of what happened." And, he went on, it didn't help that the other women had never gone to the police. There were only a handful, he said.

Even more accusers were now going public with their stories, and another Jane Doe shed her anonymity. Soon there were fifteen women, including Andrea, with alarmingly similar stories to tell. A critical mass had solidified.

At *People*, we published a package of stories with accompanying sidebars and photos of eleven of them in our December 8, 2014, issue. This time it made the cover. The national news and the influx of accusers' declarations had Marty Singer whipping out new statements as quickly as he could. Late Friday November 21 came this one:

The new, never-before-heard claims from women who have come forward in the past two weeks with unsubstantiated, fantastical stories about things they say occurred 30, 40, or even 50 years ago have escalated far past the point of absurdity. These brand-new claims about alleged decades-old events are becoming increasingly ridiculous, and it is completely illogical that so many people would have said nothing, done nothing, and made no reports to law enforcement or asserted civil claims if they thought they had been assaulted over a span of so many years. Lawsuits are filed against people in the public eye every day. There has never been a shortage of lawyers willing to represent people with claims against rich, powerful men, so it makes no sense that not one of these new women who just came forward for the first time now ever asserted a legal claim back at the time they allege they had been sexually assaulted. This situation is an unprecedented example of the media's breakneck speed to run stories without any corroboration or adherence to traditional journalistic standards. Over and over again, we have refuted these new unsubstantiated stories with documentary evidence, only to have a new uncorroborated story crop up out of the woodwork. When will it end? It is long past time for this media vilification of Mr. Cosby to stop.

Cosby had not been taken down. Yes, his TV shows had been canceled or taken off the air, as had future comedy shows in casinos in Nevada, Illinois, Arizona, South Carolina, and Washington state. But the day Singer released his statement, Cosby headlined a sold-out performance in Melbourne, Florida, and got not one but two standing ovations. And that was despite a campaign from local radio hosts offering to pay hecklers $1,000.

Cosby spoke to a reporter from *Florida Today* before taking the stage, making it clear he was not going to be apologizing anytime soon. "I know people are tired of me not saying anything, but a guy doesn't have to answer to innuendos," he told him. "People should fact check."

There was no groundswell of anger from fans, no outpouring of hatred against Cosby.

Just two protesters stood outside, with one holding a sign that said, "Rape Is No Joke."

CHAPTER FOURTEEN

THE COSBY EFFECT

It may have been a lackluster protest at Cosby's Florida show, but the accuser list continued to grow in the coming days and weeks, eventually reaching more than sixty.

Many of them were represented by famed women right's attorney Gloria Allred, who began holding press conferences with new accusers in early December. At her first one on December 3, with Beth Ferrier and Chelan Lasha by her side, she called on Cosby to either waive the statute of limitations for the allegations against him or create a $100 million fund for his accusers.

I grimaced when I heard this. Someone from our Los Angeles bureau was handling Allred while I focused on the East Coast, so she wrote our online story about the press conference, but in my opinion, asking for money like that played right into Cosby's hands. His emissaries were already questioning the motives of his accusers. Now all they had to do was point to this press conference to prove their point. Even worse, both Beth and Chelan said they had no idea Allred was going to do that beforehand.

Other women were bypassing Allred and going straight to the media with their stories. Among them were some ex-Playboy bunnies. It was shocking at the time, but perhaps, in retrospect, not surprising. Cosby had been best friends with Playboy founder Hugh Hefner since the late 1960s and had been a fixture at the Playboy clubs and mansions across the country.

The mansion in Los Angeles had been a mecca for celebrities since it first opened in 1971. Warren Beatty and Jack Nicholson were there all the time. So were Kirk Douglas, Robin Williams, and James Caan. The corridors of the second floor were lined with photos of hundreds of other celebrity visitors. There on the wall were Ralph Nader, Walter Matthau, Patty Hearst, Mick and Bianca Jagger, and Dr. Ruth. Further down you'd find Eddie Murphy, Dick Van Patten, Kris Kristofferson,

Whoopi Goldberg, and Whitney Houston. Even Cameron Diaz, who was younger than most of the other celebrities on display, made an appearance.

And, of course, Cosby. These were the circles he moved in while Camille was raising their family back in Massachusetts. He had an apartment at the bunny mansion in Chicago and often stayed at a guesthouse on the mansion's property in Los Angeles when he was in town instead of getting a hotel room. That's exactly why former Playboy bunny mother P. J. Masten felt comfortable accepting his dinner invitation in 1979. She'd worked in several Playboy clubs and resorts over the last few years and knew him well. "He was always telling us jokes," she said. She'd just seen him at an event at the Playboy building in Chicago the day before when he'd taken a guest's wheelchair and was wheeling himself around the room, hamming it up, grabbing food off of people's plates. "Everyone thought it was funny because it was Bill Cosby," she said.

When, at 7:00 P.M., she arrived at the Whitehall, a classy four-star boutique hotel on Chicago's Gold Coast where Cosby was staying in the penthouse suite, she called up to his room.

"Come on up," he said. "We'll have a drink before dinner."

Thinking nothing of it, she agreed. When she got up to his suite he was watching sports with four other men—two she recognized, two she didn't. "I'll have a Grand Marnier," she told him. Instead of calling room service, he called down to a bellman, giving him a $100 bill to go fetch a bottle of the orange-flavored liqueur. An unusual move in retrospect but one she didn't question at the time.

So was the next. He stood behind her, preparing the drink, after the bellman returned.

She took two sips. The next thing she knew it was 4:00 A.M., and she was lying naked in bed with Cosby, bruised, battered, and bloody. She slid out of the bed as quietly as she could, gathered her clothes, hailed a cab, went home to her apartment, and jumped into the shower, desperate to cleanse herself of what she feared had happened to her. "I don't know how long I was in there, but I just stood there and screamed and cried," she said.

As bunny mother, her job was to hire, train, and schedule the bunnies who were the cocktail waitresses at the Playboy Club along North

Michigan Avenue, and she had to work that day. Cosby called her a few hours later, asking her why she left. He told her he was sending her something. Not long afterward a four-foot ficus tree arrived with a note that said, "Stay healthy mentally, stay in charge of yourself." She threw away the tree but kept the card, astonished at his gall.

She told her boss what happened to her and got this as a reply: "You do know that's Hefner's best friend, right?"

"But he drugged and raped me," P. J. insisted.

"If you're smart, you'll keep your mouth shut if you want to keep your job," her boss said.

So that was that. Cosby called her private number at her office several times afterward, asking about the ficus and asking her to join him in Denver; then in California. When she refused, he'd call and ask for other bunnies by name. She'd tell him they weren't allowed to use her private line, take the message, then rip it up after they got off the phone. "My job was to protect them," she said.

The calls gradually faded away, but the aftermath of the assault didn't. She suffered from posttraumatic stress disorder, began cutting herself, and tried to commit suicide several times, doing something, anything to try to stop the pain. She still struggles today.

Sadly, she is not alone.

It is common for trauma survivors, I knew, to experience ongoing nightmares, suicidal thoughts, and terrifying flashbacks. Rape survivors are also more likely to rely on alcohol or drugs to cope.

P. J. knew all of this, yet in late 2014, when she started seeing the news reports of the other accusers, some of them also former bunnies like Victoria Valentino, she knew she had to say something, even if talking about it once again might trigger a relapse. She still can't talk about it for very long without dissolving into tears.

But it was time.

In some ways it was past time. She'd seen the news reports about Andrea's case in 2005 but was too scared to speak out. She was still frightened now, but with other former Playboy bunnies saying Cosby had sexually assaulted them too, she was no longer alone. Maybe now people would listen.

And they did. Other former bunnies contacted her to say he'd done the same to them. "They said, 'He got me too,'" said P. J., now sixty-eight.

"I spent hours on the phone with these girls." They were too scared to tell their stories publicly, but ones who had spoken publicly still had an effect. The Rape, Abuse & Incest National Network (RAINN) said calls from survivors to their sexual assault hotline surged by 50 percent that November.

Although Cosby's attorneys criticized his accusers for coming "out of the woodwork," as Marty Singer put it, sexual assault experts said this "snowball effect" is not unusual and appears to happen most frequently with sex crimes. "Hearing from someone who has survived a similar experience can be incredibly encouraging for those who have yet to come forward," explained Katherine Hull Fliftlet, a spokesperson from RAINN. In January 2016, New York police commissioner William J. Bratton held a news conference, saying there had been a huge spike in reported rapes in 2015, driven in part by victims bringing forward years-old assaults, and calling it "The Cosby Effect."

"Survivors are often fearful to come forward until someone else has, and then there's sort of safety in numbers," Lindsey Pratt, a New York City psychotherapist who specializes in sexual trauma, told me. "I think a lot of it is fearing their story will be deemed illegitimate or they're not a trustworthy source, which of course stems from victim blaming. Coming forward with sexual assault often brings the survivor's character into question. That, coupled with the fear of having to face an attacker in court and potentially lose the court battle, keeps people from taking that risk unless they have a feeling they're not alone in it."

Being the first one to go to authorities, she told me, is "incredibly brave and incredibly difficult," particularly when the offender is someone high profile and powerful.

Like Bill Cosby.

Retired FBI profiler Mary Ellen O'Toole had noticed this phenomenon decades earlier, coining the term "icon intimidation" for the way the inequality of power between an icon and his victims can act like a psychological gag, preventing them from speaking out.

"Back when I was in the [FBI's Behavioral Analysis Unit], I was looking at the reasons that people either become victims or ignore dangerous behavior," O'Toole said. "I kept seeing the same patterns, so I just started to keep track over thirty years, and it fell basically into four categories: people normalize, ignore, and rationalize behavior, and the fourth was 'icon intimidation,' where someone big and powerful was involved, and people would literally step over behavior and not see it. That's what enabled predatory Catholic priests, coaches, and others. They were icons. Predators take total advantage. They know it. They know they're looked up to."

She defines an icon as someone who has more power or influence than their victim, someone the victim reveres, respects, and wants to have reciprocal liking in return. Many have been powerful men with seemingly pristine reputations, often lauded for their charitable work and other good deeds, either by virtue of the job they hold or their own actions. They are men people look up to, honorable family men who help the unfortunate. They can be priests, rabbis, Boy Scout leaders, coaches, politicians, millionaires and billionaires, and, yes, sometimes even celebrities. Icons are different for everyone. "It depends on who you are, your age, your gender," O'Toole said.

Their carefully honed public images not only help them attract their prey but also serve as their cover, ensuring they won't get caught. Their iconic façade suggests great character, ethics, or behavior, and this is why accusations against them seem to be in stark contrast to the façade of normalcy they project. That façade is so strong that when someone does come forward with allegations against these icons, people are reluctant to believe them and may even impugn the victim.

The icon's stature and power can sway investigators, prosecutors, judges, and juries. Although O'Toole's iconic serial predators share many common characteristics, these cases have a distinct pattern, she said. They carefully hunt for the right victims, selecting ones with less power than them, and then groom them and their family members. The icons have a bevy of "sycophants" around them to do their bidding. They do this over and over again with multiple victims, sometimes for years. Some may understand that the more they offend, the more likely they can be caught. However, for other icons, their arrogance, confidence, and sense of entitlement are so strong, they feel little if any anxiety or worry about being caught. They crave the thrill and excitement that comes from the risk.

For some icons, when they are caught there is little if any remorse or guilt for their behavior. "There's anger that you've been called out on it," she told me. "You blame the victim."

The "power differential" between the predator and prey is the heart of icon intimidation and predatory behavior, O'Toole explained. The icon is confident that his power and importance blinds the victim to any potential red flags in his behavior, such as excessive attention, being made to feel special, sexual innuendos, insisting on private time together, inappropriate compliments or actions, or excessive interest in her private life.

He builds upon that trust by showering attention on them and at times even their families. "They inherently know the victim is like, 'He wants me to come to his hotel room to read a script?'" she said. "They're getting the sense he wants to mentor them, so they're really flattered by that. They have been singled out in a very special way. He's grooming them to do what he wants, yet they're feeling something very different."

Then, when something does happen, like being drugged or sexually assaulted, they blame themselves, not him. They ask themselves, *What did I do wrong?* "These guys pick women who respond to them in a certain way and develop this trust. These are women who, when something happens in their life, they don't say, 'He's a complete asshole.' They doubt themselves." So it's not surprising they don't go to the police. "They've had this trust relationship with this icon that's treated them so well and they second-guess themselves," O'Toole said. "There may be people they tried to tell, and the reaction, when they give them the name of the icon, is disbelief."

For the perpetrators it's not all about the sex. "What's exciting and arousing for many of them is the whole process: being the predator, engaging in the prey-predator chase—that is, targeting the woman, engaging with her, grooming her and her family," she said. "All of these phases can be very gratifying."

If a perpetrator likes to drug his victims before he sexually assaults them, that could be part of his MO, behavior you do over and over so you don't get caught. Or it could be his signature, the unique method he uses to commit his crimes, an act within the crime that, by itself, is gratifying to the offender, so he has to repeat it every time he commits the crime. "It also becomes part of the pleasure and the excitement and the reason they commit the crime," O'Toole said.

A signature act or behavior within a crime can be something that significantly elevates the offender's risk level. It can cause him to stay at the scene longer than he should, to be identified and/or apprehended. Nonetheless, for many offenders the higher the risk, the more exciting the crime itself can be.

An offender may drug a victim for multiple reasons, including elevating the risk level. "It can allow the offender to control the victim and fog her memory," she said. "But taking this type of risk with the victim's health demonstrates a disregard on the part of the offender, of the victim's health, even her life. And that's very callous behavior."

The sycophants, as O'Toole called them, who surround the icon are enablers who help keep these crimes secret, using whatever means necessary to keep an alleged victim from going to the police, ranging from intimidation to secret financial payments that make the victim look culpable as well. But the icon can also dupe the sycophants who help the offender get victims or access to them, she said, and therefore they are victims in their own right.

So, who were the enablers that helped keep these allegations quiet for so many years? Barbara Bowman wrote about some of them in her *Washington Post* op-ed. "Fixing this problem demands more than public shaming. For Cosby to commit these assaults against multiple victims over several years," she wrote, "there has to be a network of willfully blind wallflowers at best, or people willing to aid him in committing these sexual crimes at worst."

She went on,

When I was a teenager, his assistants transported me to hotels and events to meet him. When I blacked out at Cosby's home there were several staffers with us. My agent, who introduced me to Cosby, had me take a pregnancy test when I returned from my last trip with him. Talent agents, hotel staff, personal assistants and others who knowingly made arrangements for Cosby's criminal acts or overlooked them should be held equally accountable.

Others began weighing in as well.

In December 2014 the *New York Times* published a story titled "Cosby Team's Strategy: Hush Accusers, Insult them, Blame the Media." In the story the *Times* noted that "the aggressive legal and media strategy mounted by Mr. Cosby and his team" may have played a role in why these stories had never sparked a public outcry before.

"An examination of how the team has dealt with scandals over the past two decades and into this fall reveals an organized and expensive effort that involved quashing accusations as they emerged while raising questions about the accusers' character and motives, both publicly and surreptitiously," the paper wrote. "And the team has never been shy about blasting the news media for engaging in a feeding frenzy even as the team made deals or slipped the news organizations information that would cast Mr. Cosby's accusers in a negative light."

At the end of 2014 former NBC employee Frank Scotti revealed another silencing strategy, saying that in 1989 and 1990 he was in charge of delivering monthly payments of up to $2,000 from Cosby to eight different women, one of whom was Shawn Upshaw (now Thompson). He still had receipts from some of the money orders he gave them. They were in Scotti's name.

Scotti was the facilities manager at the Brooklyn studio where *The Cosby Show* was filmed, and he told the New York *Daily News*, "I did a lot of crazy things for him. He was covering himself by having my name on it. It was a cover-up. I realized it later."

He elaborated in an interview with the *Today* show, saying he regularly brought young women to Cosby's dressing room and guarded the door so no one could enter.

"I felt like a pimp," Scotti said. "I felt dirty."

One of the women, Alva Chinn, told NBC the monetary gifts were just "generosity" on Cosby's behalf and were to pay for her son's boarding school. "It is a shame that Dr. William Cosby's generosity is being questioned and maligned."

Singer called Scotti's claims "pure speculation so that he can get his 15 minutes of fame."

Enablers don't just have to be people who work for a sexual predator, though; they can be members of law enforcement and others who are aware of the offenses but do nothing about it. Hollywood insider Tommy Lightfoot Garrett said it was well known in Hollywood circles what Cosby was up to, saying he first heard it when he arrived in Los Angeles in the 1980s.

"Everyone who was anyone in Hollywood knew," Garrett, a long-time writer and publicist, told me. "There wasn't a party you didn't go to, there wasn't an event you didn't go to, there wasn't an awards show you didn't go to that something didn't come up. Every single time."

So why was nothing done?

"Because Bill Cosby was making money for these people and the networks and the studios," he said. "People who see him as Dr. Huxtable do not see him as what he really was—a Hollywood mogul."

In January 2015, actor and visual artist Lili Bernard was still struggling with whether to go public with her own story of being drugged and sexually assaulted by Cosby three times in the early 1990s. One day a celebrity friend of hers, who was also a Cosby victim, came over to her home in Los Angeles to try to convince her she should. The friend's fiancé came as well.

"My friend's fiancé said, 'Many people in Hollywood know. You will be supported. Don't be afraid,'" Lili said. Then he said to her friend, his fiancée, "Why don't you show her Quincy's text?"

Her friend showed her a text message on her phone. It was sent after the sexual assault allegations against Cosby had exploded into the news again in October and read, "I've been telling Bill for years to stop drugging women."

Lili looked at the message, reading it over and over. Finally she asked, "Quincy who?"

Her friend replied, "Quincy Jones."

Quincy Jones, the legendary music producer, was a longtime friend of Cosby's. They first met in the 1960s when Jones composed the score for *The Bill Cosby Show*.

"I said to my friend, 'That's some really strong evidence. Are you going to surrender that to any authorities?'"

But the friend said she wasn't. Jones was old and sick, she explained, and she didn't want to upset him. But she added that Jones was only one of several friends of hers who said they knew these things about Cosby.

"Justice is going to prevail," the friend insisted.

Lili was very interested in Jones's text—but not surprised by what it said.

"I knew a lot of the people in the industry knew about Cosby drugging and sexually assaulting women," she told me. "I was just thinking how the text could be used as evidence to vindicate his victims."

She finally went public about the text on June 15, 2017, holding a news conference on the courthouse steps in Norristown during Cosby's first trial as the jury deliberated. The *Washington Post* posted a short video and CNN even played a clip, but there was no media reaction, no public outcry.

I knew Lili had appeared as an extra on *The Cosby Show*, but I had no idea what her actual role had been until recently. I was watching the Allred documentary on Netflix when the clip was played. I was horrified. Even more than twenty years later I remembered that episode because it was one of my favorites. Her portrayal of the enormously pregnant Mrs. Minifield was so charming, her interactions with Cliff Huxtable so sweet and funny.

Oh my God, I thought. *Her too?*

STAND-UP COMEDIAN DL Hughley has said many times that what Cosby was doing was common knowledge in Hollywood. A former gang member in Los Angeles, he'd worked his way up by performing gigs in local clubs in the late 1980s, so he was familiar with the world Cosby inhabited. He was also aware that Cosby was no fan of his. Hughley was one of those comics who swore and used the n-word, something Cosby hated.

The two once got into it.

Hughley was cohosting a radio show on KISS-FM in 2009 when producers arranged for Bill Cosby to call in for a promo segment. "I was like, 'Bill don't like me, and I don't particularly care for him, so I'll let you guys do the interview,'" he told his cohosts.

"So my cohosts started interviewing him, but he was being such a d—. I finally said, 'Mr. Cosby, what is it you would like for us to know?' And he said, 'Who is this?' And I said, 'DL Hughley.'"

Cosby wasted no time and called him out for using the n-word.

"I said, 'With all due respect, Mr. Cosby, I say n—, but no co-ed has ever woke up drugged with her drawers on backward. . . . Out of all the words people have said about me, no one has ever said the word 'rape.'"

Cosby was irate, telling Hughley, "That tape will never air."

And it never did.

Ten minutes later the top honchos at Emmis, which owned the station, came down to the studio. They took the tape and asked if anyone had made a copy of it. No one had.

"If this airs, nobody in here will work in radio again," the execs said.

Hughley was disgusted. "I know that cat has the power to make people do shit."

IN THE WAKE of the tidal wave of allegations that November, journalists began doing some tough self-examinations about their own culpability in enabling Cosby.

Ta-Nehisi Coates—who had written the National Book Award–winning father-son memoir *The Beautiful Struggle* and would soon go on to write the *New York Times* best-selling history of race in America, *Between the World and Me*—was the first journalist to express regret for not paying more attention to the allegations against Cosby. Coates had profiled Cosby in 2008 for the *Atlantic*, and "in that essay there is a brief and limp mention of the accusations," he wrote on November 19, 2014, again for the *Atlantic*.

The writer had spent parts of 2006 and 2007 following Cosby around the country as Cosby was in the middle of his "callouts" about the decline of morality in black communities, yet "one of the biggest accusations of immorality was left for a few sentences, rendered invisible," he wrote. "I believed them. Put differently, I believed that Bill Cosby was a rapist." Still, he made a conscious decision to not dwell on those allegations.

"I don't have many writing regrets. But this is one of them. I regret not saying what I thought of the accusations, and then pursuing those thoughts. I regret it because the lack of pursuit puts me in league with people who either looked away, or did not look hard enough."

A few days later, in a thoughtful piece titled "Calling Out Cosby's Media Enablers," *New York Times* media columnist David Carr took it a step further, chastising not only himself but others who he felt had failed the accusers and asking why it took so long.

"What took so long is that those in the know kept it mostly to themselves," he wrote. "No one wanted to disturb the Natural Order of Things, which was that Mr. Cosby was beloved; that he was as generous and paternal as his public image; and that his approach to life and work represented a bracing corrective to the coarse, self-defeating urban black ethos. Only the first of those things was actually true."

Those "in the know" included Coates and Kelefa Sanneh, "who wrote a major profile in the *New Yorker* this past September and who treated the accusations as an afterthought, referring to them quickly near the end of the piece," he wrote. They also included Mark Whitaker, the author of Cosby's biography, "who did not find room in his almost-500-page biography to address the accusations."

And finally, "those in the know also included me," Carr wrote. "In 2011, I did a Q and A with Mr. Cosby for *Hemispheres* magazine, the in-flight magazine of United Airlines, and I never found the space or the time to ask him why so many women had accused him of drugging then sexually assaulting them."

The interview, he said, was supposed to be about Cosby's new book. "I knew when the editors of the airline magazine called that they would have no interest in pursuing those accusations in a magazine meant to occupy fliers. My job as a journalist was to turn down that assignment. If I was not going to do the work to tell the truth about the guy, I should not have let him prattle on about his new book at the time."

Carr's callout prompted Whitaker to own up to his own transgression. He sent Carr a message on Twitter, saying, "David, you are right. I was wrong to not deal with the sexual assault charges against Cosby and pursue them more aggressively."

Even investigative journalist Ronan Farrow later revealed his own shame over not asking tougher questions of Whitaker when he interviewed him for NBC upon the release of his Cosby biography. "The book omitted allegations of rape and sexual abuse against the entertainer, and I intended to focus on that omission," he wrote in a guest column for the *Hollywood Reporter*. But a producer, he said, "was one of several industry veterans to warn me against it. . . . So, we compromised: I would raise the allegations, but only in a single question, late in the interview."

Farrow went on: "The author has apologized. And reporters covering Cosby have been forced to examine decades of omission, of questions unasked, stories untold. I am one of those reporters—I'm ashamed of that interview."

Finally, I thought as I read mea culpa after mea culpa. *Some accountability.*

Then—and I couldn't help myself—I thought once again, *Where were all of you nine years ago?*

Imagine if the national media had aggressively jumped into the Cosby story in 2005 the way they did in 2014. The press is supposed to be the watchdog for the public; instead, it was Cosby's lackey. Perhaps the collective force of the media would have forced Castor to take a deeper look at the case, to maybe actually interview all those women who'd reached out back then instead of closing the investigation just as it was getting geared up.

If the investigation had gone on longer and the media coverage had been as intense as it was in 2014, maybe more of these women would have spoken up back then. Maybe more cases would have been prosecutable because the statute of limitations had not yet expired.

Still, it was an astonishing level of introspection from those in an industry that doesn't like to admit when it's wrong. Perhaps some of it was damage control, calling themselves out before others did. It was too late for Whitaker, though. While he had promised to include the allegations in a new edition of the book, several months later Simon & Schuster announced that its book would not be updated nor would it get a paperback publication. Celebrities like Jerry Seinfeld and David Letterman even asked for their endorsements on the back of the book to be pulled.

Cosby still had his defenders, though, and they were starting to bring race into the discussion.

So were his accusers.

CHAPTER FIFTEEN

YOU KNOW I'LL BE HILARIOUS

In January 2015, Cosby got ready to resume his "Far from Finished" comedy tour, with three major appearances in Canada. Though the mayor himself purposely boycotted the event, the first one in Kitchener, Ontario, was a hit. Cosby's on-stage banter clearly delighted the audience, as they left Centre in the Square having enjoyed a fun night of Cosby's classic wit.

But the mood shifted when he reached London, Ontario, for his second show. As ticket holders arrived at the Budweiser Arena, dozens of protesters stood outside in the blowing snow, yelling at them, "Shame on you!" Another group handed out flyers that read, "We stand in solidarity with abused women." Each flyer included the name of a Cosby accuser.

Local activists and residents called on Cosby to cancel his shows, but Cosby was defiant, and the venues said they couldn't afford to breach their contract with him. Even Judd Apatow, who had become one of Cosby's most vocal critics, had no effect when he took to Twitter to castigate the venues hosting Cosby's show. "Do people still find him delightful after 30 accusers?" Apatow tweeted to his two million–plus followers.

Finally settled into their seats, the audience applauded as Cosby took the stage shortly after 7:30 P.M. while wearing his trademark "Hello Friends" hoodie, a reference to his late son, Ennis, who had often greeted people with the phrase. Cosby launched into his routine smoothly, and all was well until about halfway through the performance, when a woman stood up and made her way toward the aisle.

Cosby stopped his set to ask her where she was going. The woman replied she was going to get a drink.

Cosby didn't miss a beat. "You have to be careful about drinking around me," he joked.

For a moment the crowd gasped. One heckler called him a rapist and was ejected. Then the audience "laughed and cheered, and the show went on," *National Post* reporter Richard Warnica wrote.

At the end of the night Cosby got a standing ovation. Afterward he released a statement—not about the joke but about the heckler.

Dear fans: One outburst but over 2,600 loyal, patient and courageous fans enjoyed the most wonderful medicine that exist for humankind. Laughter. I thank you . . . I'm far from finished.

It was yet another déjà vu all over again moment for me. He'd done the same thing after Castor announced he was not charging him criminally in Andrea's case, jokingly asking a woman in the audience if he'd slipped anything in her drink. But this time the rest of the media did not ignore the story. This time his off-script quip quickly caught fire. News agencies around the world, ranging from the Associated Press to ABC to the *New York Times* and CNN, picked it up.

"As both a survivor of sexual assault and as an advocate, I am appalled at Bill Cosby making a joke about drug and alcohol-facilitated sexual assault," Angela Rose, founder of the nonprofit group Promotion Awareness Victim Empowerment, said in a national statement. "This disgraceful, reprehensible act shows an absolute lack of tact."

Allred added her voice to the public outcry, insisting that the drugging and raping of women was "not a laughing matter."

His ill-timed joke prompted an even larger group of protesters to gain entrance to his third and final show in Hamilton, Ontario, and it was the most raucous of all three. A crowd outside the theater stood up and chanted "We Believe the Women" as they blew rape whistles and unveiled T-shirts with the same message.

Security escorted them out as Cosby pled for calm.

Cosby's refusal to apologize for the joke only fueled the anger of Allred and other activist groups. He had scheduled appearances in Colorado the following weekend, and plans for protests were ramping up when Cosby released another far-from-contrite statement.

Dear Fans: I have thousands of loyal, patient and courageous fans that are going to leave their homes to enjoy an evening of laughter and return home feeling wonderful . . . I'm ready! Hey, hey, hey. I'm Far from Finished.

But things didn't go much better once he got to Colorado. Protesters chanting "No means no" and "Colorado believes the women" greeted him in Pueblo, where he then performed to a packed house. His next stop was Denver, where Allred and Beth Ferrier hosted a rally and teach-in at the Crawford Hotel prior to his back-to-back shows at the Buell Theater. Then they joined a group of a hundred or so protesters outside the venue who were chanting "Rape is not a joke!"

Inside the theater, once again, Cosby received a standing ovation.

IN EARLY MARCH Cosby released a video message to his fans, his first since the scandal broke. It was timed to promote his upcoming appearances in several cities. It carried the same tone-deaf message, showing him sitting on a tan, striped chair in fuchsia pajamas, talking on a white rotary phone, and assuring his fans he was still performing. He gave it to ABC, which was still his network of choice, all these years later.

"You know I'll be hilarious," he said in the ten-second video. "Can't wait!"

While Cosby worked on improving his public image, the African American community struggled with the racial implications. Setting aside his controversial town halls, Cosby had been an outspoken advocate on their behalf for half a century, so the struggle was understandable. He started his career at a time when the media could barely mention his name without the word "negro" attached to it. Not only did the racial barriers he broke with both *I Spy* and *The Cosby Show* pave the way for other African American actors and African American–starring shows, he made hiring African Americans a priority for his productions.

As early as 1965 he was saying he wanted television to be about equality, that someday he wanted to do a family situation comedy on TV that would be a hit because people want to see what goes on in an African American home. In 1967 he wrote a lengthy piece for the *Los Angeles Times* expounding on the need for positive role models within the black community and on television, calling on Hollywood to fill roles regardless of skin color.

"Hollywood so far has been afraid to star black actors in ordinary roles which don't call specifically for a Negro. They have been afraid to chance financial losses at the box office. But, Hollywood is forgetting the large Negro population in this country that spends money at the movies and, more importantly, they are forgetting their responsibility as a medium of mass communication."

He believed his support for civil rights organizations in the sixties is what landed him on former President Richard Nixon's "master list" of political opponents, perhaps explaining why the IRS had begun auditing his and Camille's returns since Nixon took office and why FBI agents had repeatedly visited their home. He and Camille had even begun to suspect their phones were tapped.

The fear that Cosby's guilt would topple a role model in their community was real and had some African American accusers wrestling with their decision to tell their stories.

"I didn't want to take this black icon down," African American model Jewel Allison told the New York *Daily News* and later told me. Cosby had drugged and sexually assaulted Jewel in the late 1980s after he gave her a glass of wine from a bottle he said was a gift from a famous acquaintance of his, one whose name she recognized. She met Cosby through her agent, Sue Charney, who is credited with discovering former super model Janice Dickinson—though it's not how Dickinson met Cosby—and Jennifer Thompson's agent. "This was my Bill Cosby. Do you want to shatter everyone's belief system?"

She elaborated on the racial aspect of her decision in a March 2015 essay in the *Washington Post*. Her story's title and subtitle was a gut punch of a message: "Bill Cosby Sexually Assaulted Me. I Didn't Tell Because I Didn't Want to Let Black America Down. I Let Race Trump Rape." In it she wrote,

Telling *my* story wouldn't only help bring down Cosby; I feared it would undermine the entire African American community . . .

Historical images of black men being vilified en masse as sexually violent sent chills through my body . . .

I knew these women weren't fabricating stories and conspiring to destroy America's favorite dad, but I did not want to see yet another African American man vilified in the media.

Yet she did, spurred by the "vicious anger" directed at other accusers like Barbara Bowman and former *Playboy* playmate Victoria Valentino. Afterward, she confessed, "It was hard for me to look other African American people in the eye. On some level I felt that I had betrayed black America. And some of my African American friends seemed too hurt by the damage to Cosby's image to offer me any support."

African American model Beverly Johnson followed suit not long after Jewel first told her story to the New York *Daily News* in a thoughtful essay for *Vanity Fair* about watching Cosby on *I Spy*, when he was the first African American to star in a dramatic television series. "He was funny, smart and even elegant—all those wonderful things many white Americans didn't associate with people of color," wrote Beverly.

Beverly, who had been the first African American woman to appear on the cover of American *Vogue,* had her own Cosby story of being drugged at his Manhattan home one night. Cosby had invited her there to read for a part on *The Cosby Show*. She'd already attended a couple of tapings and even accepted an invitation to brunch at his home, with her daughter tagging along, so she felt comfortable going over there again.

When she arrived, he brought a cappuccino and insisted she drink it. She had a few sips and felt woozy within minutes. She somehow managed to escape without being sexually assaulted, but she was terrified and traumatized.

"As I thought of going public . . . a voice in my head kept whispering, 'Black men have enough enemies out there already, they certainly don't need someone like you, an African American with a familiar face and a famous name, fanning the flames.'"

Yet she did go public, spurred on by women like Barbara and Janice Dickinson, who were suffering the repercussions of sharing their stories. And she came forward for those who hadn't yet emerged publicly. "Over the years I've met other women who also claim to have been violated by Cosby. Many are still afraid to speak up," she wrote. "I couldn't sit back and watch the other women be vilified and shamed for something I knew was true . . ."

"Finally, I reached the conclusion that the current attack on African American men has absolutely nothing to do at all with Bill Cosby," she wrote. "If anything, Cosby is distinguished from the majority of black men in this country because he could depend on the powers that be for support and protection."

Lili Bernard also wrote an op-ed, hers appearing in the *Los Angeles Times*. "I knew that as a black woman accusing a beloved black celebrity of such heinous conduct I would come under heavy scrutiny from the black community and expose myself to possible retaliation," she said, describing herself as a black Latina and noting that one-third of his sixty-plus accusers are black.

Lili had been experiencing flashbacks, she said, and dredging up her memories and talking about them publicly was difficult on its own. What made it even more painful was the backlash from the black community. "They will contact me through my artist's website, saying, 'What kind of black woman are you, trying to take down a black man? You're not a real sister,'" she later told me.

Luckily she had supportive friends who rallied around her. One such friend had been a firm believer in Cosby's innocence—until Lili confessed to him what had happened to her all those years ago. That man was fellow actor Joseph C. Phillips, who played Denise Huxtable's husband, Martin Kendall, on the show. In a 2015 blog post titled, "Of Course Bill Cosby Is Guilty!" he wrote about the impact their exchange had on him.

"He was my boyhood idol," Phillips wrote of Cosby. "His influence on my life has been profound." But he then went on to say that although it was "common knowledge" Cosby "slept around," there seemed to be nothing untoward about it. "You didn't have to see it or hear it to know that it existed. . . . There was also the seemingly unending parade of pretty young women that streamed through the studio."

Phillips wrote that he'd recently learned from a friend that Cosby had assaulted her. "I battled my emotions," he shared. "I felt for my friend, for the violation of her trust, loyalty and body. I was angry with Bill. He had money, fame and power; he was a walking aphrodisiac! Why? I was also angry with myself for falling for the okey-doke, of putting Bill on a pedestal."

COSBY, THOUGH, WAS not without his defenders. Other African American celebrity friends rose to support him, starting with Whoopi

Goldberg, who said she had some concerns about Barbara Bowman's claims that Cosby repeatedly sexually assaulted her.

"I've been accused of a lot of stuff, and I've had friends that have been accused of a lot of stuff," she said on *The View*. "It opens the door for everybody to come out and say, 'And me, too, boss.' . . . So you have to really take a minute and follow the evidence. . . . I have a lot of questions for the lady. Maybe she'll come on [the show]."

Then Goldberg played a video clip of Barbara claiming no one believed her at the time of the incidents because of Cosby's stature. When the clip ended, Goldberg argued that the police or the hospital might have wondered why Barbara didn't have a rape kit done. Goldberg didn't seem to know that not every hospital has someone trained to conduct a sexual assault forensic exam using a rape kit or that police fail to test hundreds of thousands of rape kits. Or that less than two-thirds of women who were eligible for one completed it, and less than a third of those women released the results to the police. And even when police test and analyze the kits, what they find may not provide useful evidence, especially if the victim knows her rapist.

The View cohost Rosie O'Donnell spoke up to play devil's advocate. She pointed out that Cosby settled Andrea's lawsuit, implying guilt. "Settlements don't necessarily mean you're guilty," Goldberg argued. "I hope that there is justice for this lady. I hope somebody gets to the bottom of this. But I'm going to reserve my judgment because I have a lot of questions."

Likewise, platinum recording artist Jill Scott, a fellow Philadelphian, had a back and forth with her Twitter followers, writing, "I'm respecting a man who has done more for the image of Brown people than almost anyone EVER. From Fat Albert to the Huxtables."

And in an interview with *Entertainment Tonight* African American actor Ben Vereen urged people to "Pray for Bill Cosby. Pray for the women who are scandalizing him more so. I love the man. I support you, Bill."

Cosby himself spoke to the issue of race when he told the *New York Post*'s Page Six he expected "the black media to uphold the standards of excellence in journalism [and] go in with a neutral mind." But as Cosby was thanking these supporters, his star on the Hollywood Walk of Fame was defaced with the word "rapist."

COSBY'S WIFE, CAMILLE, was ready to speak out for her husband.

The couple had been married for forty years. She was rarely in the spotlight, rarely by his side, but she quickly made it clear where her loyalties lie.

The couple had met on a blind date when he was still a struggling young comedian. Though he was seven years her senior and her parents did not approve, she took a leap of faith and dropped out of college to marry him when she was just nineteen years old. She took over the family finances early on in their marriage, after his financial manager robbed him blind, nearly bankrupting them. "In this kind of business, you have to protect each other," she told *American Visions* magazine in a rare interview.

Once he made it big, they bought a luxurious home in Beverly Hills, but she quickly tired of the glitz and glamour and her husband's wild lifestyle. So in the early 1970s they sold their mansion, packed up, and moved the family to an 1800s New England colonial farmhouse in rustic Shelburne Falls, Massachusetts, where she still lives.

After raising their five children, she finished her degree and went on to get a master's and then a doctorate in education, slowly developing an identity of her own as a philanthropist, Broadway producer, and author. "Education helped me to come out of myself," she told *Oprah* magazine in its May/June 2000 issue.

Raised in a middle-class home just outside Washington, DC—her father was a chemist and her mother worked at a nursery—Camille maintains a regal demeanor. She rarely smiles in public and seems standoffish, yet she garners respect from those who know her. Even Oprah Winfrey, who has interviewed hundreds of women during her career and had socialized with the Cosbys at their home, admitted she was nervous before her sit-down interview for the magazine, her first ever without the comfort of television cameras.

She and Bill had gone through a rocky patch, Camille said, but about ten years into their marriage they spent a lot of time talking about what marriage means. That's "when we knew that we really wanted to be with each other," she said, "that we didn't want to live without each other."

With her husband in the glaring light of disapproval, she was ready to stand by his side in the most public way imaginable, releasing a statement comparing the media's coverage of Cosby to the recent *Rolling Stone* cover story about an alleged gang rape at the University of Virginia in Charlottesville that was already being discredited. Camille called for the same declaration of her husband's innocence. Her statement said,

I met my husband, Bill Cosby, in 1963, and we were married in 1964. The man I met, and fell in love with, and whom I continue to love, is the man you all knew through his work. He is a kind man, a generous man, a funny man, and a wonderful husband, father and friend. He is the man you thought you knew.

A different man has been portrayed in the media over the last two months. It is the portrait of a man I do not know. It is also a portrait painted by individuals and organizations who many in the media have given a pass. There appears to be no vetting of my husband's accusers before stories are published or aired. An accusation is published, and immediately goes viral.

We all followed the story of the article in the *Rolling Stone* concerning allegations of rape at the University of Virginia. The story was heart-breaking but appears to be proved to be untrue. Many in the media were quick to link that story to stories about my husband—until that story unwound.

None of us will ever want to be in the position of attacking a victim. But the question should be asked—who is the victim?

Cosby's TV wife, Phylicia Rashad, followed suit not long afterward, expressing her support for Cosby and questioning the motives behind the accusers. "Forget these women," she told *Showbiz411*, a celebrity news website. "What you're seeing is the destruction of a legacy. And I think it's orchestrated. I don't know why or who's doing it, but it's the legacy. And it's a legacy that is so important to the culture."

Rashad also said she'd never seen a hint of inappropriate behavior during all the years she'd known him, then she alluded to some sort of conspiracy that did not involve the accusers. "Someone is determined to keep Bill Cosby off TV," she said. "And it's worked. All his contracts have been cancelled."

She and Cosby were friends as well as former costars. He'd even been a groomsman in her 1985 wedding to former NFL player and sports broadcaster Ahmad Rashad. (O. J. Simpson was his best man.) In May 2018 a photo of Cosby and Simpson at their wedding began making the rounds again, finally prompting Ahmad to tell *Sports Illustrated*:

> Here's my feeling about that. Everybody has their cross to bear. Those two guys' crosses are pretty f— heavy. And that's all I have to say about it. I'm sure they knew a lot of people. Maybe you just didn't know them as well as you thought you knew them. You just don't know. I'm as devastated as everyone else with these two people. It's like, holy s—. They were in chapters [of my life]. So were a lot of other people. They weren't the main characters. I'm the main character in my own book. Those two things are just . . . maybe the most . . . oh, I can't even describe it. It's just . . . heartbreaking all around. And not so much for them, but the victims. It's like, that's f— crazy. But like I said, that's their cross.

He said he hadn't spoken to Cosby in years and Simpson since 1988.

Allred criticized Rashad's "forget these women" comment at a press conference where three more accusers came forward. Rashad responded by claiming she was misquoted.

"That is not what I said," she told Linsey Davis of ABC News. "What I said is 'this is not about the women.' This is about something else. This is about the obliteration of a legacy. I am a woman. I would never say such a thing."

Whatever she meant, there was no question about her support for Cosby. "He's a genius. He's generous. He's kind. He's inclusive," she said. "What has happened is declaration in the media of guilt. Without proof." And for those who think Rashad has a financial motive for supporting Cosby, that's not how residuals work, she explained. "The longer a show runs, the smaller the residual," Rashad told Davis.

That same month, Malcolm Jamal Warner, who played Theo on *The Cosby Show*, expressed his support for his TV father, albeit with some hedging, never fully saying what he believed to be true. "I can't speak to any of the allegations because obviously, I was not there," Warner told *Billboard* magazine. "I know he has been great to me and great for a lot of people. . . . What he's done for the black community and education is invaluable. That's the Bill Cosby I know."

Keshia Knight Pulliam, who played Rudy, also defended Cosby without stating what she believed about the allegations. "What I can say is this: I wasn't there. No one was there, except for the two people, to know exactly what happened," she said on the *Today* show on January 5, 2015. "All I can speak to is the man that I know and I love. . . . You can't take away from the great that he has done, you know, the amount, the millions and millions of dollars, that he has given back to colleges and education, and just what he did with *The Cosby Show* and how groundbreaking that was."

No one can deny Cosby had experienced racism during his career, but as his wealth and fame grew, did our nation's shameful history of false sexual assault accusations against African American men become a cloak he wrapped around himself so he wouldn't get caught?

New Yorker writer Jelani Cobb posed that very question in an essay entitled, "What Shielded Bill Cosby?" He examined the racial issues swirling around the case and Barbara Bowman's contention that her story was not considered credible until a man (Hannibal Buress) repeated it onstage. He also pointed out the racial relevancy of Buress's role in Cosby's predicament.

"Hannibal Buress, like Cosby, is a *black* man, a common heir to the body of stereotypes about sexual predation and the tormented history that accompany it. Cosby was insulated from the long trail of allegations not only by his wealth and power but by the lurid history of black men brought low by accusations, specious or not, of sexual contact with white women."

Buress, he wrote, "saw the lurid stories around Cosby not as evidence of a prominent black man being brought low but as the exposing of a serial rapist who had masterfully manipulated both the white desire for an icon of post-racialism and the black desire for the type of dignified success that Cosby represented."

So yes, race had begun creeping into the discussion and would never really disappear. But it was already becoming clear that this scandal was not going away either.

Sure, it had quieted down, but the women had not stopped revealing themselves, including many of the ones I'd been intrigued by in 2005.

The Jane Does.

CHAPTER SIXTEEN

POWERFUL, POPULAR, PRIVILEGED, PROTECTED

Therese Serignese, Jane Doe Number Ten, was one of the first to publicly shed her anonymity in 2014. She was nineteen years old when she met Cosby at the Las Vegas Hilton in the mid-1970s, she told various media outlets in November 2014. She was standing in the gift shop with her younger brother and sister when a man approached her from behind, slipped his arm around her shoulders, and said, 'Will you marry me?'"

It was Cosby, the headline act for that night's show. He offered them free tickets to his show but only she was able to go. Afterward, a staff member came to get her but instead of escorting her to the showroom's door, he took her to a room backstage, where about ten people were waiting for Cosby. After everyone left, Cosby offered her two pills, with a glass of water. She didn't know what they were, and she doesn't remember him telling her, but she took them. She was scared and intimidated. She was also passive, which Cosby somehow knew because that's how he described her in his deposition. Her memories are a patchwork after that but she remembers looking in a mirror and seeing them having sex.

Then came Kristina Ruehli, Jane Doe Number Twelve. She'd been a secretary for a Beverly Hills talent agency called Artists Agency Corporation, which represented big celebrities like George Burns and Cosby's *I Spy* costar Robert Culp, when Cosby drugged and tried to assault her. She was twenty-two years old.

Donna Motsinger, or Jane Doe Number One, was next. She told a San Francisco television station that she was working as a waitress at the Trident Restaurant in Sausalito when she met Cosby.

The Trident—owned at the time by the famous folk band the Kingston Trio—was a mecca for stars in the 1970s when Cosby saw Donna and asked her to attend one of his shows with him. They shared a drink in a limousine on the way there, after which, she claims, "I didn't feel right." She woke up in her bed the next morning and knew immediately she'd been sexually assaulted.

"These women are not lying," she told ABC7 News. "I'm not lying. It's the honest to God truth."

Jane Doe Number Four revealed herself in early 2015. Patricia Steuer first met Cosby in the fall of 1978, when she was twenty-two years old. She had just graduated from the University of Massachusetts with a degree in music, and Cosby was on campus to deliver a lecture for an educational conference, which she attended. Cosby had earned his PhD there the year before and has also been awarded a star on Hollywood's Walk of Fame. His career as a product pitchman, first for Jell-O then for Coke, was soaring.

The next day, she was walking across campus when she saw him surrounded by a small group of people and decided to wait in line to thank him for his remarks the night before. When it was her turn, she extended her hand to shake his, and he wouldn't let it go.

"He made a comedy routine out of not letting me have my hand back," she said. "The other students and teachers were laughing. I was blushing."

He invited her to a banquet that evening, where he and Jesse Jackson were speaking, and then for drinks after. She accepted, and that night, she shared her dreams of becoming a singer.

About two weeks later he invited her to a dinner party at his family home in Shelburne Falls, Massachusetts. She eagerly accepted.

She assumed she'd be dining with Camille and many others as well, but when she arrived there were two place settings on a coffee table next to his fireplace. Cosby offered her a drink, which she accepted, left to go mix it in another room, then asked her to take part in an acting improvisation: he wanted her to pretend to be an elegant queen with oatmeal dripping from her face.

"It was the weirdest thing I'd ever done," Patricia told me. "I got three-quarters of the way through the drink, and then I don't remember anything else—until he was waking me up the next morning."

When she came to, she was naked in Cosby's guest bedroom, and Cosby was standing over her in a bathrobe with a toothbrush, telling her she needed to leave. He was calm but insistent.

"What happened?" she asked him.

Cosby told her she'd thrown up in his powder room and passed out and that he'd had to wash her dress.

She believed him.

"It never occurred to me anything more had happened," she said. "I thought I had embarrassed myself in front of this powerful man. I took full responsibility for what happened."

She got dressed, gathered her things, and drove home, stopping to throw up four times on the roadside.

"I never told my parents," she said. "I was deeply ashamed."

Cosby kept in touch with her afterward, arranging for acting lessons and a gym membership for her, then he asked her to join him in Atlantic City. She met him in his suite, where he handed her two large pills and a glass of champagne.

"What will the pills do?" she asked.

"They'll relax you, like a drink," he explained.

The next thing she remembers is waking up naked in one of the rooms in his suite, feeling sick to her stomach. That's when she connected the dots from what happened in 1978. *I've felt like this before*, she thought. She was furious.

"I got dressed, and I went stalking out to the living area of the suite, where he was sitting having coffee, and I confronted him about it, asking him why he did it. He got really pissed and said, 'You're being ungrateful, and I want you to leave,'" she said. She never heard from him again. To this day she has no idea what the pills were.

Over the years she told a couple of friends, her sister, and her husband what happened, and that was all. But once she saw the news about Andrea's allegations in 2005, she knew she had to do something, so she spoke with Andrea's attorneys and a detective as well.

"It was about stopping him and helping Andrea," she said of becoming a Jane Doe. "I wanted her to know she wasn't alone."

Bill Cosby the family man being accused of multiple sexual assaults was shocking enough; the thought of him drugging women seemed inconceivable. He didn't drink or do drugs himself, at least according to his official biography by Whitaker. Yet woman after woman was coming forward, telling variations of the same story. None of them knew each other. Most had told other people along the way, defusing possible claims that they made up their stories after hearing about the other allegations on the news.

Not all the women accusing him say he gave them a pill, however. Many, like P. J. Masten, said he only gave them something to drink. Some said it was an alcoholic drink; others said it was coffee, soda, or even water. But whatever he put in P. J.'s Grand Marnier was so powerful it knocked her out after two sips.

Writer Sammie Mays had a similar experience. She was at a television conference in New Orleans in the mid-1980s, hoping to score a big coup for her hometown newspaper in Mississippi by grabbing a few quotes from Cosby. He agreed, inviting her to walk with him to his suite to continue the conversation. Along the way she asked a man to take a photo of the two of them with her camera. Once there, with his back turned toward her, he mixed her a drink. Nervous about interviewing someone so famous, she said she took two big swigs. That's the last thing she remembers. When she awoke she was slouched in the chair in Cosby's hotel suite in New Orleans, and Cosby was standing in front of her chair. Her shirt was unbuttoned, and her underwire bra was slid over to the side, exposing her breasts. The chain belt she'd worn tightly around her waist was unhooked and rehooked, left loose around her hips. There was some kind of liquid "crud" around her mouth. She thought it was drool—then she realized it was sperm.

Cosby was standing there, staring down at her.

"His eyes were flat and dead," she said. "The sparkle was gone. He'd had sparkle in them earlier, which made me believe I'd be fine."

At first she couldn't believe he hadn't called 911—after all, she'd lost consciousness.

"He drugged me, not knowing if those drugs could be fatal or not," she said. "I could have overdosed and died."

Later, of course, it made more sense, that decision not to call for help. "He had a lot to lose," she said. "He's a celebrity, a beloved father figure. That's when I knew he'd molested me."

Forensic toxicologist Anthony Costantino said Sammie was right to be concerned. It's extremely dangerous to drug someone without their consent or to give someone drugs without telling them what it is, especially if it's a central nervous system depressant. One wrong dose and someone could go into respiratory distress and die.

"You don't know the health or the condition of the person," he said. "You're assuming they're a healthy person with nothing else compromising their system, that they don't have breathing difficulty or heart problems or perhaps are already intoxicated on something else."

So what was Cosby giving them?

While it is impossible to know what drugs were used, the symptoms many of the women describe match both central nervous system depressants like Quaaludes and date-rape drugs like Rohypnol, which are dissolved into a liquid. "The primary effect they all have is loss of inhibition, intoxication to some degree, sleepiness, and memory loss," said Trinka Porrata, a former Los Angeles narcotics detective and drug-facilitated sexual assault expert. "The goal is inability to resist. You can't jump up and run away."

Quaaludes, also known as methaqualone, were the party drug of the 1970s and the early 1980s. They first became popular as a sleeping pill and sedative because they were supposedly less addictive, but people began using them recreationally because they produce an intense, euphoric high after an initial fifteen-minute drowsy phase. They were banned in the United States in 1984 after hundreds of deaths from poisonings, overdoses, injuries, and accidents, but they are still legal in Mexico and Canada. They are particularly potent when combined with alcohol, said Costantino, who is also president of DrugScan, a national toxicology lab. "You lose motor coordination, critical thinking skills, the ability to stay conscious," he said. "There are also some amnesia effects, almost like being under mild anesthesia."

Some central nervous system depressants that come in pill form, like Xanax and Valium, can also be crushed and dissolved into a drink, Costantino said. While many of the so-called date-rape drugs, like Rohypnol, can be added to drinks without changing the color, flavor, or odor of the beverage, some, like GHB, are so pungent they have to be disguised in a really strong drink. Sexual assault in and of itself is the most underreported violent crime, but drug-facilitated sexual assaults are even less likely to be reported to authorities because the drugs wipe out a person's memory as well as their resistance, so they may not even know what happened to them.

Many of these drugs leave the body quickly, within twelve to seventy-two hours, which is why, if you think you may have been drugged but can't get to a hospital, RAINN urges you to save your urine in a clean, sealable container as soon as possible and place it in the refrigerator or freezer.

"Almost any drug can be used as a date-rape drug," said Porrata, who is also the founder of Project GHB, a website that, among other things, contains advice for those who think they were drugged and sexually assaulted. "Drug rapes can happen to anyone of any age in any environment, from a private party to a cruise, or even in a hospital," she wrote on the site.

And, she warns, anybody can be a rapist.

Even America's Dad.

DESPITE ALL OF the new accusers continuing to come forward in 2015, it still seemed that many people were having trouble believing Cosby was capable of such atrocities.

While many "Far from Finished" comedy tour appearances had been canceled or indefinitely postponed and though protesters and hecklers had been hounding him at the ones that didn't, standing ovations were still the norm.

On the last day of his tour a gathering of protesters, including Lili Bernard and Jennifer Thompson—Jane Doe Number Two, who had finally felt comfortable enough to allow her name and photo to be used— stood outside the Cobb Energy Performing Arts Centre in Atlanta holding signs that said "Shame" and chanting, "We believe the women."

Members of a Facebook group called "We Support the Survivors of Bill Cosby" were there, led by Brandy Betts, the administrator of the group at the time who had also started a petition to get the event canceled.

"It's not acceptable that a very powerful, popular, privileged, protected man has been able to perform, largely unstopped, and gain wealth and power while these women put together the pieces of their shattered lives," Betts told CNN.

Cosby's public standing was not improving. And his educational philanthropy was receding along with it. He'd resigned from Temple's board of trustees the previous December, and the University of Massachusetts Amherst, where he'd earned his master's degree and PhD, severed its relationship with him. High Point University in North Carolina removed him from its national board of advisors, to which he had just been appointed earlier in the year, and the Berklee College of Music said it was no longer awarding an online scholarship in Mr. Cosby's name.

But the biggest blow, given his long relationship with the college and the historic $20 million donation he and Camille gave to it in 1988, came from Spelman College, which announced that it was suspending the William and Camille Olivia Hanks Cosby endowed professorship.

Nonetheless, championing education had always been important to Cosby, and when the nonprofit Black Belt Community Foundation invited him to come to rural Alabama in May 2015 to speak to high school students about the value of education, he agreed. After his speech he would walk hand in hand with those students in a "March for Education" across the Edmund Pettus Bridge in Selma, where, in 1965, police beat peaceful demonstrators marching in support of voting rights on what's now known as Bloody Sunday.

It was the perfect way to remind people of his long, illustrious work in both civil rights and education. Perhaps it would also help erase the memory of those other, ugly allegations that were still trickling out, though at a much slower pace.

To promote his appearances, Cosby sat down for his first big media interview since the scandal broke. But the interviews didn't work out for Cosby.

When ABC's Linsey Davis asked him what he would say to a young person in Alabama if they asked him about the allegations, Cosby evaded her questions. Instead, he said he was "prepared to tell this young person the truth about life." He went on: "I'm telling you where the road is out. I'm telling you where, as you're driving, you're going to go into water and it looks like it might only be three inches deep, but you or your car are going to go down. Now you want to go here, or you want to be concerned about who's giving you the message?"

Remarkably, he was using the same bizarre, rambling anecdote he'd used in 2005 when he sat down with ABC for his first TV interview after Castor closed Andrea's criminal case without charging him.

This time he vowed to make a comeback on TV, saying, "I have a ton of ideas to put on television about people and their love for each other."

The next day the New York *Daily News* called the interview "wacky."

CHAPTER SEVENTEEN

DISCO BISCUITS

US District Judge Eduardo Robreno had been a federal judge for thirteen years when Andrea Constand's civil lawsuit against Cosby was assigned to him in March 2005. A former refugee who had immigrated to the United States at age fifteen without his family, he was the first Cuban American in history to be appointed to the federal court system and the first Hispanic federal judge in Pennsylvania.

Until the Cosby case exploded again in July 2015, Robreno was all but unknown by the public. Within legal circles, however, he was admired for his masterful handling of a massive number of federal asbestos claims—it was the largest multijurisdictional litigation in US history, and Robreno whittled the cases down from 150,000 to 5,000.

Robreno kept busy, authoring more than a thousand opinions during his twenty-plus years on the bench. But it was the one he wrote on July 6, 2015, that will likely make the greatest impression on history.

Summer was heating up in Philadelphia when he granted a motion submitted by the Associated Press to unseal parts of Cosby's deposition in Andrea's case. This meant that the AP—and America—would be able to read some of Cosby's private testimony.

Cosby's attorneys argued against the release, saying their client was not a public figure, but the judge disagreed, pointing them to the controversial May 2004 "pound cake speech" and other public chastisements as examples of Cosby's engagement in public life.

"Defendant has donned the mantle of public moralist and mounted the proverbial electronic or print soap box to volunteer his views on, among other things, childrearing, family life, education and crime," Robreno wrote. "To the extent that defendant has freely entered the public square . . . he has voluntarily narrowed the zone of privacy that he is entitled to claim."

When the AP's story reporting on the unsealed excerpts of the deposition went out on the national wire, the contents were explosive.

In his deposition Cosby revealed that he obtained Quaaludes to give to women he intended to have sex with, then, after his attorney interceded, amended his statement to say it was just one woman he gave them to, and that he had seven prescriptions he used for this purpose, ones he got from a Los Angeles gynecologist named Dr. Amar, who'd since died. He also confirmed the account of Therese Serignese, Jane Doe Number Ten, saying they had sex after he gave her the pills at the Las Vegas Hilton in 1976.

"She meets me backstage. I give her Quaaludes. We then have sex," Cosby had said in the deposition.

He said he had obtained these prescriptions in the 1970s and kept them through the 1980s, 1990s, and into the 2000s, even though they were banned in the United States in 1984.

Elsewhere in the testimony, he recalled contacting his agent, Tom Ilius, at the William Morris agency and telling him to send money to Therese. He admitted to offering Andrea money for her "education," something he had vigorously denied when he filed his response to Andrea's lawsuit in May 2005.

He said he didn't remember whether he drugged Beth Ferrier but confirmed he'd had an affair with her and had agreed to do an interview with the *National Enquirer* in exchange for the tabloid killing her story. The *Enquirer* had also agreed to not run any stories about Cosby's extramarital affairs, drugging women, or inappropriate physical contact with any woman while she was incapacitated for two years from the date the agreement was signed. After the two years were up, they could extend it annually, provided Cosby gave the *Enquirer* two exclusive interviews per year of each yearly extension.

After the contents of the deposition were published, Cosby quickly tried to do damage control and his reps released a statement to ABC News saying, "The only reason Mr. Cosby settled was because it would have been embarrassing in those days to put all those women on the stand and his family had no clue. That would have been very hurtful."

Despite that defense, the deposition revelations cost him the support of pop star Jill Scott:

About Bill Cosby. Sadly, his own testimony offers PROOF of terrible deeds, which is ALL I have ever required to believe the accusations.

1) We live in America. Many African American men are detained &/or imprisoned for crimes without evidence. I will never jump on bandwagons 2) based on social media or hearsay. Proof will always matter more than public opinion. The sworn testimony is proof. Completely disgusted. I stood by a man I respected and loved. I was wrong. It HURTS!!!

Whoopi Goldberg was also forced to publicly (albeit reluctantly) walk back her support. "I gotta say, all the information out there kinda points to guilt," she admitted.

Washington, DC, attorney Joseph Cammarata, whose most famous case thus far had been representing President Bill Clinton accuser Paula Jones, was now representing three accusers in defamation lawsuits against Cosby. Two of the women were Tamara and Therese. I'd gone to him for comment for the stories I was writing, knowing these revelations would be key evidence for those lawsuits.

"It's an extraordinary turn of events which provides much-needed public light on Mr. Cosby's behavior," he said, noting that Cosby's deposition statements "support the victims' allegations against him."

WHEN BETH FERRIER read the Associated Press story, she was blown away. She'd suspected the tabloid had shelved her profile as part of trading up for the exclusive interview with Cosby, but now she knew for sure.

"We have been telling the truth," she told me. "Other Jane Does can come forward. It's safe now."

And a few days later one did. On July 13 Becky Cooper, Jane Doe Number Eleven, went public with her story at a press conference with Ferrier and Allred. In 1982 Becky was a twenty-eight-year-old massage therapist at a Las Vegas health club where Cosby played tennis.

Cosby had been an avid tennis player for years. He played for several hours a day while staying at Hefner's Los Angeles mansion and began participating in the celebrity tennis tournaments that were all the rage in the 1970s and 1980s. He even hosted some of his own, with the proceeds going to Cedars-Sinai Medical Center, Jesse Jackson's Operation PUSH, and the United Negro College Fund, playing with and against stars like Farrah Fawcett, Sydney Poitier, Dabney Coleman, and, in one case, O. J. Simpson.

His love for tennis even allowed him to hobnob with royalty. He met Princess Grace and Prince Ranier when he played in a tournament they were hosting and shared the court with some of the top tennis players in the world—John McEnroe, Billie Jean King, Monica Seles, Andre Agassi.

So when Cosby told Becky he had a sore elbow and shoulder, she believed him, instantly offering him a massage. "I've got time before my next appointment," she told him. "Let's do it now." Instead, he invited her to his show at the Las Vegas Hilton that Friday night and dinner afterward. Then she could massage him, he said. She agreed. She wasn't the least bit suspicious. He'd been playing tennis there every day for about a month and was always a perfect gentleman, even befriending her aunt and mother. Besides, he was nearly twenty years older than her and was married with children.

Cosby had been playing at the Las Vegas Hilton since the 1970s, performing there as many as four times a year, often staying in Room 3000, the Elvis [Presley] Suite, which was the penthouse, after Presley's death. It was five thousand square feet, larger than most homes, built to keep Presley safe from his adoring fans. Cosby shared the billing with musical acts like Ike and Tina Turner, Nancy Wilson, Ben Vereen, and Sha Na Na.

After the show he and Becky were sitting in his favorite booth at the hotel restaurant when suddenly a man appeared with a shot of Stolichnaya vodka for her, though she hadn't ordered anything. To this day she has no idea whether the man worked for the restaurant or Cosby. And she wouldn't have thought anything of it except for what happened next.

She took a sip. "No. No. Drink it down," Cosby insisted.

So she did.

A few minutes later he abruptly ended their dinner over her protests because she still hadn't eaten or even placed an order for food, and he began escorting her back to his dressing room. She was already having trouble walking. By the time they got to his dressing room, she was barely able to stand. He led her over to a chair, took her pants off, and raped her. She couldn't stop him. "It was like I was in a dream state," she told me. "I couldn't fight him off."

She somehow managed to put her pants back on and grab her massage table, dragging it as she fled down the hallway. That's the last thing she remembers. She woke up two days later in her own bed. Her roommates had found her passed out in the driver's seat of her car the previous morning. Unable to wake her, they carried her up to her bedroom, then checked on her every so often to make sure she was still breathing.

"I can't believe I was able to drive home with that drug in my system," she told me. "I could have crashed my car and died. Or killed somebody." She didn't go to the police back then, fearing she wouldn't be believed, but she did tell her sister and, many years later, her husband. "He wanted to watch *The Cosby Show* one day, and I just broke down crying and said, 'I have to tell you something. He's not the nice guy you think he is,'" she said, then she told him what happened to her.

"It just blew me away," her husband, Bob, told me. "He was one of my favorite comedians. His records just cracked me up as a kid."

But he believed her.

She told her husband if she ever heard of this happening to anyone else, she'd have to say something. She already felt guilty, wondering how many other women it had happened to after her. In 2005, when she heard about Andrea and Tamara, she immediately called Andrea's attorneys and told them her story. She wasn't yet ready to have her name revealed to the public, so she simply went by her Jane Doe number.

By 2015, with so many other women coming before her, she was finally ready to reveal her identity.

Becky and Beth wanted to know more. So they joined together and, in a motion filed by Allred, asked Robreno to unseal the entire deposition.

Meanwhile the previously released excerpts were so shocking that even President Obama addressed them at a news conference when he was asked whether he would revoke Cosby's Presidential Medal of Freedom. Angela Rose, the executive director of PAVE, as well as some Cosby accusers had been calling for the revocation.

"There's no precedent for revoking a medal," Obama said, adding that he makes it a policy not to comment on cases in which legal action is pending. Then, after a pause, he added, "I'll say this, if you give a woman or a man, for that matter, without his or her knowledge, a drug, and then have sex with that person without consent, that's rape. And this country, any civilized country, should have no tolerance for rape."

ON JULY 19 the public learned what was in the full deposition. The *New York Times*, which got hold of it through a legal loophole, published a story about its contents, which revealed that during his long career Cosby "used a combination of fame, apparent concern, and powerful sedatives" to help him seduce women and that he did his best to hide his extramarital activities from his wife.

"[H]e presented himself in the deposition as an unapologetic, cavalier playboy . . . a profile at odds with the popular image he so enjoyed, that of father figure and public moralist," said the *Times*.

During the deposition Cosby was asked about each of the Jane Does. When questioned about Beth, he admitted asking her about her father, who died of cancer, because he wanted to have sexual contact with her.

The revelations, which confirmed so much of what his accusers had been saying and he'd been denying, sent shockwaves across the country. I'd heard the contents of the deposition were explosive, but never in my wildest dreams did I imagine he'd admit to so much. I'd jumped back into the story after the AP excerpts were released and just kept on going.

Monique Pressley, a telegenic Washington, DC, attorney just hired by Cosby, quickly took to the airwaves to defend her client. "Mr. Cosby has denied the accusations that have been lodged thus far," she told ABC's *Good Morning America* on July 22. "The sheer volume or number of people who are saying a particular thing does not make it true."

Another Cosby attorney, Patrick O'Connor, filed a new motion asking the judge to keep the deposition from being released to the rest of the media. He insisted that just because Cosby admitted to giving Quaaludes to a woman he was in a consensual relationship with in the 1970s does not mean he gave other women the drugs "without their knowledge or consent" or that he "engaged in any non-consensual sex."

"Quaaludes were a highly popular recreational drug in the 1970s, labeled in slang as 'disco biscuits' and known for their capacity to increase arousal," he noted. But the women didn't ask for the drug—and it was given to most of them without their knowledge. What's more, Quaaludes were known to render a person unconscious. This prompted Troiani to raise an intriguing question: Was Cosby a somnophiliac—someone who is sexually aroused by an unconscious or sleeping person?

"Although some of the women engaged in consensual relations with Cosby, their accounts substantiated defendant's alleged predilection for somnophilia," she wrote in support of the release of the full deposition.

WHILE THE LAWYERS battled over the documents, Andrea again came under attack. A reporter from a Toronto newspaper had ambushed her, and though she hadn't granted an interview, the paper quoted her as saying, "there is so much more to say." O'Connor then filed a motion asking for sanctions against Andrea, saying she had breached her confidentiality agreement. He also pointed to some of her recent comments on Twitter—like "I won't go away. There's a lot more I will say" and "It's not that everybody forgot about [this case]. Truth is, nobody cared"— claiming that those too went against her agreement of silence.

Troiani fired back with a motion denying that Andrea violated the confidentiality agreement and revealing something that had never been made public before: Andrea's sexual orientation.

"In his narcissistic view of the world, [Bill Cosby] believes that plaintiff's every tweet must be about him," Troiani wrote. "He is as perceptive in this belief as he claims to be in his interpretation of non-verbal cues from women he wants to seduce. As defendant admits in his deposition, despite his talent for interpreting female reactions to him, he did not realize plaintiff was gay until the police told him."

She later told me she finally revealed Andrea's sexual orientation because "it was pertinent to the legal argument we were making. He kept saying how attuned he was to women in his deposition."

In that deposition Cosby also revealed himself to be a conniving predator, describing in detail how he stalked Andrea as prey, carefully working to gain her trust for months before that final sexual encounter, which he insisted was consensual.

He said he had had a "romantic interest" in Andrea since the first time he met her. His plan was to "meet her" and then "perhaps to have some moments with her that would have to do with some sort of friendship." He then nurtured their relationship by "inviting her to my house, talking to her about personal situations dealing with her life, growth, education, access and thoughts to how to acquire a more aggressive attitude, protecting oneself in business," he said.

The perfect predator, choosing and chasing his prey.

Step by step, the way he described his pursuit of Andrea was exactly how former FBI profiler Mary Ellen O'Toole said these icons operated.

THE RELEASE OF the deposition had another effect—a game-changing one. It prompted Montgomery County District Attorney Risa Vetri Ferman, who was Castor's first assistant in 2005, his number two when he had dismissed the original criminal charges, to reopen Andrea's case.

After a long hike one day in September, I saw the headline in the *Philadelphia Inquirer*: "Time Hasn't Run Out on Possible Charges Against Cosby in Pa." I read and reread the headline, amazed. Of all the things I'd thought might come out of the new publicity about the case, that wasn't one of them. I thought the statute of limitations had long passed. But aggravated indecent assault is a felony with a twelve-year statute of limitations, which would not expire until January 2016 at the earliest.

Troiani was as stunned as I was. Kevin Steele, then Ferman's first assistant, had visited her to ask whether Andrea would cooperate if they reopened the investigation. "When Kevin appeared in my office that day, I was like, 'What?' I think the first thing I said to him was, 'Isn't the statute of limitations gone? No?'" she said. "That was the surprise—that the case came back all those years later."

Ferman soon released a veiled statement that indicated the case was open once again: "I believe prosecutors have a responsibility to review past conclusions, whether their own or a predecessor's, when current information might lead to a different decision," she said.

Castor was quoted in the story. Now a county commissioner, Castor reversed his stance on the case once again, telling the *Inquirer* he didn't think much had changed since he made his decision—despite the more than fifty women who had now come forward and Cosby's admission about using Quaaludes in the deposition.

"The statement [Andrea Constand] gave police did not provide sufficient detail on which a criminal charge could be based," he told the *Inquirer*. He then posted links to the story on his public Facebook and Twitter accounts, with the comment: "Cosby victim told police much different than she told the court in her lawsuit. First I saw that in a story. Troublesome for the good guys. Not good."

Those posts would come back to haunt him in the fall.

CHAPTER EIGHTEEN

DO YOU WANT TO GO TO HEAVEN
OR DO YOU WANT TO GO TO HELL?

The Cosby case quickly became key in the contentious race for Montgomery County's top prosecutor. Steele, Ferman's first assistant, was running against Castor. Castor had decided he wanted his old job back, and Steele wasn't about to let Castor off the hook for his treatment of Cosby's criminal allegations.

On October 20 Steele released a television ad titled "Tough," attacking Castor for not prosecuting Cosby in 2005. In the ad Steele boasted of his office's "98 percent conviction rate" and the "tough sentences for sexual predators" he had earned in his position. The ad went on to refer to Castor as "the former DA who refused to prosecute Bill Cosby" and used Castor's words against him by quoting him directly from a clip from 2005: "In Pennsylvania we charge people for criminal conduct," Castor had claimed. "We don't charge people for making a mistake or doing something foolish."

The ad continued: "Many more victims came forward, and Castor admitted he could have used their testimony against Cosby." But Castor "didn't even try," the narrator said.

Castor quickly defended himself with a commercial of his own.

"By now you've heard my opponent's ad saying I did nothing to protect the other victims of Bill Cosby," he said in the ad. "These women's identities became available only after I left the DA's office and lost the power to enforce the law." But this wasn't true—thirteen other women came forward back then, and although Castor had their names and addresses, Castor's team chose not to interview most of them.

Castor went on to turn the blame on Steele, claiming he "had the power to help victims of Cosby but he sat on his hands." Again, his accusation wasn't true: as the first assistant district attorney, Steele didn't have the authority to act on the women's behalf. Only Ferman did. And she had.

Castor's comments about her in the *Inquirer* story and on his social media accounts devastated Andrea, and her attorneys were indignant and quick to act. A week before the November 3 election
they filed a defamation suit against Castor, arguing that he had "chosen to make [Andrea] collateral damage for his political ambitions"
by defaming her in public. In the lawsuit Andrea also accused Castor of trying to "thwart" the current district attorney's investigation
into the case through an interview he gave to Peggy Gibbons, a reporter for the *Times Herald* in Norristown, Pennsylvania, which ran
September 24.

"From a political standpoint, it looks really bad to move on Cosby
before the election and garner, presumably, favorable press at the time
when the district attorney knows there is no chance the viability of
the prosecution will ever be a problem," he told the reporter.

Troiani was indignant that Castor had injected politics into a prosecutorial decision and called it "unfair not only to my client but unfair to Bill Cosby." She went on, "Nobody should be arrested or not
arrested for political reasons."

Castor's campaign released a statement blaming Steele for the lawsuit, calling it a political "stunt." "The lawsuit filed today, seven days
before an election, is the cheapest of Steele's cheap campaign stunts,"
the statement said. "It is the act of a desperate candidate who is down
in the polls and headed to defeat. It is totally without merit."

Castor then told the *Inquirer* that Andrea and her lawyers were
engaging in "quite despicable behavior" in an effort to influence the
election. "It really is stunning to see the lengths that these people will
go to," he said. "I'm a lawyer. I'm not afraid of court. I think the people
who filed this lawsuit ought to be afraid."

Andrea was, in fact, afraid. Castor's threats were intimidating, and
after what she'd already been through, she couldn't imagine engaging
with him throughout another investigation. If he won the race, she
wouldn't cooperate, Troiani told me exclusively for a story I wrote for
People.com.

"He said she should be afraid of him," Troiani marveled. "He seems
to have declared war on her. Logically speaking, I don't know how a
victim could trust him."

In THE MIDST of this heated campaign, Cosby was issued a stunning defeat. A federal judge in Massachusetts had refused to dismiss defamation lawsuits against him by three accusers, including Tamara.

The defamation suits were a strategy of their lawyer, Joseph Cammarata. He knew the women couldn't bring a claim of assault against Cosby because the statute of limitations had expired. But he had also heard Cosby respond to these allegations by calling the women liars, so a charge of defamation would be within the law.

"It became clear to me that the women now had an opportunity to restore their good name and reputation by bringing a defamation claim, which would then give them an opportunity for a court to determine who was telling the truth," he told me.

Tamara's lawsuit, filed in December 2014, claimed that comments made by Cosby's representatives to the *Washington Post* and *Newsweek* that year "impugned" her reputation and exposed her to "public contempt, ridicule, aversion or disgrace." The *Post* had also included comments from Walter Phillips Jr., Cosby's attorney from 2005, in which he said Cosby didn't know Tamara and that her allegations against him were fabricated.

Seeing the truth surface was gratifying, but Tamara was still suffering from the fallout of publicly accusing Cosby. She had lost clients and even longtime friends, who looked at her claims with skepticism.

"I was really afraid," she told me. "I can't tell you of what. It was more of deep anxiety and fear. I didn't know whether somebody loved him so much I'd be in some kind of danger, but I felt much better [behind the gates of my home]." Still, she didn't regret coming forward against Cosby. "I would do it all again, even though it was very difficult emotionally, psychologically, professionally and personally because I feel that these fifty-plus women were also given a chance to be brave and come forward, and I don't think any of them would have done that if we hadn't started the ball rolling back in 2005."

As THE DEFAMATION case waited for its day in court, Steele defeated Castor in the election, beating him by seventeen thousand votes.

"You made a choice to take it forward, to fight for victims, to fight for people who have been the subject of crimes," he told supporters at a victory party. "And that is where I will continue to make a difference every day."

Castor also thanked his supporters and congratulated Steele: "I tried one more time to pull the rabbit out of the hat," he wrote, conceding he'd lost the race. "The hat was simply out of rabbits."

Neither Steele nor Castor mentioned the Cosby case that night, and over the coming weeks we were all waiting anxiously to see whether Steele would charge Cosby. He remained tightlipped about the investigation, and nearly two months passed with no news.

But that didn't mean everyone was waiting in silence. While Steele quietly conducted his internal investigation and investigators traveled to Canada to interview Andrea once again, four more accusers joined Tamara's defamation lawsuit against Cosby: Joan Tarshis, Barbara Bowman, Louisa Moritz, and Angela Leslie.

Louisa was a Cuban-born actress who would become best known for her role in the TV show *Love, American Style*. She'd also appeared as Rose in the Oscar-winning movie *One Flew Over the Cuckoo's Nest*. She said Cosby stuck his penis in her mouth backstage at the *Tonight Show* in 1971 when she was twenty-five years old.

Ex-model Angela Leslie said Cosby forced her to masturbate him in his Las Vegas hotel room in the early nineties after he asked her to pretend she was intoxicated. All said they were called liars by Cosby's representatives after going public with their claims.

And Kristina Ruehli—she'd been Jane Doe Number Twelve—filed her own defamation lawsuit against Cosby, which she later withdrew after she won a motion to dismiss. She'd proved her point. She'd pointed to a blanket statement that Marty Singer put out about all the accusers on November 21, 2014, in which he called allegations like Kristina's "fantastical" and "past the point of absurdity," for how she was defamed.

Cosby fought back against the suits, filing counter-defamation lawsuits against the seven accusers. He claimed he "never drugged nor sexually assaulted the defendants and that each defendant has maliciously and knowingly published multiple false statements and accusations" about him "in an effort to cause damage to [his] reputation and to extract financial gains."

Cosby also filed his own defamation suit against ex-model Beverly Johnson. "In cases of rape and abuse, abusers will do whatever they can to intimidate and weaken their victims to force them to stop fighting," Johnson said in response. "I ask for your support of all the victims involved."

Cosby did not, however, counter-sue Janice Dickinson, who was being represented by Lisa Bloom, Gloria Allred's daughter, in her defamation suit. Due to her celebrity status, Janice's filing brought the cases into the national media spotlight and refueled interest in Cosby's criminal past as she went on *Entertainment Tonight* to talk about her case.

"I'm suing Bill Cosby for justice and vindication," Janice announced as she insisted on Cosby's guilt and called on Cosby to stop perpetuating his lies. "Why won't you talk about the truth?" she demanded of the actor. "Do you want to go to heaven, or do you want to go to hell?"

He may have hoped his aggressive legal strategy would stop more women from coming forward with allegations about him—and it did just that. No new accusers revealed themselves after that.

The total was now sixty-three.

JANICE'S SUIT WAS filed in May. By December there was still no word from Steele about the potential reopening of a criminal case. As the year headed toward a close, I grew more and more convinced that nothing would ever come of the renewed investigation, that the ordeal would be over and the women who had come forward with their claims of sexual assault, who had been shamed and attacked, would never see Cosby to justice. There was still time, though. The statute of limitations didn't expire until mid-January, so maybe they were waiting until after the holidays. I felt comfortable taking some time off but kept a close eye on my emails and texts while doing so.

I'd been covering the story for nearly eleven years by now; it had become a part of my life to pursue the truth—for the women who had been violated and shamed and disbelieved. It looked all too possible that their truths would never be acknowledged in a courtroom. As the world prepared for New Year's Eve and the promise of a new year, I found myself wondering whether the DA's office had once again let Andrea down.

Then, on the night of December 29, I got a tip in the form of a text. The wording was cryptic, but its meaning made my heart race as my adrenaline surged.

Bill Cosby was going to be arrested.

I confirmed the tip with a secondary source, emailed my editors, and wrote late into the night.

I broke the news of his arrest at 9:35 A.M.

CHAPTER NINETEEN

I AM THE SOVEREIGN

Kevin Steele was preparing to prosecute America's Dad.

A soft-spoken yet forceful man whose silver-white hair contrasts with his youthful face, he had a Jimmy Stewart–like quality about him—even tempered, sometimes even somber. He didn't have aspirations for a higher office than the one he held; he was content to have reached the pinnacle of the county's law enforcement.

Until now Steele's most high-profile case had been that of Kathleen Kane, the state's attorney general who was charged with perjury, a felony, along with an array of misdemeanors related to her job, including official oppression, obstruction, and conspiracy for allegedly leaking grand jury information to reporters. Steele knew that with the Cosby case he'd be experiencing an entirely different level of attention and that Cosby's legal team would be coming after him with their cannons fired up. But the time had come, and Steele was ready. He would have to charge Cosby now or risk running out of time on the aggravated indecent assault case's statute of limitations. Andrea couldn't give them an exact date in mid-January, so better to be safe and charge him before year's end.

Steele's first press conference after the arrest was kept low key; I was the only national reporter in the room. Though he'd hoped to just confine it to the local media he had sent a vaguely worded alert to, he hadn't counted on me finding out about it. He kept it short, letting the details of the probable cause affidavit attached to the arrest warrant, which he distributed to the press, do most of the talking.

"A prosecutor's job is to follow the evidence wherever it leads and whenever it comes to light," Steele told the small gathering of reporters. Flanked by Cheltenham Township police chief John Norris and other law enforcement officials, Steele announced that Cosby was being charged with three counts of aggravated indecent assault, each a felony carrying a prison sentence of up to ten years.

Cosby, Steele went on, had agreed to turn himself in; he would be going to the district justice's office in Elkins Park that afternoon for his arraignment.

The affidavit was chilling in its details, many of them new. It outlined two times Cosby had come on to Andrea, only to be rebuffed by her. It also alleged that Andrea's rejection of Cosby was the reason he drugged her in January 2004.

"Cosby knew that his two prior sexual advances were blocked by the much younger, athletic victim," the affidavit stated. "He knew that further attempts at sexual conduct would likewise be unsuccessful unless he was able to prevent her from resisting. . . . He knew the victim would become sedated, and likely rendered incapable of resistance, by her ingestion of wine and Benadryl, or wine and another substance, known only to Cosby, with similar effects."

It also revealed particulars about phone calls between Andrea, Gianna, and Cosby, one of which Gianna had taped. While Castor had claimed this was an "illegal wiretap" and could not be used as evidence in the case, his legal interpretations were faulty, and the tape was deemed admissible; in fact, the tapes were a key component of the case investigators built against Cosby.

The calls took place shortly after Andrea confessed to Gianna about the night Cosby sexually assaulted her. Gianna had demanded Andrea give her Cosby's telephone number so she could "confront him" and find out what drugs he had given her daughter. She dialed his phone and left an irate message.

He called her back three days later. Although he didn't tell her he'd given Andrea Quaaludes, he admitted to fondling Andrea's breasts, placing Andrea's hand on his penis, and digitally penetrating her. The affidavit went on to say that Cosby repeatedly apologized and even offered to cover any expenses associated with Andrea's therapy.

Gianna wasn't appeased. She demanded to know what kind of drug he'd given her daughter, telling Cosby he was "a very sick man." Cosby agreed with her.

Finally, Cosby relented and said he would go upstairs to his bathroom to read the label of the prescription drug. Moments later he returned to say that he couldn't read the label because of an eye condition but that he would write it down on a piece of paper and mail it to her. He never did.

But he called again on January 17, and this time Gianna taped the conversation, hoping he would repeat what he'd said to her in the earlier phone call. She asked him if he was going to send her that piece of paper with the name of the drug he'd given her daughter. Instead, he offered to help Andrea "financially with any educational goals." He asked if she and Andrea would be willing to travel to meet with him in another city. She agreed to nothing.

The following day Peter Wiederlight from William Morris, the talent agency that represented Cosby, called Andrea and asked to arrange the meeting Cosby had mentioned. It would be in Florida, explaining that Cosby would pay for the trip. Andrea and her mom did not accept the offer. Wiederlight gave a statement to investigators on February 4, 2005, in which he confirmed Cosby had asked him to make the phone call and arrange the travel, and he also revealed that he had made similar arrangements for other women on Cosby's behalf.

We also finally learned the details of what Cosby had told police in January 2005. He said their encounter was consensual, as ABC had reported all those years ago, and that he gave Andrea one and a half Benadryl because of her tension and inability to sleep. Afterward they "began to pet (touching and kissing), then he touched her bare breasts and genitalia." She never objected, he said, never pushed him away, never told him she felt paralyzed or affected by the medication. He went to bed and woke in the morning to find her awake. They talked, he gave her a blueberry muffin and some tea, then she left.

He confirmed Gianna's account of their phone conversations, saying he had touched Andrea's breasts and vagina but guaranteed her there was no "penile penetration" of her daughter.

Investigators acknowledged the 2005 investigation in the warrant, noting that Castor had closed it on February 17, 2005, but also made it clear in his press release that he would "reconsider th[is] decision should the need arise." They also revealed that both Andrea's and Cosby's depositions from the civil suit aided their investigation. Cosby's own "evasive and conflicting" identifications of the drug he gave Andrea were a "significant factor" in the probe. She said he told her it was herbal. Cosby told police it was Benadryl. He told Andrea's mother it was some sort of prescription, though he didn't know what it was. His deliberate efforts to conceal what kind of drug he gave Andrea demonstrate his "consciousness of guilt," they wrote.

So did his apologies to Gianna and Andrea and his offer to pay for Andrea's graduate school, her therapy, and expenses for a trip to Florida. "[I]ndividuals who are falsely accused of sexual assault generally do not unilaterally offer generous financial assistance, and apologies, to their accuser and the accuser's family," the affidavit said. "To the contrary, such conduct is consistent with offenders who are seeking to make amends for wrongful behavior and prevent involvement by law enforcement."

And Cosby himself gave a telling answer when asked whether he'd had sexual intercourse with Andrea, they wrote. "Never asleep or awake," he replied, inferring that either was a reasonable answer.

The details of the warrant amazed me, as did the level of knowledge that Castor had when he dismissed the case. Castor had heard those "illegal wiretaps" but still chose to close the investigation.

Worse, Castor would soon be claiming that the press release announcing his decision was also an agreement to never prosecute Cosby for this crime, which is why Cosby was so forthcoming in his deposition. And that phrase about reconsidering his decision was about his decision not to disparage Andrea or Cosby publicly, not his decision not to prosecute Cosby.

Curiouser and curiouser.

BY THE TIME Cosby arrived at the district justice's office, it was a mob scene. There were so many members of the media that they couldn't fit inside the tiny courtroom and were spilling out into the halls and onto the property outside.

Cosby exited his car and walked toward the building with an attorney on each side holding his arms and escorting him as he walked slowly toward the courthouse. Cosby carried a cane, and though he didn't use it, it enhanced the perception that he was elderly and feeble. It was known that he had battled a rare form of glaucoma in the past and that his vision in one eye was impaired, but he'd never been seen at a public appearance with a cane or otherwise unable to function without assistance. Now he walked haltingly, his eyes seemingly clouded and distant.

The sweater-clad Cosby was arraigned at 2:30 P.M. His bail was set at $1 million, and he was ordered to surrender his passport. He did not enter a plea.

Throughout the brief appearance Cosby seemed disoriented and was fidgeting with his fingers. When the judge had completed the proceedings and gave Cosby permission to leave, he said to Cosby, "Good luck to you." Cosby replied, "Thank you."

Cosby then headed to the nearby Cheltenham Police Department to be processed and fingerprinted. When those procedures were complete, Cosby was freed on bail. He had to post 10 percent of his bail—$100,000—in cash. The DA's office released his mug shot later that day, and his lawyer released a statement to ABC News.

"The charge by the Montgomery County District Attorney's office came as no surprise, filed 12 years after the alleged incident and coming on the heels of a hotly contested election for this county's DA during which this case was made the focal point," it said. "Make no mistake, we intend to mount a vigorous defense against this unjustified charge and we expect that Mr. Cosby will be exonerated by a court of law."

Andrea was doing her best to keep her spirits up now that the media had once again descended on her hometown and photographers were following her every move. She was grateful for those who supported her, but when people maligned her in public, she took it hard. She wasn't looking forward to another bout of courtroom dates.

She got a short reprieve when Cosby's preliminary hearing was pushed back indefinitely as his attorneys filed motions galore to get the charges dismissed. The first motion attacked Steele, saying the charges were brought "illegally, improperly and unethically" and violated an "express agreement" Castor made in 2005 to never prosecute Cosby on these charges. If the charges weren't dismissed, the motion asked that Steele and the Montgomery County DA's office be disqualified from handling the case. This was the first we'd heard about that press release also being an agreement not to prosecute, though it would not be the last. My stories about the DA's race in 2015 were used as exhibits. The revelation set the stage for a two-day-long hearing in February, with Castor as the star witness.

At the hearing Castor explained why he had the power to make his press release an immunity agreement to never prosecute Cosby criminally in Andrea's case. "The prosecutor, according to Pennsylvania rules, [is a] minister of justice," he said. "And I did not believe it was just to go forward with the criminal prosecution. I wanted there to be some measure of justice."

He went on: "So I made the determination as the sovereign—and not Bruce Castor, district attorney. I am the sovereign of Montgomery County, Pennsylvania. As the sovereign, I determined we would not prosecute Cosby, and that would then set off a chain of events that I thought as a minister of justice would gain some justice for Andrea Constand."

Meaning her civil suit.

In an email to Ferman in September 2015, Castor said Andrea's attorneys had signed off on this press release also being an immunity agreement. During his six hours of testimony, he stuck to that story, saying he had asked Ferman to notify Andrea's attorneys about this agreement and assumed she had done so. Emails between he and Ferman from the fall of 2015 were included as exhibits. In them Ferman said she had no idea what Castor was talking about.

Steele spoke out in the courtroom too. He clarified that an immunity agreement was only enforceable if a judge signed it. The presiding judge for the case, Steven O'Neill, agreed. He also seemed puzzled by Castor's testimony, asking him why he didn't follow the state's immunity statute by making an agreement in writing with the plaintiff's attorney. Castor objected, invoking his power as the "sovereign" a few more times before the judge gave up questioning him.

THE NEXT DAY Troiani and Kivitz took the stand. They both disputed Castor's testimony, saying they never agreed to the press release also being an immunity agreement. In fact, they didn't even know about the press release until the media showed up at their office. For the first time Troiani also revealed what it was like questioning Cosby over those four days in 2005 and 2006.

"It was an extremely contentious deposition," she said, remembering aloud how Cosby had stormed out of the room and would only return when a judge intervened. "There was a lot of yelling and screaming and trying to divert our attention," she recalled.

She went on to describe the circumstances around the lawsuit settlement. Eventually Cosby and Andrea had reached an agreement to settle for an undisclosed amount of money, she said, but Cosby's attorneys wanted Andrea and her lawyers to agree to destroy their files on the case. What's more, Andrea would need to agree that she would not cooperate with law enforcement if the case were ever reopened.

Troiani had refused on both counts. She would not destroy her records, and Andrea would not promise to remain silent during any future follow-up investigation, noting that both were tantamount to obstruction of justice. Finally, the two parties settled on an agreement that Andrea would cooperate only if law enforcement approached her.

In the end, the judge apparently believed Troiani and Kivitz, not Castor. He denied the motion to dismiss, saying the credibility of the witnesses who testified was an "inherent part" of his ruling.

Troiani and Kivitz were relieved. Andrea had been terribly upset the day before when she'd heard about Castor's testimony about her, when he'd said Andrea had ruined her credibility with the inconsistencies in her various statements to law enforcement. They all now felt vindicated and maybe even hopeful once again. Maybe justice would prevail.

And it would.

But not yet.

CHAPTER TWENTY

THE GOOD WIFE

Throughout her fifty-plus-year marriage, Camille Cosby had done her best to stay out of the public eye. So it was no surprise that she fought hard—unsuccessfully—to avoid being deposed by Joseph Cammarata, who represented seven women suing her husband for defamation.

After Cosby's arrest I thought the case would stay quiet through the rest of the holidays and I could resume my vacation. My husband and I made plans to go out with friends for dinner on New Year's Eve, and we decided to keep them.

I should have known better.

Judges love to release controversial decisions on the eve of big holidays. I'd seen it happen in other cases I'd covered through the years.

In this case the judge denied Camille's motion to avoid testifying in her husband's civil case. After we got home from dinner I ended up working on this deep into the night, tracking down a comment from Cammarata and a copy of the judge's order.

Camille was not done fighting, however, and the dispute played out over the next several weeks with various motions and filings.

When Cammarata did finally question her in February 2016, Camille was combative, refusing to answer 166 questions, according to court filings. The exchange grew so heated that Cammarata considered asking a judge to intervene and force her to participate in the query, much like Troiani had to do with Cosby during Andrea's lawsuit a decade prior.

What Camille did reveal was eye opening. She said she had never read the criminal complaint against her husband nor his deposition in Andrea's civil suit, and initially she refused to say whether she and her husband had even discussed it.

"I don't want to answer that," she told Cammarata, indignant. "That is communication between me and my husband."

A frustrated Cammarata responded, "You don't get that privilege, that you just tell me you're not going to answer." After he threatened to call the judge, Camille complied by saying that she and Cosby had talked about the contents of his deposition, but she would not reveal what they said.

All those depositions ground to a halt, though, until after the criminal case was resolved. And as his attorneys fought the criminal charges in court over the next 16 months, Cosby battled them in the court of public opinion with a series of strategically managed interviews in the weeks leading up to his trial.

He had also started raising the issue of race. He had a flamboyant new spokesman, Andrew Wyatt, who owned his own public relations firm in Birmingham, Alabama. And he wasn't shy about saying whatever he could to defend his boss.

In September 2016, on the day prosecutors filed a motion asking the judge to allow thirteen other accusers to testify as so-called prior bad act witnesses to show a pattern of behavior, Cosby released this statement:

> Mr. Cosby is no stranger to discrimination and racial hatred, and throughout his career Mr. Cosby has always used his voice and his celebrity to highlight the commonalities and has portrayed the differences that are not negative—no matter the race, gender and religion of a person. Yet, over the last fourteen months, Mr. Cosby, and those who have supported him, have been ignored, while lawyers like Gloria Allred hold press conferences to accuse him of crimes for unwitnessed events that allegedly occurred almost a half century earlier. . . . The time has come to shine a spotlight on the trampling of Mr. Cosby's civil rights.

Allred now represented many of the thirteen women the prosecution was calling to testify and more than half of the sixty-three accusers. She continued to hold press conferences with them, which further angered Cosby. The statement went on to berate her personally.

> Gloria Allred apparently loves the media spotlight more than she cares about justice. She calls herself a civil rights attorney, but her campaign against Mr. Cosby builds on racial bias and prejudice that

can pollute the court of public opinion. And when the media repeats her accusations—with no evidence, no trial and no jury—we are moved backwards as a country and away from the America that our civil rights leaders sacrificed so much to create. Mr. Cosby is not giving up the fight for his rights.

This message that Cosby was a victim of racism would be a continuing theme throughout the case.

SOME OF COSBY'S accusers were doing what they could via the court system, but the limitations of their rights to see justice served frustrated others. Unwilling to sit quietly by, teams of Cosby accusers mounted efforts to change the statute of limitations laws on sexual assault cases. They wanted limitations extended—or even eliminated.

Lise Lotte-Lublin was the first to petition her lawmakers in Nevada. Lise, a teacher in Las Vegas, was a twenty-three-year-old model in 1989 when, she said, Cosby drugged and sexually assaulted her after her agent introduced them.

Twenty-six years later she testified before lawmakers in Nevada and successfully saw the time limitation on accusations extended from four years to twenty years.

A year later Cosby accusers Beth Ferrier and Heidi Thomas joined together in Colorado and successfully lobbied to change the limitations from ten years to twenty.

That same year four of the accusers in California, including Lili Bernard and Victoria Valentino, joined the campaign in California—called EndRapeSOL—that eliminated California's statute of limitations for rape altogether.

The women's individual and combined efforts became an important step forward for sexual assault victims. It gave them back some of the power they'd lost with Cosby. It was too late for them, but perhaps it would help others like them in the future.

Still, Kristen Houser of the National Sexual Violence Resource Center would like to see an even more aggressive revision of the law, with the time frame limits on accusations completely eliminated in all states.

"It can take decades for victims to come forward," she said. "They don't trust the rest of us to respond appropriately. There's a general fear of reaction from the public, from family, from friends."

THE FALLOUT FROM his arrest continued for Cosby. His children's book series *Little Bill* made the American Library Association's list of most-challenged books of 2016, coming in at number nine. The list of books was designed to represent the titles that parents and other community members most wish to see removed from libraries, and the ranking was based on 323 challenges reported to the ALA in 2016 by school librarians across the country.

The *Little Bill* books, which follow the adventures of five-year-old Bill Jr. as he grows up in Philadelphia and learns a variety of life lessons, were challenged not for their content but due to the "criminal assault allegations against the author." It was the first time in ALA history that a book was listed because of the status of the author.

Every so often, one of the books, called *My Big Lie*, still makes the rounds of social media for the eerily prescient words on the back cover:

What started as a tiny fib, grew and grew and GREW
into a BIG lie.

And now Little Bill is in BIG trouble!

As his trial date grew closer, Cosby's lawyers kept filing motions, trying to get key evidence in the case thrown out. His team also staged a media blitz in an effort to raise support among African Americans and to illicit emotional sympathy from the public. On the eve of trial Cosby did an interview with the NNPA Newswire, a network composed of 205 black newspapers across the country, telling them he was completely blind. And his daughter Evin, then forty and the youngest of his five children, released an emotional statement to the African American news service, assailing the "public persecution" of her father.

My father "loves and respects women," she wrote. "He is not abusive, violent, or a rapist."

Another daughter, Ensa, agreed that race played "a big role in all aspects of this scandal."

Then, during jury selection, the issue of race surfaced once again. After the prosecution eliminated some black women from the selection, Cosby's lawyers complained that the prosecution was trying to keep African Americans from serving on the jury. The judge ruled that prosecutors had other valid reasons for excluding the women.

In the end, with two black and ten white jurors, the jury was roughly 17 percent black, a percentage that was established as slightly higher than the demographic of the county itself.

The trial was expected to last two weeks. The weekend beforehand I immersed myself in reporting and writing an analysis of the long, tangled history of the case to run online on the first day of the trial.

Then, on Sunday night, I got exclusive information that Cosby was going to make a splashy entrance on the first day of the trial, accompanied by a very special guest.

PART
THREE
(JUNE 2017–SEPTEMBER 2018)

If we take a downer, it kind of makes us sleepy and we
think we feel good. . . . Say "no" to pills.

—Bill Cosby Talks to Kids About Drugs, 1971

CHAPTER TWENTY-ONE

THIS IS WHERE THE TRUTH HAPPENS

On Monday, June 5, 2017, shortly before 8:30 A.M., Cosby arrived at the courthouse in Norristown, Pennsylvania, a massive limestone building built in 1847. With him was Keshia Knight Pulliam, who played the adorable Rudy on *The Cosby Show*. Her career had been a mixed bag since the show folded. She'd joined *Tyler Perry's House of Payne* in 2008, playing Miranda, the new wife of Calvin Payne, for which she'd won two NAACP image awards, but her other roles had mostly been on reality TV shows. She'd won a celebrity version of *Fear Factor* in 2002 by racing junkyard cars and retrieving hockey pucks from the bottom of a snake-filled tank, and appeared on *Celebrity Apprentice*, *Celebrity Big Brother*, and ABC's celebrity diving show *Splash*.

On that warm morning in early June a beaming Pulliam walked arm in arm with Cosby as they passed the hordes of reporters gathered in front of the building. Cosby had a gentle smile on his face as he leaned toward Pulliam to hear what she was saying.

Although the event was clearly staged, the affection between the two seemed real. And it seemed like a good strategy. "The goal is to ensure that at least one or two jurors who hear Cosby's trial will remember the good side of the man when they pass judgment," Gene Grabowski, a crisis management expert, told me. "This strategy has proven to have worked. Even in murder trials, it can lead juries to impose life sentences rather than the death penalty. In many cases, it can lead to hung juries." Pulliam escorted him all the way up to the courtroom, where he sat down at the defense table, laughing and chatting with his attorneys.

"I came to support [Cosby] because this is where you hear the facts. This is where the truth happens," Pulliam later told reporters. "Ultimately, it's easy to support someone and to be in their corner when things are great. When things are good. But . . . true family, friendship, integrity is how people show up and support when things aren't looking so great, when they aren't shining."

There was an air of excited anticipation when I'd arrived earlier that morning. The streets outside the courthouse were lined with satellite trucks from all the major networks. News helicopters hovered in the air while on-air correspondents did live shots on the plaza area outside. It was the highest-profile criminal trial in recent memory, and nobody wanted to miss it. Cameras aren't allowed in the courtrooms in Pennsylvania, so there would be no live streaming of the trial like there was with O. J. Simpson's in 1994, a trial many were drawing comparisons to for its intertwining themes of race, power, fame, gender, and crime, though Simpson, of course, was charged with murder, not sexual assault.

The case had been assigned to Courtroom A, a stately room with tall ceilings, majestic walnut wainscoting, eight elaborate chandeliers, and purple carpeting, its crème walls lined with portraits of current and former judges, regally posed in their judicial robes. On the front wall was a massive portrait of the first session of the Court of Common Pleas, convened in 1784 in the barn of the Barley Sheaf Inn, a few miles from Norristown. It was the largest courtroom in the courthouse, and it still felt cramped. The eight rows of padded wooden benches on either side were filled, and we were all jammed in, shoulder to shoulder. Local reporters got preferential seating, one row each behind the defense and prosecution side, while national reporters were assigned to the rows behind them. The rest were for the public.

Halfway down the hall, in Courtroom C, other observers and reporters could watch via a video hookup to a large TV in the room. It wasn't ideal, but it was the best they could do. Judge O'Neill, who was presiding over the criminal case, had issued a decorum order, with strict guidelines for the media. We had to be in our seats by 8:45 A.M., though we didn't get started until 9:30 A.M., which meant getting in line as early as possible, so I was getting up at 5:30 A.M. to make sure I was in line by 7:30 A.M. If you left the courtroom while court was in session, you couldn't come back in until the next designated break. We were allowed to have our laptops in the courtroom but were not allowed to transmit emails, tweets, or stories or even be on the internet. If we were caught doing that, we were thrown out. Cell phones were to be turned off and put away, out of sight.

I was grateful we were allowed to have our laptops in the courtroom because I ended up filing two or three stories a day, depending on the news developments. Because we only had short breaks, I'd start writing my story during testimony, then run outside during a break and transmit it. Most days I ate a breakfast bar during the lunch break while I filed because I didn't have enough time to grab lunch and write and file my story during the sixty or so minutes we got.

Gloria Allred, who represented the one other accuser O'Neill had allowed to testify, actually got in trouble that week for forgetting to turn her cell phone off, and it rang during testimony. She was booted from the courtroom for the day. Attorney Joseph Cammarata was there as well to monitor what was going on and get a glimpse of what he'd be up against once his lawsuits were allowed to move forward again.

O'Neill was equally protective of the jurors, who'd traveled nearly three hundred miles from their homes in Allegheny County across the state, warning reporters to leave them be and to not even try to get video or photos of them. They were sequestered for the duration of the trial in a nearby hotel, though we didn't know which one or where it was. Inside the courtroom a huge screen blocked our view of most of the jurors. It was supposedly there so the jurors could get a better view of any exhibits that were shown, but it was such a distraction that a radio reporter did a separate story about it, calling it a "monstrosity."

Pulliam sat in the second row, on the defense side, along with some of Cosby's other supporters, including some male comedians I had never heard of but who Andrew Wyatt told me Cosby had mentored. Wyatt also told me Phylicia Rashad planned to come sometime during the trial, though that never happened. Pulliam, with a fuchsia scarf draped around her shoulders, black pants, and a white shirt with black polka dots, was hard to miss. She appeared to be paying close attention throughout the proceedings, then left during the lunch break and never returned.

Cosby's social media team made the most of her presence, tweeting "Thank you to Cliff and Claire's 4 year old daughter (Rudy) and the brilliant Spelman Alumnus #TheCosbyShow #KeshiaKnightPulliam" along with a photo of her leaning over and hugging his neck near a water cooler in the courthouse during the lunch break.

Nowhere in sight was Camille or the Cosbys' four daughters, though Pulliam was probably more recognizable than any of his real children. While every so often their troubles made headlines and though two of them had recently very publicly come out in support of their father, for the most part they'd stayed out of the public eye throughout their lives.

Also in the courtroom were several Cosby accusers, including Lili Bernard, Barbara Bowman, Victoria Valentino, Jewel Allison, and Therese Serignese, who stayed until the end.

I was eager for it to get underway, to see and hear Andrea testify. I had no idea what to expect. She'd never done any media interviews, at least ones that she knew were interviews, so it would be the first time any of us heard the story from her lips. There was still so much we didn't know as well: why she waited a year to go to police; why she had the dates of the assault mixed up initially, saying it was in mid-March and then saying it was mid-January; and why some of her statements to law enforcement seemed to contradict one another. I knew the defense was going to use these points to discredit Andrea, because they'd already done so at the preliminary hearing a year ago, so the prosecution needed to make sure she explained all of this when she testified. In Pennsylvania in a sexual assault case a jury can convict a defendant based solely on whether they find the alleged victim's testimony credible.

So these were important holes to fill. I probably knew this case better than anyone other than the lawyers on both sides at this point, and I still didn't know the answers to those questions. I'd interviewed some former prosecutors before the trial to see what they thought would happen, and they were unsure too. One thought the prosecution had the edge due to all of the publicity surrounding all of the other accusers, while another predicted a hung jury.

The atmosphere became more sober as Assistant District Attorney Kristen Feden began her opening statement, in which she portrayed Cosby as a manipulative sexual predator who gained Andrea's trust by first posing as her mentor and then betraying her by drugging and sexually assaulting her.

"Truth, betrayal, and the inability to consent—that's what this case is about," she said, walking over to stand behind Cosby.

"This case is about a man," she said. "This man, who used his power and his fame and his previously practiced method of placing a young, trusting woman in a trusting state so she couldn't say 'No.'"

Her delivery was stilted at times, unnecessarily strident at others. I was surprised she gave the opening argument instead of Steele but wondered whether he thought it was better for a woman, especially an African American woman, to lead, given Cosby was already saying racism was behind his prosecution.

Then Cosby's charismatic lead defense lawyer, Brian McMonagle, took his turn to address the court. His opening was powerful, his lengthy trial skills evident. Before he'd become a criminal defense attorney, he'd been a prosecutor himself. But when his wife became pregnant with the first of their four children, he left the Philadelphia district attorney's office for private practice so he could better provide for his family. Since then he'd represented some of the most high-profile criminal defendants in the area, including mobsters, politicians, and the Roman Catholic archbishop of Philadelphia, who was accused of covering up multiple child sexual assault allegations against priests over the years.

McMonagle was also friends with Castor. He'd even held a fundraiser for Castor when he ran for district attorney in 2015, though it was before Cosby hired McMonagle. He'd been invoking Castor and his decision not to prosecute Cosby a lot in pretrial hearings and continued to do so throughout the trial. He insisted Cosby was an innocent man who had been wrongfully accused, and he characterized Andrea as a scheming liar, saying there were many inconsistencies in her statements to authorities and that is why Castor did not charge Cosby in 2005.

He dangled one other tantalizing tidbit: Andrea had called Cosby fifty-three times after the assault, he said, though she initially told law enforcement she'd had no contact with him afterward. "Sexual assault is a terrible crime," he said. "The only thing worse than that is the false accusation of sexual assault."

It's "an attack on human dignity," he said, his voice rising. "It can destroy a man. It can destroy his life. It can destroy his future." Opening and closing arguments are not evidence, but they hold a powerful effect on the jury, and McMonagle's opening argument was especially convincing. Cammarata was shaking his head in disappointment as we filed out of the courtroom for a break afterward. The consensus seemed to be that the prosecution had been outlawyered in that first round. I couldn't disagree.

But prosecutors rallied with their first witness. Steele had petitioned the court to allow thirteen accusers to take the stand during the trial, but the judge had only permitted one, Kelley Johnson, who identifies as African American. O'Neill didn't state why he chose her when he issued his order, but it was most likely because her assault occurred in 1996 and was the most recent of all the accusers besides Andrea.

Kelley, who'd been known publicly only as "Kacey" prior to the trial, spent nearly three hours on the stand. At first she was calm and composed, but over time she grew teary, and she visibly shook as she told the court how Cosby had drugged and sexually assaulted her after he first gained her trust through mentorship and friendship.

She met Cosby in 1990 while working as an assistant to Tom Ilius, then Cosby's agent at the William Morris Agency, who was also the man who sent Therese Serignese, Jane Doe Number Ten, $5,000 at Cosby's request. That was the same year Cosby topped *Forbes*'s list as the richest entertainer in the world. Since the mid-1980s he'd routinely topped lists of the highest-paid performers in the world, beating out both Oprah and Michael Jackson.

The eighties had been kind to him. Not only was he the most admired man in America in 1986, beating out President Reagan, he was lauded as a hero by adults and teens alike, and named one of *USA Today*'s 53 people who made a difference for being a "black man who refutes the stereotypes about black men's commitment to fatherhood" with his portrayal of Cliff Huxtable and his bestselling book *Fatherhood*. He'd signed on as a spokesman for brokerage firm E. F. Hutton to help repair their image in the wake of fraud allegations while also representing Kodak.

The Cosby Show was still wildly popular, though nearing its end, and it seemed as though nothing could touch his Teflon image. Nor could anyone match his power. Even after *The Cosby Show* went off the air in 1992, Cosby was so wealthy from the syndication deal he'd negotiated that he began exploring buying NBC with a team of investors, even though the network wasn't for sale. The reported price tag? Four billion dollars.

The week after his move to buy the network failed, Cosby bemoaned the poor depiction of African Americans on television, telling *Newsweek* that TV writers and producers still think of blacks as "living cartoons."

"It's the same image most of the writers and producers still have of us: the funny minstrel," he said. "Someone at the top has to say, 'Enough of this.'"

So in the 1990s Cosby was one of the agency's most important clients, Kelley said, possibly *the* most important. They developed a casual friendship in which he'd call her and chat, sometimes asking her to switch from her office phone to a personal line and call back.

"He'd call and ask me about my life, like in a fatherly, Dr. Huxtable kind of way," she said. He eventually befriended her family, inviting her parents and sisters to come along with her to one of his performances in Las Vegas.

One day in 1996, Cosby called Kelley and invited her to lunch at the Bel Air Hotel to "discuss my life, my career." She didn't think anything of it and agreed to meet him there. At the last minute, though, he changed the location to a private bungalow instead of the hotel dining room.

When Kelley arrived at the bungalow Cosby answered the door, wearing a bathrobe and slippers, she said. "I thought it was a little odd," Kelley testified. "I thought he'd get dressed and we'd go have lunch as planned." Instead, Cosby told her he was having lunch delivered to the bungalow, and he offered her wine and water. When she declined both, he told her she needed to relax.

Kelley, a thirty-four-year-old mom at the time of her testimony, broke into tears when she described what happened next.

"He had his right hand like this," she said, demonstrating by holding her right hand palm side up. "And there was a large white pill in the palm of his hand." Cosby encouraged her to take it, insisting it would help her relax. She resisted, but he repeated his implorations, though he would not tell her what the pill was. Finally, feeling pressured, she took the pill from Cosby, put it under her tongue, and pretended to swallow it with water. Her ruse didn't work.

"He leaned forward and said, 'Open your mouth. Lift up your tongue,'" she said, her voice shaking at the memory. "And I did. And there it was."

Kelley, afraid, swallowed the pill. Then she quickly excused herself to the bathroom to try to gather herself. In the bathroom the counter by the sink was "covered with prescription bottles," she said. She tried to read the bottles, hoping to figure out what he gave her, but she was already having trouble focusing. "I felt like I was underwater," she said as she wiped the tears from her eyes with a tissue.

She slowly made her way back to the living room and sat on the couch. The next thing she remembered was waking up in the bungalow's bedroom on the bed. Her dress was pulled up from the bottom and down from the top, and her breasts were exposed. Cosby was standing by the bed.

"I could see a bottle of lotion on the corner of the nightstand," she said, pausing and putting a hand to her mouth to try to compose herself. "He put lotion in my hand . . . and he made me touch his penis."

That was the last thing she remembered. She had no idea how she got home that night.

She never saw Cosby again, but not long afterward, while she was at work, she overheard a phone conversation between Cosby and Ilius, her boss, and Cosby was complaining about her. He'd called on her boss's private line, the one only Cosby used, and she'd picked up the phone to answer it. Part of her job was to listen in on Ilius's phone calls with his clients and take notes. "I heard [Cosby] say, 'She's always away from her desk.'" He went on to criticize her job performance: "She's messing up her work. . . . She's a problem. This is a problem. You need to get rid of the problem."

Stunned, Kelley hung up the phone, tears streaming down her face. She walked to a pay phone and called her mother, certain she was about to be fired. She told her she just wanted to leave. "No. Go to human resources," her mother said.

She did, stumbling and crying as she tried to explain what she'd overheard and what Cosby had done to her. Before she could get the whole story out, the woman in human resources interrupted her and told her to go home to rest, as she seemed stressed out. Kelley later filed a workman's compensation claim, alleging job stress. She settled with them for less than $10,000 and was eventually fired.

Her mother, Dr. Patrice Sewell, a retired educator, took the stand the next morning. She testified that after her daughter was fired, she was depressed, anxious, and withdrawn. Cosby appeared to be listening intently as she spoke, furrowing his brow a little at times. Sewell got visibly upset as she started to tell the story. McMonagle objected to what she was about to say at one point, prompting a sidebar with the judge we couldn't hear. As he walked toward the judge, he looked over at reporters and threw up his hands as if to say, *Can you believe this?*

Her mother also shared that it took Kelley months to tell her parents what happened, and even then Kelley only said she'd been drugged, not sexually assaulted.

"I didn't know until much, much later that wasn't all of the story, that she'd told her sister more details," her mom said, her voice shaking as she fought off tears. Then she whispered, "I told her sister I didn't want to know."

WHEN THE TIME came for Andrea to take the stand on the second day of trial, the courtroom was completely silent. She did not testify at any of the earlier hearings—including the preliminary hearing—so this was the first time we would hear what happened from her directly, in her own words.

Andrea had changed quite a bit since 2005. She no longer had long, flowing, curly red hair, nor did she have that happy, carefree smile she bore in the widely circulated photo of her holding a basketball at age nineteen. Her hair was now chopped fairly short, and the expression on her face was serious.

Andrea seemed nervous as she sat down and, with her left hand on the Bible, pledged to tell the truth, the whole truth, and nothing but the truth. Troiani and Kivitz, along with Kivitz's daughter, a Miami prosecutor, were there for moral support, as was her sister, Diana, all of them sitting on the prosecution side. As she settled into her seat on the witness stand, Cosby swiveled his chair so he could face toward her as she testified, his chin resting on his hand, a thoughtful expression on his face. He seemed to be listening intently, leaning forward in his seat with his head cocked to the side and pointed toward Andrea, while at the same time not seeming to take it very seriously, smiling at the more emotional points of her testimony, like when she spoke of when she and her mother called to confront him. The jurors seemed to be paying close attention while she spoke.

Andrea's voice was soft but firm as she began telling the story of how she first met Cosby. She remained calm as she described how he began to call her at her office at Temple University, at first to talk about the women's basketball team. Slowly they began to build what she thought was a friendship and mentorship.

Andrea went on, saying Cosby invited her to his Elkins Park home a couple of times, and that during one of her visits he casually placed his hand on her thigh as he sat next to her. She moved her body away from his without saying anything, she said. It happened again, though, at another dinner at his home a few months later, and this time he reached toward the zipper of her pants. She gently pushed his hand away, and this time she was direct: "I said, 'I'm not here for that. I don't want that,'" she said.

Thinking the issue was behind them, Andrea kept accepting social invitations from Cosby, including a trip to a Connecticut casino where he invited her up to his room late at night to give her some baked goods to take back home.

"I trusted him," she said. "He had never disclosed to me that he . . . was interested in a romantic interaction with me."

Andrea went on to reveal all of the details of the night in January 2004, most of which I'd written about in 2005, but it was riveting to hear them from her now, in the courtroom.

Andrea arrived around 8:30 P.M. She and Cosby sat down at his kitchen table, where he had about a quarter of a glass of wine poured for her. "I told Mr. Cosby I was on an empty stomach and I didn't want to drink wine . . . and he said, 'Just taste it. It's an old bottle.' And so I tasted the wine," she said.

They chatted about her career for about twenty or thirty minutes, after which he went upstairs and came back with three blue pills. "He said, 'These will help you relax. They're your friends,'" she recalled. "I said, 'What are they? Are they herbal?'" Cosby nodded. "He gave me water. I said, 'I trust you.' I swallowed the pills."

Within thirty minutes she began to slur her words and had trouble seeing.

"I wasn't able to speak without getting a buildup of white stuff around the edges of my mouth," she recalled. He grabbed her by the arm, guided her to a couch, and put a pillow under her neck. She woke up to find him lying behind her.

"I felt Mr. Cosby's hand groping my breasts under my shirt," she said, blinking back tears. "I also felt his hand inside my vagina moving in and out. And I felt him take my hand and place it on his penis and move it back and forth." She could not move or speak, she told the jury. "I was frozen," she said. "I wasn't able to fight in any way."

The next thing she recalled was waking up on the couch between 4 and 5 A.M. Her bra was up higher, around her neck. She walked to the kitchen, and Cosby was there. He motioned for her to sit down.

"'There's a muffin and tea,'" she said he told her. She took two sips of the tea, grabbed the top of the muffin, rolled it up in a napkin, and left without saying a word to him.

"I felt really humiliated, and I was very confused. . . . I just wanted to go home."

Andrea struggled for weeks trying to understand what had happened to her while still maintaining a professional relationship with him, as he was on the board of trustees and she still worked for Temple. She kept a distance personally for a while, but then, desperate for answers, she accepted an invitation from him for dinner with local high school students at a Chinese restaurant.

"I didn't think I'd really be able to talk to him, but I took the chance," she said.

After the dinner, when they all stood up to leave, she told him she'd like to speak with him. "Come up to the house and I'll talk to you," he replied. She agreed and drove to his home.

Once she arrived, she stood in the doorway, afraid to go in any further. "What did you give me that last time to put me into that state?" she asked him. "And he said, 'I thought you had an orgasm, didn't you?' I said, 'I did not. I just want to know what you gave me.'"

He tried to get her to come further into his home, but she refused and left. "I was very uncomfortable," she said. "I realized at that point that he was not going to tell me what he gave to me that night."

Then it was time for her to be grilled by Cosby's defense attorneys, who'd already made it clear they weren't going to go easy on her.

CHAPTER TWENTY-TWO

THE TAPES

When it came time for Angela Agrusa, one of Cosby's defense attorneys, to cross-examine Andrea, she exhausted every possible angle. For nearly seven hours spread over two days, Agrusa aimed questions at Andrea.

She asked why Andrea tried to engage a lawyer before she went to police. She asked about the fifty-three phone calls Andrea made to Cosby after he assaulted her, including one on Valentine's Day, insinuating a romantic component to the call. She asked Andrea why she went with her parents to one of Cosby's concerts in Toronto in August of that same year. She asked Andrea about wearing "a midriff-bearing top" to Cosby's home one time.

Andrea patiently responded to each query. She called attorneys before and after she went to police because she was afraid and because she didn't understand how the criminal justice system worked in the states. The fifty-three calls to Cosby were work related, including the one on Valentine's Day; he was influential among her employers, and she couldn't refuse to return his calls. She went to the concert because her father wanted to go, and Andrea hadn't yet had the courage to tell her parents what Cosby had done to her. And so on.

Agrusa got more personal, again trying to demonstrate for the jury that Andrea and Cosby were involved in a consensual relationship. She asked why Andrea had gifted Cosby with incense; Andrea answered that he had requested it. Agrusa asked why Andrea had once delivered bath salts to Cosby; Andrea explained they were a gift for Cosby and his wife from a Temple supporter. Why did she keep seeing him alone, even after he'd twice made passes at her? Andrea said she trusted him and that she thought she could fend him off again, as she already had, if he made another sexual advance toward her.

Finally Andrea was dismissed, and she stepped down from the witness stand. Hearing Andrea's story directly from her, after all of these years, made it real in a way that cold, hard words in a legal document never could. Andrea was not an emotional person by nature, and to see her fight off tears and to hear her voice tremble was wrenching.

Andrea's resilience on the stand also moved Kristen Houser. As Houser watched the trial, she blogged about it for the public, trying to educate readers about sexual assault. After watching Andrea's cross-examination, she posted an entry called "It's Called Grooming, Not Romance":

> Many people who perpetrate sexual assault test boundaries before-hand—this is sometimes called grooming. Perpetrators may judge how a person reacts to suggestive comments, unnecessary physical touch, or offers to spend time in private. They are testing whether their actions will be actively or verbally discouraged or if they will be tolerated or ignored in the way that many women are socially conditioned to respond to unwanted advances that aren't "overly in-trusive." . . . It is important that the difference between demonstrat-ing "romantic interest" and testing a person's boundaries is noted.

Next, it was Gianna's turn, and she took her place in front of the court. Under questioning by Steele, Gianna detailed how she placed a call to Cosby to confront him about what he did to her daughter and to ask what medication he gave her. She was worried. "Why would you drug her? . . . What if she had died?" she asked him, quaintly referring to the sofa where Andrea slept that night as a "chesterfield." "I mean, in so many hours, if somebody's sleeping, how did he not know that she dropped dead? . . . Why didn't you call 911?" She said that Cosby—who called her "Mom" during their two-plus-hour phone conversa-tion—told her in graphic detail about his sexual encounter with her daughter, implying it was something both he and Andrea had wanted.

Andrea was also on the line, Gianna told the court, when Cosby said, "Oh, Andrea, don't you remember? Mom, she even had an orgasm."

Later in the call, she said, Cosby asked what he could do for Andrea. "I said, 'The only thing I'd like from you is an apology.' . . . He said, 'I apologize to Andrea, and I apologize to you, Mom.'"

The next time she spoke to Cosby it was again over the phone. This was the call that Gianna had taped, using a recorder she had bought from Radio Shack, and the tape was played in the courtroom. In this call Cosby offered to pay for Andrea's graduate school, and Gianna told him she'd have to discuss it with Andrea. Then the court heard the two discuss the drug Cosby had given Andrea: "I just wanted to ask you one quick question because I'm a little worried. Are you really going to send that piece of paper with the name of that stuff or not? Or were you joking?" Gianna demanded to know.

"We can talk about what you asked for later," Cosby said. Then, "I don't think so. I wouldn't even worry about that."

When it ended, Steele asked her to tell the court why she sounded so aggressive in the phone call with Cosby. "I was very upset because I knew that Mr. Cosby had mentored her, and they were good friends," she said. "She viewed him like a father. He's ten years older than her own father. I was obviously very distraught at the fact [of] what he did to her . . . that he betrayed her."

On the stand Gianna wept. But the testimonies unfolding in front of him did not seem to move Cosby. He leaned back in his chair as Andrea and then Gianna testified, occasionally making a comment to McMonagle, who sat beside him. At one point McMonagle wrote something on a legal pad and showed it to Cosby, who looked at it and nodded—it would seem he wasn't so blind, after all.

During the breaks Cosby also seemed relaxed, even clowning around outside the courtroom. One day, as the sheriff shouted to the reporters to put their cell phones away, Cosby ducked and covered his head in mock fear. Another day he yelled out the Fat Albert catch phrase "Hey! Hey! Hey!" as he walked out of the courthouse. This kind of brazen behavior belied the situation he was in. Maybe he felt he hadn't done anything wrong except, of course, getting caught. Could that be?

How could a man under scrutiny for vicious, premeditated acts demonstrate such cavalier behavior? I turned to forensic psychologist J. Reid Meloy for some insight. "If I were evaluating Mr. Cosby, I would carefully evaluate for both narcissism and psychopathy, among other characteristics," he said. "Individuals with such personalities, often because of their sense of entitlement, believe they are above the law. The Achilles heel of such personalities is their sense of impunity, which typically leads them to take greater risks and eventually leads to their downfall."

ON THE FOURTH day of the trial, Sergeant Richard Schaffer took the stand. Schaffer had been one of the detectives assigned to investigate Cosby in 2005, when Bruce Castor announced he would not pursue a criminal case against the comedian. Schaffer testified that he was shocked when he learned of Castor's decision, in part because that very morning they had met and come up with a list of leads to follow up on.

The reference came and went so quickly that it would have been easy to miss had I not covered the case for as long as I had. The exact chain of events that led Castor to not prosecute Cosby in 2005 had been cloaked in secrecy, and this was the first time anyone in law enforcement confirmed that the investigation was *still going on* the day Castor announced his decision, so I quickly filed a story about it during the next break. It was another piece of the puzzle snapping into place, though many were and are still missing.

What came next in the courtroom was graphic. It was a close review of the deposition Cosby gave during Andrea's long-settled civil suit, in which Cosby described in detail what happened between them sexually—or at least his version of it—as well as the statement Cosby gave police in 2005. They'd had a romantic relationship beginning the second time she came to his home, he said. On the night in question they were "petting"—kissing and fondling each other—something they'd done three times prior. He did not have sexual intercourse with her. He had never known Andrea to be untruthful.

During that taped phone call with Gianna he felt the conversation was "threatening," which is why he brought up paying for Andrea's education, an offer that was not accepted. He said he wanted them to fly to Miami at his expense to meet "face to face" and talk things through. The subsequent phone calls to them from Marty Singer and Peter Wiederlight at William Morris, who both left messages that were played in court, were to set that up and to put the details of any agreement they reached in writing.

In the deposition Cosby said he had a romantic interest in Andrea from the first moment he met her but that he didn't let Andrea know. Asked why, Cosby replied, "Don't do it that way. Wanted to build up trust."

He described one of their sexual encounters at his home when he tried to unzip her pants. "I don't hear her say anything," he said. "And

I don't feel her say anything. And so I continue and I go into the area that is somewhere between permission and rejection. I am not stopped."

The courtroom also heard the portions of the deposition in which Cosby discussed obtaining and giving Quaaludes to women he wanted to have sex with, but in his statements he insisted he never gave the drugs to any woman without her consent. "What was happening at the time was that Quaaludes happened to be the drugs kids, young kids, were using to party with, and there were times I wanted to have them just in case," he said.

By now Montgomery County detective James Reape had taken over from Schaffer, reading aloud from the transcript of the deposition. Cosby appeared to be enjoying his own responses, even laughing as the detective read certain parts aloud.

The prosecution wrapped its case on Friday afternoon with two lackluster expert witnesses—one sexual assault expert and a toxicologist. Andrew Wyatt was dangling to reporters the possibility of Cosby testifying, though that seemed unlikely. If not, we would go straight to closing arguments on Monday.

As I LEFT the courthouse on Monday afternoon after the closing arguments I took a mental assessment of the two legal teams.

Agrusa, who had questioned Andrea for the defense, had stumbled over her words and facts, often getting dates, locations, and other details wrong. At times she framed her questions as statements, and the judge had to interject to remind the jury that an attorney's questions to a witness are not evidence, that only the witness's answers are.

McMonagle had more than made up for her stumbles in his closing argument, though. He was forceful, passionate, and articulate, attacking Andrea's credibility for the discrepancies in her various statements to police, something the prosecution had never allowed Andrea to adequately explain. It would be difficult to imagine he hadn't had an impact on the jury.

Camille had even shown up, staying long enough to hear McMonagle's closing argument Monday morning then leaving before it was Steele's turn. Watching Andrea on the stand, I'd felt like I was in a time warp, back in 1991, watching Anita Hill as she was grilled over her claims that US Supreme Court nominee Clarence Thomas sexually harassed her while he was her supervisor at the Department of Education and the EEOC.

Why didn't you report his behavior to someone?

Why did you keep working for him?

If he did this to you, why did you still speak to him after you left those jobs?

The hostile cross-examination of Hill so enraged women across the country that it led to the so-called Year of the Woman in politics in 1992, with a record number of women running for office. Had we learned nothing in the past twenty-six years?

Unlike the Anita Hill hearings, however, Cosby's trial wasn't televised. No one but those of us sitting in the courtroom were there to watch yet another woman be torn apart. Kristen Houser had blogged again, furiously trying to dispel all of the rape myths the defense trotted out in court as truth.

Some victims may tell others that they were sexually assaulted right away, but most do not.... When reports are made, delayed and partial reports are normal and should be expected. This is especially common in non-stranger sexual assault. When the assailant is a person in a position of power or trust, reporting is even more unlikely.... In addition to denial, there are many reasons why someone might not disclose what was done to them: fear of not being believed; worries about retaliation; concern that their social circle and supports will be disrupted if the perpetrator is a mutual friend or family member; fears of privacy invasion and being made the subject of gossip and slander, and even distrust of law enforcement.

Steele recovered some ground they'd lost with a masterful closing argument, but McMonagle had been compelling as well. But would they matter? Would the evidence or the testimonies? Did the deposition of Cosby admitting he'd given drugs to women he wanted to have sex with make an impact on the jury? Or had the jury already decided before the very first day in court?

There was no way to know. We just had to wait for the verdict.

CHAPTER TWENTY-THREE

DEADLOCKED

Judge Steven O'Neill had been a Montgomery County judge for nearly fourteen years by the time the Cosby criminal case was assigned to him. A former county solicitor and county prosecutor, O'Neill said at his swearing-in ceremony that the three most common questions he'd been asked were whether he intended to continue whistling as he walked down the courthouse hallways, if he would keep his beard, and whether he would don his St. Patrick's Day attire next year, as he had for the past twenty, when he visited the courthouse and county offices.

"My answer to all three is 'Yes,'" he said, surrounded by his wife and three children. "I'm fulfilling a dream, not changing who I am."

Part of his dream was to create systems to help nonviolent drug offenders find their way back to productive lives. In 2006, he began presiding over the newly established county drug court, sentencing nonviolent drug offenders to court-supervised treatment programs instead of jail. "Offering a hand up, offering treatment and recovery as opposed to incarceration for people who suffer a life claiming disease was the right thing to do," O'Neill would later say when the Supreme Court of Pennsylvania awarded the program accreditation. O'Neill has a "heart of gold," said Supreme Court Justice Kevin Dougherty at a ceremony bestowing the honor. "Montgomery County citizens, you don't know how fortunate you are to have people who truly care about the way of life in this county." Well-earned high praise—for creating programs to rehabilitate offenders rather than simply punishing them is no easy task.

His genial manner and quiet respect for the well-being of his constituents would be tested throughout the Cosby case, and far more than he expected. Because after the jury deliberated for fifty-two hours without reaching a unanimous decision, Judge O'Neill was forced to declare a mistrial.

The jury had wrestled. Agonized. Debated. Voted, revoted, and then revoted again. For more than five days they congregated in the jury room, returning time and again to the open court to have nearly the entire trial read back to them before all was said and done. They asked questions, listened, asked more questions, called for more recitations of the trial transcript, and retreated again for more deliberation.

But they couldn't reach a decision.

O'Neill pushed the jury hard to work through their differences, insisting they keep trying when they came to him on Thursday morning, after thirty hours of deliberations, and said they were deadlocked. But as time dragged on inside the jury room, the crowds outside the courthouse grew—and became chaotic, unruly.

First, activists from the National Organization for Women, seeking to shine a light on drug-facilitated sexual assaults, gathered on the steps of the courthouse carrying signs that read, "Stop Drug-Rape Now" and "Speak Truth to Power."

Then Andrew Wyatt, Cosby's spokesman, doing his best to steer the narrative to favor his client, read a statement from Marguerite "Margo" Jackson, a Temple academic adviser and former colleague of Andrea's who claimed Andrea told her she planned to set up Cosby. According to the statement Wyatt read aloud, Andrea and Margo were sharing a room during an out-of-town basketball game when Andrea told Margo her plan was to "get money [from Cosby], go to school, open up a business."

Wyatt went on to announce that the judge would not allow the defense to call Jackson to testify at the trial. "This court has not given [Cosby] a fair and impartial trial," Wyatt complained to reporters outside the courthouse. "That's all we were looking for. Just a fair shot."

Tempers flared again when Wyatt announced that the jury's ongoing deliberations "pleased" and "vindicated" Cosby—as if the trial was already over. That was how the crowd took it, at least, and there was an uproar. Accuser Jewel Allison broke down in tears. She and Lili Bernard, both African American, confronted black Cosby supporters who were chanting "Free Cosby now!" and holding signs saying the charges against him were racially motivated.

"I understand your pain," Lili told them, "because I experienced it firsthand when he *drugged* me, when he *raped* me, when he threatened me to silence!"

Cosby's angry defenders circled her, and one shouted, "It hurts me to see a blind man go to prison for thirty years!"

Lili began reading Bible passages aloud. Jewel faced off with an African American woman holding a sign that said, "Bill Cosby is innocent," but ended up having a heart to heart with her, holding hands for nearly forty minutes as a crowd formed around them.

"It was an extremely spiritual, enlightening experience," Jewel told me later. "I told her, 'I would be you standing out here if I had not been in a room alone with him.' It would have been very difficult for me to believe."

The distress was palpable everywhere. Capitalizing on the anguish around him, Wyatt called for a mistrial, claiming the record had been broken for the longest deliberations in the county, though no such record exists.

O'Neill rebuked Wyatt—more than once, in fact. But the judge couldn't ignore the dead-end deliberations much longer.

It was a gloomy Saturday morning when the jury told O'Neill they were hopelessly deadlocked. Exhaustion showed on the jurors' faces as they filed into the courtroom; one seemed to be holding off tears. They had hoped to arrive at a resolution but were now admitting defeat.

A weary-looking O'Neill officially declared a mistrial. And then the room erupted.

Troiani, who had rushed to the courthouse as soon as she heard there was a decision but was unable to reach the courtroom in time, was waiting in a side hallway when Steele emerged.

"We're doing this again" was all he said. He'd already talked to Andrea. She was on board.

Outside the courthouse a jubilant Wyatt ignored the judge's clarification that this was neither "vindication nor victory" for anyone when he declared it a victory for the defense and immediately released a scathing statement from Camille Cosby attacking Steele, the judge, and the media:

How do I describe the district attorney? Heinously and exploitatively ambitious.

How do I describe the judge? Overtly arrogant and collaborating with the district attorney. How do I describe the counsels for the accusers? Totally unethical.

How do I describe many, but not all, general media? Blatantly vicious entities that continually disseminated intentional omissions of truths for the primary purpose of greedily selling sensationalism at the expense of a human life.

Historically, people have challenged injustices. I am grateful to any of the jurors who tenaciously fought to review the evidence; which is the rightful way to make a sound decision. Ultimately, that is a manifestation of justice, based on facts, not lies.

Throughout the trial O'Neill had done all he could to protect the sequestered jurors' identities. Once the trial was over, he still refused to release their names. But media agencies quickly filed motions to intervene to force the release of the names, and they won their request. Though it's rare for jurors' names to be withheld from the press, it had become more common in recent years to protect jurors from retaliation, especially in high-profile cases. But under the First Amendment jurors' names are generally considered public information, said Eli Segal, arguing on behalf of the media.

"The impartiality of jurors is absolutely essential to a fair trial," Segal said. "We can be confident that jurors are in fact impartial if we know who they are and there is no veil of secrecy hanging over their identities."

After their names were released and reporters began interviewing them, I began to understand why the jury of twelve couldn't agree on a verdict—they couldn't even agree on what they disagreed about or how many voted each way, though it's possible they voted more than once. One juror told ABC News that the vote was ten-to-two to convict; another told the Associated Press the vote was evenly split. Another told the Philadelphia newspapers that he couldn't understand why Andrea went to Cosby's house at all, let alone wearing a top that exposed her midriff and bringing him incense and bath salts.

Still another said the jury remained at a deadlock because the language of the charges themselves confused some of the jurors. They would go to the judge and ask for definitions of the phrases in the charges, like "without her knowledge," "reckless," and "unreasonable doubt." "What *is* unreasonable doubt?" asked the juror. "We spent a lot of time trying to figure these words out."

The one thing the jurors all seemed to agree on was that emotions ran high in the cramped room. The experience was exhausting and frustrating, and at times there were jurors in tears. One juror even punched a concrete wall.

Bobby Dugan, twenty-one, the only juror to allow his name to be used in an interview, told ABC News that the sticking point was the lack of evidence in the case. "We all said it a million times in the room," he said. "If there's other evidence, more substantial evidence, we would have had a better verdict than deadlock."

THE JURORS WERE still making news when Wyatt and his fellow spokesperson, Ebonee Benson, stirred up controversy again, telling a Birmingham, Alabama, TV station that Cosby was planning a series of town halls "to talk to young people" about "sexual assault" to protect them from being falsely accused.

"Because this is bigger than Bill Cosby," Wyatt announced. "This issue can affect any young person, especially young athletes of today. And they need to know what they're facing when they're hanging out and partying, when they're doing certain things that they shouldn't be doing. And it also affects married men. . . . Anything at this point can be considered sexual assault, and it's a good thing to be educated about the laws."

Days later, after an outcry from Cosby accusers, Benson backpedaled, telling CNN the town hall meetings were not about sexual assault after all. Cosby himself weighed in too, saying there would be no sexual assault tour and that it was all "propaganda." As if his own PR team hadn't floated the idea.

WHILE THE MEDIA and the courts scrambled to determine next steps for the case, I had to figure out some moves of my own. The day after the case went to the jury I was told my position had been eliminated at

People, though I could still freelance for the magazine if I chose. I was one of three hundred people laid off companywide that day, the latest in a seemingly endless series of downsizing moves that began shortly after I was hired.

I was sad to leave the magazine that had been my home for twelve years, and I can't say I didn't wonder for a moment if my aggressive Cosby coverage had landed me on the layoff list. But I quickly pushed aside any worries and rallied. Honestly, I'd been through worse, and I had a lot on my side. I had a husband I adored, good health, and a house filled with rescue animals who would be very happy to have me not working those crazy hours anymore, not jumping on a plane at a moment's notice to cover the latest horrific tragedy.

And there was a freedom I longed for that I could now have as a freelancer, without a boss to assign or approve the stories I wrote. With nearly a year's severance pay thanks to our union—which was helpless to save our jobs but could at least make sure we were well taken care of when we lost them—to tide me over, my next project was up to me. And the one thing I knew was that I wasn't ready to give up the Cosby case. I decided right away that I'd stop reporting the story when there was nothing more to say—and not a word before.

The Jane Does had always fascinated me, so I decided to find out how many of them had spoken publicly about their experiences with Cosby. If there were some who still had not revealed their identities, maybe they'd do so now. And maybe that would be enough "news" to keep the story going—and the truth at the forefront of the national conversation.

I spent several days digging through old court documents from Andrea's civil lawsuit, and I finally found an early filing that listed the Jane Does by numbers and the towns where they had been living in 2005. I cross-referenced those with mentions of the various Jane Does in Cosby's deposition, and eventually I had the names of all of them.

Four of them had never spoken to media, and their stories had never been shared publicly. I set out to track them down, and I was making nice progress when the #MeToo movement exploded.

On October 5, 2017, the *New York Times*, followed quickly by the *New Yorker*'s Ronan Farrow, revealed that Hollywood movie executive Harvey Weinstein had sexually harassed or assaulted nearly two dozen women over a thirty-year period, including actresses Rose McGowan and Ashley Judd. The revelations prompted actress Alyssa Milano to tweet, "If you've been sexually harassed or assaulted write 'me too' as a reply to this tweet." Thousands of women from around the world responded with tales of their own. Before long, allegations against more than a hundred famous men would be lodged by their victims.

Matt Lauer. Charlie Rose. Al Franken. Louis C.K. Jeremy Piven. Kevin Spacey. Tavis Smiley. One by one, high-profile men were being called out for their transgressions.

With fascination I watched the movement grow, and like most of America, I became engrossed in the daily updates. I wondered whether the revelations would have an effect on Cosby's second trial. Would potential jurors have a better understanding of sexual assault? Would they be more likely to convict? Would more accusers be allowed to testify this time?

I redoubled my efforts to find the Jane Does and make their stories heard too. I wanted them to know that even with all the publicity surrounding new accusations by new accusers against a new powerful man each day, their bravery in coming forward all those years ago had not been forgotten.

At least by me.

CHAPTER TWENTY-FOUR

ASK FOR SEYMOUR

I knew from experience that sometimes, after enough time has passed, sexual assault victims are ready to talk. My approaches were gentle and nonintrusive. I sent letters or emails or called them, depending on what contact information I could find for each.

Even if I found them, I knew it might take them a while to feel comfortable enough with me to agree to speak, especially on the record, and I was more than willing to invest that time to let them get to know me. Building up a trusting relationship takes time. It had taken me years sometimes to bring in an interview I wanted.

If, after all that, they preferred to stay quiet, I would understand.

But I was determined to at least offer these women a chance to tell their stories. I believed they deserved to be recognized for having the courage to come forward in 2005, back when no one wanted to believe Cosby was capable of the type of atrocities he was being accused of and those who did speak out were vilified.

It took me several months to find each woman and build up enough trust that they felt comfortable telling their story to me.

A source told me Patte O'Connor, Jane Doe Number Six, was dead, but I insisted on confirming that myself and found her, alive and well, in Toledo, Ohio. Virginia Bennett, Jane Doe Number Nine, was still living in California, fighting an aggressive form of multiple myeloma and had just been released from the hospital, where she'd been receiving blood transfusions for anemia related to her treatment and illness, but she called me back, saying she would talk to me when she was stronger. And she did.

I also found Denise Ferrari, Jane Doe Number Eight, in Colorado. She agreed to speak with me but at first did not want her full name used. After the #MeToo movement exploded she changed her mind.

When I learned the details of Denise's story in 2017 it sounded vaguely familiar to me, so I went through the notes of my 2005 interview with Beth Ferrier and saw that Beth had first briefly mentioned her to me back then. She couldn't remember Denise's last name, so it was impossible for me to follow up at the time. And I had no idea that the woman she mentioned was one of the Jane Does. Neither did Beth.

I was having the most difficult time finding Jane Doe Number Three. None of the phone numbers I found for her turned her up, nor did the letters I sent to addresses I got seem to reach her. When I finally did find a good email address for her in December 2017, she called me within a few minutes.

She was fragile. Though she'd had a near-miss with Cosby, she'd been a victim of a violent crime more recently and had a multitude of health issues. She agreed to do an interview with me if she were identified simply as Jane Doe Number Three. We spoke many times over the next ten months, but in September she decided not to participate and dropped out of sight. I haven't been able to reach her since.

I decided to just mention her briefly, using only the details of her story from Cosby's deposition, which were already public anyway. She'd given a statement to Andrea's attorneys, and Troiani had used that statement to question Cosby.

I felt strongly that it was still important to include her. She's a part of the history of this case. She'd changed her mind a couple of times during the time we spoke, and I knew she could change it again and it might be too late.

She said she met Cosby through her sister and her sister's best friend in the late 1960s, early 1970s, and he was going to help her become an actress. She became friendly with his secretary, Marlene, who told her Cosby wanted to throw her a birthday party at the Brentwood home he was renting. Instead, when she arrived, he "tried to fondle her breasts and tug on her pants with his fingers." She got Marlene to take her home. When Jane Doe Number Three told her roommate what happened, that she'd rebuffed Cosby's overture, her roommate, who was from a famous Hollywood family herself, warned her that Cosby might now offer to fly her to meet him in another city. If she refused to have sex, he'd abandon her there.

Three days later Marlene called her and invited her to join Cosby at an event in Philadelphia to make amends for what happened at the birthday party. Jane Doe Number Three declined.

She also revealed the fake name Cosby was using at the time: Seymour Rapaport.

Asked about this in his deposition, Cosby confirmed that "Seymour Rapaport" was a name he used in the 1970s and 1980s when he was staying at a hotel or "in humor with friends." And he did once have a secretary named Marlene. But when he was told Jane Doe's real name, he said he did not remember her.

That was the answer he gave for the other three women as well, though all of their accounts were chillingly similar to those of so many of his accusers.

Patte O'Connor, Jane Doe Number Six, said she had been at her job as student activities director at Clemson University less than two months in October 1984 when she got a very important assignment: Comedian Bill Cosby was flying into town on his private jet, and she was to pick him up at the airport at 2:00 P.M. He was scheduled to perform at eight or nine that evening during a weekend of homecoming festivities.

"It was cool," O'Connor, now fifty-nine at the time of this writing and a full-time caregiver for her mother in Toledo, Ohio. "I was waiting with the police escort. He was wearing the same red Adidas top and pants that he was dressed in in the opening credit of *The Cosby Show*. I'll never forget it. He said, 'I'm hungry! Let's go back to the hotel room. What's the best place to get some burgers?'"

They got some burgers and Cokes from a local burger place and brought them to his hotel room. A gift basket with a bottle of wine was in his room as well.

"He asked me if I wanted something to eat, and I didn't, so he was eating, and we just kinda settled into talking."

There were two twin beds in the room with a table between them, and at one point he said, "'This bed is my bed and this bed is your bed.' And I thought, 'That's bizarre. Why would you say that?' I remember thinking how odd it was. But, of course, I was like, 'What am I going to say?'" So they just kept talking.

"He was very smart, very intellectual," she said. "We were talking about philosophy and the merits of education. It was a nice, deep conversation. He was asking me about my family, and I said, 'My cousin in Toledo is getting married [tonight].' He said, 'Really? Let's call!' I thought, 'How fun is that?'"

By this time the gift basket was open, and Cosby asked her if she wanted some red wine. "I said, 'Okay,' so he gave me a glass, and I never noticed that he didn't drink, that he kept filling my glass, but I got pretty relaxed and drunk quite quickly because I had been up since 4 or 5 A.M. I don't think I ate breakfast, and I didn't eat lunch."

They tried to call her cousin at her wedding, but they couldn't reach her. They finally tracked down a phone number for the wedding reception hall, and soon Cosby was chatting amiably with her very surprised parents. "It was hilarious," she said.

At some point Cosby began serving her coffee and Kahlua as well. "I don't know where the coffee came from," she said. "He just kept making me these coffee drinks with Kahlua in them." Then he said, "'Are you tired? I'm exhausted. Do you want to take a nap?' So he points to his bed. He says, 'Let's take a nap.' We'd been together for hours, so I felt comfortable with him. He was like an old buddy."

They laid down together, and he said, "'Do you like tummy rubs or back rubs?'" she told me.

"I'm, like, well, that's an odd question . . . um, back rubs." He gave her one without taking her shirt off, then told her it was his turn and that he wanted a tummy rub.

"So he lifted up his shirt right away, brought my face close, and kissed me on the lips," she said. "That startled me. I said, 'No. No.'"

That's the last thing she remembers. She woke a few hours later to the phone ringing in the room. The shower was running, so she answered the phone. It was her boss.

"My boss was screaming, 'What is going on? Where are you?'" she said. "I was so out of it. We were running late."

The next thing she remembered—it seemed like within minutes, but she wasn't sure how much time had lapsed—there was a banging on the hotel room's door. "It was my boss. He was pissed." They were late for the performance.

She only remembers pieces of the rest of the night: riding in the back of the police escort car seated in between her boss and Cosby; squeezing her boss's hand because she couldn't speak; walking down a huge, long corridor to get to the locker room, where they'd set up a photo op with the president of the university and other bigwigs;

getting her photo taken with Cosby and her boss; and hearing her boss screaming at Cosby.

"He was yelling, 'What happened? Why is Patte like this? What did you do?'" Then she remembers Cosby walking by her on the way to the stage and mouthing, "I'm sorry." She heard the roar of the crowd as he took the stage. She couldn't drive, so the police took her home. After that, it's all blank until she woke up in the middle of her steps leading up to the second floor of her townhouse around 3:00 or 3:30 A.M. Her next memory is waking up in her bed, though she had no memory of getting from the stairs into her bed.

In a panic she called her boss to apologize.

"I was upset and crying, and he said, 'Don't worry.'"

For years, she thought of that incident as her "funny Bill Cosby story"—until 2005, when she saw news reports about Andrea's claims that the entertainer drugged and sexually assaulted her. "It hit me. Oh sweet Jesus, that wasn't a funny story. That couldn't have been just alcohol. How could I have blacked out so much?"

She also came to realize he had probably sexually assaulted her while she was unconscious. "I thought to myself, 'There is no way on God's green earth that he had a woman to himself with his history, passed out, and he didn't do anything,'" she said. "It took a long time for me to process that. . . . I was a victim of sexual assault. I had to have been."

She called Andrea's attorneys and offered her assistance, though she did not want her identity revealed, so she became a Jane Doe in the civil suit.

"I did a lot of soul searching, and it was very painful," she said. "A friend of mine told me if I did allow my name to be used, I'd have reporters at my door, that my whole life would change, and this is what I would be known for. And it scared me."

Now, she says, she's ready to be open about her identity. "I've heard other women's stories. I admire their courage and their bravery and putting themselves out there for people's opinions," she said. "I want to stand up for women and support my sisters. Maybe somewhere down the road I can help women at any age to stand up for themselves with sexual predators."

Patte still has the photo she and her boss took with Cosby that night. Cosby told Troiani during his deposition that he did once have a private plane, he recalled being at Clemson, but he could not remember whether he flew to Clemson on a commercial flight or in his own plane. Nor did he remember Patte.

VIRGINIA BENNETT, JANE Doe Number Nine, also has a photo of Cosby, a studio shot autographed by him, though she says she has no idea why she kept it. "Even back at the time I thought, 'I don't need a picture of this creep,'" she said. "For some reason, unbeknownst to me, I ignored the instinct to rip it up and throw it out."

Virginia was a flight attendant for Western Airlines in the late 1960s when she struck up a conversation with Bill and Camille on a flight out of Las Vegas, and he invited her to the Los Angeles studio where he was taping *I Spy*.

"We started speaking to one another," said Virginia, seventy-one at the time of this writing. He gave her an autographed photo of himself, though she hadn't requested one. "But he asked if I wanted to come by the set. I really wanted to meet Robert Culp, so I accepted."

Virginia went there on her first day off. *Why wait?* she figured. If she put it off, he'd probably forget her.

When she arrived she was taken to a lounge area, where Cosby greeted her. "He said, 'Well, Culp isn't here today,' and the filming had either been canceled or delayed," she said. He offered her a nonalcoholic drink, which Virginia accepted. The next thing she knew, he was sitting next to her and pushing her face down toward his penis.

"I just remember feeling really shocked," she said. "I'm just thinking, 'How did this happen?'"

Virginia's memories are hazy—she doesn't know if that's because she was drugged or if it was just the trauma of what happened to her— but she somehow got off the couch and found her way to her car. "It seems like I wasn't able to drive right away," she said. "I had to hang out and get myself gathered together. All I remember is I didn't just storm out, as it would have been my nature to do."

For many years Virginia told no one of what happened to her. "I finally told a girlfriend here in Santa Cruz because we were doing a lot of healing work," she said. "And one afternoon, after some of that work we'd been doing, I just burst into tears and said what happened back then. She was very supportive—but really shocked I'd held it in all those years."

Virginia had just shoved it away, deep inside of herself, appalled by what had nearly happened to her. "It was almost like denial," she said. "I was a very strong woman and mother of a young child and a flight attendant. I was very independent and strong willed and capable. I was just horrified that I could have let myself get into such a situation."

She never even thought about going to police at the time. "I was just too embarrassed and too chagrined that I had let myself get into that position," Virginia said. "It was like I'd done something wrong to get in that position."

When she saw something on the news in 2005 about Andrea's allegations, she just knew she had to come forward to support her. Virginia called Andrea's attorneys, becoming Jane Doe Number Nine in Andrea's lawsuit against Cosby.

"I wanted her to know she wasn't alone, that she wasn't making anything up, that he was very capable of doing that," Virginia said. Even today, in the midst of fighting an aggressive cancer and undergoing chemotherapy treatments, she is still clearly very angry and says she gets mad anytime she sees something about the case on television. "Every one of us is coming out of the woodwork to tell our story," she said. "Let him try to deny it."

Asked about her at his deposition, Cosby said he didn't remember her.

For all of these years the only details I knew about Jane Doe Number Eight were heartbreaking. Her husband was awaiting a bone marrow transplant, one 2005 court filing said, explaining why she hadn't yet obtained an attorney to file a motion to protect her anonymity. I knew from experience dealing with cancer among some of my family that this meant her husband was deathly ill. No wonder she didn't have time to get her own lawyer.

Finally, though, I had all the pieces of the particular story, which was one of the only ones I knew of with two other corroborating witnesses.

It was around midnight in September 1984 when Tony Hogue got a frantic phone call from Denise Ferrari, Jane Doe Number Eight, the fashion director for JF Images, the Denver-based agency he and Beth Ferrier modeled for.

"She was crying. She was whispering, 'Tony, I need your help. You have to come get me,'" said Hogue, now sixty and living in Barnegut, New Jersey, running his own graphic design company.

"She said, '[Cosby] keeps trying to kiss me, and his breath is horrible because of the cigar. It's just making me sick. My clothes are just a mess, they're undone. I really don't know what's going on.' She sounded scared."

Hogue jumped in a cab, went over to Cosby's Manhattan townhome, and banged on the front door. Cosby answered.

"He was fine. He didn't look upset," Hogue said. "I said, 'I'm just here to get Denise. She said she wasn't well.' I was trying to be careful not to accuse him."

He pushed past Cosby and walked upstairs, where he found Denise slumped on a chair. "She was just a mess," he said. "She wasn't really coherent. She had this flat look on her face, a drugged look."

Hogue walked over, placed her arm around him because she had no bodily control of her own, and said, "Let's go. Can you walk?"

When she said she could, he gently led her out of Cosby's home and took her back to the apartment where they'd been staying that belonged to an employee of Farrell's. Denise collapsed in bed when they got there and flew home the next day. Hogue and Denise did not speak again for nearly thirty years.

Hogue, Beth Ferrier, and Denise had come to New York that week at the request of Jo Farrell, owner of JF Images, and Farrell had connected them with Cosby, who was showing them around. Mostly, though, his attention was focused on Beth, with whom he began a romantic relationship that week. On the night in question he'd invited all of them over to his townhome for dinner that evening, but Hogue had begged off.

He gave each of them a Sambuca, said Beth, who was there that night as well. It had no effect on her, but within a few minutes Denise, who was sitting next to her in the great room, "crumbled."

"She started slurring and acting all giddy, and then she just slumped over on me," she said. "Cosby acted like it was nothing, like no big deal."

She helped Cosby carry her into the bedroom he shared with Camille to lay her on their bed.

"He said, 'Let her sleep it off. The night is still young,'" she said. "'We'll keep an eye on her and get to know one another.'"

Every fifteen minutes or so he'd go to check on her, Beth said.

Denise remembers none of this.

"I remember very little other than Cosby giving me a licoricey-tasting drink," said Denise, now fifty-eight and the owner of Ferrari Films, a production company in Monument, Colorado. "I remember standing by this big cappuccino machine, and that's when he kissed me."

The next thing she remembers is waking up in the apartment where they were staying. By the time she got back to Denver, Cosby had already called her parents' home, she said.

"I went over to see them, and my mother said, 'Bill Cosby is trying to reach you,'" Denise said. "She was so excited because she'd talked to him on the phone. I called him back, and he said he wanted to make sure I hadn't misunderstood anything. I probably apologized for having had too much to drink. I was still in such a fog."

When she went back to work, she told Farrell and Annie Maloney, one of her agents, "Something fishy might be going on," she said. "They both just looked at me like I was nuts. The look was, 'Well, no one will believe that. Everyone believes he is Cliff Huxtable.'"

There had been another model too who abruptly dropped out of the business after spending time with Cosby. Enough was enough. Denise left the job not long afterward and started a casting company with Dixie Webster, a friend from JF Images. Cosby was a reference for her for the loan she took out at the bank, she said. In 1996, she and her husband, Ted Ferrari, formed Ferrari Films.

For years, she just thought she'd had too much to drink. Then Hogue, whom she'd lost touch with over the years, saw coverage of Andrea's case in 2005 and called Andrea's attorneys to let them know what had happened to Denise, which is how she became a Jane Doe in the lawsuit.

They reached out to her at the time, but her life was in turmoil, so there wasn't much she could do. She'd only recently recovered from breast cancer, and now her husband had leukemia and was waiting to undergo a bone marrow transplant, which meant they'd be moving to Seattle once that happened.

"We were trying to fight for my husband's life," she said. "It was horrible."

Her husband died the following year, and she didn't think about the case again until 2014, when Hogue did an interview about what happened to her with the *Daily Beast*. Denise gave them a few comments via email but would not allow them to use her name. Now, after the #MeToo movement, she's ready to be identified.

"I realize I have nothing to be ashamed of," she said. "I didn't do anything wrong."

In his deposition Cosby said he did recall having dinner with a male model, whose name he could not recall, and Beth in New York City, but at a Chinese restaurant, not his home. He said he did have an affair with Beth but could not recall when it started.

He did not remember Denise.

As I WRAPPED up my interviews with the Jane Does, I marveled at the sheer volume of accounts I'd been told over the previous weeks—and years. For so long I had wondered who the twelve Jane Does were and what their stories were, and now I knew. Their stories were so similar to those of the dozens of women who'd come forward in 2014 and 2015.

What I didn't understand, though, was why Cosby's accusers hadn't triggered a movement in the way the #MeToo accusers had.

Maybe it was because their story hadn't been told first in the *New York Times*, lending gravitas and seriousness to their outrage by giving them space in the paper of record.

Maybe it was Allred's call for Cosby to create a $100 million fund for the victims, which made people question their motives for coming forward.

Maybe it was because with the Weinstein accusers there was a paper trail that the other reporters could follow, something I'd never had back in 2005, as several women had signed nondisclosure agreements with Weinstein in exchange for money and their silence.

Or maybe it was because none of the accusers were famous. Weinstein and some of the others were accused by women who were household names—celebrities in their own right who soon became celebrated for their brave uprising against institutional sexism and violence.

On December 6, 2017, *Time* magazine named the women of the #MeToo movement—or "The Silence Breakers," as the magazine called them—its "Person of the Year" for 2017. The story included interviews and photographs of women like Hollywood-icon accusers: Taylor Swift, Selma Blair, Rose McGowan, Ashley Judd, and more.

None of the sixty-plus Cosby victims were included; their stories had been told too long before the #MeToo movement erupted on Twitter.

But that was okay.

All eyes would be on them once again in a few short months.

Cosby would be the first powerful man accused of sexual misconduct to be tried in a post-#MeToo world.

Would the outcome be any different this time?

Nobody knew.

CHAPTER TWENTY-FIVE

POSSIBLE ERRORS IN JUDGMENT

One evening in early January 2018 Cosby did something he hadn't in a long while: he went out for dinner with some childhood friends at Ristorante La Veranda in Philadelphia, one of the city's landmark Italian restaurants.

The outing was unusual in part because Cosby had been keeping a low profile since his mistrial in June and the public relations debacle afterward. But even more odd was the fact that someone from his team had tipped off a select group of local reporters, photographers, and videographers in advance, and they were waiting for him at the restaurant with notepads, tape recorders, and cameras at the ready. Now, with his retrial just three months away, Cosby clearly wanted to be in the public eye.

For the second trial Cosby would have a local jury—not one from hundreds of miles away, like the first one—and he wanted people to remember he was a hometown Philly boy. Dressed casually in a yellow sweater over a checked button-down shirt and tan khaki pants, with his cane in one hand while he held onto Andrew Wyatt with the other, he chatted and joked with other diners as he headed toward his table in the largely empty dining room of the tony restaurant on the city's waterfront.

"You were the funniest man in the world," one man called out to Cosby as he passed white-clothed tables toward his friends. "And you still might be!" he added. Cosby paused by the fan's table, bowing over in laughter at that last line.

After dinner, as he headed toward his waiting limo, Cosby was warm and chatty with reporters, sharing childhood memories and answering questions about what he had for dinner—penne with garlic, black olives, sausage, and cheese—and how he felt about being home in Philadelphia.

"The feel of this city at this time, for me, with the snow and all, it's just a great, good crisp feel," Cosby opined.

The atmosphere was amiable as the reporters lightly bantered with the comedian. Then Cosby made his way toward the door. Before leaving he turned to a female *Philadelphia Inquirer* reporter, grabbed her hand, and said, "Please, do not put me in #MeToo," he told her. "I just shook your hand like a man."

THE #METOO MOVEMENT had dominated the headlines through the end of the year, and Cosby was clearly worried about its impact on his retrial.

Oprah Winfrey's powerful speech at the Golden Globes added heat to the already growing fire: "For too long, women have not been heard or believed if they dared to speak their truth to the power of those men. But their time is up," she pronounced, and cheers filled the air. Her chosen expression, "time's up," was a nod to a new initiative founded by three hundred prominent Hollywood women, including Shonda Rhimes and Reese Witherspoon, to fight sexual harassment in the workplace. The plan also included a defense fund to help women in blue-collar industries, like nurses and factory workers, to protect themselves from sexual misconduct.

A couple of months later, after pre-trial hearings for Cosby's second trial were underway, the *Daily Beast*, a news-and-opinion website, ran an intriguing story. In the wake of the #MeToo movement, one of their reporters asked veteran actress Lynda Carter if she had ever been sexually harassed or abused. She said she had, though she wouldn't say exactly what happened to her or name the man, other than to say he was presently facing some sort of punishment and justice.

"He's already being done in," she said. "There's no advantage in piling on." Then she added, "I believe every woman in the Bill Cosby case."

Meanwhile Bruce Castor still seemed like he was trying to help Cosby. In November Castor had filed a defamation lawsuit against Andrea and her attorneys, saying they organized a smear campaign against him when he ran for DA in 2015 to get Cosby convicted and destroy Castor's political and legal career. In it, he revealed she got "well into the millions of dollars" in her settlement with Cosby. At that point only Cosby, his attorneys, Andrea and her attorneys knew the exact amount. The timing of his defamation suit seemed suspect, coming as it did only a few months before Cosby's retrial, and its potential to prejudice the jury pool against Andrea. The only other journalist who seemed to grasp this besides me was Diana Moskovitz. "Ex-DA Bruce Castor Is All but Officially on the Cosby Defense Team Now" was the headline for her story in *Jezebel*, which noted that the complaint, with its "three-page, Excel-type chart of Andrea's 'inconsistencies,'" was a blueprint for Cosby's legal team. Moskovitz emailed Castor and his attorneys asking for comment, writing she'd update her story if they got back to her. They apparently didn't, because her story still didn't reflect a response from them. Nor did Castor nor his attorneys respond to my requests for comment. In fact, he didn't respond to multiple requests for comment from me for this book.

And trust me, I wasn't about to go knocking on his door to try to get one. In December 2015, after Cosby's arrest, Castor got so angry when a reporter knocked on the door of his Schwenksville, Pennsylvania home when his wife was home alone that he posted this on his public Facebook page:

> 30+ years in public life and today is the first time a reporter came to my HOUSE! My wife, home alone, did not like it. A stranger coming to our very remote home, with all the criminals I helped send to prison, quite literally takes his life into his own hands. This reporter will never know the danger he was in. Elizabeth is very well trained to protect herself and our family, and she takes our privacy very seriously. I am retired from government. The DA's Office speaks for the Commonwealth in Montgomery County, not me any longer. . . . I have said everything that needs saying about this case. I have nothing to add. So reporters: stop calling my elderly parents, and never even consider coming to our house uninvited, especially on a work day when my wife is alone, except for Mr. Ruger.

Cosby was clearly concerned the #MeToo movement could hurt him at his second trial. He would be the first powerful man accused of serial sexual assault to face trial since #MeToo became a phenomenon, and no one could say how deeply it would impact the case—or if it would at all. And so Cosby spent the intervening months hanging out in a local barbershop, clad in Philadelphia Eagles gear. He made sure reporters knew in advance he was performing his first comedy show in years at a Philadelphia jazz club so they could attend.

And he circulated videos and photos of all this on his social media sites.

"Bill Cosby's current litigation strategy is to try and appeal to potential Philadelphia jurors as a hometown kid who's just a regular guy even though he's achieved fame and fortune," observed crisis management expert Gene Grabowski. "He's also reminding people that he's a legendary comedian whose substantial life's work shouldn't be erased because of some possible errors in judgment."

AT THE END of February Cosby suffered a tragic loss. His daughter Ensa, forty-four, had died from renal disease. Cosby and his family buried her on their property in Shelburne Falls, Massachusetts, next to Ennis.

Although he was still grieving, Cosby was present on March 5 when trial preparations began with a series of hearings. The hearings would determine various rules for the trial, such as how many of the accusers would be allowed to testify and whether Cosby's deposition testimony could be used as evidence. By then I was covering the case for the *Daily Beast*, and I followed the back-and-forth over each decision with growing fascination. The arguments seemed endless. He'd replaced his legal team yet again, and his new attorneys were even more aggressive than all of his previous ones put together.

The prosecution had asked the judge to allow nineteen accusers to testify at the second trial, and Cosby's attorneys were especially adamant that none should be allowed to testify this time, insisting that in light of the #MeToo movement, it would bias the jury. "The purpose would just be to enrage the jury this time, fueled by even more prejudicial . . . 'Me Too' accusations that have nothing to do with Mr. Cosby at all," argued Becky James.

But Assistant DA Adrienne Jappe felt otherwise. She insisted that all nineteen women should be allowed to testify because Cosby's drugging and sexual assault of Andrea was part of a "sadistic sexual script" that Cosby perfected over decades, so much so that it became his "signature."

The conflict grew so contentious that Judge O'Neill issued an order telling both sides to file separate memorandums of law on the issue, and he would then review their written arguments.

Steele's memo focused on the right to allow victims to seek justice in court. With statistics provided by the advocacy group RAINN, he demonstrated the value of having the women testify. Their testimony, he wrote, could help to mitigate juror prejudice toward rape victims, especially ones who delay reporting the crimes to law enforcement.

"Out of every 1,000 rapes, only 310 will be reported to law enforcement," he detailed. "This is especially concerning given that in the United States, another individual experiences sexual assault every 98 seconds. Among the chief reasons victims cite when explaining a decision to avoid altogether or delay a report to officials: fear of being disbelieved."

Cosby's attorneys took another stance. They felt the accusers had all been influenced by one another and had motives to lie. "The commonwealth's argument . . . necessarily rests on the question of 'what are the chances' that so many accusers are fabricating their reports of sexual assault," they wrote. "In this case the chances are quite high."

Three days later O'Neill made his ruling: five of the nineteen women would be allowed to testify at the trial. The judge went on to explain that prosecutors could choose the five women themselves, but only from cases from 1982 forward. The women would be testifying as "prior bad act" witnesses to demonstrate a specific pattern of behavior.

Celebrity lawyer Tom Mesereau, who was most famous for getting singer Michael Jackson acquitted of child sexual abuse charges, and the others filed motion after motion, challenging nearly every aspect of the case. He even filed a motion demanding O'Neill recuse himself, arguing that because O'Neill's wife worked with sexual-assault survivors, O'Neill would be biased against the defendant.

O'Neill's wife, Dr. Deborah O'Neill, was a psychotherapist at the University of Pennsylvania in Philadelphia, coordinating a team of counselors who cared and advocated for student sexual-assault survivors. She had dedicated her PhD dissertation on college-acquaintance

rape to her husband, which the defense used to claim they had discussed sexual-assault issues and therefore that made him an inappropriate judge for the case.

They also pointed out that his wife's name was on a $100 donation
to Women Organized Against Rape, a group that said it would protest
outside the courthouse during Cosby's trial. But O'Neill clarified that
it was a donation from his wife's employer, not her, and dismissed the
allegations that his wife's work compromised his judgment. He would
not recuse himself, he announced, and the proceedings moved forward.

By THE TIME the pretrial arrangements were complete, it was clear to
everyone that this trial was not going to be a simple repeat of the last
go-around.

This time Cosby had a new, hard-hitting, seven-member legal team.

This time six accusers would be testifying, not two, with Marguerite "Margo" Jackson being called as a defense witness.

And this time the judge insisted that Bruce Castor's 2005 decision
not to prosecute Cosby could not be mentioned in the courtroom,
while information about Andrea's civil suit, including the whopping
$3.38 million she received in the settlement, could.

Even the jury profile was different. For the second trial the jury
was younger and came from the same county as Cosby. They were also
more affluent and more educated.

That's not to say the jury selection was drama-free. An overwhelming majority of potential jurors in all three jury pools said they had
heard of the case and the #MeToo movement, but all of the ones who
were chosen said they could render a fair and impartial verdict. The
defense was worried, but there was little they could do about it.

By the third day both teams were anxious and tensions were high.
At one point Steele incited an outburst from the defense team when
he used one of his peremptory strikes to exclude Potential Juror Number Nine from the second pool of candidates. The candidate was African American, and Kathleen Bliss, one of Cosby's attorneys, objected
to the strike, saying the woman had been unconstitutionally rejected
because of race.

"She passed every single stage as a fair and impartial juror," Bliss angrily told the judge. "There is thus no explanation other than her race."

Steele, equally heated, denied her claim. He couldn't say it in public, but he didn't want the woman on the jury because the DA's office had an open fraud investigation on her, which wasn't a reason to strike her for cause, but it still made him unwilling to seat her. She'd also been prosecuted by his office in the past and referred into a diversion program. So Steele used a peremptory strike, which didn't require a reason. He also pointed out that two African American jurors had already been chosen for the panel and that the prosecution hadn't objected to either of them.

The dispute halted jury selection for three full hours and led to headlines like "Cosby Team Alleges Racial Prejudice in Jury Selection."

It took four days and three jury pools totaling 359 people, but finally a jury was selected. There were twelve jurors and six alternates who were ready to go to court on Monday. Potential Juror Number Nine wasn't done making news, though.

She had reached out to Cosby's defense team to say she overheard the man who would become Juror Number Eleven in the case say, "I just think he's guilty." The defense filed a motion late Friday night asking for the juror to be removed. The beginning of the trial was delayed for five hours on Monday while both sides met with the judge outside the courtroom. We were never told what happened, but when the trial finally got underway that afternoon, Juror Number Eleven was still seated.

Curious about what had transpired, after the trial I ordered transcripts of the so-called in-camera hearing, which means it is on the record with a court reporter but not in the actual courtroom, so it is public record. While Potential Juror Number Nine swore under oath she'd heard Juror Number Eleven make that statement, he denied it under oath and three other jurors (Nine, Ten, and Twelve) who were in the same room said they did not hear him say anything.

That is also how I learned the details about why Steele didn't want her as a juror.

ON THAT BITTER cold Monday morning, part of an unseasonably brisk spring that even brought snow on the first day of jury selection, a topless protestor hopped the barricades and jumped out of the bushes at Cosby as he walked into the courthouse, escorted by Wyatt and Benson. Cosby openly gaped at her.

Her body was covered with the names of the Cosby accusers along with the words "Women's Lives Matter," "Cosby Rapist," and "Semen."

"Hey, hey, hey!" she yelled to the masses around her. "Convict Cosby! Rapist!"

The police quickly apprehended her. She held her fist in the air as they escorted her away; she was arrested and charged with disorderly conduct. We learned later that she had appeared on several episodes of *The Cosby Show* as a child.

"The main goal was to make Bill Cosby feel uncomfortable because that is exactly what he has been doing for decades to women," she told reporters, saying she was a member of the European feminist group Femen, which is known for staging topless protests around the world.

Andrew Wyatt was not impressed. "That's not about the victims. That's about yourself," he said. "And if you are going to protest rape, you shouldn't rip your clothes off."

While the second trial wasn't attracting the crowds, the protesters, the number of accusers, or even the media attention of the first, the incident put Wyatt on edge, and he urged court officials to increase security. Officials agreed and added a second row of barricades. Still, the message was not lost on countless supporters and accusers who watched the woman's outburst and cheered her on.

This time around, expect the unexpected.

CHAPTER TWENTY-SIX

YOU REMEMBER, DON'T YOU, MR. COSBY?

No one had wished for a second trial. But because there was going to be one, Kevin Steele and his team figured they should use the do-over to their advantage by reviewing the play-by-play of the first trial to improve their strategies for the second go. They studied courtroom transcripts, evaluated testimonies, reviewed witness lists, and spoke to jurors, making careful notes about how they reacted to various aspects of the proceedings.

This time the prosecution decided to put a sexual-assault expert on the stand first instead of waiting until later in the proceedings. That way, the jury would be educated about rape and prepared for the testimonies of the six women accusers before they took the stand. Their stories might seem odd to jurors if they weren't first educated about sexual assault victims' behavior. And they opted not to bring Kelley Johnson back, knowing Cosby's new defense team could look at her testimony from the previous year to provide a roadmap for how to cross-examine her.

As logical as this was, it was a relatively new practice to put a sex-crime expert on the stand. In fact, Pennsylvania had only recently started allowing the practice, and it was the last state in the country to do so. The new law was enacted after Penn State defensive coach Jerry Sandusky was convicted of sexually abusing ten young boys in 2012. Before that, there was no opportunity to counteract a defense team's barrage of insinuations that the rape victim—or victims—were to blame.

Steele hoped that by educating the Cosby jury in a similar way, they'd be better prepared to comprehend the victims' testimonies—and less likely to buy into the defense team's inevitable pretense that Andrea was to blame.

The aging courtroom was freezing cold that first day, so much so that it felt like someone had turned on the air conditioning instead of the heat. The jury was shivering as well, and many of them came back in after the first break with their winter coats on to keep warm. Throughout the trial the ancient heating system was kicking out something into the air that had some of us sniffling and sneezing. Toward the end I was so congested that I could barely breathe through my nose and nearly lost my voice at one point, though I was still squeaking out radio interviews about the trial. The days were long. Like the first trial, I was getting up at 5:30 A.M., leaving my house by 6:30 A.M., and not getting home until after 7 P.M., so there was no time to get to a doctor.

The courtroom was barely half filled this time, which surprised me. I thought the #MeToo movement and six accusers testifying instead of two would generate more media interest. Perhaps more media weren't here because they thought this trial would end the way the last had. That I could understand. I had interviewed several legal experts for one of my stories and couldn't find one who thought Cosby would be convicted.

It quickly became clear to me, though, that this was a different trial and was being prosecuted more skillfully than the first. Even their sexual-assault expert was better, her testimony more on point. Feden struggled with the expert they used the first time, asking her questions so specific to Andrea's case that it gave the defense plenty to object to—these experts are supposed to talk in general terms, not specific, and to be objective. And it didn't help that the previous expert had a post on her business's Facebook site that seemed to be cheering on the prosecution.

Dr. Barbara Ziv, a forensic psychiatrist specializing in sex crimes, took the stand and, after an exhaustive cross-examination of her credentials, began her testimony shortly before noon. "Sexual assault is one of the most misunderstood crimes," she announced, and from there she then listed all the ways this was true. She pointed to the prevalence of rape—saying one in five women and one in seven men in the country have been sexually assaulted—to demonstrate that, while many people know someone who has experienced sexual assault, and many have strong feelings about it, much of what they believe about sexual assault is wrong. Yet people cling to these so-called "rape myths," which place blame on the victim and more or less excuse the perpetrator's actions. She then went on to list and dispel each of them.

Most sexual assaults—a full 85 percent—are perpetrated by somebody the victim knows. I knew this might surprise some jurors, and it certainly surprised me, as it's commonly imagined that rapes are like muggings—a stranger accosts a woman in the dark of night.

Another rape myth, Ziv told the courtroom, is that rape victims tend to file police reports right away. "That's not true," she instructed. "A delayed reporting is the norm, not the exception. Delayed reporting can go from days to weeks to months to years."

One more point she was clear about: we tend to blame sexual assault victims for not reacting afterward the way we expect them to, for not becoming this "broken creature hiding under your covers." For instance, she said, "If an athlete, a football player, gets hit hard on the field and then gets back up again, or if a skier has a huge fall and gets back up again, you applaud them. But if a victim of sexual assault moves on with their life and gets back up again, the common response is, 'Well, then nothing happened.'"

I thought about that. It struck me that if a woman "seemed fine," there was a perception that the rape was no big deal. But not all scars are visible. Meanwhile, not only does society blame victims, but victims blame themselves as well. It doesn't help that if a date-rape drug is used, it can leave a woman with a spotty recollection—or no recollection—of what happened.

"People's memories are impacted," Ziv confirmed. "They may be impacted by substances, but they are also impacted by the sexual assault itself. People talk about feeling disassociated . . . having out-of-body experiences." Their memory may come back in out-of-sequence pieces.

She went on, dispelling another rape myth, that most victims fight back against an assailant's sexual advances or attacks. "A lot of people who are victims of sexual assault describe themselves in a state of being frozen." And if the rapist is someone they know, they may try to see him again. The rape itself creates confusion. How could this person I know, this friend, do this to me? What happened? "If this is a trusted relationship that's important, a woman's first impulse is to try to find a way to make it make sense," she said.

Even if they put together a timeline of events, Ziv clarified, it's still common to not report the crime, especially if she knows her rapist. If the perpetrator is someone in a position of power over the victim and has an otherwise good reputation, the likelihood that the woman will feel she can speak out about what happened to her becomes minimal—at best.

Putting Dr. Ziv on the stand first proved to be a smart decision. One reason she was invited to the stand early was to educate the jury; another was to preemptively undermine the defense team's attack on Andrea and the five other accusers who would be testifying. That was the strategy Cosby's defense team had planned, and they weren't happy about Dr. Ziv's testimony; in fact, they had tried to bar such expert testimony in both trials, but O'Neill overruled the objection.

That didn't stop Mesereau. A startling sight with a shock of white hair and a golden tan, he launched the second trial with a formidable blame-the-victim tactic. If I thought the defense in the first trial was vicious, it looked like they would be far worse now. During his opening statements Mesereau's arguments were explosive, playing on every rape myth in the book. He called Andrea a "con artist" and a "so-called victim," and he claimed Andrea had invented drugging and sexual assault allegations to extort money from Cosby.

To me this argument simply wasn't logical. If she were just after Cosby's money, she got it in 2006, so why did she subject herself to not just one but two criminal trials? But Mesereau's style hinges on emotion and theatrics—it was a strategy that had worked well for him in Michael Jackson's case—so he stuck to the plan.

"She was madly in love with his fame and money," Mesereau told the jury. He also said Andrea had purposely played on Cosby's vulnerabilities in the wake of his son's death. "[Mr. Cosby] was lonely and troubled, and he made the terrible mistake of confiding in this person . . . that he had never recovered from his son's murder."

Was he really trying to use Ennis to earn the jury's sympathy for Cosby? I marveled at the ploy. Prior to the first trial, Cosby had tweeted about Ennis, urging him to "keep fighting in spirit." And here it was again. But it was still early in the trial, so there was plenty of time for the truth to come out. I put the moment out of my mind and concentrated on what came next.

For the next two days, one after the other, the women came forward and presented chilling portraits of what happened to them at the hands of a man they had trusted and revered. The first accuser to take the stand was Heidi Thomas. As she took her seat, the courtroom quieted, and her story began.

IN 1984 BILL COSBY was charming America in Coca-Cola commercials and starring in the first season of *The Cosby Show* when Heidi Thomas, a twenty-four-year-old aspiring actress, got a call from her agent at JF Images, the same Denver agency that had represented Beth Ferrier and Barbara Bowman. Her agent told her Cosby wanted to mentor her. He called her at home first, even chatting with her parents to put them at ease, and arrangements were made for Heidi to meet Cosby in Reno, where he was performing at Harrah's.

However, when she arrived at the airport, instead of taking her to her hotel, the driver took her to a home on the outskirts of the city, where she was told paparazzi wouldn't stalk Cosby. Although she was his only guest, she wasn't worried. After all, he was Bill Cosby, the family man, the humanitarian. He'd just testified before Congress on behalf of the poor, urging members not to cut funding for programs for needy families, like the ones who had helped his family when he was growing up. "Without that check coming on the 15th and 30th of every month I, my mother and my brothers would have been out on the street or we would have been living with relatives," he told a congressional subcommittee.

Inside the house Cosby welcomed Heidi and prompted her to practice for an audition by reading from a script. The script called for her to pretend to be intoxicated, so Cosby encouraged her to take a sip of wine—for the benefit of her performance, he explained.

"I took a sip . . . and I can tell you it was a *sip*," said Heidi, a striking figure with chin-length blondish-gray hair who was calm and collected during her hours on the stand. "After that I don't remember. I have little snapshots of the next four days."

In one flash of memory she woke up in bed with Cosby naked and forcing his penis into her mouth. In another, Cosby was at the head of the bed and her head was at the foot of the bed. "I heard his voice saying—and he always referred to himself in the third person or as 'Mr. C' or 'your friend'—he said, 'Your friend is going to come again.'"

Heidi went back home after that weekend without confronting Cosby, she said. And she told no one else about it when she got home, blaming herself. But a few months later she decided to try to talk to him to find out what happened. She met him at a dinner in St. Louis where he was eating with friends, but she never got a chance to ask him her questions.

"He wasn't very happy with me, and at that point it was pretty clear that whatever this mentorship thing was, it wasn't happening," she said. That was the last time she had any contact with him. She dropped her acting dreams and pursued teaching instead. She kept a scrapbook of the photos she'd taken that weekend, of the travel documents, and even that photo of her with him at that dinner in St. Louis. She really had no idea why at the time, but it certainly came in handy thirty-four years later.

NEXT ON THE witness stand was Chelan Lasha. Chelan was crying as she approached her chair—it was an emotional day for her, seeing Cosby again after all this time. She had been so young when he had violated her and seeing him in the room brought her back to that frightening time. Chelan began her story.

She was a fifteen-year-old aspiring model when she first met Cosby in 1984 through her stepmother, she said. America was already in love with Cliff Huxtable. Cosby was so popular that the FBI had asked him to record a series of three-minute videotaped messages warning children to be alert about potentially dangerous situations like walking alone or getting in a car with a stranger, videos they played at FBI headquarters in Washington, DC. He wasn't yet wealthy enough to buy NBC, so he was trying to purchase a piece of one of its competitors, an ABC station in Detroit.

Chelan's stepmother, in fact, worked for a production company that Cosby was affiliated with, so she gave Cosby a photo of Chelan explaining that her stepdaughter wanted to pursue a modeling career. Chelan and her older sister were being raised by their grandparents in Las Vegas because her mother was in prison, so he called Chelan in Vegas, inviting her and her grandmother to one of his shows. He also said he would introduce her to people he knew at the Ford modeling agency. Chelan was overjoyed.

Even better, Cosby struck up a friendship with her grandmother, and he spent time with her family at their home. He'd come for dinner or with ice cream to share. One time her grandmother cooked him one of his favorite soul food meals—oxtail, rice and greens, and cornbread, with a homemade peach cobbler made fresh with the fruit from a tree in their backyard for dessert. He even brought Jell-O pudding pops for the kids. "I'll never forget that day," she told me later. "Everyone thought I was a star because I knew Bill Cosby."

This was a familiar part of Cosby's pattern—grooming the family members as well as the victim herself to gain their trust. And it worked. By the time he invited Chelan to his penthouse suite at the Las Vegas Hilton for a photo shoot for her portfolio, in 1986, she had known him for a couple of years and was not even a little bit suspicious. "I wanted to be a model and actress and was going to school, and he wanted to . . . help my career," she said, weeping.

Chelan had a bad cold that day, she told the court, and she had arrived sneezing and coughing. Cosby offered her what he said was an antihistamine, and she took it. Within a few minutes she was woozy.

"He said, 'You need to lay down,' and he walked me to the bedroom and . . . laid me on the bed," she said. "I couldn't move." He lay down next to her. "He kept pinching my breasts and humping my leg . . . and grunting," she said between sobs. "I was thinking, 'Dr. Huxtable, what are you doing, and why are you doing this to me?' I couldn't say nothing."

What felt like hours later, Cosby woke her up and told her she had to go home. She left, but she went straight to her guidance counselor's home and told her what happened. She also told her sister and eventually her grandmother.

When Chelan finished telling her story, Bliss spent two hours hammering away at her, asking about a 2007 conviction for lying to law enforcement, claiming she was motivated by money, mentioning the $100 million victim fund her attorney, Gloria Allred, had wanted Cosby to set up. Sobbing, Chelan denied it. "I have a roof over my head, food in my mouth, and a family that loves me," she said, crying. "That's all I need."

Finally the judge called for a break, and Chelan was free to step down. Before leaving the stand, though, Chelan stared straight at Cosby and burst out: "You remember, don't you, Mr. Cosby?"

Cosby's response: No words. Just a smile.

JANICE BAKER-KINNEY TOOK the stand next. She was working as a bartender at Harrah's in Reno in 1982, she said, when a coworker invited her to a pizza party at the casino owner's home—a party hosted by Bill Cosby. She knew that celebrities who were performing at the casino either stayed in a luxurious penthouse suite at the resort or at Harrah's home, so this didn't seem odd to her. She'd even been to a party Wayne Newton had hosted there before. Cosby had been performing at Harrah's since the late 1960s and had even purchased one of Bill Harrah's Rolls Royces for $35,000 back then.

Janice had met a few celebrities through her job, including Loretta Lynn and Smokey Robinson, so she wasn't starstruck. She just thought it'd be fun to go to a party and had no reason to be suspicious of Cosby, who at the time was hawking pudding pops on TV, talking to moms across America about how Jell-O brand pudding was made with fresh milk, "so you know it's wholesome!"

But when she arrived, she quickly discovered it was just the three of them—Cosby, her coworker, and herself.

"I kinda thought, 'Oh, it's just us. Not a real party,'" she said. "I didn't think to say, 'I'm not staying if it's just the three of us.' I thought I'd stay for a while, have a beer or two and a couple of slices of pizza." Instead, Cosby offered her a Quaalude, followed by another. "I took one from him, and he put a second one in the palm of my hand, closed my hand, and said, 'No. Take two of them. It'll be okay,'" she said. So she did. "I thought, 'Well, if Bill Cosby says it's okay to take these, it must be okay," she said. "I trusted him."

They sat down to play backgammon.

"We weren't that far into the game, and I was looking down at the board, and I was getting very dizzy," she said. "Everything was blurry, and my head was spinning. I recall vividly saying, 'This game isn't fair anymore,' and he asked me why. I said, 'Because I can no longer see the board.' And I fell forward and passed out."

The next thing she remembered was waking up on a couch with her shirt unbuttoned and her pants unzipped. Her coworker saying her good-byes to Cosby had woken her. "Mr. Cosby came over and sat down on the couch with me. He sat in the corner, and he leaned my back into his chest, kinda like he propped me up. . . . He had one arm over me and placed his other arm inside my shirt and was fondling me and then kinda went downward into the top of my panties."

Then she recalled Cosby helping her up the steps to a bedroom. After that, everything went black until she woke up the next morning when the phone rang. She and Cosby were in bed together, naked.

"I apologized to Mr. Cosby because I was so mortified that I had passed out," she said. "There was a sticky wetness between my legs, and it felt like I'd had sex the night before."

During a forceful cross-examination by Mesereau, Janice said she didn't think about it as rape until other women began coming forward in 2014 and 2015. Rape was being dragged into an alley by a stranger with a knife. Plus, "I blamed myself for taking the drugs," she admitted. She didn't realize those drugs took away her ability to consent and that is what made it rape, not until she heard other women with similar experiences speak out. Mesereau was openly contemptuous of Janice, at one point even rolling his eyes at her, which she called him out on. "Are you rolling your eyes at me?" she demanded.

"Yes," Mesereau replied.

He did his best to portray Janice as a party girl who loved to drink and take drugs, and in fact she did admit to using different drugs at various times in her life but said that while she was living in Reno she only drank alcohol. As with the others, Mesereau also insinuated she was fabricating her story for money, once again citing her representation by Allred and the $100 million victim fund, a claim Janice flatly denied.

Allred helps her with media appearances, she said, and that's it.

He also tried to discredit her for remaining silent for thirty long years. "So for thirty years you didn't suspect someone had sexually assaulted you?" Mesereau demanded.

Janice paused before she replied. "For thirty years I didn't think about it," she admitted. "I didn't want to think about it."

I could understand why.

FORMER SUPERMODEL JANICE DICKINSON was the next accuser to testify and possibly the witness most anticipated by the room. Janice was well known for her colorful behavior, and she didn't let anyone down in the courtroom. She cursed and bantered, refusing to kowtow to Mesereau in what was the most contentious of all the cross-examinations.

But she was dead serious when she told her story.

In 1982 Janice had finally made it as a model and wanted to try her hand at acting when her agent at the Elite Modeling Agency told her Cosby wanted to mentor her.

"I was excited," she said. "He was very well respected from being on TV to being a happily married man with five children."

They met up at his Manhattan townhome, where they discussed her acting aspirations. Not long afterward she was on a photo shoot in Bali when she got a call from Cosby, who invited her to come to Lake Tahoe, where he was performing, to talk about her career. After a little bit of haggling—he wanted her to fly economy, she insisted on first class—she agreed to go.

When Janice arrived at the hotel there were several outfits for her laid out around her room, purchased at the boutique in the hotel. Cosby had provided them for her because she only had summer attire with her in Bali.

That night they had dinner with Stu Gardner, who later wrote and produced music for *The Cosby Show*. "I started to get menstrual cramps," she said. "I put my hand on my stomach and mentioned that. . . . Cosby said, 'I have something for that,' and I was given a blue pill."

Shortly afterward she started feeling "woozy and dizzy" and "slightly out of it." They finished dinner and Gardner left. "Cosby said, 'We'll finish this conversation upstairs,' so I followed him to his room."

They arrived in his room. She was feeling lightheaded, so she sat down on his bed. That's when he raped her, she said.

"He smelled like cigars and espresso and his body odor," she said. "I couldn't move. I felt like I was rendered motionless. Just immobile." That's the last thing she remembered before passing out. "I woke up the next morning in my room. I didn't know where I was. . . . I looked down and I noticed semen between my legs, and I noticed I felt anal pain. . . . I remember having my pajamas halfway on, halfway off, with no bottoms on and thinking, I am disgusted, and I am in shock and humiliated."

Afterward she went with Cosby to a house near Reno owned by the Harrah's casino owner—it seemed to be the same house where Heidi and Janice Baker-Kinney said they were raped.

"I said, 'Do you want to explain what happened last night? Because that wasn't cool,'" she said. "And he said nothing and he looked at me like I was crazy. . . . I wanted to punch him in the face."

Janice went on to reach new levels of fame and that same year wrote a memoir, *No Lifeguard on Duty*. She tried to include the rape story in the book, but the publisher's lawyers pressured her to remove it. She said she had sworn statements from her publisher, Judith Regan, and her ghostwriter, Pablo Fenjves, saying she told them what really happened.

Mesereau seized on that discrepancy as the two got into the most heated debate of the entire trial. "You tell a completely different story in the book, right?" he demanded.

"Today I'm under a sworn Bible!" she snapped back.

Finally her time on the stand came to an end. She got confused when the defense attorney said she was "subject to recall," meaning they could ask her back to testify if they needed her to. "You mean I have to stick around?" she asked.

Judge O'Neill explained the legal concept to her, but seeming to feel she was growing frustrated, he added, "I'm just trying to advise you."

She was quick to reassure him. "I think you've been great!" she blurted out, as the courtroom burst into laughter, adding before stepping down: "*Law & Order* is my favorite program."

BY THE TIME Lise Lotte-Lublin, the fifth and final accuser to take the stand, began to testify, it was Thursday afternoon, the fourth day of the trial. I could tell that the stories were weighing on everyone in the room, but the jury still seemed to be paying close attention just the same, furiously scribbling notes as each woman spoke.

As Lise began her story, few in the room could have been surprised by the way it unfolded—it was uncannily similar to the previous tales. Lise was now a sixth-grade teacher, married with two children, and had a master's degree in computer technology. She also coached track and field and archery, and her archery team had been the state champions in Nevada for the last seven years. In fact she was missing their national tournament in Salt Lake City to testify at Andrea's trial.

Lise told the courtroom that she was a twenty-three-year-old model in 1989, when her agent told her that Cosby wanted to mentor her. *The Cosby Show* was in its fifth year as the number-one comedy in America, and Lise was jubilant to meet the superstar. He'd written two best-selling books, one about fatherhood. Why should she be suspicious?

She went to meet with him at the Las Vegas Hilton.

"When I walked in I saw several headshots—some of the girls I recognized—on the table," she said. "We talked for a bit. He said he'd send my photos to New York and have a modeling agency look at them and see what would be best for me, runway or commercial."

The second time she met with him her sister was with her and they all took a photograph together. He got to know her entire family, she said. "He had a relationship with my mother where he would just call her on the phone and they would banter back and forth because she was in the field of psychology," she said.

He even introduced her around as his daughter, she said.

So when he invited her to the Elvis Suite at the Las Vegas Hilton—where Chelan said she'd been invited and where he often stayed while in town—to discuss her modeling career in 1989, she thought nothing of it. She had no idea, no preparation, for what was about to happen to her.

First they looked at her new headshots. Then he insisted she have a drink "to help her relax." She did, and then she blacked out. She woke up two days later in her own bedroom with no idea how she got there.

For years Lise thought she had a bad reaction to alcohol. But after seeing a Janice Dickinson interview in November 2014, she came to believe he had drugged and sexually assaulted her, so she reported it to the police. "I realized something else had happened after I blacked out," she said, gasping and fighting off tears. "I don't know what it was, but I believe I know what it was. There was a purpose for me to black out." She stuck to her story throughout a ninety-minute grilling by Bliss. Though represented by Allred, Lise insisted she was not part of her efforts to get Cosby to pay his victims through a fund. All she wants from him are an apology and for him to "take responsibility for his actions. Some remorse."

Hearing those stories, one after the other, was compelling. I couldn't imagine there was anyone in the room who wasn't affected by the painful details of each woman's story. But who really can know how another person is interpreting details, processing emotions? Was the jury feeling the anguish of the women, and if they were, did it matter? I didn't know. I felt a different vibe from this jury. The defense attorneys' attacks on the women did not seem to be sitting well with them, judging by the expression on some of their faces. That massive screen was back, blocking our view of some of the jurors, but I could still see a few of them. They were already starting to remind me of the Sandusky jury.

It was still early, though, and the most important witness was about to take the stand: Andrea.

CHAPTER TWENTY-SEVEN

PACK OF WOLVES

Prosecutor Kristen Feden eased Andrea into her testimony by asking questions that would allow the jury to get to know her a bit, something they really hadn't done at the first trial. She asked Andrea about her life as a basketball player and about her job as a massage therapist working with cancer patients. And she asked that question that had never been asked of her publicly before: Why are you here?

"For justice," Andrea replied.

It was a powerful moment. It was already evident to me that the prosecution had learned from its mistakes in the first trial. Feden herself was much more seasoned, more confident. They masterfully built their case piece by careful piece, leaving no questions unanswered this time and making sure Andrea was clear and forceful about what Cosby had done to her so the jury could correctly apply her testimony to the law.

Her testimony was far more detailed and graphic than it had been in the first trial, and it was more emotionally gripping too. She was calm and composed as she testified, but she became visibly sadder as she talked about the day she told her mother what Cosby did to her and why she went to police.

"I didn't want it to happen to anyone else, what had happened to me," she said. And she needed some answers. "I really wanted to know what Mr. Cosby gave me and why he did that to me. And I was never my whole Andrea, not knowing the answers to those questions."

She agreed to cooperate when Steele wanted to reopen the investigation in 2015, though it was not an easy decision to make. "This was a matter that was tugging at my heart because I had moved on and I had healed an open wound, and now I could slowly feel this wound opening again," she said to a rapt room.

Soon the dynamic lost its friendly façade when Mesereau stepped up to cross-examine Andrea. Right away he dug into a fierce attack. He was openly contemptuous of her and spent hours trying to catch Andrea in inconsistencies in the accounts she gave various police departments and her own deposition in her civil suit against the entertainer.

Andrea had expected this; she managed to stay even-tempered, explaining herself patiently. "I was just trying to recall an enormous amount of information, and I was very nervous, and I was trying to piece it together," she said. "It was just confusion on my part."

And that Valentine's Day phone call with Cosby in 2004 that Mesereau wanted the jury to believe was proof they'd had a romantic entanglement? Phone records showed it was the same day there was a Temple women's basketball game so the call was work related.

Cosby smiled several times as she spoke and as Mesereau led Andrea through certain parts of the settlement agreement. He asked her why she signed off on a provision in which Cosby admitted no guilt for what he did to her. "It was a very painstaking process for my family," she testified. "It tore my family apart, and we just wanted it over."

When Mesereau finished his interrogation, Andrea stepped down, and Gianna took her place on the stand.

Gianna was the same fierce mama bear she was at the first trial, describing how furious and concerned she was when her daughter told her Cosby had drugged and sexually assaulted her. She described their phone calls: "I guess I was very combative and I kinda yelled, 'What did you give my daughter? What did you do to her?'" And she said she told Cosby, "Only a sick man would do that."

Cosby replied that he too felt he was "a sick man, and it took Andrea to stop him," Gianna said. She also reported that Cosby admitted what he'd done and apologized.

Gianna was at turns indignant, frustrated, and flustered under cross-examination by Bliss, who started off by taking a gentle approach but then became increasingly forceful.

"Don't talk to me like that. Please." Gianna said at one point, at times putting her hand to her throat when she got upset. "Why are you asking me in that voice?" she asked Bliss another time. The defense attorneys were unfazed, and Bliss accused Gianna of benefiting from her daughter's lawsuit and asked her whether Andrea bought her a home with the money.

"I didn't benefit a thing," Gianna said forcefully, saying she didn't even know how much money her daughter got until it became public for this trial. "This isn't about money, Miss Bliss."

A particularly poignant moment came at the very end of her testimony, shortly before 6:00 P.M. as we were about to adjourn for the day. As Steele gently asked her if she had any health issues, Gianna revealed she had Parkinson's disease as she sobbed into her handkerchief.

THE REST OF the prosecution's case involved detectives reading Cosby's statements into the record, the same as they had for the first trial, and the same forensic toxicologist they used before testified once again. Sergeant Richard Schaffer spent three hours on the stand going through the statements Andrea made to him as well as her and Cosby's phone records.

Mesereau and Schaffer butted heads during Mesereau's forty-five-minute cross-examination on everything from the number of phone calls Andrea made to Cosby, especially after the alleged sexual assault, to inconsistencies in Andrea's various statements to police.

"She is employed by Temple University at this time," Schaffer replied. "This is one of the most powerful men on the Temple campus. If he calls, she's answering his calls. . . . She is compelled to call him back."

Mesereau asked Schaffer about Andrea saying in one statement that she sat on the corner of Cosby's bed in his hotel room at Foxwoods Casino in November 2003, while in another statement she said she laid down on the bed. "Were you in the room with Miss Constand and Mr. Cosby?" a frustrated Mesereau finally asked.

"Things would have gotten weird if that was going on," Schaffer said as the courtroom erupted in laughter—a rare release of tension after hours of fraught combat.

MONTGOMERY COUNTY DETECTIVE James Reape came next. He took the stand and read excerpts from Cosby's deposition in Constand's civil suit against him. The jury seemed to be paying close attention, reading along as Reape and Steele read the excerpts aloud.

Outside the courtroom Wyatt and Benson were making sure TV reporters got good sound bites for their shows by holding daily press conferences during the lunch break and after court adjourned for the day. The accusers traded in "poetic licensing, otherwise known as alternative facts," Wyatt said one day. Andrea and her mother seemed to be "more colorful and more embellished" than they had been in the first trial, Benson said on another.

In one particularly heated moment Wyatt got into a verbal scuffle with Allred, who represented three of the accusers who testified. He began calling her Gloria "Awful-red." Her daughter, who was there as Janice Dickinson's attorney, was dubbed Lisa "Blasphemous" Bloom. Together they are "two of the greatest extortionists of the twenty-first century," he said before confronting Allred about the $100 million victim fund she'd asked Cosby to create.

"You need to listen and don't interrupt," she demanded.

"I'm not your child," Wyatt snapped back.

The following day O'Neill issued a new order banning press conferences from the steps of the courthouse. But Wyatt and Benson just moved their daily show to another site nearby.

It's hard to convey how over the top Wyatt and Benson's behavior was. No cameras were allowed in the courtrooms, and the prosecution wasn't making comments outside of what was said in court, so they had free rein to say whatever they wanted, with no one to contradict them. The TV reporters needed people talking on camera for their segments, so they had to use whatever Wyatt and Benson said. For a while they had Allred as a counterpoint, but she did not stick around for the entire trial, so Lili Bernard and Victoria Valentino jumped in where they could.

I didn't have time to run out to hear what Wyatt and Benson were saying during the breaks because I was busy filing my stories. Like the first trial, members of the media had to be in the courtroom by whatever time the judge said or we would be locked out. If we left for any other reason than O'Neill calling a break, we couldn't get back in, so we never strayed too far. Luckily, there were plenty of videos. Reporters were shooting them themselves with their cell phones and posting them on Twitter with their stories.

Though he'd been representing Cosby for various fundraising events and college visits since 2010, Wyatt seemed to come out of nowhere as Cosby's new spokesperson in early 2015, first merely issuing press releases and, later, releasing motions in the criminal case through his Birmingham, Alabama–based PR firm. Wyatt spoke with *PRWeek* about his media strategy in October 2016, admitting he'd had to use some "unorthodox" methods.

"We can't just put messages out because anything we say we could possibly be sued [for]," he said, clearly referring to the various defamation lawsuits that several of Cosby's accusers had filed against him. "Our statements have to come through the motions our attorneys file. We can't just ultimately go out there and do interviews and speak freely."

Clearly he'd abandoned that particular strategy by the time the trials rolled around.

THE WITNESSES CONTINUED their parade, and soon Judith Regan was called to the stand as a supporting witness for Janice Dickinson.

During her long, illustrious career in book publishing, Regan had never shied away from controversial subjects, editing a number of best-sellers, including those written by shock-jock Howard Stern and conservative radio host Rush Limbaugh. But it was the book she never published, O. J. Simpson's confession, *If I Did It*, that got her fired from her imprint at HarperCollins by NewsCorp chief Rupert Murdoch in 2006. She sued and won a multi-million-dollar settlement.

During her testimony the famed book publisher confirmed that she asked Janice to remove the rape story from her memoir because the publisher's lawyers were concerned Cosby would sue.

Mesereau, in full attack mode, asked Regan about everything from her time working for the *National Enquirer* as a human-interest writer to her attempt to publish Simpson's book, and he did all of it in a way designed to taint her credibility. He'd ask a leading question he knew she was not allowed to answer due to the parameters of her testimony—"Did you help hide the money [from the O. J. Simpson book]?"—then triumphantly watch the judge shut her down before she could answer.

She was fuming, later telling me Mesereau's questions were "a desperate attempt to smear me" and a "sleazy" lawyer technique. She was so furious, in fact, that her spokesperson called me after she got back to New York City and offered me an exclusive interview with Regan. If the judge wouldn't allow her to answer Mesereau's questions, she'd take her testimony to the public through me. She also gave me ghost-writer Fenjves's contact information so I could interview him; he confirmed Janice's account, as well.

When I asked Mesereau and Wyatt for a response, Wyatt made it clear he couldn't care less that Regan was angry with this bizarre statement: "Saint Peter has been given direct orders from JESUS and HIS Father, not to let Judith Regan near the pearly gates," Wyatt wrote in an email to me. "However, they have informed Satan that he will have a guest by the name of Judith Regan coming in on a rocket and she's wearing gasoline stilettos."

Did he really just say Judith Regan is going to hell? I thought to myself, incredulous, as I read it.

Wyatt's response only infuriated her more when she read it in my story. She issued a statement blasting his "perverted, misogynistic, and frankly bizarre" comments to me. "His shameful and derogatory slur is representative of this pack of wolves' predatory views of women," she said.

THE STAR WITNESS for the prosecution was Marguerite "Margo" Jackson, the Temple employee who testified that Andrea told her in February 2004 she was going to set up a "high-profile" person to get money. I kept waiting for the defense to present the smoking gun, the proof she'd at least shared a room with Andrea when they traveled with the women's basketball team, which is when Jackson said the conversation occurred. There should be receipts somewhere.

That proof never came. Instead, it was the prosecution that found records showing that Jackson had submitted expense reports for travel with the team in February 2003, not 2004.

Their other witnesses spent an inordinate amount of time going over various itineraries for Cosby for parts of December 2003 and January 2004, going through records from when he had a private plane in order to show that Cosby was not in his home when Andrea said the assault occurred. They said Cosby and Andrea's encounter was in mid-December 2003, meaning the statute of limitations had expired by the time Cosby was arrested, even though Cosby said in his deposition it happened in 2004. But there were gaps in these timelines—which weren't official documents, anyway; they were simply itineraries his staff typed up, with no independent confirmation.

And on it went. Their toxicology expert's credentials were so suspect that it prompted one local TV reporter sitting near me to blurt out, "My pharmacist at CVS knows more about drugs than this guy."

By the time we got to closing arguments on Tuesday, April 24, I was exhausted. It had been a grueling few weeks, during most of which I'd been sick, and the gloomy, cold weather that had settled over us matched the temperament of the room. Cosby's attorneys had continued to file motions throughout the trial, so the judge kept us until six in the evening each day to make up the time. The network morning shows, which often drive the coverage of the rest of the national media, had done little on the second trial. Their reporters dropped in and out, never sticking around for long. It surprised me, especially in light of the #MeToo movement.

Some other members of the national media that were there, the ones who sat near Wyatt in the courtroom, had made it clear to me that they believed Jackson. It had me shaking my head. After ignoring or disparaging the story in 2005, many had jumped on the anti-Cosby bandwagon in 2014, and I'd always known they were just as likely to jump off at any point. I was watching it happen.

As she did for the first trial, Camille Cosby arrived in time for the defense's closing arguments. She entered the courtroom and walked to her husband at the defense table; Cosby stood up and smiled, and then they touched foreheads for a few seconds.

He whispered to her, they kissed, and she found her seat in the front row on the defense side. She sat regally, wearing a gold brocade top that matched her oversized glasses as she listened intently to the closing arguments.

Cosby's defense team chose to blast the #MeToo movement. It seemed like a risky strategy, but it fell in line with what they'd been doing for the entire trial, openly mocking the accusers, questioning them with voices dripping in contempt and attacking them so viciously that at times it felt like the movement had never happened.

"Mob rule is not due process," announced Bliss, who shared the closing with Mesereau. "And just as we have had horrible, horrible crimes in our history, we've also had horrible, horrible periods of time where emotion and hatred and fear have overwhelmed us. Witch hunts. Lynchings. McCarthyism. When you join a movement based primarily on emotion and anger, you don't change a damn thing."

Mesereau joined in. "It's a very, very serious moment where an eighty-year-old man who's legally blind and had a very successful career is looking at ruin. Absolute ruin."

They demolished the five other accusers who testified, calling Janice Dickinson a "failed starlet" and an "aged-out model."

Heidi was described as "living the dream" by going on speaking tours and appearing on TV shows to speak out about Cosby and the dangers of rape.

Chelan was discredited because she "has been convicted before of lying to the police."

Lise only participated because she "wants to be part of something," and Janice Baker-Kinney "heard about this case and joined the movement. Must have been #MeToo."

The attacks were so vicious that I actually saw a couple of the jurors wince.

The prosecution took its turn next. Feden turned around the defense's opening arguments that Andrea is a "con artist," saying it was Cosby who was the con artist and admonishing the defense for attacking the accusers.

Cosby seemed to find her amusing, chuckling as she defended the victims.

"He's laughing like it's funny!" Feden said, outraged. She flew across the room and glared at him. "But there's absolutely nothing funny about drugging a woman. There's nothing funny about *that*, Mr. Cosby. There's nothing funny about no permission, and there's nothing funny about intoxicating an individual so he can get what he's after."

It was a powerful moment and one that was clearly unrehearsed. How in the world could you predict Cosby's laughter? And, finally, she laid to rest one issue that had been dogging them for their entire investigation: Castor's decision not to prosecute Cosby in 2005. Though it wasn't their fault or even their call back then, she apologized to Andrea.

"We take full responsibility for it," she said. "We failed Andrea Constand back in 2005. We failed her."

I actually got chills when I heard her say that. Maybe it was because I thought Andrea deserved an apology for how she was treated in 2005, though not from anyone who was currently involved with the case. Or maybe it was because it was a masterful move and a powerful, emotional moment. The prosecution's performance this time was smooth and flawless, unlike the first trial.

It still remained to be seen if any of that would matter.

DURING THE PROSECUTION'S closing statements, Andrea sat two rows in front of me. She had left town after her testimony and had clearly been somewhere warm, because she was now sporting a dark tan, still visible though she was dressed for the cool April weather in a dark blue blazer with a white shirt underneath and light dress pants.

As she turned around to talk to someone behind her, our eyes met.

"Nicki?" she mouthed, the hint of a smile on her face.

After all this time, we'd never met, never even spoken. We'd connected on Facebook before the criminal case reopened, so she knew what I looked like, but I'd always gone through her attorneys for anything official. And yet I felt like I knew her, and I wished I could tell her that I'd believed her all those years ago. I'd done the research. I knew who she was before all of this happened, and I knew it didn't remotely match the way Cosby's attorneys portrayed her. On the outside she'd seemed so strong and calm, but I couldn't imagine how she was feeling on this day when she might be disappointed yet again.

I smiled and nodded.

"It's been a long time," she mouthed back. And it had. We'd traveled a long journey together, yet separately.

I nodded again. "It has," I agreed.

Thirteen and a half years.

CHAPTER TWENTY-EIGHT

INSIDE THE JURY ROOM

No one explains to a jury exactly how they are supposed to deliberate. Jurors are given lengthy, detailed instructions about what the law is, how to apply it, and how to decide whether a witness is credible. But beyond that, they are on their own to sort through the testimonies and evidence and come to an official conclusion.

That fact alone might explain why the first jury struggled as painfully as they did: with a case this complex, trying to reach a consensus of twelve could quickly become unruly. So when the judge dismissed the courtroom for the last time on Tuesday evening and the jury was set free to begin their work of determining Cosby's guilt on three counts, a quiet anxiety filled the courthouse as we wondered how the jury would manage the job in front of them. Would they too become indefinitely mired in tangled facts and complicated emotions? Or would they find a way to methodically review the case, part by part, until they reached a uniform conclusion?

Luckily this jury was far more able to manage the task. When they gathered Wednesday morning to begin their work, their deliberations were as methodical and cordial as the first trial's jury was chaotic and acrimonious. The foreperson, Cheryl Carmel, then fifty-nine, was vice president of cybersecurity and privacy for an international emergency notifications firm, and her organized, deliberate, and patient manner helped keep emotions in check and conversations focused. So did the jury's decision early on to take their time.

"We committed to not rushing to judgment," said Dianne Scelza, then sixty, a healthcare consultant. "We decided we wanted to go through the case step by step, meticulously. We went through every witness, every charge, every count, every question somebody had."

They also set ground rules: one person at a time, cover one topic at a time until it is settled, raise hands to be recognized, and be respectful of others.

At first it was just a relief to the jurors to be able to talk to one another. During the trial the jurors had been sequestered at a local hotel, where they were forbidden to discuss the testimony with anyone—even each other. They could only see family members on prearranged Sunday visits; in fact, their families weren't even told where they were staying. On Sundays a sheriff's deputy came to their hotel and took them to another location, where they would meet their families. It's a lonely experience, and for these jurors it had been three long weeks of isolation.

After establishing the ground rules for deliberation, they took the next hour and a half to release pent-up emotions. "It was a free for all," Carmel said. "We just kinda spilled everything."

After that, the group agreed that they were not ready to vote and that they wanted to dig into the case. First, they turned their attention to the three charges, reading each aloud, word by word, to ensure they were in sync on the definitions of the terms and lingo. There were three separate charges of aggravated indecent assault, each with slightly different elements to them saying Cosby digitally penetrated Andrea: (1) without her consent, (2) while she was unconscious, and (3) after drugging her without her knowledge to wipe out her resistance.

The judge told them that in order to find Cosby guilty of this first crime, they needed to be convinced beyond a reasonable doubt that four elements were proven, including that she did not consent to what happened. For the second one, that she was unconscious when it happened and thus unable to consent and that Cosby recklessly disregarded that. And for the third, that Cosby not only gave her drugs that wiped away her resistance but that he then "recklessly" disregarded that impairment while assaulting her.

Their first real debate was over the definition of consent. This was the heart of the case: Cosby said what happened between him and Andrea was consensual, and she said it was not. This is also where Carmel's job came in handy: she'd just been dealing with this very issue for a new European data protection law that was about to take effect.

"This is the most far-reaching law anywhere in the world for individual privacy," she said, "and the basis of the law centers around an individual's 'consent.'"

The definition of consent in this privacy law states it must be freely given, specific, informed, and unambiguous. It must be given by a clear affirmative act; it must be demonstrated that each of the above tests occurred, and it must be able to be withdrawn at any time. She explained this to her fellow jurors. "This is the *privacy* definition," she said. "Surely there is a specific legal definition of *consent* for criminal acts such as aggravated indecent assault."

It turns out there isn't, at least not in Pennsylvania.

The jury sent a note to the judge, requesting a definition of the word.

The judge replied in open court. His reply was perplexing to the jury; they were informed that there isn't a definition—that is, Pennsylvania law does not offer a definition of "consent," and the judge advised the jury to define the word for themselves.

In the end they went without defining it at all.

"Cosby did not deny performing the act of penetration," Carmel said. "Constand said explicitly she did not consent."

That was key. In Pennsylvania, in sexual assault cases, believing the victim, finding her credible, is enough to convict.

AFTER THAT, THE JURY continued this way through the charges, repeating them several times, and parsing each phrase to make sure they fully understood the essences and implications of each word. "It's almost like diagraming sentences and flowcharting charges," Scelza said. "We were trying to decipher what these charges really meant because it's complex legal language. We wanted to make sure we really understood what we were being asked."

Several hours passed in this way, and then the jury shifted their focus to the witnesses. They discussed and debated which ones they found credible, which ones they found not credible, and which were just irrelevant.

They all agreed they found Andrea credible, and they all agreed that the five accusers were credible too. "Together they showed a pattern," Scelza said. "Some of them were quirky, but I say, 'So what? Who amongst us is perfect?' I don't care if somebody took drugs. I don't care if somebody kept a photo album or memorabilia. None of that had any-thing to do with the fact they were sexually assaulted."

But they were not in agreement about Margo Jackson. Some felt she was believable; others were unsure. "I really did not buy Margo's tes-timony," Scelza said. "There were several reasons, including the fact that she did not have an expense report for 2004 but did for 2003. . . . She wouldn't even look at us while she was testifying."

And they also wanted to make sure they understood what Cosby said happened because his statements were so disjointed and ram-bling. Of course, Cosby wasn't an actual witness—he was never on the stand—but his deposition excerpts offered the jury an opportunity to read Cosby's testimony under oath.

So the jury returned to the courtroom to rehear Cosby's deposi-tion testimony, which took two hours, and then they returned to the courtroom again the next morning to hear Jackson's testimony re-peated too.

They listened closely, and then they again adjourned to the jury room. After hearing Jackson's testimony once again, the jurors who had believed her changed their minds. They all now agreed she was not credible.

Not long after that, the jury was ready—they wanted to vote.

Each of the three charges was read aloud, and charge by charge, the group voted by raising their hands.

The votes were unanimous on all three offenses.

Knowing the defense or prosecution could ask to poll each juror in-dividually, Carmel read each charge again and had each juror respond verbally before she put a single mark on the verdict sheet.

Nothing changed.

OUTSIDE THE COURTROOM reporters, lawmakers, and other officials could only wonder how the jury was faring, but one thing we expected was for the deliberations to last several days, if not weeks. But after only fourteen hours of jury deliberations, we were notified that court would reconvene at 1:30 P.M. That was in fourteen minutes. Could it be a verdict? Was it another mistrial? No one was saying.

Stunned, everyone rushed to the courtroom.

The courtroom was completely silent as we watched the jury file in, looking somber. Carmel's hands shook as she handed the verdict sheet to the court official, who read three charges aloud and asked Carmel to declare the verdict for each.

Guilty.

Guilty.

Guilty.

Each time she said the word *guilty*, the courtroom erupted with gasps. I'm pretty sure some of them were mine. By the third time Carmel was calm and steady, confident in the decisions the jury had made.

"I know it's the right decision," she told me later of why her hands were shaking at first. "But at the same time, I know what it means to this American icon we have known as Dr. Huxtable, and to the victims, knowing that their voices are finally heard."

It was an emotional moment for her—and for many in the room. Lili Bernard was so overcome that she had to be escorted out of the courtroom. Andrea was stoic. She didn't let any emotions show until she was out of the courtroom with Troiani by her side, hugging her as she smiled. Camille was nowhere to be found.

I just sat there, stunned. I'd thought maybe it was possible they'd convict him on one count, but all three? It was truly hard to absorb. But I had to shift my attention back to the courtroom because we weren't done yet, and I wanted to make sure I didn't miss anything.

Steele immediately moved to revoke Cosby's bail. If the judge agreed, Cosby would no longer be able to live at home until his sentencing, as he had since he was arrested on December 30, 2015, when he paid 10 percent of a $1 million bail. Steele wanted him in jail and argued to the judge that Cosby was a flight risk.

"This is somebody who has unlimited wealth," he said. "I don't think any amount of bail can be assured under these circumstances. We'd ask that bail be revoked under these circumstances."

O'Neill wasn't convinced and asked Steele why he thought Cosby might flee.

"Your Honor," Steele replied, "he has the wealth to go any place in the world. He's got a plane."

Cosby was listening to this exchange and suddenly burst out, yelling at Steele.

"He doesn't have a plane, you asshole!" he shouted. Then he muttered, "I'm sick of that guy."

It was the only time I'd seen him lose his composure. For just a moment, I thought, the mask slipped, and we saw the real Bill Cosby.

O'NEILL DENIED STEELE'S MOTION. Sentencing would be scheduled later, after Cosby underwent various psychological evaluations. Cosby could remain at his Elkins Park home until then on house arrest, which meant wearing an ankle monitor.

There's something poetic about him being confined to the home where he drugged and sexually assaulted Andrea, I thought.

Camille lived at their home in Massachusetts, and even Cosby himself was rarely at their Pennsylvania home.

Now he couldn't leave it.

Mesereau wasn't satisfied and vowed to appeal.

"We don't think Mr. Cosby is guilty of anything, and the fight is not over!" he told reporters.

Meanwhile the jurors were quickly taken back to their hotel in nearby Plymouth Meeting, with the media in pursuit. When they arrived at the hotel they had to be escorted through the shipping entrance and up the freight elevator to the top floor of the six-story building. The jurors gathered on the balcony overlooking the courtyard and watched the media swarm below.

The reporters, seeing the jury peering over the balcony ledge, called up to them with questions. When that didn't work, they set off to stalk the jurors at their homes. Someone had leaked their identities to select members of the media, so it wasn't long before eager reporters swarmed jurors' neighborhoods. The jurors were bewildered—they'd been told their names wouldn't be released for another few weeks. Instead, many returned to their neighborhoods to find news vans parked in front of their homes.

The media didn't let up for several days. Even when jurors were clear that they didn't want to be interviewed, they were contacted over and over again, by text message, email, social media, and at their front doors. When that didn't work, the media reached out to neighbors, friends, and family.

"They were all showing up at my door," Carmel said. "Then they were calling my family members, even my husband's ex-wife."

Carmel had just walked into her home when a producer for *Good Morning America* showed up, telling Carmel that she had a limo waiting outside and inviting her to come to New York City for an interview. Carmel politely declined.

The next morning, Andrew Wyatt and Ebonee Benson called the verdict a "public lynching" on *Good Morning America* and said one of the jurors was a "racist." "I think these jurors got it wrong," Wyatt said. And some news outlets were speculating about whether the jurors were swayed by the #MeToo movement or hailing it as the first victory of the movement.

Organizer that she is, Carmel quickly arranged for the group to hold a conference call, and during that call the jurors decided to release a statement to the media. In the statement they said their verdict was based on the evidence they heard in court—and *only* the evidence.

Scelza reiterated that when I spoke with her, saying the jury was committed to doing "the right thing," and "doing the right thing was looking at all the evidence from both sides and delivering the right verdict." She was adamant on this. "If there were any doubts in that room," she said, "we made sure we cleared them up."

SEVERAL DAYS LATER Camille Cosby released a statement of her own. In it she lashed out at the media, at Steele, and at the entire prosecution team. She compared her husband's case to that of Emmett Till, a fourteen-year-old African American boy who was lynched in 1955 Mississippi after being falsely accused of leering at a white woman, and Darryl Hunt, an African American man who served nineteen years in prison after being falsely convicted of raping and murdering a white woman in North Carolina in 1984.

"These are just two of many tragic instances of our justice system utterly and routinely failing to protect African Americans falsely accused in so-called courts of law and the utterly unfair court of public opinion," she said in her statement. "In the case of Bill Cosby, unproved accusations evolved into lynch mobs. . . . I am publicly asking for a criminal investigation of that district attorney and his cohorts. This is a homogenous group of exploitive and corrupt people whose primary purpose is to advance themselves professionally and economically at the expense of Mr. Cosby's life. If they can do this to Mr. Cosby, they can do so to anyone."

I struggled with this message. Of course, I knew Cosby had been found guilty. And I couldn't help but think that with all his wealth and power, he wasn't the profile of a typical African American male convicted of a sex crime. There's no doubt the criminal justice system is vicious to black men—they get longer sentences for their crimes and are imprisoned at five times the rate of white men. Five times! And for black men serving time for sexual assault, they are three and a half times more likely to be innocent than white defendants; the bulk of those wrongful convictions stem from white victims mistakenly identifying their African American assailant. It's a depressing statistic and a horrible reality for the African American community—for everyone, really.

And yet . . . that wasn't the case here. There was no mistaking Cosby for someone else. Nor are the Cosbys a typical African American family, with their reported worth of $400 million and multiple higher-education degrees. All I knew was that race is an entrenched injustice in our country and that it was a sensibility Camille held onto—tightly.

IN PENNSYLVANIA SENTENCING must be imposed within ninety days of a verdict. Cosby's seven lawyers, who would soon be out of a job, successfully lobbied to have it pushed back to late September, citing their conflicting schedules.

There was a lot at stake. Cosby was facing up to thirty years in a state prison. Few sexual assault victims see their attackers arrested and convicted. Even fewer see their attackers go to prison. Although just 5.7 percent of rapes end in an arrest, only 0.7 percent result in a conviction and 0.6 percent result in incarceration.

Whether Cosby went to prison depended largely on one person.

Andrea.

CHAPTER TWENTY-NINE

NO ONE IS ABOVE THE LAW

For nearly fourteen years Andrea kept to herself, seeing few people and talking to almost no one outside of her family and clients.

First, she was muzzled by her own confusion over what had happened to her, how her beloved mentor and friend had betrayed her in the worst way possible. Then the criminal investigation put strict boundaries around what she could say and when and who she could talk to or be seen with. And then, again, the same restrictions were demanded of her during her lawsuit, which ended with her signing a confidentiality agreement stipulating that she could never speak publicly about what happened to her. Nor could her parents.

For all those years Andrea lived alone, with two dogs for company. Her trust had been shattered, so she let few people in. Her life revolved around her work helping people with Parkinson's disease, arthritis, diabetes, and cancer cope with the ravages of age, chemotherapy, and radiation. She had her family, and she practiced yoga and meditation. But she had been stuck in a dark, lonely place for many years.

With all this silence, only Andrea and those close to her knew what her life had been like since her assault. But Cosby's sentencing hearing allowed her—finally—to speak out about her feelings. Cosby's attorneys and spokesperson had vilified her for years, calling her a liar and a con artist, claiming she made up the drugging and sexual assault allegations to extort money from him. I hoped that finally being able to speak her truth about the devastating effects of sexual assault might help her get at least some of her confidence back.

The first day of sentencing was unseasonably gloomy and cold, much like the entire April retrial. It was as though the weather remembered the dark chill in the air as Bill Cosby was tried for his crimes and came back to witness the final pronouncements for what he had done.

Outside the courtroom on September 24 there was a heavy media presence. The satellite trucks were back. Reporters and camera crews gathered on the front steps, ready to hear the outcome and catch the reactions to it. They had their lenses trained on the accusers in particular—Janice Dickinson was there, along with Chelan Lasha, Lise Lotte-Lublin, Cindra Ladd, Therese Serignese, Lili Bernard, and Victoria Valentino. And, of course, Andrea.

One attendee I'd been looking forward to seeing that day was Tamara Green. She'd told me she was coming, but she'd also said that about the retrial and then changed her mind.

But she got a spark to be in the room to witness Cosby's sentencing, so nine days before, she'd climbed into her RV and headed east from her southern California home. The road trip gave her time to reflect on this final reckoning of the man who traumatized her and her life— that is, until her RV broke down in rural Tennessee and she then had to fly the rest of the way. But she was there and ready to witness Cosby's final moment in the courtroom.

I didn't recognize her at first. Though I knew her hair was now shorter and gray because I'd seen more recent photos of her, in my head she was still the red-haired, vibrant, outspoken woman who'd held her own while being pummeled unmercifully on live TV for telling the truth. On the day of Cosby's sentencing she seemed smaller somehow and quieter— though she still had her witty sense of humor, joking that she actually was smaller because she'd lost a couple of inches in height since 2005.

In all the years I'd been covering the case, Tamara and I had spoken many times but had never met in person, so I was eager to talk with her that day. I wanted to see her and to thank her. She'd trusted me to tell her story all those years ago, and I wanted her to know I was grateful and that what she had done was brave and important. If she hadn't, most of the Jane Does wouldn't have come forward, and we might not be here today to watch Cosby finally pay the price for his sins.

I found her in the crowd and tapped her on the shoulder. Her eyes widened when she saw me and I introduced myself since I didn't know if she knew what I looked like, she flashed a huge smile, and we hugged for a long, long time.

I also got to speak with Andrea for the first time. Our eyes had met during closing arguments and we'd exchanged a silent few words in the courtroom, but I'd never really spoken with her. Now I could! During one of the first courtroom breaks of the day I found her.

After all these years we were finally face to face. Andrea smiled her enigmatic half-smile, saying again, "It's been a long time," the same words she'd mouthed to me at closing arguments. She was serene and beautiful, with a gaze that made me feel she was staring right into my soul. There was so much I wanted to say, and at the time there was too much to say. She just isn't the type of person you have small talk with. Instead, I asked, "Have you ever met Tamara Green?" She hadn't.

This was someone she should meet. The only person who had paid a heftier price for coming forward than Andrea was Tamara. She was sitting a few rows back and on the other side of the room, so I called out to Tamara and introduced the women and watched as they hugged each other tightly. They traded murmurs of kindness and love, and Andrea gave Tamara a jade bracelet from her arm.

"She said it would bring me luck and peace," Tamara told me later that week. "I'm still looking at it."

I introduced her to Gianna too, and Kivitz and Troiani, who had never met her in person. She went to dinner with all of them, including Andrea and her family, after the sentencing. It lifted her spirits.

"We would drink a toast to me and what I did, and pretty soon I was feeling pretty heroic," she told me. "They were deeply grateful."

So was she. She'd had bouts of suicidal depression after the way she was ripped apart in 2005. "Frankly Bill Cosby has saved my life a couple of times because I refused to die and give him my life," she said.

Being with all of them, feeling their warmth, knowing she'd made a difference after all had helped her to start healing in a way nothing else could.

It was surreal to sit in the courtroom, all of us together in one room. Dolores Troiani. Bebe Kivitz. Andrea. Andrea's family. Tamara. And Cosby, for that matter. We'd been there together at the beginning of this nearly fourteen-year journey, and here we were now, nearing the end. It was a full-circle moment.

As the judge called the room to order on Monday morning Andrea sat in the second row, behind the detectives and prosecutors, with her sister and her parents. Her tousled, curly hair—once long and wild—was now even shorter than it was at the second trial, with playful deep gold highlights on the top. She had always exuded a calm, serene presence in the courtroom, whether she was being cross-examined or sitting quietly and listening to the prosecution's closing arguments. Sometimes she even closed her eyes and seemed to be meditating. And she was just as composed today, but she seemed lighter somehow. Happier, I hoped.

At 2:00 P.M., wearing a crisp blazer over a pale blue dress shirt, Andrea took the stand.

She began by talking about a four-and-a-half-page victim-impact statement, which she'd given to prosecutors earlier in the summer. Today she was not going to read it aloud in court. She was submitting that statement for the record, to stand as her testimony, to share her experience of how what happened forever changed who she is:

> When the sexual assault happened, I was a young woman brimming with confidence and looking forward to a future bright with possibilities.
>
> Now, almost 15 years later, I'm a middle-aged woman who's been stuck in a holding pattern for most of her adult life, unable to heal fully or to move forward . . .
>
> Bill Cosby took my beautiful, healthy young spirit and crushed it. He robbed me of my health and vitality, my open nature, and my trust in myself and others.

But she said none of that in the courtroom. Cosby didn't deserve to see her bare her soul. Andrea sat straight in her chair and spoke with clear, unhesitating tones. "I have testified," she said to the room, her red-rimmed bifocals perched on her nose. "The jury heard me. And now all I am asking for is justice as the court sees fit."

After Andrea's moment on the stand, the others followed. One by one, her mother, father, and sister gave statements to the courtroom. Gianna went first. She couldn't bear to think about how the crime changed her daughter, so she focused on the devastating impact it had on her as well, causing a multitude of physical ailments.

"I deal with my own trauma on a daily basis," said a teary Gianna, her shoulder-length dark brown hair now sunbleached a lighter shade and held off her face with a small barrette. "From the time our daughter opened up about the incident our lives became a rollercoaster that never came to an end. . . . Bill Cosby for years through his lawyers and the media, used every powerful tool at his disposal to destroy our reputations, [and] physical and mental state of minds to protect and shield his reputation."

She went on to describe how they found themselves under siege, with reporters tricking them into interviews and trapping them in their own homes by camping out on their doorsteps, preventing them from going to work. But then she brought the message back to the women and to Andrea. "The victims cannot be unraped," she lamented. "All we can do is hold the perpetrators accountable."

Then it was Andrea's father's turn. A handsome, silver-haired man wearing a dark suit and tie, he spoke of how Andrea was different after she moved back home in April 2004. Once Andrea finally revealed what had happened to her, he too went through a deep transformation, feeling "an immense pain that most probably only a father having been through this kind of situation can comprehend." The psychological pain so interfered with this sleep, he confessed, that he began taking a sedative to get some rest and still relies on the medication to help him cope with the past.

"The thought of what happened to my daughter Andrea will always be with me forever like a dark cloud hanging over my head," he said, his voice shaking at times. "I feel profound love and compassion for my daughter . . . so many years of trauma she has gone through."

Andrea's older sister, Diana Parsons, described the sister she knew growing up together, raised by two loving, amazing, supportive parents who instilled values and morals in them both at an early age. "She was full of energy and had a sweet personality but, more importantly, had an unbelievable zest for life," she said. But the sister who returned home in April 2004 was not that woman. Instead, Diana saw "a frail, timid, nervous, weak, reclusive" woman. When she found out what had happened to her, she felt so shocked and helpless. As tight as her family is, the impact will never go away.

"Many people always ask me how my sister is doing," she said. "I always answer, 'She's doing fine. Thank you.' Then I ask myself, I wonder how she really is doing? How can she handle being called a pathological liar? . . . How did she have the courage to come forward and tell our mother what happened to her? And how will she ever trust again?"

No ONE FROM Bill Cosby's family was by his side in court. Not his children, not Camille.

But Camille was still vocal and outraged. In fact, the week before, she had hand delivered an ethics complaint about Judge O'Neill to the state's Judicial Conduct Board. Her complaint claimed that O'Neill had a grudge with Castor dating back to 1999 when they both ran for district attorney and O'Neill dated a woman in Castor's office.

She also called O'Neill "arrogant," "corrupt," and "unethical" and revealed she'd hired a retired FBI agent to investigate the judge.

If she thought this would intimidate the judge into delaying sentencing, she was wrong. O'Neill was there, if a little weary. Which I could understand. It had been nearly thirty-four months since he took the case—more than enough time to wear on one's being. And there was a grave task in front of him: soon he'd be sentencing America's Dad to prison for what could be the rest of his life.

BEFORE O'NEILL COULD sentence Cosby, he had to determine something else: whether or not Bill Cosby should be classified a "sexually violent predator." The classification would require that Cosby participate in monthly counseling for the rest of his life and lifetime registration as a sex offender. And it was the judge's decision to make.

In order to be labeled a sexually violent predator, a person has to be diagnosed with a "mental abnormality" or "personality disorder" that makes him likely to repeat his crimes. But Cosby wouldn't cooperate with a psychiatric evaluation, so Dr. Kristen Dudley, a forensic psychologist and member of the state's sex offender assessment board, had to rely on trial transcripts and police reports to make a diagnosis. In court, she shared her findings: she concluded that Cosby suffered from a mental disorder that gave him uncontrollable urges to have sex with women without their consent—and that he would likely do it again.

Cosby's new lawyer, Joseph Greene, objected, saying Cosby was too old to be a threat. To support his claim, he put his own expert on the stand—Dr. Timothy Foley, a forensic psychologist. But it didn't take long to see that Foley wasn't solidly familiar with the case. He hadn't read the trial transcripts or the police reports or even his client's own deposition. And he'd only spent three hours with Cosby by way of assessing him;

during that time, he admitted, he wasn't allowed to ask Cosby any questions about Andrea or any of the other women who accused him.

Still, he said he believed Cosby wasn't a threat and that he posed no danger of hurting anyone.

"He's eighty-one years old," Foley said. "He's been convicted of a sex offense. Sex offense recidivism declines as you age, and after seventy it becomes virtually negligible."

Foley returned to his seat, and then it was time for O'Neill to pronounce. He acknowledged the opinions of the witnesses and then told the room that he had reached a decision.

He was designating Cosby as a sexually violent predator.

There was little time for the room to react because the judge and the defense team immediately launched into a discussion over the rules and policies required of a sexually violent predator. Among other restrictions, Cosby would need to adhere to Megan's Law, which required him to notify the state police if he moved.

That designation prompted a series of questions and answers between O'Neill and Cosby's then co-prosecutor Stewart Ryan and Cosby, the only times Cosby spoke during the entire two days.

O'Neill told him he had the right to speak on his own behalf if he chose, which Cosby declined.

"No," Cosby said firmly. "I don't need any more discussion on that."

Ryan, at the prosecution table in the front of the courtroom, then turned toward his right to face Cosby, who was sitting at the defense table and had turned toward him. Ryan asked him a series of questions.

A couple of times, Cosby asked his own. "If I went from a city to another city, even if it's just overnight, do I have to get in touch with the state police?" Cosby wanted to know. You should ask your lawyer but yes, he was told. He went on to ask more questions about the law's requirements: Who would be notified of his status as a predator? Who was responsible for making those notifications? And so on.

It was an unusual back and forth, Ryan told me later. Typically a defendant would ask his or her attorney, not the prosecutor.

"I found it interesting that he wanted to ask me lots of questions and make sure that I knew—and everyone else knew—that he was paying close attention," Ryan said. "With the perpetrator, as much as it's about sex, it's also about power. There were many instances in the case where I was reading a statement from him or his deposition, and you could see he wanted to remain in control.

"I don't think there was much difference when he wanted to question me on the ins and outs of Megan's Law," he said. "I don't think I've ever had a situation where the questions were that complex."

After that, only the sentencing itself was left.

IT WAS TIME. Cosby's day of reckoning was finally here, and the lawyers stood up to address the judge. Steele argued that Cosby should be sentenced to five to ten years in a state prison. Greene said he shouldn't be imprisoned and should remain on house arrest.

O'Neill heard both men and then made his pronouncement. He said he had put a great deal of weight on the "devastating trauma" Cosby had caused Andrea and her "extraordinary" family. "Nobody is above the law, and no one should be treated differently or disproportionately because of where they live or who they are in terms of wealth, fame, celebrity, or even philanthropy," he said. "It is time for justice."

And with that, he sentenced Cosby to three to ten years in a state prison, bail denied.

Andrea, who had remained stoic throughout the proceedings, turned around and hugged Lise Lotte-Lublin, who was sitting behind her and her family with accusers Stacey Pinkerton, Janice Dickinson, and Chelan, who had taken out loans so she could be at his sentencing. I'd seen Chelan pacing up and down the middle of the courtroom before sentencing began, giving herself a quiet pep talk as she fought off tears.

"This is going to be big for me. This is going to turn my life back around to the way it was when I was seventeen, before this happened," she said. Soon she was openly weeping.

When we spoke many weeks later she was still hopeful that could happen, that she could get back the life he stole from her.

"He took my special away," she said, sobbing. "He took my innocence. That man broke me but I got my strength back when I was finally able to look at him in court and say what he did to me."

A few rows back accusers Victoria Valentino, Therese Serignese, and Lili Bernard held hands and cried.

Cosby, who'd been smiling during most of the two days, was silent. Avoiding eye contact with anyone other than his lawyers, he began preparing himself to be escorted to prison. Even though his incarceration was inevitable, he tried to control what he could, while he could. He slowly removed his suit jacket and his tie, leaving just his white dress shirt held up by red suspenders. He rolled up his sleeves, preparing himself for the handcuffs, smiling and joking with Andrew Wyatt and his attorney all the while. When Janice Dickinson looked straight at Cosby and laughed out loud, a deputy sheriff came over and told her to quiet down or she'd need to leave.

Then court officials allowed him one last courtesy: they ushered everyone out of the courtroom while they placed the handcuffs on him. Eventually, though, he was led out of the courtroom, with his cane clutched awkwardly between his shackled hands while hundreds of onlookers watched and pool photographers and videographers captured the moment. Everyone was quiet; you could even hear the dull hum of normal courthouse activity in the background.

As Cosby walked out of the courtroom, flanked by sheriff's deputies, his eyes down and smiling an odd smile, I couldn't tell if he looked frightened, confused, or defiant. Maybe he was just in shock. After decades of wealth, celebrity, and power, he wasn't used to not getting his way.

Tamara was also there, watching as the Cosby procession made its way down the hall. Trembling, she raised her right fist in the air. Then, for all her bravado and quips during the last two days, she dissolved into tears.

"Watching him be dragged somewhere he didn't want to go, I kept thinking, 'That's how I felt, you son of a bitch,'" she said. "Unable to save myself. Unable to do a goddamn thing. Utterly helpless."

Though the hall outside the courtroom was bursting with people, there was dead silence for a moment after he was gone.

For me it was a dreamlike sight—unreal and so very real at the same time. In all my time covering this case I don't think I'd ever imagined this scenario. But this was not about me.

It was about Andrea.

She'd said she wanted justice as the court saw fit.

I hope she feels she got it.

A NEW LEGACY

The afternoon of the sentencing brought an outpouring in more than one way. After Cosby was led away in handcuffs, his spokespeople gathered on the front steps of the rain-drenched courthouse to address the sprawl of reporters and camera crews. Standing under a wide umbrella, an outraged Andrew Wyatt called Cosby "one of the greatest civil rights leaders" of the last fifty years and said the trial was "the most sexist and racist" in the history of the United States.

"Mr. Cosby knows God is watching over him," Wyatt shouted to the crowd. "He knows that these are lies. They persecuted Jesus, and look what happened. Not saying Mr. Cosby is Jesus," he added, "but we know what this country has done to black men for centuries."

Race had always been a haunting backdrop to this story, and even at the end it was still all around us. Wyatt was hoping Cosby's downfall would invoke memories of so many tragic cases in which innocent African Americans were wrongly accused or convicted. And for some his imprisonment brought to mind a raw awareness of the injustices black men in America so commonly experience. It was sad to think of who should be free and who shouldn't and how often we get it wrong. This time we got it right, but that didn't make the other cases any less tragic.

Hannah Giorgis, who covers culture for the *Atlantic*, wrote about this in the Cosby aftermath. "There are countless black men in America whose interactions with the criminal-justice system have been marred by the specter of racist policies, practices and ideologies." But, she said, "Bill Cosby's story is simply not one of them. He is a man whose prestige finally stopped overshadowing his predation. To lose sight of that is its own injustice."

Even for those African Americans who don't particularly care for Cosby, like comedian DL Hughley, his prison sentence stirred up strong emotions. Hughley wrote about it on Twitter and Facebook, calling Cosby's mug shot "one of the saddest things I've ever seen."

Then, a few days later, Hughley posted about another recent case: a white doctor raped a heavily sedated patient and was sentenced to ten years' probation, no prison time. He pointed to the case as further evidence of entrenched racism in the criminal justice system. His post: "Proof: #Justice means #Justus."

I had also felt a lingering sadness when I thought about Cosby. It started when I saw those red suspenders he was wearing when he removed his suit jacket, remnants of a bygone era, something Cliff Huxtable used to wear. I was exhausted and overwhelmed, so it took me a couple of days to figure out why. But then it hit me: I was sad because it was finally clear to me, after all this time, that Cliff Huxtable, America's most beloved dad, was never anything more than fiction. A character. A persona Cosby invented and then skillfully used to get what he wanted, at anyone's cost. He was nobody's hero, and perhaps he never should have been.

Jewel Allison wrote beautifully about this in her essay for the *Washington Post* in March 2015:

> Cosby was once a source of hope for many African Americans. But fictional icons like him should not wield so much power over our collective spirit. Our nation's greatest African Americans have been on the front lines of civil rights efforts, not in our television sets. They are in the mothers and fathers who fought real-life challenges to raise us and in the teachers and professors who worked long hours to educate us. Bill Cosby did not lead the March on Washington, and *The Cosby Show* didn't end racism. The only legacy at stake is one of entertainer, not of black manhood, as I once feared.

There's no doubt that legacy is now in tatters.

Most of his sixty-plus honorary degrees have been revoked, including the one from Temple University. The Kennedy Center Honors for lifetime achievement and the Mark Twain Prize for American Humor were rescinded. The Academy of Motion Picture Arts and Sciences voted to expel him. Some buildings that once bore the Cosby name have been rechristened. And, in one final indignity, the Television Critics Association rescinded his 2002 career achievement award, for the first time in its history.

One honor that likely won't be taken from him, though, is his star on Hollywood's Walk of Fame. Protesters called for it to be removed, but the local chamber of commerce refused, saying the star was a testament to his professional accomplishments, not his personal life.

But that doesn't mean it's safe. Since 2014 it's been defaced more than once with the words "rapist" and "serial rapist."

Recently someone else added another phrase: #MeToo.

IN THE WEEKS after the trial I kept in touch with some of the victims. The sentencing was closure for many of them, I found, but not the end of their suffering. Many were experiencing flashbacks, triggered by all of the publicity about the case or simply by talking about what happened to them again. The aftereffects of what happened to them would likely linger for the rest of their lives. For them it would never really be over.

After the sentencing, a few blocks away from where Wyatt was defending Cosby, a group of Cosby's accusers held a news conference. Many of them hadn't been allowed to speak in court about the impact the sexual assault had on them, and each one wanted a chance to have her story heard. The drumming rain underscored their powerful, heartbreaking stories.

Sunni Welles was a seventeen-year-old virgin when she said Cosby drugged and raped her in 1965. She's now seventy and single, with PTSD and night terrors. She couldn't bring herself to say Cosby's name and simply addressed him as "B.C."

"You have, in essence, destroyed so much of my life," she said, fighting off tears. "Not only who I am today at seventy years old but who I was and could have been or would have become in this world."

Lili Bernard spoke of her multiple suicide attempts, night terrors, panic attacks, and PTSD, saying Cosby threatened her life if she told anyone what he'd done. "Bill Cosby has taken away years of peace from me," she said. "Fear consumed my life."

AND STACEY PINKERTON, who had never before revealed her identity, was there, too. She is victim number sixty-four by my count.

She spoke briefly, simply saying Cosby had drugged and sexually assaulted her in 1986 and that the experience left a permanent mark. "No matter what, these things stay with you," she said. "It affects your health and your trust. I tried to block it out and kept going."

In late December 2018, she told her whole story to me, the first time she has made it public.

Stacey was a twenty-one-year-year-old flight attendant when she met Bill Cosby. She'd shared a ride from her hotel to the airport with one of Cosby's assistants, who then introduced her to Cosby on the plane, and the two struck up a conversation, in which Cosby encouraged her to pursue modeling and acting.

When Stacey reached home two days later, there were messages on her answering machine from Cosby and his assistant, inviting her to New York, which she happily accepted. In New York, Cosby began mentoring her, even getting her a role as an extra on *The Cosby Show*.

Cosby was generous with his time and attention, so Stacey had no reason to be suspicious when he invited her to dinner in Chicago with some friends a few weeks later. At dinner, she sat next to Cosby, chatting and drinking a glass of wine; at one point, she left her chair to talk to some guests at the other end of the table. Then, a little while later, she went to the ladies room—and returned to find Cosby and the other dinner guests gone and the maître d' waiting for her.

"Where is everyone?" she asked him. She was in a dreamlike state, unsure how long she'd been in the bathroom. He only replied that "the driver knows where to take you," and he ushered her into a limousine, which drove her to the Drake Hotel.

Inside the hotel, she asked the front desk staff where the Cosby party was, thinking maybe Cosby and his dinner guests had moved their get-together to the hotel. The desk staff was no help; they offered her no information and refused to tell her if Cosby was even staying there.

Suddenly, she remembered something that had happened at the restaurant—before she had left the table for the ladies room, Cosby had shoved a key in her hand. He wouldn't tell her what it was for, though she'd asked—maybe that was the clue to where he and his friends had gathered. So she made her way to the room number that matched the key, and found herself in Cosby's suite. He arrived a few minutes later. Alone.

Cosby offered her a glass of champagne, which she accepted, and took a couple of sips. Then he told her he had a present for her, an oversized Philadelphia 76ers sweatshirt signed by Larry Bird, and asked her to put it on. After she did, he pushed her on the bed and started to rape her. "I kept saying, No! No!" but she couldn't fight him off. "It was as if I was completely paralyzed," she said. The last thing she remembers before she passed out is seeing his face two inches from her own. She woke up hours later and fled.

After that night, her stability was shattered. She moved from city to city, finally settling in Spain in 1989, where she's been ever since.

"It affected me enough I left my career, my friends, my family," she said. "No place was far enough away from Mr. Cosby."

But when news of Cosby's conviction reached her, she knew she had to attend his sentencing, for her own sense of justice, and maybe some closure, too. Both days, she sat in the courtroom with Lise, Chelan, and Janice Dickinson, listening to the testimonies. Then, after the sentencing, she spoke at the victims' press conference. "It was liberating," she said. "And with him behind bars, I feel safer."

Still, much of that night is still missing from her memory. She'll never know for sure exactly what happened that night. Did he put something in her glass of wine at the restaurant? Did he drug her again with the glass of champagne? Like so many of the other women, she will never know the whole truth of what he did to her.

Of course, not all the victims were there that day. Some couldn't come; others didn't want to. And for all we know, there are still victims who haven't come forward, who watched the press conferences on their TV sets, silent and separate. P. J. and Beverly Johnson say they know of others who Cosby drugged and assaulted but are too scared to come forward.

After everything these women endured, I could understand why.

Still, Dolores Troiani says she's received a number of phone calls from sexual assault victims since the case reemerged in 2014. "Some have just said, 'I've never told anybody about this, and I want to tell you,'" she said. "It's very sad. I'm glad that they can call here. And I never, ever say to them, 'You've got to tell the police.' I don't think anyone should ever second-guess those choices. . . . Unlike every other crime, this is a very personal choice."

Could someone have gotten in a car accident and died after he drugged them, too intoxicated to be at the wheel? Both Becky Cooper and Tamara Green aren't quite sure how they escaped that fate. Could someone have accidentally overdosed? We'll likely never know.

What we do know is that for the foreseeable future Cosby will be known simply as Inmate NN7687. Housed in a medium-security state prison in Skippack Township, Pennsylvania, he has his seven-by-thirteen cell to himself but eats and socializes with the other inmates. He is one of the oldest inmates, one of a small number of men in their eighties. Outside the prison walls his appeals will go on, as will the various lawsuits for and against him. They may drag on for years.

I wasn't able to talk to Andrea; she is still bound by the confidentiality agreement she signed in 2006 when she settled her civil case. But I was happy for her. I hope finally seeing justice served will allow her to move forward and give her that second chance to be the person she was meant to be—the person she spoke of in her statement. She deserves to be happy. She deserves to enjoy a life filled with laughter and love.

I also hope her family finally finds peace and gets their old Andrea back, the daughter with the appetite so big that they joked she had a hollow leg, the sister with a zest for life who chased her nieces and entertained them with funny antics, pretending to be Cruella de Vil.

Andrea spoke of the burden she carried being the only one of the sixty-plus victims whose case could be tried in a court of law. She felt responsible for the future mental and emotional well-being of every one of Cosby's sexual assault victims who came before her. Though she never showed it publicly, the attacks on her integrity and her character caused debilitating stress and anxiety. It was the most difficult thing she has ever done, she said, and she did it not once but twice—for one reason only. It was the right thing to do.

Andrea can rest now. And she can go to sleep each night knowing she helped not only all the others who Cosby victimized but also all the sexual assault victims out there who haven't seen justice.

Cases like hers are hard to win. But she proved it can be done.

ACKNOWLEDGMENTS

Throughout this journey there have been so many who have helped make this book possible. First and foremost, I am deeply grateful to all of the Cosby survivors who trusted me to tell their stories through the years. I wish I had room to include all of them but that simply isn't possible. I want to give a special shout out to Tamara Green and all 12 of the original Jane Does. Without their courage in coming forward in 2005, I don't think Andrea would have found justice. Tamara and Beth Ferrier (Jane Doe Number Five) trusted me to tell their stories to the world first and, now, Patte O'Connor (Jane Doe Number Six), Denise Ferrari (Jane Doe Number Eight), and Virginia Bennett (Jane Doe Number Nine) have as well. I am honored. A special thanks also to the other accusers and Jane Does I've come to know, including: Lili Bernard, Becky Cooper, Tony Hogue (he is almost an honorary Jane Doe for first bringing Denise Ferrari's story to the attention of Andrea's lawyers), P. J. Masten, Sammie Mays, Kristina Ruehli, Therese Serignese, Patricia Steuer, Joan Tarshis, Heidi Thomas, Jennifer "Kaya" Thompson, Stacey Pinkerton, Jewel Allison, Janice Baker-Kinney, Lise Lotte-Lublin, and Chelan Lasha.

I also want to thank Andrea's attorneys, Dolores Troiani and Bebe Kivitz. You've proven time and again you were telling the truth all those years ago. Though you are both still shockingly humble about what you have accomplished, I'm sure Andrea knows how lucky she was to get the both of you as her attorneys.

As a first-time author I had no idea what to expect from a book editor, but it was clear from the beginning that I struck gold with Seal Press's Laura Mazer. Not only did she share both my vision and passion for this book, she is a brilliant editor who helped hone and shape this into one that I think manages to enlighten and inform, while also giving you the entire sordid history of this case. Her guidance, razor-sharp editing skills, and keen intelligence helped me in more ways than I can count. She was there when I needed her and let me be when I didn't. Her kindness, sense of humor and unflappable demeanor helped me navigate a series of crushing deadlines. Along the way, she also patiently answered my questions so I could better understand how the editorial process works, newbie that I am. (I still need to ask her what "second pages" are.) She is easily the best editor I have worked with and I have worked for some amazing ones. I mean it when I say this book would not have been possible without her.

Nor would it have been possible without my agent, Sharlene Martin of Martin Literary Management. I first thought about writing a book about this case back in 2005, but ultimately decided not to. The agent I approached was lukewarm about the idea; unwilling to be the one to dismantle the Cliff Huxtable/ Bill Cosby myth and, after the intimidation tactics Cosby's attorney used against me, I wasn't convinced it would ever get published. When that same agent came back to me in November 2014, now eager to pursue that book, I was the one who had to say "No." I just didn't have time with the demands of my job at *People*, especially since our staff was smaller than ever after yet another round of layoffs. I realized I may have missed my chance but so be it. And then came Sharlene, who finally made it happen. Like Laura, she shared my passion for this subject. She also shared her theory about the possibility that a woman could have died after being drugged by Cosby, which I explored as best I could and have not yet given up on. Someday, Sharlene. Someday!

I was extraordinarily lucky to get a dynamic publicist, Seal Press's Sharon Kunz. She was hard at work lining up opportunities to publicize the book while I was still toiling away writing it. Project manager Christine Marra, copyeditor Josephine Mariea Moore, and attorney John Pelosi helped make sure everything passed muster grammatically and legally, while Hachette's design team came up with a powerful cover design that I just know will catch people's eyes, whether they are strolling through a bookstore or trolling the Internet.

I had some go-to experts along the way as well. Back in 2005, it was Delilah Rumburg and, when she wasn't available, Karen Baker from the National Sexual Violence Resource Center and the Pennsylvania Coalition Against Rape. In recent years, it was Kristen Houser from the same groups. Time and again, they were fierce advocates for the sexual assault victims they help each and every day, educating the public about victim behavior and rape myths and calling out those who use smear tactics against them. Survivors who need help can find it at https://www.nsvrc.org/find-help.

Former prosecutor Dennis McAndrews, who owns his own law practice in Berwyn, Pennsylvania, helped me fact check legal issues and became my go-to legal analyst for my stories after his friend, colleague, and fellow former prosecutor Joe McGettigan passed the baton to him. A special thanks to Ally McAndrews for always making sure I connected with Dennis.

Former FBI profiler Mary Ellen O'Toole skillfully took me into the mind of a serial sexual predator so I could better understand "icon intimidation" and how it factored into this case. A special thank you also to forensic psychologist J. Reid Meloy; forensic toxicologist Anthony Costantino; Trinka Porrata; Lindsey Pratt; Gene Grabowski; and former Montgomery County prosecutor Stewart Ryan for lending their expertise as well.

Jurors Cheryl Carmel and Dianne Scelza were invaluable in helping me understand how they deliberated and came to make the gut-wrenching decision to convict America's Dad. Until I spoke with them, I never really thought about the fact that no one tells a jury HOW to deliberate once they get back in that jury room. This jury was the epitome of what you hope you get in our system—smart, thoughtful, and courageous, unwilling to be swayed by anything but the evidence.

I can't say enough about the bravery of the editors at my former employer, the *Philadelphia Daily News*. Kurt Heine was the city editor and is the one who set me loose on the story, then just sat back and let me go. He trusted me completely, making sure to run things up the flagpole when needed but never interfering with what I was reporting or writing. Thank you for your faith in me, Kurt. And a special thanks to Michael Days, who was the editor of the paper at the time, for never backing down. This story was so difficult on so many levels, but it could not have been in better hands.

At *People*, I was lucky enough to have many talented colleagues who helped cover the story, but I want to single out Jeff Truesdell for his sensitivity, compassion, and professionalism. Editor Betsy Gleick was a champion for our 2006 story while Samantha Miller and Alicia Dennis were total pros who oversaw our later coverage.

In late 2014, a young journalism graduate student named Kate Walz reached out to me. She was writing her thesis about Bill Cosby and the media. She thanked me for all of my early coverage, saying I was a role model for her and without my stories from 2005, she would have had virtually nothing to work with from that time period. Now it's my turn to thank her. She sent me her paper, which was such a thorough history of Cosby's entire life she had even turned up articles from the 1960s: I would never have known about these articles, since the databases I have access to don't date back that far. So, thank you, Kate. I had two months to write this book and your research helped guide me, saving me so much time.

When I was growing up, my parents, Bill and Roni Weisensee, taught me how to dream big. From the time I was a little girl they made it clear to me that my gender should never be a barrier to what I wanted to accomplish; that I could be anything I wanted to be. While my mother came to rue that advice at times, often fretting about me working too much and neglecting my personal life, especially when she knew she was dying, I know she truly wanted me to have it all, in love and in life. Her words continued to guide me after her death in 1994 and still do to this day. My father not only instilled in me a strong work ethic, as well as the mantra "work hard, play hard," he taught me about strength, resilience, loyalty, compassion, and honor. And how, when times get tough, humor can sometimes be the best way to cope. I watched how tenderly he cared for my mother for the two and a half years she was sick, especially those last few months when she could no longer swallow food and had to get her nutrients by IV. Knowing how fiercely independent she was, he prepared her food each day himself, never complaining. Together, they showed me what a marriage should be, that I should settle for nothing less. And I didn't.

Which brings me to my husband, Sean Egan, who has my deepest love and gratitude. He has lost me time and again to this story, sometimes for months at a stretch. He's put up with late nights, early days, and weekend work and a distracted wife so hyper focused on making sure her work was mistake free, that she sometimes had him lower on her priority list than he deserved to be. Sean may not have understood my obsession with finding out the truth or why I refused to let the story go, but he never tried to stop me from chasing it. He's always supported my dreams and been proud of my accomplishments. I owe him more than I will ever be able to say. I don't know where I'd be without him in my life. Certainly, it wouldn't be where I am now. I love you.

SOURCES

Transcripts of all of the court proceedings as well as all of the documents associated with the Cosby criminal case can be found at "Commonwealth v. William Henry Cosby, Jr.," Montgomery County, Pennsylvania, www.montcopa.org/2312/Common wealth-v-Willliam-Henry-Cosby-Jr, the official court website for the case. It also links to the sites for the courts that are handling his appeals. I used these transcripts and documents to double-check my own note taking. Documents for the various civil lawsuits can be found at pacer.gov, except for Castor's defamation lawsuit against Andrea and her attorneys, which Castor has since withdrawn, but can be found at: https://courts.phila.gov.

For details about Cosby's life, career, and upbringing, my primary source was *Cosby*, Mark Whitaker's 2014 biography of the comedian, because Cosby himself cooperated with him, giving him access few writers have been able to get.

So I don't have to laboriously include each and every one of my hundreds of Cosby stories below, you can find many of them on my website, NicoleWeisensee Egan.com, which is also where you can watch videos of most of my 2005 national television appearances. The stories from 2005 remain difficult to find on my former newspaper's website, but they are all on mine and in LexisNexis. I also list them here. My *People* stories are even more difficult to find. The magazine does not put its stories into LexisNexis and many of my online stories were lost when *People* redesigned its website in 2016 and migrated to a new system. I've included what I can find below.

"9 to 5 Boss Dabney Coleman Cops Cosby's Celebrity Net Tourney." *Jet*. July 2, 1981.

Abrams, Dan. *Abrams Report*. MSNBC. January 26, 2005; February 8, 2005; February 18, 2005; March 9, 2005; May 10, 2005.

Adams, Val. "Bill Cosby of 'I Spy' Series Wins TV Emmy; First Negro Cast in a Lead Role." *New York Times*. May 23, 1966.

Allison, Jewel. "I Let Race Trump Rape." *Washington Post*. March 6, 2015.

Allyn, Bobby. "Bill Cosby Makes Surprise Stand-Up Appearance Ahead of Retrial." NPR. January 23, 2018.

——. "Jurors in Cosby Trial Out of View Thanks to Screen 'Monstrosity.'" WHYY .org. June 10, 2017.

"Arizona Wins Women's NIT." United Press International. March 23, 1996.

Armstrong, Mark. "Cos Cracks 'Enquirer.'" Eonline.com. March 8, 2000.

Associated Press. "Ban on Quaaludes Approved." June 17, 1984.

Associated Press. "Bill Cosby Demands Retraction of Enquirer Sex-Abuse Story." March 6, 2000.

Associated Press. "Bill Cosby Retrial: 'Goal Was to Make Bill Cosby Feel Uncomfortable,' Says Topless Protester." April 9, 2018.

Associated Press. "Cosby Sells in Los Angeles." November 20, 1986.

Associated Press. "Reagan Loses Out to Cosby as Most Admired Man." October 10, 1986.

Associated Press. "The Latest: Lawyer Accuses Cosby Team of Smear Attempt." April 9, 2018.

Associated Press International. "Bill Cosby Jokes Woman Should Be Careful Drinking Near Him." January 9, 2015.

Associated Press Online. "Cosby Says Allegations Won't Stop Activism." June 29, 2005.

Aurthur, Kate. "18 Moments That Led to Bill Cosby's Stunning Downfall." *Buzzfeed*. November 21, 2014.

———. "Bill Cosby #CosbyMeme Hashtag Backfired Immediately." *Buzzfeed*. November 10, 2014.

———. "Bill Cosby Tells a Woman 'Be Careful About Drinking Around Me' During His Standup." *Buzzfeed*. January 9, 2015.

Bahadur, Gaiutra, and Chris Gray. "Montco DA Well Poised for State Campaign." *Philadelphia Inquirer*. December 2, 2002.

Baker, Katie. "Barbara Bowman Speaks About Bill Cosby Sexual Allegations." *Newsweek*. February 12, 2014.

———. "Tamara Green Talks About Bill Cosby." *Newsweek*. February 7, 2014.

Baker, Katie J.M. "Another Woman Comes Forward Accusing Bill Cosby of Rape." *Buzzfeed*. March 3, 2015.

Barclay, Dolores. "The Rise and Fall of a Much-Abused Drug." Associated Press. November 18, 1983.

Barnes, Tom. "Campaign 2004: GOP Race for Attorney General Gets Rough." *Pittsburgh Post-Gazette*. April 21, 2004.

Basile, George. "Temple Rescinds Cosby's Honorary Degree." *The Tab*. April 27, 2018.

Bauder, David. "NBC Nixes Cosby Project, TV Land Pulls Reruns." Associated Press. November 21, 2014.

———. "NBC, TV Land, Netflix Pull Plug on Cosby-Related Entertainment." Associated Press. November 20, 2014.

Baum, Matthew A., Dara Kay Cohen, Yuri M. Zhukov. "Does Rape Culture Predict Rape? Evidence from U.S. Newspapers, 2000–2013." *Quarterly Journal of Political Science* 13, iss. 3 (August 30, 2018).

Beck, Lia. "Model Jewel Allison Accuses Bill Cosby of Sexual Abuse & Her Story Follows a Familiar Pattern." *Bustle*. November 24, 2014.

Belloni, Matthew. "Charlie Sheen, Sharon Stone, Arnold Schwarzenegger Toast Marty Singer at Wild Lawyer of the Year Dinner." *Hollywood Reporter*. April 18, 2012.

Berlet, Bruce. "UConn Women Land One Recruit, Lose Two." *Hartford Courant*. November 13, 1991.

———. "UConn Women Ranked 17th in AP Poll." *Hartford Courant*. November 19, 1991.

Berman, Taylor. "Hannibal Buress Called Bill Cosby a Rapist During Set." *Gawker*. October 20, 2014.

Bernard, Lili. "I'm One of Bill Cosby's Accusers. His Defense Strategy Is Reprehensible." *Los Angeles Times*. June 7, 2017.

"Best Sellers: Hardcover Nonfiction." *New York Times*. October 12, 2014.

Bever, Lindsey. "Bill Cosby's 1970s Anti-Drug Album for Kids: Say 'No to Pills.'" *Washington Post*. July 23, 2015.

Bianculli, David. "Can Bill Cosby Make TV History Again?" *CNN Wire*. January 23, 2014.

"Bill Cosby Awarded the Presidential Medal of Freedom." 2002. White House. YouTube.

"Bill Cosby Awards." IMDb.com.

"Bill Cosby Celebrity Tennis Tournament to Benefit Medical Center." *Jet*. May 3, 1973.

"Bill Cosby Exclusive Interview." *ABC News, Nightline*. May 15, 2015.

"Bill Cosby Fast Facts." CNN Library. September 26, 2018.

"Bill Cosby Hollywood WOF Star Defaced . . . with 'Serial Rapist.'" *TMZ*. September 27, 2018.

"Bill Cosby Paid to Keep Affairs Secret: Deposition." *ABC News*. July 19, 2015.

Blake, Meredith. "Bill Cosby's 'Drinking' Joke Incurs More Gloria Allred Wrath, Fresh Outcry." *Los Angeles Times*. January 10, 2015.

Bollag, Sophia. "Inspired by Accusations Against Bill Cosby, California Lawmakers Move to Lifetime Limits on Rape Cases." *Los Angeles Times*. August 30, 2016.

Botkin, Ben. "Cosby Sexual Assault Bill Signed; Statute of Limitations Extended." *Las Vegas Review-Journal*. May 27, 2015.

Bowerman, Mary. "Jill Scott No Longer Supports Bill Cosby, 'Completely Disgusted.'" *USA Today*. July 7, 2015.

Bowley, Graham. "Prosecutors Want Cosby 'Spanish Fly' Comments as Evidence at Trial." *New York Times*. March 30, 2017.

Bowley, Graham, and Sydney Ember. "Cosby Detailed Many Affairs in Testimony." *New York Times*. July 19, 2015.

Bowley, Graham, and Jon Hurdle. "A Tenacious Team of Two in the Cosby Case." *New York Times*. February 16, 2016.

Bowman, Barbara. "Bill Cosby Raped Me. Why Did It Take 30 Years for People to Believe My Story?" *Washington Post*. November 13, 2014.

Bradley, Diana. "How Bill Cosby's Defense Team Is Defending Its Client in the Press." PRweek.com. October 2, 2016.

Brady, James. "Brady's Bunch." *Advertising Age*. November 4, 1991.

Brodesser-Akner, Taffy. "Hannibal Buress Was Funny Long Before Bill Cosby Wasn't." *GQ*. July 22, 2015.

Brokaw, David. "Statement from The Brokaw Company: Bill Cosby Responds to Media Criticism." *PR Newswire*. May 22, 2004.

Brown, Stacy. "Former DA's Bombshell Affidavit Could Clear Bill Cosby." *Blackpress USA*. October 23, 2018.

——. "NNPA Newswire Exclusive: Bill Cosby Finally Breaks His Silence." *NNPA Newswire*. April 26, 2017.

——. "Paranoid Bill Cosby Fears His Drink Will Be Spiked Before Trial." *New York Post*. May 27, 2017.

——. "Upbeat Cosby Expects 'Black Media' to Stay Neutral." *New York Post*. December 13, 2014.

Bryan, Kenzie. "Bill Cosby Mounts Bizarre P.R. Campaign in Philadelphia." *Vanity Fair*. January 23, 2018.

Bueno, Antoinette. "Exclusive: Janice Dickinson Details Bill Cosby Sexual Assault: He Raped Me." *Entertainment Tonight*. November 18, 2014.

——. "Keshia Knight Pulliam Supports Bill Cosby on First Day of Sexual Assault Trial: Pics." Ew.com. June 5, 2017.

"Business Report: On Media and Advertising: Study Links Celebrities, Products." *Atlanta Journal and Constitution*. October 29, 1991.

Cabrera, Ana. "Cosby's Denver Show Draws Protests." CNN.com. January 17, 2015.

Cady, Jennifer. "Exclusive: Janice Dickinson Suing Bill Cosby for Defamation." ETonline.com. May 20, 2015.

Callas, Toni. "Cosby Visit Surprises Students; Don't Become 'a Nobody Living Amongst Nobodies,'" He Urged Them." *Philadelphia Inquirer*. June 22, 2006.

"Camille Cosby." *Contemporary Black Biography*. Vol. 80. June 2010.

"Camille Cosby Tells the Tabs What She Thinks." [San Jose, California] *Mercury News*. February 7, 1997.

Campisi, Gloria. "Cosby's 'Call-Out' Comes to Philly." *Philadelphia Daily News*. December 21, 2006.

Carlson, Cheri. "Media on Watch for Venturan Who Says Cosby Fondled Her." *Ventura County Star*. February 10, 2005.

Carr, David. "Calling Out Bill Cosby's Media Enablers, Including Myself." *New York Times*. November 24, 2014.

Carroll, Linda. "Police Get Rape Kits in Small Percentage of Cases." Reuters. August 7, 2018.

"Castor to Revisit Rabinowitz Murder on Upcoming TV Show." *MainLine Times*. January 24, 2012.

Celebrity Justice. "CJ Obtains Confidential Document in Cosby Case" January 27, 2005.

——. "Cosby Accuser's Mom Contacted Cosby Before Cops?" February 7, 2005.

——. "Cosby's Attorneys Claim Accuser After Cash." February 9, 2005.

Chang, Juju. "Judging Cosby: Inside the Tense Jury Room." *Nightline*. June 26, 2017.

Chen, David. "Bill Cosby Was Target of Extortion." *New York Times*. January 21, 1997.

Chinchilla, Rudy. "Hollywood Chamber of Commerce Rejects Calls for Bill Cosby's Walk of Fame Star Removal." NBC-4. September 25, 2018.

Chuck, Elizabeth. "Bill Cosby Conviction Is the First Big Win of the #Metoo Movement." NBCNews.com. April 26, 2018.

Cieply, Michael. "Guard Dog to the Stars (Legally Speaking)." *New York Times*. May 21, 2011.

City News Service. "Gloria Allred Presents 3 More Women Claiming Sexual Abuse by Bill Cosby." *San Bernardino Sun*. January 7, 2015.

Cleveland, Claire. "Gov. Hickenlooper Signs Bill Extending Rape Statute of Limitations, Inspired by Cosby Allegations." *Denver Post*. June 10, 2016.

Coates, Ta-Nehisi. "The Cosby Show. Declining to Seriously Reckon with the Rape Allegations Against Him Is Reckless. And I Was Reckless." *Atlantic*. November 19, 2014.

Cobb, Jelani. "Harvey Weinstein, Bill Cosby, and the Cloak of Charity." *New Yorker*. October 14, 2017.

——. "What Shielded Bill Cosby?" *New Yorker*. November 24, 2014.

Colford, Steven. "How to Find the Right Spokesman." *Advertising Age*. October 28, 1991.

Corey, Dan. "A Growing List of Sexual Misconduct Since Weinstein." Associated Press. November 8, 2017.

Cornfield, Josh. "Cosby Accuser Also Testified Against Marv Albert." The Associated Press. Dec. 6, 2014.

Corriston, Michele. "Bill Cosby's Wife Camille Defends Him." People.com. December 15, 2014.

Cosby, Bill. "Comedian Cosby Sees Identity Negroes' Biggest Need." *Boston Globe*. September 17, 1967.

——. "For a Touch of Color." *Los Angeles Times*. September 17, 1967.

Cosby, Camille. "Camille Cosby Says Vote for Justice, Equality and Democracy." *BlackpressUSA*. November 5, 2018.

Cosby, Rita. "The Big Story." Fox News Channel. February 12, 2005.

——. "On the Record." Fox News Channel. February 12, 2005.

"Cosby Accuser's Credibility Questioned by News Show." WENN Entertainment News Wire Service. February 14, 2005.

"Cosby Accuser's Mom Called Him Before Cops." UPI. February 8, 2005.

"Cosby Controversy Hits Campuses; Sexual Assault Accusations Against Bill Cosby." *Diverse Issues in Higher Education*. May 7, 2015.

"Cosby: No Brotherly Love. Philly Media Boycott, Toilet Paper Top Comic's Concert Demands." *Smoking Gun*. September 23, 2005.

"Cosby Show Theatre Picketed by Protesters over Rape Allegations." *Western Morning News*. January 18, 2015.

"Cosby Unraveled." Newsworks. WHYY-FM. May 24, 2017.

"Cosbys Clash with the 'Enquirer.'" *USA Today*. February 7, 1997.

Crook, Lawrence III, Walter Imparato, and Eric Levenson. "Bill Cosby Juror Speaks: 'We Had No Real Evidence.'" CNN. June 23, 2017.

Dale, Maryclaire. "Attorney: Cosby Lawyer Denies Fondling Allegations by Second Woman." Associated Press. February 9, 2005.

——. "Bill Cosby's Wife Wants Ethics Board to Investigate Judge." Associated Press. September 17, 2018.

——. "Cosby Attorney Questions Why Accuser Took So Long to Come Forward." Associated Press. January 21, 2005.

——. "Cosby Said He Got Drugs to Give Women for Sex." Associated Press. July 7, 2015.

——. "Prosecutor: Bill Cosby Won't Face Charges in Alleged Sexual Misconduct." Associated Press. February 17, 2005.

——. "Prosecutor Cites Weaknesses in Woman's Allegations Against Cosby." Associated Press. January 26, 2005.

——. "The Cosby 13: Meet the Women Being Asked to Testify at Trial." Associated Press. December 3, 2016.

Dalton, Meg. "Is the News Media Complicit in Spreading Rape Culture?" *Columbia Journalism Review*. October 26, 2018.

Davis, Linsey. "ABC News Exclusive: Phylicia Rashad Speaks." *Nightline*. January 7, 2015.

——. "Bill Cosby Speaks to Fans in New Video." *ABC News*. March 9, 2015.

——. "Exclusive: Bill Cosby Breaks Silence About Sexual Assault Allegations." *ABC News*. May 15, 2015.

——. "Inside the Cosby Jury: Jurors Describe Tense Deliberations." *ABC News*. June 22, 2017.

De Moraes, Lisa. "Petition Demanding Return of Bill Cosby's Medal of Freedom to Trigger White House Action at 100k Signatures." *Deadline*. July 10, 2015.

DeHuff, Jenny. "Castor to Run Again for DA." *Philadelphia Daily News*. January 8, 2015.

Dent, Mark. "Bill Cosby's Fall: How an Extra Ticket, an iPhone and a Six-Month-Old Comedy Bit Changed How We View a Comedy Legend." BillyPenn.com. December 3, 2014.

——. "'Complete Nonsense': Ex-D.A. Bruce Castor on His Undisclosed Tie to Bill Cosby.'" BillyPenn.com. February 25, 2016.

DePaulo, Lisa. "Why Did Bruce Castor Pass on a Chance to Lock Up Bill Cosby?" *Bloomberg*. November 26, 2014.

Depper, Jenny. "Bill Cosby's Daughters Release Statement to Try and Prove Their Father's Innocence." Aol.com. May 15, 2017.

Derschowitz, Jessica. "Bill Cosby's Walk of Fame Star Vandalized." *CBS News*. December 5, 2014.

Devlin, Frank. "Drew Lewis Accused Again of Drunk Driving." [Allentown] *Morning Call*. August 15, 2001.

Dillon, Nancy. "Trolled Models: Cosby Got 'Dates' via Fashion Agent." [New York] *Daily News*. July 24, 2015.

Dillon, Nancy, and Sasha Goldstein. "Joke's on Us. Cos Dodges Assault Questions in Wacky Sitdown." [New York] *Daily News*. May 16, 2015.

——. "Bill Cosby Rape Accusers Asking Judge to Unseal Full Transcript of 2005 Testimony." [New York] *Daily News*. July 13, 2015.

Dorfman, Dan. "Cosby's NBC Bid Belittled. Reported Quest Draws a 'No Sale' from GE." *USA Today*. June 15, 1993.

Dorsey, Tom. "Cosby's Cliff Huxtable Is the Top Post on List of Best TV Dads." [Louisville, Kentucky] *Courier-Journal*. June 18, 2005.

Dougherty, Philip H. "Advertising: Bill Cosby to Appear for Kodak Colorwatch." *New York Times*. December 24, 1986.

"Drew Lewis Expected to Plead Guilty in DUI." [Norristown, Pennsylvania] *Times Herald*. January 9, 2002.

Durham Regional Police Department Incident Report. January 13, 2005.

Dyson, Michael Eric. *Is Bill Cosby Right? Or Has the Black Middle Class Lost Its Mind?* New York: Civitas Books, 2005.

Eady, Brenda. "A New Book Says Doctorates in Education—Including Actor Bill Cosby—Are a Joke." *People*. November 18, 1985.

Edgers, Geoff. "Bill Cosby to Baltimore Hecklers: We Are Here to Enjoy My Gift." *Washington Post*. March 28, 2015.

"Editor's Choice: Recent Books of Particular Interest." *New York Times*. September 28, 2014.

Edwards, K. M., J. A. Turchik, C. M. Dardis, N. Reynolds, and C. A. Gidycz. "Rape Myths: History, Individual and Institutional-Level Presence, and Implications for Change." *Sex Roles* 65 (2011): 761–773.

Egan, Nicole. "A Jane Doe in Cos Case Seeks Time to Protect ID." *Philadelphia Daily News*. June 11, 2005.

——. "Accuser Andrea Constand's 2005 Statement Read in Court as Bill Cosby Ordered to Trial." People.com. May 24, 2016.

——. "Accuser Described as Outgoing, Forthright." *Philadelphia Daily News*. March 9, 2005.

——. "All About Bill Cosby's Accusers—and the Fall of a TV Icon." People.com. November 24, 2014.

——. "Andrea Constand on Why She Finally Told Her Mother Bill Cosby Allegedly Drugged and Sexually Assaulted Her." People.com. June 2, 2016.

——. "Another Cosby Accuser Speaks Out: Jane Doe No. 5." *Philadelphia Daily News*. June 23, 2005.

——. "Bill Cosby Accuser Beth Ferrier Says She Lost 'Everything' After Going Public in 2006." People.com. November 21, 2014.

——. "Bill Cosby Accuser Tamara Green Is Ready for Her Day in Court. People.com. October 29, 2015.

——. "Bill Cosby Accuser Tamara Green Files Defamation Lawsuit." People.com. December 20, 2014.

——. "Bill Cosby's Accuser Taped Calls with Him." *Philadelphia Daily News*. February 5, 2005.

——. "Bill Cosby Admits He Gave Woman Quaaludes Then Had Sex in Newly Released 2005 Court Papers." People.com. July 6, 2015.

——. "Bill Cosby Drops Breach-of-Contract Lawsuit Against Sex Assault Accuser Andrea Constand." People.com. July 28, 2016.

——. "Bill Cosby Says He's Blind, While Daughter Defends Him in Essay." People.com. April 26, 2017.

——. "Bill Cosby Sexual Assault Trial Begins Monday: How He Went from 'America's Dad' to Defendant." People.com. June 5, 2017.

——. "Bill Cosby Steps Down from Board of Trustees at Temple University." People.com. December 1, 2014.

——. "Bill Cosby: From Mentor to Sexual Predator?" People.com. May 2016.

——. " Bill Cosby: I Did Not Give Women Drugs or Have Sex with Them Without Their Consent, New Court Docs Say." People.com. July 21, 2015.

——. "Bill Cosby's Attorney Threw a Fundraiser for Former Prosecutor Who Declined to Bring Charges Against the Comedian, Court Documents Say." People.com. March 18, 2016.

——. "Bill Cosby's Lawyer Says Former District Attorney Made Promise Not to Prosecute Him. 'A Promise Is a Promise.'" People.com. February 3, 2016.

——. "Bill Cosby's Sex Assault Investigation Was Abruptly Shut Down in 2005, Detective Testifies." People.com. June 8, 2017.

——. "Camille Cosby Can be Deposed but Can Refuse to Answer Certain Questions, Judge Rules." People.com. February 11, 2016

——. "Camille Cosby Never Read Deposition in Which Bill Cosby Admits to Offering Women Quaaludes, New Court Docs Say." People.com. March 9, 2016.

——. "Camille Cosby Wants Second Deposition Canceled After She Was Asked 'Offensive' Questions About Her 'Sexual Relations', Politics and Son's Death." People.com. March 16, 2016.

——. "Camille Cosby's Attorneys File Emergency Motion to Stop Her Deposition Wednesday." People.com. January 4, 2016.

——. "Chilling New Details of Bill Cosby's Alleged Sexual Assault of Andrea Constand Revealed in Complaint." People.com. December 30, 2015.

——. "Cos Accuser's Lawyers: There's More to Tell. They Seek to Add Statements from Ten More Women." *Philadelphia Daily News*. April 9, 2005.

——. "Cos Challenges Anonymity of Accusers." *Philadelphia Daily News*. June 22, 2005.

——. "Cos Discusses Scandal." *Philadelphia Daily News*. March 3, 2005.

——. "Cos Met Accuser's Parents After Alleged Incident?" *Philadelphia Daily News*. January 25, 2005.

——. "Cos Offered $ to Accuser. Mom Alleged Recorded Call Made After Claim Was Filed." *Philadelphia Daily News*. February 7, 2005.

——. "Cos Says He Did Give Woman Pills—Benadryl." *Philadelphia Daily News*. May 10, 2005.

——. "Cosby Accuser Sues Him." *Philadelphia Daily News*. March 9, 2005.

——. "Cosby Accuser Taking the Heat." *Philadelphia Daily News*. February 10, 2005.

——. "Cosby Accusers Now Number 13." *Philadelphia Daily News*. April 27, 2005.

——. "Cosby Attorneys Want Documents Sealed." *Philadelphia Daily News*. April 28, 2005.

——. "Cosby Jokes on Stage About Doping Drink." *Philadelphia Daily News*. March 8, 2005.

——. "Cosby Puts Career on Hold in Wake of Groping Allegations, He Cancels Two More Appearances." *Philadelphia Daily News*. January 22, 2005.

——. "Cosby Wants Data on 9 Accusers." *Philadelphia Daily News*. April 19, 2005.

——. "Cosby's Lawyer Under Fire." *Philadelphia Daily News*. January 29, 2005.

——. "Cosby's Lawyers Deny He Has Refused to Be Deposed." *Philadelphia Daily News*. April 23, 2005.

——. "Court Papers: Cosby Declines Deposition." *Philadelphia Daily News*. April 20, 2005.

——. "DA's Dad Aided Mansion Buy." *Philadelphia Daily News*. February 19, 2005.

——. "Date Rape Alleged 'Nova Sophomore Accused." *Philadelphia Daily News*. February 14, 2001.

——. "Democrat Kevin Steele Wins District Attorney Race Where Decade-Old Bill Cosby Case Became the Issue. People.com. November 4, 2015.

——. "Exclusive: Alleged Victim of Bill Cosby Will Cooperate with Prosecutors If Charges Are Brought Against Him." People.com. September 22, 2015.

——. "Exclusive: Arrest Warrant Issued for Bill Cosby for Alleged January 2004 Sexual Assault of Andrea Constand. People.com. December 30, 2015.

——. "Exclusive: Bill Cosby Accuser Andrea Constand Files Defamation Lawsuit Against Former Prosecutor." People.com. October 26, 2015.

——. "Exclusive: Bill Cosby Accuser Andrea Constand Threatens to Withdraw from Criminal Investigation." People.com. October 27, 2015.

——. "Exclusive: New Criminal Charge Against Bill Cosby Is Not Something Alleged Victim Andrea Constand Sought Out, Source Says." People.com. January 6, 2016.

——. "Exclusive: Some of Bill Cosby's TV Family from *The Cosby Show* Will Support Him in Court During Sexual Assault Trial." People.com. June 4, 2017.

——. "Ex-Trooper Cops a Plea." *Philadelphia Daily News*. October 4, 2000.

——. "Former Prosecutor Who Declined to Charge Bill Cosby in 2005 Says He Believed Accuser Andrea Constand." People.com. February 2, 2016.

——. "Four More Women Join Defamation Lawsuit Against Entertainer Bill Cosby." People.com. November 13, 2015.

——. "Grope Accuser Says More Coming Forward." *Philadelphia Daily News*. February 11, 2005.

——. "Jane Does in Cosby Case Seek Secrecy." *Philadelphia Daily News*. June 14, 2005.

——. "Joan Tarshis on Bill Cosby Sexual Assault Allegations: 'I Was Sickened, Embarrassed and Humiliated.'" People.com. November 19, 2014.

——. "Judge Grants Motion to Delay Deposition of Bill Cosby's Wife, Camille." People.com. January 5, 2016.

——. "Judge Refuses to Dismiss Sexual Assault Case Against Bill Cosby." People.com. February 3, 2016.

——. "Montco Authorities Meet with Cosby and His Lawyer." *Philadelphia Daily News*. January 27, 2005.

——. "New Bill Cosby Attorney Blasts Accusers." People.com. July 22, 2015.

——. "New Campaign Ad Criticizes Pennsylvania Prosecutor for How He Handled the Bill Cosby Case in 2005." People.com. October 20, 2015.

——. "No Criminal Charges Against the Cos." *Philadelphia Daily News*. February 18, 2005.

——. "Pennsylvania District Attorney Candidates Battle It Out over the 2005 Bill Cosby Sexual Assault Allegations." People.com. October 22, 2015.

——. "Physical Evidence Against the Cos?" *Philadelphia Daily News*. September 27, 2005.

——. "Setback for Jane Does in Cosby Suit." *Philadelphia Daily News*. July 8, 2005.

——. "Tamara Green Exclusive Interview. My Cosby Story." *Philadelphia Daily News*. February 8, 2005.

——. "The Surprising Reason a Bill Cosby Accuser Withdrew her Lawsuit Against Him—One Day After Legal Victory." People.com. June 27, 2016.

——. "They Want to Talk with Cos. Montco Authorities Notify His Lawyer About Grope Claim." *Philadelphia Daily News*. January 26, 2005.

——. "Trend a Bitter Pill; Women in Fear of Date-Rape Drug Spikings." *Philadelphia Daily News*. April 2, 2002.

——. "Two Other Accusers Joining Tamara Green's Defamation Lawsuit Against Bill Cosby." People.com. January 5, 2015

——. "Woman Accuses Coz of Groping Her. Ex-Temple Employee Claims She Was

Doped, Assaulted at Comedian's Montco Home." *Philadelphia Daily News*. January 21, 2005.

Egan, Nicole, with Aurelie Corinthios, Patrick Gomez, Mary Green, Steve Helling, Elizabeth Leonard, Hugh McCarten, Liz McNeil, Lynette Rice, Janine Rayford Rubenstein, and Jeff Truesdell. "The Fall of Bill Cosby." *People*. December 8, 2014.

Egan, Nicole, and Christine Pelisek. "Massachusetts Judge Refuses to Throw Out Defamation Suit Against Bill Cosby Filed by Three Alleged Victims." People. com. October 6, 2015.

Egan, Nicole, and Diane Herbst. "Camille Cosby Arrives for Deposition in Husband's Defamation Case After Judge Strikes Down Last-Minute Motion to Delay." People.com. February 21, 2016.

——. "Bill Cosby's Wife Camille Continues Deposition Today." People.com. April 19, 2016.

——. "Judge Rules Cosby's Wife Camille Can Be Deposed Again, but Scolds Opposing Lawyer for 'Crossing the Line' with Personal Questions." People.com. April 12, 2016.

Egan, Nicole, and Elizabeth Leonard. "Bill Cosby's Wife Camille Stands by Him, Says Source." People.com. January 5, 2016.

Egan, Nicole, and Greg Hanlon. "Bill Cosby's Lawyers Allege Racial Bias in Sex Assault Claims: He 'Is No Stranger to Discrimination.'" People.com. September 6, 2016.

Egan, Nicole, and Kathy Ehrich Dowd. "All about Bill Cosby's Accusers—and the Fall of a TV Icon." People.com. November 24, 2014.

——. "Bill Cosby's Original Accuser Andrea Constand Calls Him a 'Narcissist' Who Missed Cues That She's Gay." People.com. July 28, 2015.

Egan, Nicole, and Ramona Smith. "ABC: Probe Focusing on If Cos Contact Was Consensual. Philly Police Investigate Leak of Confidential Police Report." *Philadelphia Daily News*. January 28, 2005.

Egan, Nicole, and Tara Fowler. "CNN's Don Lemon Apologizes after Telling Bill Cosby Accusers How to Avoid Rape." People.com. Nov. 19, 2014.

Elber, Lynn. "Cosby's Life of Achievement Stained by Assault Conviction." Associated Press. April 26, 2018.

Ellis, Ralph. "Bill Cosby Sues Supermodel Beverly Johnson for Defamation." CNN. com. December 22, 2015.

Ember, Sydney, and Richard Perez-Pena. "Cosby Jury Named as Report Says It Leaned Toward Conviction." *New York Times*. June 21, 2017.

"Entertainment News." UPI Newstrack. February 10, 2005.

Erdely, Sabrina Rubin. "Lucky Man." *Philadelphia* magazine. December 2002.

Farberov, Snejana. "'You Raped Women, Bill Cosby': Comedian Hannibal Buress Lashes Out Against Legendary Sitcom Star, 77, During Stand-Up Performance in Philadelphia." *Mail Online*. October 21, 2014.

Farrow, Ronan. "My Father, Woody Allen, and the Danger of Questions Unasked." *Hollywood Reporter*. May 11, 2016.

——. "Sexual Assault: Harvey Weinstein's Accusers Tell Their Stories." *New Yorker*. October 20, 2017.

Finke, Nikki. "Bill Cosby's Big Adventure." *Vanity Fair.* January 8, 2015.

Finn, Natalie. "Camille Cosby Defends Husband Bill Cosby, Compares Coverage of Sexual Assault Allegations to Rolling Stone's UVA Rape Story." Eonline.com. December 15, 2014.

——. "Bill Cosby Ordered to Stand Trial in 2004 Sexual Assault: A Timeline of an Epic Downfall." Eonline.com. May 24, 2016.

Fiorillo, Victor. "Kristina Ruehli Says Bill Cosby Drugged and Tried to Sexually Assault Her, Too." Phillymag.com. November 21, 2014.

Fisher, Luchina. "10 Celebrity Responses to Bill Cosby Sexual Assault Allegations." ABCnews.com. January 22, 2015.

Fisher, Luchina, Joe Ruffolo and Lesley Messer. "'The Cosby Show' Turns 30: 30 things You May Not Have Known About the Show." ABCnews.com. September 20, 2014.

Fisher, Kendall. "Keshia Knight Pulliam Defends Her Continued Support for Bill Cosby on the First Day of His Sexual Assault Trial." Eonline.com. June 5, 2017

Fleishman, Jeffrey. "Will Hollywood Lawyer Martin Singer's Pitbull Tactics Still Work in a Post-Weinstein Era?" *Los Angeles Times.* November 3, 2017.

Forgette, Richard, and Jonathan S. Morris. "High-Conflict Television News and Public Opinion." *Political Research Quarterly* 59, no. 3 (September 2006): 447–456.

Fowler, Tara, and Diane Herbst. "Bill Cosby Released on $1 Million Bail After Being Charged in Alleged 2004 Sexual Assault." People.com. December 30, 2015.

Fox News Network. "Is the Media Giving Bill Cosby a Pass?" Fox News Watch. April 30, 2005.

France, Lisa Respers. "Conspiracy Claims Surround Bill Cosby Debate." *CNN Wire.* January 8, 2015.

Friedman, Megan. "Here's the Full Transcript of Oprah's Inspirational Golden Globes speech." *Harper's Bazaar.* January 7, 2018.

Friedman, Roger. "Clearing Up What Phylicia Rashad Said, Meant, and How I Wrote It." Showbiz411. January 7, 2015.

——. "Phylicia Rashad: Stop Before You Attack Her—Bill Cosby Could Be Anybody." Showbiz411. January 7, 2015.

Friends of Tom Corbett. "Castor Continues to Defend Unethical Treatment; Pennsylvania DAs Question Castor's Actions." April 23, 2004.

Gajewski, Ryan. "Ex-NBC Employee Claims Bill Cosby Paid Off Women." *Hollywood Reporter.* November 23, 2014.

Galivanes, Grace. "Some of the Craziest Playboy Mansion Stories." People.com. September 28, 2017.

Gardner, Chris. "Bill Cosby Bio Loses Endorsements from Jerry Seinfeld, David Letterman." *Hollywood Reporter.* July 22, 2015.

Gardner, Paul. "Comic Turns Quips into Tuition; Bill Cosby, Student at Temple, Featured at Gaslight Café. Philadelphia Negro Aims Barbs at Race Relations." *New York Times.* June 25, 1962.

Garvin, Glenn. "Bill Cosby Does Florida: Standing Ovation, Little Protest." *Miami Herald.* November 21, 2014.

Gay, Verne. "Bill Cosby Booking on 'Late Show with David Letterman' Canceled." *Newsday.* November 14, 2014.

Gayle, Stephen. "Commercial Success: Celebrities Such as Bill Cosby and Gladys Knight Are Selling Their Image to Pitch National Brands." *Black Enterprise*. December 1981.

Gennis, Sadie. "Malcom-Jamal Warner: It's 'Painful' to Watch Bill Cosby 'Go Through This.'" NBC-4 WCMH. January 23, 2015.

Gentile, Don. "Cosby Accused of Sex Attack." *National Enquirer*. March 14, 2000.

Gibbons, Margaret. "Montgomery DA Candidate Castor Urges Delay in Cosby Case Until After Elections." *Bucks County Courier Times*. September 24, 2015.

——. "'Regular Guy' Sworn In as County Judge." *The Reporter*. July 30, 2002.

Gibson, Jeremy L., and Jonathan Gore. "Is He a Hero or a Weirdo? How Norm Violations Influence the Halo Effect." *Gender Issues* (December 1, 2016): 299–310.

Giles, Matt, and Nate Jones. "A Timeline of the Abuse Charges Against Bill Cosby." *Vulture*. December 30, 2015.

Gillies, Rob. "Bill Cosby Returns to Stage for 1st Time Since November." Associated Press. January 7, 2015.

——. "Promoters Say Bill Cosby's Canadian Shows Will Happen." Associated Press. January 3, 2015.

——. "Protesters Shout at Fans as Cosby Returns to Stage in Canada." Associated Press. January 8, 2015.

Giorgis, Hannah. "Bill Cosby Is Not an Anti-Racist Martyr." *Atlantic*. September 26, 2018.

Gore, Leada. "Bill Cosby's Alabama-Based Spokesperson Compares Client to Jesus." AL.com. September 25, 2015.

Grace, Nancy, and Jean Casarez. "Cosby Cracks a Rape Joke on Stage." CNN. January 12, 2015.

Gray, Emma. "Therese Serignese, Florida Nurse, Says Cosby Drugged and Raped Her in 1976." *Huffington Post*. November 20, 2014.

Greene, Bob. "From Silver Screen to Teens' Top 10." *Chicago Tribune*. December 22, 1986.

——. "A Room at the Top—And Elvis Lived in It." *Chicago Tribune*. August 13, 1989.

Greene, Teri. "Bill Cosby Finds Supportive Crowd in Selma." *Montgomery Advertiser*. May 15, 2015.

Gregory, Kia. "Fit the Bill? Media Watchers Wonder Whether the *Daily News* Has It in for Cosby." *Philadelphia Weekly*. February 16, 2005.

Griffiths, Kaden. "Bill Cosby's Lawyer Slams Rape Claims in New Statement that Breaks Silence on the Allegations." *Bustle*. November 21, 2014.

Gross, Samuel R., Maurice Possley, and Klara Stephens. "Race and Wrongful Convictions in the United States." National Registry of Exonerations. University of California Irvine. March 7, 2017.

Grossman, David. "Albert Campbell Too Strong for Rest of the Competition." *Toronto Star*. November 30, 1988.

——. "Field Hockey Upset Possible, Coach of Favored Team Insists." *Toronto Star*. November 5, 1991.

——. "High School All Stars." *Toronto Star*. November 29, 1991.

——. "Hoops Star Set for World Stage." *Toronto Star*. August 12, 1997.

——. "Metro Hoopster Arizona Bound." *Toronto Star*. November 20, 1991.

——. "Top High School Cagers Shooting for Scholarships, Campbell's Star Headed for Arizona." *Toronto Star*. November 21, 1991.

Grossman, Samantha. "Jill Scott on Bill Cosby: 'I Stood by a Man I Respected and Loved. I Was Wrong.'" *Time*. July 7, 2015.

Grove, Lloyd. "'I Saved My Friend from Bill Cosby.'" *Daily Beast*. December 3, 2014.

Hairston, Harry. Interview with Sirius/XM Host Joe Madison. November 19, 2014.

Hairston, Harry. "Woman Makes Groping Allegations Against Bill Cosby." *NBC 10 News*. January 20, 2005.

Hanlon, Greg. "Bill Cosby Lawyer Files Motion to Dismiss Charges, Claims Prosecutor Is Politically Motivated." People.com. January 11, 2015.

Hanlon, Greg, and Tara Fowler. "Bill Cosby and Wife Camille Photographed for First Time in More Than a Year." People.com. November 24, 2015.

"Hannibal Buress Announces His National Stand-up Comedy Tour, Comedy Camisado." *PR Newswire*. September 4, 2014.

"Hannibal Buress on Moving to New York with $200 and Dreams." NPR. April 10, 2014.

"Hannibal Buress: Not High, Just Cooler Than You. The Comedian Who Toppled Cosby Stops by to Talk Fame, Jokes and the Future." Howardstern.com. October 21, 2014.

Harris, Chris. "Bill Cosby Files Defamation Suit Against 7 of His Accusers." People.com. December 14, 2015.

Harris, Dan. "Protestors Confront Cosby; Angry Mob Interrupts Show." *Good Morning America*. January 10, 2015.

Hart, Ariel. "Atlanta's Spelman College Ends Professorship Tied to Bill Cosby." *Atlanta Journal-Constitution*. July 25, 2015.

Haynes Danielle. "Bill Cosby Wasn't in LA at Time of Alleged 2008 Assault." UPI. January 16, 2015.

Haynes, Danielle. "Bill Cosby Interview with Queen Latifah Cancelled." UPI. October 31, 2014.

Haynes, M. L. "Philadelphia Stands Staunchly Behind Bill Cosby." *Pittsburgh Post Gazette*. February 19, 2005.

Herbst, Diane. "Bill Cosby's Wife Camille Completes Second Day of Testifying Under Oath About Her Husband in Defamation Lawsuit." People.com. April 19, 2016.

——. "Bill Cosby's Wife Camille Testifies in Defamation Case Against Him Following Judge's Order." People.com. February 22, 2016.

——. "Camille Cosby Defends Husband Bill in Newly Unsealed Deposition." People.com. May 21, 2016.

Heinze, Justin. "Cosby Team Claims Racial Prejudice in Jury Selection: Report." Patch.com. April 4, 2018.

Hess, Amanda. "Why Did the AP Suppress the Sexual Assault Portion of Its Bill Cosby Interview?" *Slate*. November 20, 2014.

——. "Why Doesn't Anyone Care About the Sexual Assault Allegations Against Bill Cosby?" *Slate*. February 13, 2014.

Hessler, Carl Jr. "Montgomery County's Drug Treatment Court Gains Accreditation." *Montgomery News*. January 5, 2017.

Hester, Jere. "'We've Got to Laugh.' Cos Works Through Pain; Wife Craves Justice." [New York] *Daily News*. January 27, 1997.

Hibberd, James. "Hannibal Buress Answers Questions About Bill Cosby Joke, Then Shuts Down Reporters." Ew.com. January 17, 2016.

Hinkelman, Michael. "Arguments in Cosby Case Heating Up." *Philadelphia Daily News*. May 4, 2006.

——. "Cos' Attorneys Cry, 'O Canada.'" *Philadelphia Daily News*. April 13, 2006.

——. "Cosby Accuser Assails Enquirer." *Philadelphia Daily News*. May 9, 2006.

——. "Cosby 'Stonewalled.'" *Philadelphia Daily News*. April 28, 2006.

——. "Court: Cos Must Answer Queries About Article." *Philadelphia Daily News*. February 2, 2006.

——. "Dismiss It, Asks Lawyer Sued by Cos Accuser." *Philadelphia Daily News*. May 11, 2006.

——. "Judge Refuses to Drop Tabloid from Suit Filed by Woman in Cosby Case." *Philadelphia Daily News*. June 10, 2006.

——. "Judge Won't Lift Seal on Records in Cosby Sex Case." *Philadelphia Daily News*. January 14, 2006.

——. "Woman Files Suit v Cosby Lawyer, Tab." *Philadelphia Daily News*. February 3, 2006.

Hitchen, Alexander. "Bill Cosby Knows What He Did." *National Enquirer*. February 14, 2005.

Holt, Lester, and Stephanie Gosk. "Tonight for the First Time, We're Hearing from a Juror in the Bill Cosby Sexual-Assault Case." *NBC Nightly News*. June 22, 2017.

Hornaday, Ann. "Bill Cosby: A Study in Contrasts." *Washington Post*. September 21, 2014.

Horowitz, Julia, and Daniel Weiner-Bronner. "Matt Lauer Interviews Worth Rewatching." *Money*. November 29, 2017.

Huber, Robert. "Dr. Huxtable & Mr. Hyde." *Philadelphia* magazine. June 9, 2006; November 2006.

Husted, Bill. "Cosby Feels Mile High Heat from Ex-Models." *Denver Post*. December 13, 2006.

Hutchinson, Earl Ofari. "Can Even Cosby Make a Case He's Racially Targeted?" *Huffington Post*. June 1, 2017.

Iredale, Jessica. "Can Hannibal Buress Conquer Comedy?" WWD.com. February 20, 2011.

Isenberg, Barbara, and Laker, Barbara. "At Temple, Bill Cosby Remains 'the Cos.'" *Philadelphia Daily News*. February 24, 2005.

Ivie, Devon. "42 Universities on the Status of Bill Cosby's Honorary Degrees." *Vulture*. June 19, 2018.

Izadi, Elahe. "Camille Cosby Breaks Her Silence, Compares Allegations Against Her Husband to *Rolling Stone*'s Campus Rape Story." *Washington Post*. December 15, 2014.

Jackson, Adam. "Kitchener Cosby Show Goes Off Without a Hitch Despite Protest." *Kitchener Post*. January 7, 2015.

Jang, Meena. "Former 'Cosby Show' Actor: 'Of Course Bill Cosby Is Guilty.'" *Hollywood Reporter*. July 14, 2015.

Johnson, Beverly. "Bill Cosby Drugged Me. This Is My Story." *Vanity Fair*. December 11, 2014.

Johnson, Kevin. "Hannibal Buress Addresses Cosby Controversy at Pageant Concert." *St. Louis Post-Dispatch*. October 26, 2014.

———. "Hannibal Buress Keeps Much Cooking Including 'Comedy Comisado' Tour." *St. Louis Post-Dispatch*. October 24, 2014.

Johnson, Martenzie. "Ahmad Rashad Gave the Best Response About O. J. Simpson, Bill Cosby." *The Undefeated*. June 29, 2018.

Johnson, Richard. "Al Sharpton: Bill Cosby 'Has to Answer to Someone.'" *New York Post*. November 20, 2014.

———. "Cosby Leaked Story About Daughter's Drug Problems." *New York Post*. November 24, 2014.

"Judd Apatow's Fresh Cosby Swipe." *Belfast Telegraph*. January 16, 2015.

"Judd Apatow Slams Ontario Venues for Keeping Bill Cosby Shows." Thespec.com. January 7, 2015.

Kagan, Daryn. "A Look at 'Homegrown Terror'; Allegations Surface Against Cosby." *CNN Live Today*. January 21, 2005.

Kantor, Jodi, and Megan Twohey. "Harvey Weinstein Paid Off Sexual Harassment Accusers for Decades." *New York Times*. October 5, 2017.

Kelsey, Eric. "Under Fire, Academy of Motion Pictures Expels Cosby, Polanski." Reuters. May 3, 2018.

Kennedy, James. "Cosby Tops Forbes List of Richest Entertainers." Associated Press. September 7, 1987.

Kennedy, Merrit. "California Eliminates Statute of Limitations on Rape Cases." NPR. September 28, 2016.

Kim, Kyle, Christina Littlefield, and Melissa Etehad. "Bill Cosby: A 50-Year Chronicle of Accusations and Accomplishments." *Los Angeles Times*. September 25, 2018.

King, Larry. "Ennis Cosby's Death; Family Friends Share Their Sentiment." *CNN Larry King Live*. January 17, 1997.

Kingstone, Jonathan, and Ian Robertson. "Bill Cosby 'a Mentor' to Accuser." *Toronto Sun*. January 22, 2005.

Kinneally, Tim. "Bill Cosby's Lawyer Blasts Janice Dickinson's Sexual Assault Claims as 'Outrageous,' 'Defamatory.'" *The Wrap*. November 18, 2014.

Klara, Robert. "Throwback Thursday: Bill Cosby, O. J. Simpson, Playboy Bunnies and a Tennis Tournament." *Adweek*. June 25, 2015.

Klein, Michael. "Court TV to Focus on Inn Slaying." *Philadelphia Inquirer*. November 13, 2005.

———. "Rabinowitz Murder Will be Court TV Fare." *Philadelphia Inquirer*. December 15, 2005.

Kovaleski, Serge, and Colin Moynihan. "Well Before Scandals, Cosby's Wife Faulted Treatment of Blacks." *New York Times*. January 20, 2015.

Kranes, Marsha, and David K. Li. "Cos Groped Me: 'Tainted' Lawyer." *New York Post*. February 9, 2005.

Lachman, Sheldon J., and Alan R. Bass. "A Direct Study of Halo Effect." *Journal of Psychology* 119, no. 6 (November 1985): 535–540.

Lagrone, Sam. "Navy Rescinds Bill Cosby's Honorary Chief Petty Officer Title." News.usni.org. December 4, 2014.

Lange, Ariane. "Comedian Hannibal Buress Called Bill Cosby a Rapist During Set." *Buzzfeed*. October 20, 2014.

Laskaris, Sam. "Basketball Stars Eye Mexico Trip." *Toronto Star*. August 20, 1992.

——. "Skribe Among Players Hoping for Mexico Trip with Junior Squad." *Toronto Star*. August 6, 1992.

LeBeau, Marc, and Ashraf Mozayani. *Drug-Facilitated Sexual Assault: A Forensic Handbook*. San Diego, CA: Academic Press, 2001.

Lee, Esther. "Hannibal Buress Calls Bill Cosby a Rapist During Stand-Up, Rehashes Comic's Sexual Assault History." *Us Weekly*. October 21, 2014.

Lee, Felicia. "Cosby Defends His Remarks About Poor Blacks' Values." *New York Times*. May 22, 2004.

Leonard, Lizz. "Bill Cosby Lawyer Slams New Accusations as 'Utter Nonsense.'" People.com. November 20, 2014.

Leopold, Todd. "Hannibal Buress: I've Gotten Death Threats over Cosby." CNN. March 20, 2015.

Leslie, Keith. "Bill Cosby Worried About Possible Disruptions During Upcoming Ontario Shows; Cosby Urges Canadian Fans to Remain Calm." Canadian Press. January 6, 2015.

Letsch, Corinne, Kerry Burke, and Larry McShane. "Exclusive: Bill Cosby Accused of Sexually Abusing Another Model, Jewel Allison, in '80s." [New York] *Daily News*. November 24, 2014.

Levenson, Eric, and Stephanie Becker. "Bill Cosby Says He Isn't Planning a 'Sexual Assault Tour.'" CNN. June 27, 2017.

Levenson, Eric, and Shachar Peled. "Bill Cosby Jurors Give Conflicting Accounts of Deadlock." CNN. June 22, 2017.

Levin, Gary. "Bill Cosby's Legacy: From America's Dad to America's Rapist." *USA Today*. April 26, 2018.

Levine, Barry. "Bill Cosby Ends His Silence: My Story." *National Enquirer*. March 14, 2005.

Levy, Marc. "Generous Gift Helps Castor to Lead AG's Race in Funds." Associated Press. April 17, 2004.

Lewis, Andy. "Controversial Cosby Bio Won't Get New Editions." *Hollywood Reporter*. July 22, 2015.

Lewis, Hilary. "Bill Cosby Releases First Video Messages Since Rape Scandal." *Hollywood Reporter*. March 9, 2015.

Li, David, and Dareh Gregorian. "Mama Minnelli, 95, Beats Liza in Fight over House." *New York Post*. March 1, 2004.

Lisak, David, Lori Gardinier, Sarah Nicksa, and Ashley Cote. "False Allegations of Sexual Assault: An Analysis of Ten Years of Reported Cases." *Violence Against Women* (December 2010).

Lozano, Alicia Victoria. "Sex Crimes Take Front Seat at Cosby Trial." NBCPhiladelphia.com. June 13, 2017.

Malone, Noreen. "'I'm No Longer Afraid': 35 Women Tell Their Stories About Being Assaulted by Bill Cosby, and the Culture That Wouldn't Listen." *New York Magazine*. July 26, 2015.

Mancuso, Vinnie. "Hannibal Buress Opens Up About Comedy, 'Breaking Out,' and His Problem with Ninjas." *New York Observer*. September 15, 2014.

Mandak, Joe, and Michael Rubinkam. "Cosby Panel Was Concerned About 'Politics' of Case." Associated Press. June 23, 2017.

Mangan, Dan. "Cos Groped Me: 'Tainted' Lawyer." *New York Post*. February 9, 2005.

———. "Cos in 'Hush-Up' Offer: Accuser." *New York Post*. February 10, 2005.

Manly, Lorne. "Cosby Makes a Joke About Drinking Around Him." *New York Times*. January 9, 2015.

Manly, Lorne, and Graham Bowley. "Cosby Team's Strategy: Hush Accusers, Insult Them, Blame Them the Media." *New York Times*. December 29, 2014.

Maraschiello, Tony. "US Scouts Take Notice." *Toronto Sun*. October 9, 1996.

Marcius, Chelsia Rose. "Exclusive: Ex-NBC Employee Frank Scotti Claims He Paid Off Women, Invited Young Models to Dressing Room as He Stood Guard." [New York] *Daily News*. November 23, 2014.

Margolick, David. "Hollywood Lawyer Marty Singer Can Make Any Problem Go Away—Except Bill Cosby's." *Vanity Fair*. February 6, 2017.

"Mayor to Boycott Bill Cosby's Hamilton Show." Thespec.com. January 2, 2015.

McCrystal, Laura. "Bruce Castor's Unpredictable Path to Attorney General." *Philadelphia Inquirer*. August 29, 2016.

McCrystal, Laura, and Jeremy Roebuck. "Cosby Juror Says He Didn't Believe 'Well-Coached' Constand." Philly.com. June 23, 2017.

McCrystal, Laura, and Jessica Parks. "Steele Tops Castor in Contentious Montco D.A. Race." *Philadelphia Inquirer*. November 4, 2015.

McCrystal, Laura, and Michaelle Bond. "VIDEO: Tempers flare as threat of Cosby mistrial looms." Philly.com. June 16, 2017.

McDonald, Soraya Nadia. "Bill Cosby Agrees to Offer Refunds for Two Sold-Out New York Shows." *Washington Post*. December 1, 2014.

———. "Cosby Biographer Mark Whitaker Says He Was Wrong to Exclude Rape Allegations from Book." *Washington Post*. November 26, 2014.

———. "'Cosby Show' Actress Phylicia Rashad Defends Bill Cosby; 'Forget These Women,' Rashad Said." *Washington Post*. January 7, 2015.

———. "Is the World Starting to Turn Against Bill Cosby?" *Washington Post*. October 31, 2014.

———. "Whoopi Goldberg Now Thinks the Information Against Bill Cosby 'Kinda Points to Guilt.'" *Washington Post*. July 14, 2015.

McDowell, Edwin. "Best Sellers Are Year-Round Affair." *New York Times*. June 12, 1986.

———. "'Fatherhood' and 'It' Top Sellers of '86." *New York Times*. January 5, 1987.

McFadden, Cynthia. "Bill Cosby Update on Misconduct Allegations." *ABC News*. January 27, 2005.

McGinnis, Susan. "Criminal Charges Will Not Be Filed Against Bill Cosby." *CBS News*. February 18, 2005.

McGlynn, Katie. "Bill Cosby to Receive Johnny Carson Award at 2014 'American Comedy Awards.'" *Huffington Post*. April 21, 2014.

McKelvey, Wallace. "Everybody Hates Bruce Castor, and the Acting AG Couldn't Care Less." Pennlive.com. August 9, 2016.

McLaughlin, Eliot. "Who Shows Up with Bill Cosby to Court?" CNN.com. June 13, 2017.

McLaughlin, Katie. "Bill Cosby Interrupted Twice During Last Live Show of Tour." CNN. May 3, 2015.

McQuade, Dan. "Hannibal Buress on Bill Cosby: 'You're a Rapist.'" Phillymag.com. October 17, 2014.

Means, Sean. "Comedian Hannibal Buress Says He's More of a 'Weirdo' Than an Oddball." *Salt Lake* [Utah] *Tribune*. September 4, 2014.

Mehta, Diana. "Bill Cosby Forced to Confront Abuse Allegations in Midst of Ontario Show." Canadian Press. January 8, 2015.

Meloy, J. Reid, and Mary Ellen O'Toole. "Icon Intimidation and Sexual Predation." Psychologytoday.com. January 16, 2018.

Merida, Kevin. "Cos and Effect: Bill Cosby Has Always Been One to Speak Out. Now He's Really Hearing It." *Washington Post*. February 20, 2005.

Meyer, Dick. "Cosby Stands His Ground." *CBS News*. July 2, 2004.

Micek, John. "In Montco, Lynn Swann Studies the Field; Scranton, Piccola and Castor Also Seek GOP Nod in Governor's Race." [Allentown] *Morning Call*. April 15, 2005.

Mickle, Paul. "Hamilton Actress, Model Who Accused Cosby in 2000 Wants to Leave It Alone." *Trentonian*. December 1, 2014.

Mifflin, Lawrie. "CBS Says It Would Be Unseemly to Broadcast Cosby Interview." *New York Times*. January 31, 1997.

Mills, Jeffrey. "Bill Cosby Urges Congress to Reject Cuts Hurting the Poor." Associated Press. March 3, 1982.

Mitchell, Kirk. "Denver Woman Claims Bill Cosby Drugged and Sexually Assaulted Her." *Denver Post*. August 14, 2015.

Mizrahi, Robin, and Patricia Shipp. "Cosby Drugged Me, Too!—Says the Mom of His 'Love Child.'" *National Enquirer*. February 14, 2005.

Mondics, Chris. "Cardinal Bevilacqua's Defense Attorney Connects Easily with Juries; Razor Sharp on Cross-Examination." *Philadelphia Inquirer*. September 19, 2011.

Moore, Frazier. "Bill Cosby's Guest Shot with Letterman Canceled." Associated Press. November 15, 2015.

——. "Netflix Goes for Laughs with New Stand-Up Specials." Associated Press. August 14, 2014.

Moore, Tina. "10 Witnesses Give Reasons for Anonymity." *Philadelphia Inquirer*. June 14, 2005.

——. "Cosby Accusers Can't Stay Unnamed." *Philadelphia Inquirer*. July 8, 2005.

——. "Cosby Lawyer Says Anonymity OK, If Allegations Secret." *Philadelphia Inquirer*. June 23, 2005.

——. "Judge Orders Cosby to Answer Questions on Sex and Drugs." *Philadelphia Inquirer*. February 1, 2006.

——. "Sileo Guilty of First-Degree Murder in General Wayne Inn Shooting." Associated Press. August 2, 2001.

——. "Women in Cosby Case Must Be Named." *Philadelphia Inquirer*. June 3, 2005.

Moore, Tina, and Keith Herbert. "Phone Callers in Cosby Case Slow Investigation." *Philadelphia Inquirer*. February 17, 2005.

Morelli, Lana. "Cosby Admission Read in Court: 'My God, I'm in Trouble.'" Court-house News Service. June 9, 2017.

Mosbergen, Dominique. "Smithsonian Posts Disclaimer for Bill Cosby's Art Collection." *Huffington Post*. July 15, 2015.

Moskovitz, Diana. "The Bill Cosby PR Machine Is Out in Full Force, and the Judge Is Not Amused." *Jezebel*. June 16, 2017.

——. "Documents Show How Hard Ex-DA Bruce Castor Worked to Help Bill Cosby Avoid Charges." *Jezebel*. October 20, 2017.

——. "Ex-DA Bruce Castor Is All but Officially on the Cosby Defense Team Now." *Jezebel*. November 2, 2017.

——. "Jewel Allison Set Out to Change the Minds of Bill Cosby Supporters One at a Time." *Jezebel*. June 15, 2017.

Moyer, Justin Wm. "Cosby Show Cast Member Turned Conservative Commentator: 'Of Course Bill Cosby Is Guilty." *Washington Post*. July 16, 2015.

Naff, Lycia. Exclusive: "'Bill Cosby Pinned Me Down on His Bed and Pinned Me by My Neck.'" MailOnline.com. October 27, 2014.

Nakamara, David. "Obama on Cosby Scandal: Drugging a Woman for Sex 'Is Rape.'" *Washington Post*. July 15, 2015.

"Names & Faces." *Washington Post*. February 19, 2005.

National Sexual Violence Resource Center. *Crime Reports of Sexual Violence*.

Neal, Rick, and Mike Nunez. "Cosby Gets Sellout Support at Florida Event." *USA Today*. November 21, 2014.

Nedego, Jethro. "'Queen Latifah Show' Says Cosby Wasn't Canceled." TheWrap .com. October 31, 2014.

"Net-Minded Stars Sign for Cosby Tourney." *Los Angeles Times*. April 14, 1973.

Neuman, Scott. "In NPR Interview, Bill Cosby Declines to Discuss Assault Allegations." NPR.org. November 15, 2014.

Newhouse, Sam. "Bruce Castor Goes Radio Silent on Social Media After Cosby Badgering." *Metro*. January 5, 2016.

Newsweek. "Someone at the Top Has to Say 'Enough of This.'" December 6, 1993.

Newton, Paula. "Rape Allegations Vex Bill Cosby's Second Canadian Show." *CNN Wire*. January 9, 2015.

Nightline America in Black & White. ABC News Transcripts. June 29, 2005.

Norman, Tony. "Will Cosby's Image Survive Latest Allegations?" *Pittsburgh Post-Gazette*. February 11, 2005.

North, Anna, Constance Grady, Laura McGann, and Aja Romano. "252 celebrities, Politicians, CEOS, and Others Who Have Been Accused of Sexual Misconduct Since April 2017." *Vox*. October 8, 2018.

Nunez, Mike. "Bill Cosby to Florida Today: I Won't Mention Allegations." *Florida Today*. November 21, 2014.

O'Connell, Ryan. "The View's Rosie O'Donnell vs. All of Her Co-Hosts over Bill Cosby Rape Allegations." Thewrap.com. November 20, 2014.

O'Toole, Mary Ellen. "ICON Intimidation and Predatory Behavior: From Hollywood, 'to the Newsroom,' to the Halls of Congress." *Violence and Gender* 4, no. 4 (2017).

Office of the District Attorney Bruce L. Castor, Jr. Press Release. January 24, 2005; February 17, 2005.

Oldenburg, Ann. "Cos and Effect. At 61, Self-Made Bill Cosby Is Being Made a Kennedy Center Honoree." *USA Today*. December 4, 1998.

Ordine, Bill. "Johnston May Be Up to His Old Tricks from Decoys to Diversions, the Family Led a Devious Criminal Network." *Philadelphia Inquirer*. August 15, 1999.

Ordine, Bill. "Escape Renews Johnstons' Horror." *Philadelphia Inquirer*. August 8, 1999.

Ortiz, Jen. "The GW+A: Comedian Hannibal Buress on His Worst-Ever Gig." *GQ*. March 24, 2014.

Pagano, Penny. "Messages to Be Videotaped; FBI Enlists Bill Cosby in Search for Missing Kids." *Los Angeles Times*. June 12, 1985.

Parker, Ryan, and Meredith Blake. "Bill Cosby's 'Drinking' Joke Incurs More Gloria Allred Wrath, Fresh Outcry." *Los Angeles Times*. January 9, 2015.

Parks, Jessica. "Bruce Castor Seeks Return as Montco DA." *Philadelphia Inquirer*. January 8, 2015.

Paunescu, Delia. "Bill Cosby's Massive Social Media Fail." *New York Post*. November 10, 2014.

Pearle, Lauren, and Tom Liddy. "Bill Cosby Admits to Giving Quaaludes to Woman, Seeking the Drug for Others, Court Documents Say." *ABC News*. July 6, 2015.

Peipert, Thomas. "Cosby Takes Stage Despite Protest over Sex-Assault Claims." Associated Press. January 18, 2015.

——. "Protesters Direct Chants at Cosby Before Comedian's Show in Denver." Associated Press. January 18, 2015.

Pelisek, Christine. "Bill Cosby's Wife Camille Must Testify in Defamation Lawsuit Brought by 7 Women Against Him." People.com. December 31, 2015.

——. "Three Cosby Accusers Step Forward, Demand $100 Million Victim Fund for Alleged Victims." People.com. December 3, 2014.

Petski, Denise. "Bill Cosby Kennedy Center, Mark Twain Award Rescinded." *Deadline*. May 7, 2018.

Peyser, Marc, and Allison Samuels. "Death of a 'Hero.'" *Newsweek*. January 27, 1997.

Phillip, Abby. "Bill Cosby Issues a Defiant Message to His Critics Ahead of Protests Planned for His Boston Show." *Washington Post*. February 7, 2015.

——. "Judd Apatow Slams 'Monster' Bill Cosby in an Epic Twitter Rant. 'Guys Who Rape a Lot Aren't Cool,' Apatow Declared During His Weekend Tweetstorm." *Washington Post*. December 29, 2014.

Piccola, Sen. Jeffrey E. News Release. January 28, 2005.

Podheiser, Dan. "Bill Cosby, Tom Brokaw Honored by National Football Foundation." NESN.com. August 18, 2010.

Porch, Scott. "How the World Turned on Bill Cosby: A Day-by-Day Account." *Daily Beast*. December 1, 2014.

PR Newswire. December 23, 1986.

"President Obama on Revoking Bill Cosby's Medal of Freedom." C-Span. July 5, 2015.

Prigge, Matt. "Interview: Hannibal Buress Talks 'SNL,' Ex-Girlfriends and Not Doing Serious Acting (Yet)." [Boston] *Metro*. October 14, 2014.

Puente, Maria. "Bill Cosby Says, Again, 'I'm Far from Finished.'" *USA Today*. January 15, 2015.

——. "Camille Cosby Demands Investigation of Bill Cosby's Judge for 'Unethical' Judicial Behavior." *USA Today*. September 17, 2018.

——. "'I'm Far from Finished,' Cosby Says." *USA Today*. February 26, 2015.

Pukalo, Mark. "Hawks Confident This Time Around." *Hartford Courant*. November 16, 1991.

Quinones-Miller, Karen. "Lewis Draws Special Program. His Sentence for DUI: He Cannot Drive and He'll Go to Safe-Driving Classes." *Philadelphia Inquirer*. May 22, 1996.

Rappleye, Hannah, and Tracy Connor. "Cosby Trial: Defense Wanted to Use Evidence Andrea Constand Is Gay." NBCnews.com. June 8, 2017.

Rayman, Graham. "Bill Cosby Effect: Bill Bratton Says Rape Reports Are Up in NYC Because More Victims Coming Forward About Attacks from Years Ago." [New York] *Daily News*. January 5, 2016.

Redmond, Alana. "How Millennials Are Changing Rape Culture." Socialworkhelper .com. February 19, 2017.

Rennison, C. M. *Rape and Sexual Assault: Reporting to Police and Medical Attention*, 1992–2000 [NCJ 194530]. Retrieved from the U.S. Department of Justice, Office of Justice Programs, Bureau of Justice Statistics. 2002.

Rice, Lynette. "Bill Cosby's Wife 'Supports Him on Every Level' During Sexual Assault Scandal, Says Source." People.com. November 26, 2014.

Richmond, Ray. "Cosby and Effect." Associated Press. March 2, 2007.

Ritter, Kara. "Cosby Says Youths Need Tougher Rules." *Philadelphia Inquirer*. December 22, 2006.

Robertson, Ian. "Hoops Made Andrea a Star." *Toronto Sun*. January 22, 2005.

Roberts, Kimberly. "Cosby to Receive Johnny Carson Award." *Philadelphia Tribune*. May 5, 2014.

Rocheleau, Matt, and Eric Bosco. "UMass Amherst Cuts Ties with Bill Cosby." *Boston Globe*. November 26, 2014.

Rodriguez, Meredith. "Playboy Bunny on *New York Magazine* Cover Said Cosby Raped Her in Chicago." *Chicago Tribune*. July 28, 2015.

Roebuck, Jeremy. "Bill Cosby Performs at Germantown's La Rose Jazz Club in His First Public Performance Since Abuse Allegations Put His Career on Hold Two Years Ago." *Philadelphia Inquirer*. January 23, 2018.

——. "Walter M. Phillips Jr., 76, Prosecutor of Corrupt Politicians." *Philadelphia Inquirer*. February 9, 2015.

Roebuck, Jeremy, and Laura McCrystal. "Cosby Returns to Philly, Says 'We're Ready' for Retrial." *Philadelphia Inquirer*. January 12, 2018.

——. "Nearing End, Cosby Probe Could Be Shaped by Election." *Philadelphia Inquirer*. October 27, 2015.

——. "Time Hasn't Run Out on Possible Charges Against Cosby in Pa." *Philadelphia Inquirer*. September 13, 2015.

Roig-Franzia, Manuel. "Race Dominates Fraught Jury Selection in Bill Cosby Sexual-Assault Trial." *Washington Post*. May 23, 2017.

Roig-Franzia, Manuel, and Karen Heller. "Bill Cosby's Own Words Provide Scandalous Details of His Hidden Life." *Washington Post*. July 23, 2015.

Roig-Franzia, Manuel, Scott Higham, Paul Farhi, and Mary Pat Flaherty. "Accusations Recast an American Cultural Icon." *Washington Post*. November 23, 2014.

Romeo, Tony. "Bruce Castor Eyes Possible 2014 Primary Challenge to Gov. Corbett." *KYW News Radio*. December 5, 2012.

Rosenbaum, Philip. "Cosby Tops List of Richest Entertainers." Associated Press. September 14, 1992.

Rothenberg, Fred. "The Cosby Show Off to Successful Start on NBC." Associated Press. September 21, 1984.

Rothman, Michael. "Bill Cosby Jokes About Allegations During Comedy Show." *ABC News*. January 9, 2015.

Rutenberg, Sharon. "More Quaalude Deaths from Injuries Than Overdose." UPI. February 3, 1983.

Sales, Nancy Jo. "Hugh Hefner's Roaring 70s." *Vanity Fair*. March 30, 2011.

Sanders, Craig. "Arizona Has Critical Test at Oregon." *Arizona Daily Wildcat*. February 22, 1996.

——. "Pantoja and Constand Depart After Taking Program to Next Level." *Arizona Daily Wildcat*. March 7, 1996.

Scherstuhl, Alan. "Here's the 1969 Bill Cosby Routine About Wanting to Drug Women's Drinks." *Village Voice*. November 17, 2014.

Schmidt, Tom. "The Cos Speaks Volumes." *Philadelphia Daily News*. December 22, 2006.

Schogol, Marc. "After 18 Days, Tired Johnston Stumbles into Grasp of Police." *Philadelphia Inquirer*. August 21, 1999.

School District of Philadelphia press release. "Statement from the School District of Philadelphia on Its Partnership with Dr. Bill Cosby." January 21, 2005.

Schumaker-Matos, Edward. "Asking Bill Cosby If He Is a Serial Rapist." NPR. November 20, 2014.

Scocca, Tom. "Who Wants to Remember Bill Cosby's Multiple Sexual-Assault Allegations?" *Gawker*. February 4, 2014.

Sedensky, Matt. "Florida Woman Latest to Accuse Cosby of Forced Sex." Associated Press. November 20, 2014.

Segers, Grace. "Here Are Some of the Questions Anita Hill Answered in 1991." CBSnews.com. September 19, 2018.

Severance, Ryan. "Cosby's Pueblo Show Relatively Quiet." *Pueblo Chieftain*. January 17, 2015.

Shallwani, Pervaiz. "Montco DA Ponders Race for Congress; GOP Wants Castor to Take on Rep. Schwartz, but He's Undecided." [Allentown] *Morning Call*. July 27, 2005.

Shaw, Jessica, Rebecca Campbell, Debi Cain, and Hannah Fenney. "Beyond Surveys and Scales: How Rape Myths Manifest in Sexual Assault Police Records." *Psychology of Violence* 7 (2017): 602–614.

Shields, Jeff. "Big Gift to Castor Ruffles Pa. GOP; The $600,000 Gift Is One of the Largest to Anyone in a State Race. Rival Tom Corbett Cries Foul." *Philadelphia Inquirer*. April 21, 2004.

Shiffman, John. "Cosby Signed Contract with Tabloid; His Deal with the National Enquirer Gave Him the Right to Edit a Story as He Defended Himself Against Sex-Abuse Charges." *Philadelphia Inquirer*. January 10, 2006.

———. "Judge Rules Cosby Files Will Remain Sealed." *Philadelphia Inquirer*. January 14, 2006.

Siemaszko, Corky. "Cosby Accuser's Father Vouches for Her Honesty." [New York] *Daily News*. February 8, 2005.

———. "Sez Cos Groped Her, Too. Atty': Did It 30 Years Ago." [New York] *Daily News*. February 9, 2005.

Simon, Scott. "Cosbys Start a 'Conversation' with African-American Art." NPR's *Weekend Edition*. November 15, 2014.

Sisak, Michael. "Ex-Prosecutor Bruce Castor: Cosby Paid Constand Millions of Dollars." November 3, 2017.

———. "Prosecutors Hope These 19 Women Can Help Convict Bill Cosby." Associated Press. February 12, 2018.

Sisario, Ben. "Prosecutors Won't Charge Cosby." *New York Times*. February 19, 2005.

Smith, Alan, and Patricia Shipp. "The Mistress: Shocking Story of Love, Lies—and Money." *National Enquirer*. February 11, 1997.

Smith, Doug. "Women's Team Looks Familiar." *Toronto Star*. August 15, 1997.

Smith, Elmer. "Cosby Places Phone Call to a Tick Bird on His Back." *Philadelphia Daily News*. June 6, 2006.

———. "What Bill Cosby Says Is Tough, but It's Definitely Love." *Philadelphia Daily News*. May 23, 2006.

Smith, Sally Bedell. "Cosby Weighs Stake in ABC Station." *New York Times*. June 8, 1985.

Smith-Shomade, Beretta. *Watching While Black: Centering the Television of Black Audiences*. New Brunswick, NJ: Rutgers University Press, 2013.

Sola, Katie. "Two More Women Say They Were Drugged and Assaulted by Bill Cosby." *Huffington Post*. May 1, 2015.

Spencer, Sheldon. "Husky Women Finish Strong." *Seattle Post-Intelligencer*. February 2, 1996.

Stamey, Mark. "Actress Bombshell: 'Cos' Rubbed Me the Wrong Way." *New York Post*. March 2, 2000.

Starr, Michael. "Cosby: Tabloid Lied." *New York Post*. March 8, 2000.

State Bar of California. "Attorney Licensee Profile. Tamara Lucier Green #13460."

Stedman, Alex. "Bill Cosby's Lawyer Calls Assault Allegations 'Ridiculous,' Three New Accusers Come Forward." *Variety*. November 20, 2014.

Steiner, Amanda Michelle. "Joseph C. Phillips: Bill Cosby Is Guilty, He Writes on Personal Website." EW.com. July 15, 2015.

Stelter, Brian. "How Bill Cosby Tried to Keep AP Interview Under Wraps." CNN Business. November 20, 2014.

Stone, Matthew. "Questions for Judge Eduardo C. Robreno." *Philadelphia Lawyer*. Winter 2013.

Stroh, Mark, and Lea Sitton Stanley. "Drew Lewis Pleads Guilty to DUI Charge." *Philadelphia Inquirer*. January 10, 2002.

Stump, Scott. "Ex-NBC Employee Says He Sent Money to Women for Bill Cosby." *Today*. November 24, 2014.

Susman, Tina. "More Accuse Cosby." *Newsday*. February 12, 2005.

Swant, Martin. "Bill Cosby to Advocate for Education in Rural Alabama." Associated Press. May 14, 2015.

"Tamara Green Discusses Her Allegations That Bill Cosby Sexually Molested Her 30 Years Ago; NBC News Transcripts." *Today Show*. February 10, 2005.

Tanford, J. Alexander, and Anthony J. Bocchino. "Rape Victim Shield Laws and the Sixth Amendment." *University of Pennsylvania Law Review* 128, no. 3 (January 1980): 544–602.

Teeman, Tim. "'Wonder Woman' Lynda Carter: This Is My #MeToo story." *Daily Beast*. March 12, 2018.

Temin, Davia. "Les Moonves Makes No. 700 on the #MeToo Index." *Forbes*. September 12, 2018.

"Temple Alumnus Bill Cosby Dedicates 'Fat Albert' Premiere to Coach Staley." Owl sports.com. December 17, 2004.

Temple University Women's Basketball 2003–04 Media Guide.

"Temple's Bill Cosby to Be Honored with National Football Foundation's Top Award." Owlsports.com. August 18, 2010.

Thompson, Charles. "Law Allows Experts to Testify on Sex Abuse." Pennlive.com. June 29, 2012.

Timpane, John. "Bill Cosby Wins Marian Anderson Award." *Philadelphia Inquirer*. December 23, 2009.

"Top 7 Black Philanthropists." *Newsone*. December 1, 2011.

"Toronto Hoop Star Jumps to Italian Club." *Toronto Star*. September 6, 1997.

Tresniowski, Alex, Vickie Bane, Nicole Weisensee Egan, Mary Green, Lorna Grisby, Maureen Harrington, Jeff Truesdell, and Michelle York. "Bill Cosby Under Fire." *People*. December 18, 2006.

Trott, William. "HEROES." UPI. December 31, 1986.

Truesdell, Jeff. "Bill Cosby Accuser Jane Doe No. 2 Reveals Her Identity: 'I Decided to Speak My Truth.'" People.com. March 4, 2015.

——. "Bill Cosby Urges Son Killed in 1997 to 'Keep Fighting' in Tweet Ahead of Upcoming Sex Assault Trial." People.com. May 15, 2017.

——. "Florida Woman: Bill Cosby Told My Parents He'd Take Care of Me, Then Pressured Me for a Sex Act." People.com. November 25, 2014.

Truman, J. L., and L. Langton. "Criminal Victimization, 2013." US Department of Justice, Bureau of Justice Statistics (2014): 1–19.

Tyler, Carolyn. "Former Bay Area Woman Accuses Cosby of Rape." ABC 7, San Francisco. November 26, 2014.

Vadala, Nick. "Bill Cosby's Marian Anderson Award Rescinded." Philly.com. May 3, 2018.

Van Dam, Andrew. "Less Than 1% of Rapes Lead to Felony Convictions." *Washington Post*. October 6, 2018.

Van Dyke, Michelle Broder. "Bill Cosby Pressured AP reporter to 'Scuttle' Interview of Sex Assault Questions." *Buzzfeed*. November 19, 2014.

Van Susteren, Greta. *On the Record with Greta Van Susteren*. Fox News Channel. February 7, 2005; February 8, 2005; February 9, 2005; February 10, 2005.

Vecsey, George. "Cosby Can Laugh Now, but Football Was Serious Business." *New York Times*. December 4, 2010.

Venama, Rachel M. "Police Officer Schema of Sexual Assault Reports: Real Rape, Ambiguous Cases and False Reports." *Journal of Interpersonal Violence*. November 12, 2014.

Walker, Dave. "Tina Fey, Amy Poehler Clobber Cosby as Just-OK Hosts." [New Orleans] *Times-Picayune*. January 12, 2015.

Walters, Patrick. "Cosby Lawyers File Motion Denying Assault Allegations." Associated Press. May 12, 2005.

Warmington, Joe. "Exclusive: Bill Cosby Sex Case: Toronto Woman Speaks to Sun." *Toronto Sun*. July 8, 2015.

Warnica, Richard. "Bill Cosby Makes a Joke About the Sexual Assault Allegations Against Him During His London, Ontario Show." *National Post*. January 8, 2015.

——. "Cosby Tour an Oasis for Accused Rapist." *Calgary Herald*. January 10, 2015.

Wells, Jeffrey. "Another Cosby Victim Comes Out." *Hollywood Elsewhere*. November 16, 2014.

Wenzel, John. "Gloria Allred Joins Growing Anti-Cosby Chorus in Denver." *Denver Post*. January 14, 2015.

Wenzel, John, and Noelle Phillips. "Protesters, Fans Greet Bill Cosby at Denver Shows." *Denver Post*. January 17, 2015.

"What 29 TV Shows Have Been #1 in the Annual Nielsen Ratings?" TVtalkingheads .com. December 13, 2016.

Whitaker, Mark. *Cosby: His Life and Times*. New York: Simon & Schuster, 2014.

Williams, Timothy. "Did the #MeToo Movement Sway the Cosby Jury?" *New York Times*. April 26, 2018.

Winfrey, Oprah. "Oprah Talks to Camille Cosby." *Oprah*. May–June 2000.

Winship, Frederick. "Cosby Makes Comeback as World's Highest-Paid Entertainer." UPI. September 14, 1990.

"WSU Women End Skid." Lewiston [Idaho] *Morning Tribune*. March 1, 1996.

Yahr, Emily. "Cosby Loses Two Stand-Up Gigs in Las Vegas and Comedy Central Pulls Stand-Up Rerun from the Schedule." *Washington Post*. November 21, 2014.

Yoder, Michael. "Convicted Ex-State Police Trooper Accused of Indecent Assault of Berks Teen." *Reading Eagle*. September 8, 2018.

Zacharek, Stephanie, Eliana Dockterman, and Haley Sweetland Edwards. "Person of the Year 2017: The Silence Breakers." *Time*. December 18, 2017.

Zinoman, Jason. "Off-Kilter, Laid-Back Standup." *New York Times*. November 4, 2011.

NOTES

INTRODUCTION

You can watch Theo's Gift at "The Cosby S So6E05 Theo's Gift," Daily Motion, www.dailymotion.com/video/x6x5pgp. *The Cosby Show* still appears on TV One, which is where I watched it. • A list of all of the episodes are at "The Cosby Show," IMDb, www.imdb.com/title/tt0086687/. • I say half a century because the earliest known accusations against him are from 1965—Sunni Welles and Kristina Ruehli. An *LA Times*, September 25, 2018, story has a fifty-year timeline. • The Tony Norman column I quote is from his February 11, 2005, column. • Countless stories refer to Cosby as America's Dad, including the April 26, 2018, *USA Today* story and my June 5, 2017, People.com story. • Cosby's friendship with Jackson is mentioned in the January 17, 1997, *Larry King Live* interview on CNN; the July 2, 2004, CBS story; the May 27, 2017, *NY Post* story, and the June 1, 2017, *Huffington Post* story. His friendship with Sharpton is mentioned in the November 20, 2014, *NY Post* story and the May 27, 2017, *Post* story. Whitaker writes about Cosby's friendship with Nelson Mandela in his biography. • The "halo effect" is explained in the 1985 *Journal of Psychology* study by Lachman et al. and the 2016 *Gender Issues* article. • Cosby's numerous awards are listed in the September 26, 2018, CNN story. In 2011 *NewsOne* named him as one of their top seven black philanthropists. The October 14, 2017, *New Yorker* story discusses his reputation as both humanitarian and philanthropist. The May 5, 2018, Deadline.com story discusses him getting the Mark Twain and Kennedy Awards and them both being rescinded. The 2002 YouTube clip shows him getting the Medal of Freedom in 2002. • The December 30, 2015, Vulture.com story says Cosby had received nearly sixty honorary degrees and more than thirty had been rescinded so far. • His Emmys and the rest of his entertainment awards are listed on his IMDb site: "Bill Cosby," IMDb, www.imdb.com/name/nm0001070/. • The quote about Cosby being a great pitchman is from the December 1981 article in *Black Enterprise* magazine. • Many stories through the years have discussed him breaking racial and cultural barriers, most recently the April 26, 2018, AP and *USA Today* stories. • The NAACP Image Hall of Fame Award info is from the March 2, 2007, AP story. The National Football Foundation Award information is from the August 28, 2010, NESN.com story, the December 2010 *New York Times* story, and the August 2010 blurb on Owlsports.com; the Owlsports.com blurb is where the excerpted quotes are from. The May 5, 2018, Deadline.com story discusses the Mark Twain Award; the information about the Johnny Carson Award is from the April 21, 2014, *Huffington Post* story. The December 4, 2014, USNI.com story discusses his 2011 award from the Navy as well as it being rescinded. • The information about how Cosby operated as a sexual predator comes from documents in the criminal case and both trials. • Mark Whitaker's book also details all of his accomplishments, his reputation, his best-selling books, and many of his awards.

CHAPTER 1

I didn't know many of these details of how Andrea told her mother what happened until after Cosby was arrested on December 30, 2015, and after she and her parents and sisters gave victim-impact statements at Cosby's sentencing on September 24 and 25, 2018. These quotes from Andrea and her mother are from various court proceedings and the details about her massage-school training triggering her subconscious is from interviews I did with her attorney, Dolores Troiani, in 2005. In the first trial Andrea said in her testimony that she told her mother that Cosby had given her three blue pills and that he sexually violated her without her consent (June 6, 2017, 192–193). Gianna testified that Andrea told her he drugged and raped her (June 7, 2017, 173–174), so I used Gianna's quotes because the way she phrased it was more succinct. Neither woman was allowed to testify about this conversation in the second trial due to defense attorneys objecting to it as hearsay. While Andrea called attorneys after she talked to her mother that morning, she didn't speak to any before she and Gianna talked to police that evening after her mother got home from work, Andrea testified at the first trial (June 6, 2017, 194–195). • Gianna testified about how she and Diana went to see Cosby perform in both trials. Photos of them with Cosby were introduced as exhibits. • The details of the path the case took before ending up at the Cheltenham Township Police Department were given by Sergeant Schaffer at Cosby's first trial. • In Harry Hairston's interview with Joe Madison he said he was tipped off by Philadelphia police. Initially he reported that she said Cosby touched her breasts and put her hand on his penis, which is what the Philadelphia Police Department's Special Victims Unit said in its report on the complaint. Andrea had told her local police that she "could only say that something foreign was in her body." Some initial details were wrong, like when she said the incident occurred. She said she told Cosby she was stressed, so he gave her pills that made her dizzy and sick and made her legs feel like jelly. • I printed out Hairston's story from the Channel 10 website on January 20, 2005. All the police reports are available on the Cosby criminal case website. They were exhibits during various court proceedings, including the trials. I still have a printout of the Philadelphia Police Department's "white paper" because it got leaked to *Celebrity Justice*, which it posted online. • The exposé I wrote on the spike of drug-facilitated sexual assaults in Philadelphia ran in 2002. The details about how the drugs work came from the experts and police I interviewed for that story. • The former colleague from Temple I interviewed on January 20, 2005, gave me a lot of these details about Andrea, Dawn Staley, and Cosby's work on behalf of Temple, the commercials, and so forth, which I included in my first story about the case. He also told me about the signed photo of Cosby in Staley's office and Cosby dedicating the Philadelphia premiere of the *Fat Albert* movie to Staley, which I also verified through an Owlsports.com blurb from December 2004. • Joan Ballast, a donor to the Temple women's basketball team, introduced Cosby to Andrea in the fall/winter of 2002, according to Andrea's testimony during the trial. • I still have my notes from those interviews, so I also used some tidbits I didn't have space for back then. I found other details about Cosby and Staley from the Temple women's basketball media guide, which I later consulted and still have in my possession. • The Bryan Pardo quote is from the November 21, 1991, article in the *Toronto Star*. • The information about which teams were recruiting Andrea back then was from the November 13, 1992, *Hartford Courant* article, while UConn's ranking is from an article by the same writer on November 19, 1991. The details about her many sleepless nights deciding where to go and the quotes from her about why she chose Arizona, with its abysmal record, are from the November 20 and 21, 1991, articles in the *Toronto Star*. Joan Bonvicini's paraphrased quote about Andrea being popular on and off the court is from an interview I did with her on January 24, 2005. Her quote about Andrea's honesty is from the January 21, 2005, Associated Press story. • Andrea testified about how she met Cosby at both trials. These differing points of view on their relationship are from their own statements to police, depositions in the civil case, and, in Andrea's case, testimony at both trials. • The hair straightening/head shot information and how he encouraged her sports broadcasting career aspirations are from her testimony and statements to police as well as her deposition. Purna Rodman Conare and R. M. Stinemen, her two friends who lived across the hall from her in 2005, confirmed that to me. His account is from his statement to police in 2005 and his deposition in her civil suit in 2005 and 2006. • The details about Cosby's upbringing, his experiences with alcohol and drugs, why he gave the pound cake speech, the excerpts from the pound cake speech, how he met Camille, why he dropped out of college, how he became a comedian, and why he came to avoid racial issues in his comedy are from Whitaker's biography. • In the text of the book Whitaker says the *New York Times* article about Cosby was from July 26, but in the endnotes the date is June 25, 1964. I double-checked with NYTimes.com, and it came up as June 25, 1962, which I cite above. The excerpt I used from the article is one I fact-checked myself. The entire lead is: "The Gaslight Café, a Subterranean Coffeehouse in Greenwich Village, Is Featuring a Young Negro Comic Who Is Working His Way Through College by Hurling Verbal Spears at the Relations Between Whites and Negroes." • The Spanish fly references from the album and book were used by prosecutors in a March 30, 2017, filing, which is on the criminal case website. The *Village Voice* also wrote about it on November 17, 2014. • You can listen to a segment from the *Bill Cosby Talks to Kids About Drugs* album here: https://www.youtube.com/watch?v=7RoQTCtm5Ok. The *Washington Post* also wrote about it on July 23, 2015. • University of Pennsylvania professor Michael Eric Dyson was Cosby's most vocal critic and subsequently wrote a book about it. • The excerpt from Cosby's public statement came from a press release by his then-spokesman, David Brokaw, issued on May 22, 2004, and the backlash information came from a May 22, 2004, article in the *New York Times*.

CHAPTER 2

The details of Andrea's search for attorneys are in her trial testimony. • The first quote from Dolores Troiani is from my interview with her on August 6, 2018. In that same interview she told me they weren't ever intimidated by Cosby or his attorneys. • Former Governor Ed Rendell, who was Philadelphia's district attorney from 1978 to 1986 and worked with Troiani there, told the *New York Times* in February 2016 that she rarely negotiated a plea deal. In that same story former

Philadelphia district attorney Lynne Abraham, who knows both women, described Kivitz as having "a softer approach." • Kivitz and Troiani detailed their history as prosecutors and former law partners in their testimony on February 3, 2016. • The description of Phillips as an "anticorruption scourge" is from his obituary in the *Philadelphia Inquirer* on February 9, 2015. • Phillips gave that first "bizarre and preposterous" quote to my former colleague, Gloria Campisi, who was helping me reach out to people that first night because we were on a tight deadline, as well as other reporters who contacted him. She sent it to me via email, which I still have. • The excerpt is from the January 21, 2005, Associated Press story. • I still have the press release from the School District of Philadelphia, which I used for this excerpt. • I interviewed Thornhill Cosby, who is now deceased, on January 20, 2005. • The quote from Phillips about the postponements is from my notes from my interview with him on January 21, 2005. • On January 20, 2005, Barbara Isenberg, one of our interns, went to Cosby's Elkins Park home and emailed me a description saying iron gates surrounded the home and were closed. A staff member opened them to speak with her. I still have the printout of Isenberg's email with that description. • Bebe Kivitz revealed the flower deliveryman ruse in documents to me in a February 3, 2005, interview. It was also included in one of the filings for the civil suit Andrea filed against Cosby on March 9, 2005. I reached out to the *Enquirer* and the reporter himself for comment, but they did not respond. • Neither Jonathan Kingston nor Ian Robertson responded to my requests for comment about their tactics, information I confirmed through my reporting. The quotes from the Constands are all from that January 22, 2005, story in the *Toronto Sun*. I also asked the *Sun* what their policy is about using the names of sexual assault victims without their consent, but they did not respond to that question either. In the United States, news organizations do not reveal the identity of a sexual assault victim without their consent. • Harvey Levin from *Celebrity Justice* was already speculating about whether Andrea Constand wanted money from Cosby, asking on CNN on January 21, 2005: "Did this woman make any contact with Bill Cosby trying to get any money before the police in Toronto were contacted? That's always a question." • The quotes from Kristen are from my September 3, 2018, interview with her. The information about sexual assault victims not being believed, especially in high-profile cases, comes from her as well as the 2002, 2011, and 2016 rape studies I cite in my Sources. • The information about the media not revealing the names of sexual assault victims comes from the NSRVC's media packet, which cites the Associated Press stylebook, the guide for most US news organizations.

CHAPTER 3

I knew this information about Bruce's cases, what he preferred being called, and his love of the limelight from my coverage and my newspaper's coverage of him over the years as well as the December 2002 profile of him in *Philadelphia* magazine. The information about the coverage, the books, and the movies comes from various newspaper and Associated Press stories cited in my source list as well as the *Philly* mag profile. Castor did not respond to several requests for comment from me for this book. On November 20, 2014, I reached out to him for comment for our cover story for *People*. He sent me this email back, which I still have: "[A]fter the [federal judge's son] story at the DN and you not believing me concerning an eyewitness statement, I said I was through talking to you. That has not changed." • He was referring to a story I was looking into in 2001 that never ran. Nonetheless, I always try to get a comment from him when I'm writing something about him. He did give a comment to my former colleague, Mary Green, for our cover story. • The General Wayne Inn murder was featured on *Forensic Files* on February 8, 2006. The Caleb Fairley case was also featured on *Forensic Files* ("Shopping Spree," IMDb, www. imdb.com/title/tt4017424/) and was the subject of Katherine Ramsland's book, *The Vampire Trap*. • The Rabinowitz case was on ID (the story is cited in Sources) and *Forensic Files*. It was also the subject of the book *Everybody's Best Friend: The True Story of a Marriage That Ended in Murder* by Ken Englade. • I examined Castor's campaign finance records myself in November 2018 and found the contributions from Drew Lewis and his wife, Marilyn. Drew gave Castor's campaign fund $100,000 on April 19, 2004, and his wife gave the campaign fund $250,000 on March 29, 2004, and April 6, 2004. • The criticism of his actions comes from the April 21, 2004, *Post-Gazette* story and the press release from Corbett's campaign on April 23, 2004, which includes several critical comments from district attorneys across the state questioning why Lewis went to a rehab instead of jail and Castor's decision not to refer the case to the state attorney general's office, as Lewis was a friend. The donation was front-page news in the *Philadelphia Inquirer* and was also covered by the Associated Press. The *Allentown Morning Call* and *Norristown Times Herald* also wrote about Lewis's DUI arrest and sentence in 2001 and 2002 at the time, as did the *Philadelphia Inquirer*, which also wrote about his first DUI arrest in 1996, articles I cite in my Sources. • Castor defended his actions in 2002, saying Lewis would be treated "no more and no less severely than anyone else," and the contributions in 2004. His spokesman told the *Pittsburgh Post-Gazette* Corbett's claim that the contribution was a tradeoff for the DUI sentence was "untrue, ludicrous and outrageous." There is no limit on how much an individual can contribute in Pennsylvania, then or now. • In my Sources list I cite a few news stories from 2005 that talk about Castor's aspirations for higher office. • The information about the Evans case and the other date-rape case as well as the quotes from Castor and Ferman and the information about Evans's defense attorney's plans come from stories cited in my Sources. Evans was recently arrested again and charged with indecent assault involving a 15-year-old girl. The September 1, 2018, *Reading Eagle* story about his arrest is cited in my Sources. • I still have Castor's first press release, and the information about the three reporters who worked out of the courthouse getting the release the previous night is from my January 26, 2005, story. • We sent our reporter, Ramona Smith, to his press conference. The quotes from Castor come from the story I coauthored with her, the January 26, 2005, AP story about the press conference, and excerpts of his news conference played on various TV shows, including the *Abrams Report*. I spoke with Phillips and Troiani on January 26, 2005. • The law enforcement skepticism info comes from the 2017 study in *Psychology of Violence* and the 2014 one in the *Journal of Interpersonal Violence*. • The public probably being skeptical of Andrea's claims comes from a January 23, 2005, reader poll published by the *Toronto Sun*, asking people to call in response to this statement: "I believe the allegations Andrea Constand has leveled against Bill Cosby." One phone number was given for those who agreed and another for those who disagreed. Of the 123 people who phoned in 76 percent said they disagreed with the statement while just 24 percent agreed. Various sexual assault studies I cite throughout this book support this statement as well. • The information about Andrea's therapy and flashbacks came from my January 26, 2005, interview with Troiani. • The statistics about sexual assault being the most underreported violent crime and the actual underreporting stats came from my January 28, 2005, phone interview with Rumburg, the National Sexual Violence Resource Center's media packet, the Truman study, and the Rennison study. • I still had Senator Piccola's press release, so I used that as a reference. The quote from him is from my January 28, 2005, interview with him. • The quote from Governor Rendell's spokeswoman, Kate Philips, is from my interview with her on January 28, 2005. • The conspiracy theory quote is from Tony Norman's February 11, 2005, column. • Harvey Levin's comments about the show posting the police report with Andrea's name on it are from my January 27, 2005, interview with him. I also interviewed Inspector William Colarulo, head of public affairs for the Philadelphia Police Department, that same day. He told me about the Internal Affairs investigation into how the document was leaked. I have printouts of all of the CJ stories I cite as well. • The other media that used Andrea's name and photo after Andrea did that include New York's *Daily News* on Tuesday, February 8, 2005, with excerpts from her parents' comments that were in the January 22, 2005, *Toronto Sun* story. Other news organizations that ran her name back then without her consent were UPI, *Newsday*, and the *New York Post*. • Levin then went on Greta Van Susteren's show on February 8, 2005, and Greta herself said "the parents of Bill Cosby's accuser have publicly identified their daughter as thirty-one-year-old Andrea Constand, a former University of Arizona basketball star," even though that story had come out three weeks prior. They all seemed to be belatedly using that interview with Andrea's parents as a reason to identify her rather than acknowledging that the police report with her name on it had been up on *Celebrity Justice*'s website more recently. And Andrea was an adult at the time. She and her attorneys are the only ones who could give the media permission to use her name and photo, not her parents. • The other news organizations that mentioned *Celebrity Justice*'s story that Andrea tried to get money out of Cosby before going to police were New York's *Daily News*, *Newsday*, UPI, and the *Pittsburgh Post-Gazette*. • Marty Singer's quotes are from his *Celebrity Justice* interview. • Cynthia McFadden reported the consensual exclusive on *Good Morning America*. • Van Susteren played the excerpts from Castor's radio interview on her show on February 9, 2005, when I was a guest as well. • I was on Rita Cosby's show talking about Castor's threats to have me arrested on February 12, 2005. "He issued threats to me, basically, through the local media that if I spoke about these taped conversations . . . I could be arrested and put in jail," I told her. "I mean, I find his behavior, frankly, as intimidating as anything I've ever seen, and as intimidating and repulsive as what the Cosby people have been doing to Tamara and what they tried to do to our newspaper before we published the story."

CHAPTER 4

Everything from Tamara Green in this chapter is from my February 3, 9, 10, and 18, 2005, interviews with her, some of which I didn't use in 2005. • This Rumburg interview was on February 9, 2005. I still had my notes, so I used unpublished portions of her interviews as well as Tamara's. • To corroborate that Tamara told people what happened to her long before 2005, I spoke with Jean Blackburn, her then-estranged husband, Ben Housouer, and another friend of Tamara's before my story ran on February 8, 2005. I don't have the notes from those conversations, but Housouer's quote is in my February 8, 2005, story. At the time he confirmed Tamara told him about it before Andrea's allegations made the news. In November 2018 I spoke with Roy Waterhouse, a longtime friend of Tamara's; her cousin, Lauren Scott; and her longtime friend Jean Blackburn, all of whom verified that Tamara told them what happened to her long before 2005. Scott and Blackburn said she told her in the early 1970s and was visibly distraught about it still. Waterhouse said she told him and his wife around 1979 or 1980. Housouer, who told me in 2005 she'd told him what happened long before Andrea's story made the news and that she wasn't a bullshitter, now said he couldn't remember when she told him. • The quote from Troiani is from my February 3, 2005, interview with her. The Phillips quote is from a phone interview with him that same day. • I was receiving a lot of phone calls from Marty Singer. I didn't learn about the letters to my newspaper until my former boss, Kurt Heine, told me when I was working on a proposal for this book. He sent me this via email on February 7, 2018:

> I remember a multi-page letter . . . It was quite threatening. I remember thinking it was unusual to get a legal threat with this kind of detail—most of the stuff we got was the garden variety "If I read that in the paper I'll sue." We ran the letter up the flagpole and the only instruction I remember was the usual—make sure everything is solid. I don't recall they were seriously worried about it. . . . As far as I can remember, there was no outside pressure that influenced in any way what went into the paper. The stories followed the usual process, and we published them as soon as they were ready and the front page became available.

The stats about false rape reports are from the 2010 David Lisak study. The articles about Tamara and Lee Minnelli are cited in my Sources section. • In his deposition for Andrea's civil case, Cosby said Dr. Amar gave him seven prescriptions for Quaaludes. Cosby also described a time Amar got mad at him over something that happened with Tamara Green. I wove in more details from that deposition in which Cosby was asked about Tamara. • The information about the power of cable news talk shows comes from the 2006 *Political Research Quarterly* article, which also cites a 2004 study about the state of the news media by the Pew Research Center for the *People and the Press*. • The video of my February 8, 2005, appearance on Dan Abrams's show is on my website, as are all of my 2005 appearances on Greta Van Susteren's show and Rita Cosby's show. The quotes are taken from those videos. • The quotes from Tamara's appearance on the *Today* show are from NBC transcripts of that interview. • I refer to that email from David Walk in my February 10, 2005, story. The cite for the *NY Post* story is listed in my Sources. • I double-checked the dates of Tamara's disciplinary issues with the California bar more recently online and confirmed that her license was active when we spoke back then. She told me it was later suspended for six months due to that infraction, but that was not until 2006, which the records confirm. The title of the diversion program back then was the "Program for Respondents with Substance Abuse and/or Mental Health Issues." • On February 8, 2005, I spoke with Kathleen Beitiks, a spokeswoman for California's state bar, who also faxed me the complaint, which I still have. • Transcripts of Tamara's appearances on the various networks show up in a search on LexisNexis. I have videos on my website of the shows we were on together. • Kurt Heine, my boss, is quoted in the February 9, 2005, AP story defending our story. • While Tamara was handling the attacks very well, I had no idea how vicious they truly got until I did a deeper search in LexisNexis for this book. In its CBS February 18, 2005, story, CBS described her as "a woman with a history of treatment for substance abuse or mental health problems." • Tamara also spoke with the *Washington Post* for their February 20, 2005, story. • Tamara revealed her DUI to Dan Abrams on the *Abrams Show* on February 10, 2005. I included what she said in my February 11, 2005, story, which I also used in this chapter. She told me about it in my initial interview with her on February 3, 2005.

CHAPTER 5

The rape-shield law information is from my February 9, 2005, interview with Rumburg. The 1991 article I cite is a good overview of rape-shield law. • The quotes from Kristen Houser are from my September 5, 2018, interview with her. • All of these details about Cosby's achievements are from the Whitaker book. • The excerpt from Cosby's thesis is from Beretta Smith-Shomade's 2013 book. • The criticism of his PhD from the member of his dissertation committee is from the 1985 *People* magazine story about a book by the member, cited above. • I spoke with Jennifer on February 10, 2005, and again on September 26, 2018, and she gave me permission to use her name and her interview. She sent me the excerpt from her poem via email on September 22, 2018. She first revealed herself as "Jena T" and allowed a photo of her to be used by Jeff Truesdell for People.com on November 25, 2014. On March 4, 2015, she allowed Truesdell to use her full name and photo for a story on People. com. She was also in our December 8, 2014, cover story, identified only as "Jena T." • Sue Charney died in 2011. • The *New York Times*, *Vanity Fair*, the *Los Angeles Times*, and the *Hollywood Reporter* have all done stories about Marty Singer and his tactics. The articles are cited in my Sources section. • These details about Troiani's experiences as a prosecutor were included in her testimony on February 3, 2016. • Troiani's work on the Johnston brothers was written about in the *Philadelphia Inquirer* when he escaped in August 1999 and was on the lam for eighteen days. The August 8, 1999, story mentions the Sean Penn movie. • TV bookers told me about the Cosby people pressuring them to keep me off their shows while also introducing me to the phrase "trading up" and explaining it to me when I was wondering why the rest of the media was backing away from the story. I was quickly replaced on Greta's show, but Dan Abrams had me on one more time—on May 10, 2005, the day Cosby filed his response to Andrea's allegations in the civil suit. In that response, Cosby said he gave her Benadryl and denied anything sexual happened between them. • These are my best recollections of the nature of those calls. The exchange where I use specific quotes from he and I is still seared into my memory all these years later. Normally I can defuse tense conversations like this with a joke. Not with him. • I spoke with Kia Gregory on October 22, 2018, and she said she didn't remember how she got the story but thought an editor assigned it to her. Tim Whitaker, the editor of *Philadelphia Weekly* at the time, told me via email on October 22, 2018, he could not remember if he assigned it to her. Four months later Gregory did a story for *Philadelphia Weekly* where Cosby called up the weekly to chat about an issue with the Philadelphia schools ("History Repeats," June 29, 2005, www.philadelphiaweekly .com/news/history-repeats/article_6c683c50-0ec6-58c2-b7a8-705ef9e09233.html). Gregory told me she didn't remember how that came about. Neither did Whitaker, though he did say he's never spoken to Cosby himself. • I reached out to both Brennen and Woods, the journalism experts quoted in the story, to see if they felt differently about our coverage now. Woods, who is now vice president of diversity and training at NPR, did not get back to me. Brennen, who is now a professor emeritus at Marquette University, sent me this response via email:

> You pose a tricky question. On one hand, based on all of the evidence that has come out against Cosby, I definitely feel differently about him and his role at Temple and in the Philadelphia community. But what I was trying to get at in my interview, all those years ago, was that the nature of the coverage was so sensational—the blaring headlines, the accusations with quite limited evidence (at that time), the fact that he was such a beloved celebrity at Temple and in Philadelphia (at that time), and the rebuttals by Cosby supporters that Cosby was being targeted—all of it troubled me. I continue to feel that scoops should be based on solid evidence even if it takes a little longer to get them published. Of course this is why I'd never make it in journalism these days.

The information about how the news media's sexual assault coverage influences the public is from the 2018 study on rape culture and the media. I asked Michael Days for comment for this story a couple of times. He kept saying he'd check to see if he still had any notes from back then. I guess he didn't have any, because he never got back to me. • On April 30, 2005, Fox News aired a segment about the dearth of media coverage of the case titled, "Is the Media Giving Bill Cosby a Pass?" noting that the *New York Times*, *USA Today*, and *NBC News* had not covered the case and that even *Inside Edition*, a tabloid TV show, had only run two reports on the subject. • The excerpt from Tony Norman's column is from the February 11, 2005, one. • I didn't know the details of these women's stories back then. They are from interviews I did more than a decade later, so that's where these details come from, which I elaborate on later in the book. • I still have the printouts of the emailed tips as well as the letters people sent me.

CHAPTER 6

On February 2, 2016, Castor testified about the unusual nature of his press release, down to the fact he typed it up himself and faxed it to the media. • Sgt. Richard Schaffer, who was a detective in Cheltenham on the case, testified about the investigation still being open that day at the first trial on June 8, 2017. In his deposition for Andrea's defamation lawsuit against Castor (case # 2:15-CV-05799), former

Cheltenham Township Police Chief John Norris also said the investigation was still ongoing on February 17, 2005, and none of the investigators knew Castor was going to close the case. In that same lawsuit, a copy of Castor's earlier press release is an exhibit. These two paragraphs were deleted after consultation with Ferman, she said in her deposition:

> District Attorney Castor is aware of the unauthorized (and perhaps criminal) release of some aspects of the investigation apparently in an attempt to influence his decision . . . The District Attorney again highlights those provisions of Pennsylvania law which make it a felony to disclose the existence or contents of so-called wiretap evidence. Additionally, the law creates a civil cause of action for any aggrieved party who is injured by an illegal disclosure. Pennsylvania law is especially clear on these points, and the District Attorney is duty bound, and would not hesitate, to enforce those provisions should he believe such action warranted.
>
> District Attorney Castor has seen published reports and media broadcasts critical of him for stating that the law looks unfavorably upon alleged victims of sexual assault who delay reporting. It is self-evident that the District Attorney applies the law as it exists, not as some others would prefer the law to be. The District Attorney does not have the discretion to change the law to fit a particular set of circumstances.

I still have a copy of Castor's press release from that day, referenced above. • In her deposition for Andrea's defamation lawsuit against Castor, Ferman, now a Montgomery County judge, told Kivitz she'd researched the issue and told Castor she did not believe Gianna's taped call was an illegal wiretap. She also discussed the first press release and said she asked Castor if she should call Troiani and Kivitz about the decision not to prosecute Cosby. She said he told her not to, that he was going to fax them the press release. When Castor testified at a criminal court proceeding on February 2, 2016, he said he told Ferman to "communicate" the decision not to prosecute to Troiani and Kivitz. He did not mention an earlier version of his press release. A copy of it is an exhibit in this case as well. • Troiani testified under oath about what happened that day on February 3, 2016, but also told me in an interview on February 17, 2005. On February 3, 2016, Kivitz testified about giving more names to Castor's office just six days prior, which would have been February 11, 2005. • These interviews with Cosby's childhood friends, other Philadelphians, Clarence Page, and so forth are from the February 19, 2005, *Pittsburgh Post-Gazette* story and a February 24, 2005, *Philadelphia Daily News* story. The details about Cosby's long relationship with Temple came from the *Daily News* story. • The quotes from Tamara are from my February 17, 2005, interview with her. The quote from Phillips is from my February 17, 2005, interview with him. • The quote from Troiani in my section about Castor's dad helping him are from my February 18, 2005, interview with her. The quotes from Lawless are from my interview with him from that same day, as is the quote from Phillips. Castor's response is from the February 25, 2016, *Billy Penn* story I cite in my Sources.

CHAPTER 7

I tracked down and ordered the *Enquirer* issues about the murder and the affair with Shawn. Her last name was Thompson in 2005. The stories are cited above. • Shawn's account of how she met Cosby and everything else is from my March 4,

2005, interview with her. Back then her name was Shawn Upshaw, so that's how I refer to her. I'd called her to ask for her comment about another story I was working on, which I reference later in the book. I spoke with her again to fact-check on December 31, 2018. • David Brokaw initially saying Cosby barely knew Autumn Jackson is from the Whitaker book and the January 1997 *New York Times* article I cite above. • Cosby's account of how he found out about Shawn's pregnancy is from the Whitaker book. • The details about Ennis's murder are from the Whitaker book and a January 27, 1997, *Newsweek* story. • All of the information about the twenty-year-old actress from Trenton, New Jersey, comes from the *Enquirer* stories I cite above or the *New York Post* story I cite above. When the story made news again in 2014 the *Trentonian* tried to get her to speak, but she still wouldn't. Her mother told the *Trentonian* her daughter wouldn't be joining the rest of the accusers who were going public, saying she had put it behind her and wants to keep it behind her. In 2005 her mother had this reaction to Andrea's allegations: "I was like, 'Oh my God, here the same thing happened to my daughter almost five years ago,'" she told the *Philadelphia Inquirer* for a story that ran on February 17, 2005. Cosby's threats of suing the *Enquirer* for $250 million over the story were reported in the *New York Post* and Eonline, cited above, as well as other publications. • I unsuccessfully tried to reach the twenty-year-old woman myself to fact-check and see if she was OK with her name being used. Since I could not reach her we did not use her name in this book.

Camille Cosby's comments about her fears for Ennis came from her Oprah interview in 2000, and the ones about hiring an investigator are from the Whitaker book and the Oprah interview. • The details about how Cosby reacted when his family moved to Massachusetts and the size of their property where Ennis was buried and his interview with Rather and its fallout, including the first part of Camille's statement and op-ed, is from the Whitaker book. So is the information about the *Enquirer*'s cover story about her alleged nervous breakdown and her subsequent op-ed in *USA Today*. • I could not find the original op-ed she wrote in LexisNexis, but I found more excerpts of it as well as Steve Coz's response in the *San Jose Mercury News* story in February 1997, the February 7, 1997, *USA Today* blurb, and the January 20, 2015, *New York Times* story. Details about Cosby's Rather interview and its fallout were also in the January 27, 1997, New York *Daily News* story and other news stories I cite above. • Cosby talked about cooperating with the *Enquirer* and why he did so about Erinn in the 1998 *USA Today* story I cite above. The *NY Post* story from 2014 is cited as well. • I spoke with David Brokaw and Tamara Green about Cosby's interview with the *Enquirer* on March 2, 2005.

CHAPTER 8

I spoke with Stuart Zakim on March 2, 2005. The David Brokaw comment is from my March 2, 2005, interview with him. • I still had my notes of that March 4, 2005, exchange with Singer, which is how I was able to recreate it word for word. • Cosby was asked about the terms of his agreement with the *Enquirer* during his deposition and confirmed these were the terms. • I cite several profiles of Singer in my Sources section. His fame was still growing back then, and all of these profiles were written after the Cosby case. Some of the famous clients I list are ones he helped after the Cosby saga. • The Karen Baker interview is from March 3, 2005. The Dolores

Troiani interview was from March 7, 2005. Neither were included in the story that ran, though they were in the version I submitted to my editors. • I'd originally called Upshaw to make sure her interview in the *Enquirer* was a real interview and to get her account of him slipping a drug into her drink. I ended up doing a lengthy interview with her about her relationship with Cosby, and I got her reaction to the joke. We only included one short comment from Upshaw about the joke, saying it had been in "poor taste. He's making light of it as damage control. He's trying to make the community think he didn't do it; that's why he can joke about it." • Former *Philadelphia Daily News* city editor Kurt Heine told me about the threatening letters in 2018.

CHAPTER 9

I included Troiani and Kivitz's statement in my March 9, 2005, story. This account is from the lawsuit, which can be found on pacer.gov, Case # 2:05-cv-01099. • Most of this profile of Andrea is what I published in 2005. I interviewed Anthony Simms in February 2005. I also interviewed her friends and former neighbors in Philadelphia in 2018 to fill in more details about her life. I spoke with Stineman and Codare on September 10, 2018. They also helped me with the description of Andrea's apartment and steered me toward some photos online. I also wove in details from Andrea's victim-impact statement as well as her mom's, dad's, and sister's. Any quotes from any of them are from their victim-impact statements. Any quotes of Andrea's about her basketball career through the years are from news stories I cite above. • Claudia Brassard, one of her former Arizona teammates, sent me a comment via email on February 2, 2005, describing her as "tough and aggressive" on the court. In my interview with Bonvicini on January 24, 2005, she was described as popular and well liked. • I interviewed Traci Waites in February 2005; I don't have the exact date. • I interviewed the Temple player in February 2005. She didn't want her name used because Temple players were being told not to talk to the media. I commented on how the media had violated its own rules on this case on Greta's show on February 10, 2005: "It's just been interesting that a lot of media organizations have violated their own policy of revealing sexual assault victims' identities without their consent and have revealed the identity of the Canadian woman. It's just sort of been fascinating to see all the rules broken in this case." • For the discussion with Troiani about revealing Andrea's sexual preference, I relied on my memory. Her interview with Abrams was on February 18, 2005. The transcripts are on LexisNexis.

CHAPTER 10

I was covering each step of the civil case for the *Daily News*, so these details are from my stories, cited above. • The Beth Ferrier interview is from June 17, 2005, material I did and didn't use back then, along with some additional details I got from her in 2018 when we fact checked. The information about the majority of the Jane Does not being interviewed by police was in a footnote in a May 9, 2005, filing in *Constand v. Cosby*. • In his deposition Cosby admitted to the affair with Beth but said he didn't remember whether he drugged and sexually assaulted her. • The Father's Day poll information was in a number of news sources. I cited one above. The *New York Times* said *Fatherhood* was the number-one-selling hardcover of 1986. •

The Cosby show background information about Marcy Carsey and Tom Werner is from the Whitaker bio. • The information about the ratings is from various news sources cited above. • When Cosby says five or six models were sent to him each week by a modeling agency, he's referring to ones Sue Charney sent him. • I could not reach Jo Farrell in 2005 or or her daughter, Kathleen, in 2018.

CHAPTER 11

In June 2005 Beth faxed me a copy of her lie detector test and agreement with the *Enquirer*, which I still have. • The details about what happened to Andrea while she was being deposed came from her victim-impact statement. • I cite the *Nightline* interview and *Smoking Gun* sources above, as I do the Elmer Smith coverage and the graduation story. Dolores Troiani also spoke about how contentious it was when she testified on February 3, 2016. • The discord over civil negotiations was being covered in the *Philadelphia Daily News* (by me for a while), the *Inquirer* and the Associated Press in 2005 and 2006, stories I cite above. Though I didn't know it at the time, Therese Serignese, Jane Doe Number Ten, had also agreed to have her name and photo used for our story but only bits and pieces were used without her name being attached to it and her photo was not included. She revealed this publicly on her Facebook site in 2017, which is how I learned about it. I did not know that because one of my colleagues interviewed her. Our beats were broken up by geography then, and she was in Florida. I always thought Therese wasn't yet ready to go public in 2006. I was allowed to interview Tamara Green, even though she was in California and I lived in Pennsylvania, because she'd refused to participate in the story otherwise, unhappy with how *People* had portrayed her in a 2005 story, before I began freelancing for them. • Barbara Bowman's account of what happened is from the November 2006 *Philadelphia* magazine story and the December 18, 2006, *People* story. Her account is also in the defamation lawsuit she filed against Cosby. In his deposition Cosby said he did not remember Barbara and denied having tried to rape her. For Farrell he said, "From time to time Jo Farrell would send some of her clients to see me perform in Denver. We would have dinner between those." • I could not reach Farrell for comment, but in 2006, when asked about introducing Beth and Barbara to Cosby she told *People* she only supplied him with tapes and portfolios of her clients. "He wanted to look at children and girls for his show. I wasn't in on personal interviews." • In 2014, when more models who were introduced to Cosby by Farrell came forward with similar allegations, her daughter, Kathleen, told the *Washington Post* in a story I cite in my Sources that her mother was suffering from dementia and Alzheimer's but knew nothing about anything untoward between their clients and Cosby. She said Cosby worked with many of their young clients through the years, taking them on outings and asking them to auditions. Her mother never heard any complaints about Cosby, she said. If she had, she would have ended the relationship with Cosby "to protect the girls. Nobody ever addressed with her that there was an issue," she said. "She's a mother hen; she would have addressed it." • In 2015 Kathleen told the *Denver Post* in a story I cite in my Sources that her mother was eighty-three years old and in no condition to discuss the allegations. "This has been an ongoing frustration, and it has not helped her health issues," Kathleen said.

CHAPTER 12

I cite the various news stories about the Netflix special, the comedy tour, the NBC deal, and the Comedy Central special viewership in my Sources section. We also included the information in our 2014 cover story in *People* and got it from the networks themselves. • Cosby receiving the Marian Anderson Award is from a May 3, 2018, Philly.com story. It was rescinded on May 2, 2018, according to another *Inquirer* story. • The information about what Tamara, Beth, Andrea, Dolores, and Bebe were up to is from my own interviews and reporting. I spoke with Tamara on September 27, 2018; Beth on May 5, 2018; Troiani on August 6, 2018. What Barbara Bowman was doing is from her October 27, 2014, interview with the *Daily Mail*. • The description of the Cosby/Pouissant book is from a *Publisher's Weekly* blurb on its Amazon.com description. • The background on Buress and all the information about his interviews before and since his Cosby routine and the backlash are from sources I cite in my Sources list. The joke is from the Phillymag.com post. The quotes from McQuade, Lange, and Hess are from Mark Dent's December 3, 2014, *Billy Penn* story, cited in my Sources. Buress's tweet was embedded in the October 21, 2014, *Us Weekly* story I cite and in other stories I cite. The link to the Howard Stern interview with Buress and tout of his appearance is listed in my Sources. • Buress did not respond to repeated requests for comment from me. • I cite the various online sites' coverage of the Buress comments—*Gawker*, *Newsweek*, *Buzzfeed*, *Slate*, the *Daily Mail*, and so on—in my Source list. • Articles about Cosby's meme contests and some of those memes are cited in my Sources. • The December 1, 2014, *Daily Beast* story said the Twitter traffic for "Bill Cosby" had been running at a thousand to fifteen hundred mentions a day and spiked to nine thousand mentions when Cosby's website started the meme generator.

CHAPTER 13

Prior to canceling the *Letterman* appearance, Cosby had also postponed an appearance on Queen Latifah. • Cosby talks about how he started their collection of African American art in Whitaker's book. • The exhibit became so controversial after Cosby's deposition was released that the museum was forced to post a disclaimer about it on the website. It said, "The National Museum of African Art is aware of the recent revelations about Bill Cosby's behavior. The museum in no way condones this behavior. Our current 'Conversations' exhibition, which includes works of African art from our permanent collection and African American art from the collection of Camille and Bill Cosby, is fundamentally about the artworks and the artists who created them, not the owners of the collections." • Castor made the comments about the other accusers to Lisa DePaulo from *Bloomberg*, a story I cite in my Sources. • My interview with Tamara in November 2014 is no longer on People.com, but I still had a copy of what I'd written. Joan's first interview was with the website Hollywood Elsewhere, cited above. I interviewed Joan Tarshis on November 18, 2014, and spoke with a friend of hers, who did not want his name made public, confirming she'd told him about the incident twenty years after it happened. I included those interviews for our cover story for the magazine as well. I also wove in details from the defamation lawsuit she filed against Cosby a year later. • I saw Schmitt's statement myself and included it in my November 19, 2018, story about Joan Tarshis. The

November 21, 2014, *Buzzfeed* story has a screenshot of the amended statement and text of the original Schmitt statement. It also has Singer's statement regarding Louisa Moritz in its entirety. The May 24, 2016, Eonline.com story has these statements as well. • Troiani told me in our August 6, 2018, interview that she never had any intention of weighing in on the new claims until Schmitt released that statement and posted it on Cosby's website. I have a copy of the letter she wrote Schmitt. His statement about Linda Joy Traitz and excerpts from her Facebook post are in Lizz Leonard's November 20, 2014, story. It is also in a November 21, 2014, *Bustle* story, which also includes his response to the Traitz allegations. I also still have printouts of some of them. • You can listen to Janice Dickinson's 2006 interview with Howard Stern at "Listen to Janice Dickinson Discuss Bill Cosby in 2006," Howard Stern, November 19, 2014, www.howardstern.com/news/2014/11/19/janice-dickinson-on-bill-cosby-in-2006. • I also wrote a story about Don Lemon's apology to Joan Tarshis, cited above. • The AP interview with Cosby is cited in the November 20, 2014, *CNN Money* story. The interview can be found at "Full Cosby Exchange with AP on Allegations," YouTube, November 19, 2014, www.youtube.com/watch?v=RI6z97Efw3I. Amanda Hess wrote about it for *Slate* on November 20, 2014. • I interviewed Beth Ferrier on November 21, 2014. • Singer sent that November 21, 2014, statement to the media. • The "rape is no joke" anecdote is from various media coverage cited above, including our cover story. Our reporter was there and said just two protesters showed up, which was in the cover story.

CHAPTER 14

Beth, who later ended her relationship with Allred, told me many times she had no idea Allred was going to ask for that fund to be created when she agreed to the December 3, 2014, press conference, which my former *People* colleague Christine Pelisek wrote about for People.com. Chelan testified about this at the second trial and told me that herself when we spoke on January 3, 2019. I reached out to Allred for comment. Via email on November 12, 2018, Allred said she could not answer this question about whether Beth or Chelan knew about the fund beforehand because it was attorney-client privilege and that she did not regret asking for it because "Mr. Cosby was convicted of 3 felonies and is now in prison." • I interviewed P. J. Masten myself on September 5, 2018. She sent me a photo of Cosby's note that came with the ficus tree on October 19, 2018. Cosby has never responded to P. J.'s allegations but the December 6, 2014, AP story noted P. J. was a surprise witness at the 1997 trial of sportscaster Marv Albert saying he tried to sexually assault her in a Dallas hotel room in 1994. Albert pleaded guilty to assault and battery the day after her testimony, but denied her accusations. • The information about the guests and the photos at the Los Angeles Playboy mansion are from the 2011 *Vanity Fair* story and the 2011 People.com story, cited in my Sources. Cosby also talks about his friendship with Hefner in the Whitaker book. P. J. told me Cosby stayed at the mansions in L.A. and Chicago. Other former bunnies did as well. • Frank Scotti, the ex-NBC employee, died five months after these interviews. He was ninety-one. • The RAINN spokeswoman's comment is from a press release I still had in my possession. Bill Bratton made those comments at a news conference in January 2016, referring to the previous year. The New York *Daily News* wrote a story, cited above, as did other media. • I interviewed Lindsey Pratt on July 12, 2018. I interviewed Mary Ellen O'Toole on January 26, 2018; July 18, 2018; September 21, 2018, and November 12, 2018. I also reference a study she wrote in my Sources and an article she cowrote on *Psychology Today*'s website. • I interviewed Tommy Lightfoot Garrett on July 11, 2018. • I interviewed Lili Bernard on July 12, 2018, and again on November 14, 2018. I also spoke with her throughout the second trial and the sentencing. You can watch her talk about the Quincy Jones text during deliberations for the first trial here on this video by the *Washington Post*: "Bill Cosby Accuser Speaks After Deadlock," YouTube, June 16, 2017, www.youtube.com/watch?v=aiQg_UoMoo8. CNN also played the clip on Ashleigh Banfield's show *Primetime with Ashleigh Banfield* on June 15, 2017. The transcript is in LexisNexis. • Cosby reveals how he met Quincy Jones in the Whitaker book. Reached by email on November 14, 2018, Quincy Jones's attorney told me he could not comment on the text. Joseph Cammarata subpoenaed Jones in Tamara Green's defamation lawsuit. • You can watch one of DL Hughley's interviews about this at "Flashback: DL Hughley on Calling Cosby a Rapist when Bill Called His Show," YouTube, April 29, 2018, www.youtube.com/watch?v=FUpRJuwPb8Y. He did not respond to requests for comments from me. • You can still find Whitaker's tweet to David Carr, dated November 24, 2014, 5:25 PM, https://twitter.com/marktwhitaker/status/537009180839014401.

CHAPTER 15

There was enormous media coverage of all three performances in Canada, Judd Apatow's tweets, the joke about the drink and the reaction to it, as well as his performances in Colorado. I cite all the stories in my Sources list. • The statements Cosby released before and after these performances, including the video he gave to ABC, were widely reported as well and are in the Sources I list. • As Cosby was being taunted by protesters in Canada, Bruce Castor, who'd been fielding questions and doing interviews about why he didn't charge Cosby in 2005, announced he was running to get his old job back as Montgomery County's district attorney. • The 1966 and 1964 *New York Times* stories I cite use the word "Negro" before his name. • Cosby talks about being audited, the FBI visits, phone tapping, hiring African Americans for his shows, and being on Nixon's master list in Whitaker's book. Camille Cosby also wrote about this in an op-ed after Cosby was sentenced to prison. • The quote from Lili Bernard about being contacted by people through her website is from my July 12, 2018, interview with her.

Joseph C. Phillips's blog post "Of Course Bill Cosby Is Guilty" has since been taken down from his website, but multiple news organizations published excerpts from it, which I cite in my Sources. • I reached out to him, Jewel Allison, and Beverly Johnson in the summer of 2018 via Lili Bernard, who is friends with all of them, but they declined to be interviewed. Jewel subsequently spoke with me on December 21, 2018. • You can watch Whoopi defend Cosby at "Whoopie Goldberg DEFENDS Bill Cosby Against RAPE Allegation on 'The View,'" YouTube, November 17, 2014, www.youtube.com/watch?v=oCon5BbfDdc. These comments got lots of media coverage as did comments by other African-American celebrities supporting Cosby. I've cited some in my Sources. • RAINN says not every hospital has someone who can perform a sexual assault forensic exam here: https://www.rainn.org/

articles/rape-kit. The August 2018 Reuters story I cite in my Sources has the statistics about how many women complete a rape kit and how many agree to release that information to police. In addition, Jen Pierce-Weeks, the chief executive officer of the International Association of Forensic Nurses, told me only 16 percent of hospitals have SANE nurses, who are specially trained to deal with sexual assault victims and can also conduct rape kits. You can find more rape kit statistics at "Evidence Ignored, Inaccessible—Rape Kits," National Organization for Women, New York City, http://nownyc.org/violence-against-women/evidence-ignored/. • You can also find rape kit statistics at "Statistics," Natasha's Justice Project, https://natashas justiceproject.org/about/statistics/, as well as "Untested Evidence in Sexual Assault Cases," National Institute of Justice, www.nij.gov/topics/law-enforcement/investi gations/sexual-assault/Pages/untested-sexual-assault.aspx. • Camille Cosby's comments to *American Visions* magazine were mentioned in the June 2010 bio of her in *Contemporary Black Biography*, which I found in LexisNexis under "Biographies." Her education history is there as well. Her statement in defense of her husband in December 2014 has been on many media accounts, including ones I cite in my Sources. • Bill Cosby discusses buying a home in Massachusetts and Camille living there with the kids in the Whitaker biography. • Phylicia Rashad's "Forget these women" quotes were originally reported by *Showbiz 411*'s Roger Friedman, but when she said they were taken out of context he admitted he misinterpreted them and ran a clarification.

CHAPTER 16

Therese spoke with a local radio and TV station (https://www.youtube.com/watch ?v=dcwfMHQWL_0&feature=youtu.be&fbclid=IwAR0XeHWllmly6b-eGfKzYULr PyZHvl-s2eI-OSd2NUv5qv568Au7_PKL8iM) then the *Huffington Post*, a story I cite above. Cosby described Therese as "passive" in his deposition. Cosby was asked about each of the Jane Does in his deposition. For Donna he said he'd met a lot of waitresses at the Trident Restaurant and used to go there about four or five times a year but that he did not remember her. He said he met Jo Farrell (who represented Beth Ferrier and Barbara Bowman) and her partner, Annie Maloney, when he performed at Turn of the Century, a nightclub in Denver, but he did not have an arrangement with her to send him models. He did not remember Kristina Ruehli. • I interviewed Patricia Steuer and her husband on July 30, 2018. I also interviewed her friend on July 31, 2018, and she verified she told them about this long before 2005; and her sister, whom I interviewed on July 31, 2018, verified Cosby called their house once and she answered the phone. In his deposition Cosby said he didn't know who she was, even after reading the statement she'd given Troiani. • In 2017 Therese posted on Facebook that she had agreed to do an interview and photo shoot with *People* in 2006 but it was not included in our story. I did not know that. • Kristina Ruehli first told her story to Phillymag.com on November 21, 2014, then us. And I interviewed her on July 9, 2018. • Cosby talks in Whitaker's book about the celebrity tennis tournaments he hosted. There was other coverage I cite as well, including *Adweek*, where I found an old flyer for the O. J. Simpson match from 1981, and *Jet* magazine. • The info about Cosby staying at the Las Vegas Hilton and who he was billed with is from Whitaker's book. The description of the Elvis Presley suite is from Bob Greene's 1989 column. • The *Los Angeles Times*'s fifty-year history of accusations story says Cosby got his star on the Hollywood Walk of Fame in 1977. The other biographical details are from the Whitaker book. • I interviewed Sammie Mays on October 1, 2018. She first spoke out at a May 1, 2015 news conference with Allred and Lili Bernard, which various media outlets covered, including the *Huffington Post*, whose story I cite in my Source list. Sammie's statement can be found here: https://www.gloriaallred.com/Gloria-s-Videos-and-Statements/Bill-Cosby-05 -01-15-Statement-of-Sammie-Mays.pdf. • I interviewed Tony Costantino on September 28, 2018. • I interviewed Trinka Porrata on September 5, 2018. • The 1983 AP story I cite above has the stats on Quaalude deaths. • RAINN info on preserving evidence for drug-facilitated sexual assaults can be found at "Drug-Facilitated Sexual Assault," RAINN, www.rainn.org/articles/drug-facilitated-sexual-assault. • Project GHB info is available at "Drug Rape," Project GHB, www.projectghb.org/drug-rape. • CNN covered the Lili Bernard/Brandy Betts/Jennifer Thompson disruption at Cosby's concert in Atlanta. • I wrote about him stepping down from the Temple Board of Trustees, and we included the High Point development in our cover story.

CHAPTER 17

I got all the biographical info on Robreno from the Winter 2013 *Philadelphia Lawyer* story. • You can read Robreno's decision at "Case 2:05-cv-01099-ER," Document Cloud, www.documentcloud.org/documents/2158930-cosby-order.html. • I have copies of the unsealed documents and Cosby's entire deposition. • The July 7, 2015, *Time* story embedded Jill Scott's tweets. • You can watch Whoopi walk back her support after talking to Dan Abrams at "Whoopi Goldberg Discusses Bill Cosby's Allegations with ABC News' Dan Abrams," YouTube, July 14, 2015, www.youtube.com/watch?v=IoHrUtURyes. • I interviewed Joseph Cammarata on July 12, 2018. • The other quote from him is from an interview I did with him on July 6, 2015, for a story I posted on People.com that same day. • I spoke with Becky Cooper, who was referred to as Rebecca Lynn Neal in various news accounts, on October 22, 2018. I also spoke with her husband, whom she told what happened, as well as her friend and her sister on November 10, 2018. In his deposition Cosby said he played tennis at the health club where she said she worked but did not remember Becky or recall any of the circumstances she described. • You can see a photo of Cosby with O. J. Simpson at "Bill Cosby," Getty Images, www.gettyimages.ca/detail /news-photo/comedian-bill-cosby-chats-with-o-j-simpson-at-his-celebrity-news -photo/139000866. • An ad for the Princess Grace tennis tournament can be found at "Classic Film: 1974 Fashion Ad, Vogue, Wear-Dated by Monsanto, Featuring Princess Grace, Bill Cosby, Lloyd Bridges," flickr, www.flickr.com/photos/29069717@ No2/28356208532. • *Adweek* did a story about Cosby, the Playboy bunnies, O. J., and the tennis tournament in June 2015. • Whitaker's book talks about Cosby's celebrity tennis tournaments. • You can see a photo of Cosby and Farrah Fawcett at a tournament at "Golden Girl: Farrah Fawcett," *Daily Beast*, June 24, 2009, www.the dailybeast.com/golden-girl-farrah-fawcett. • The *Los Angeles Times* covered the tournaments as well as *Jet*. All are cited above. • I was writing about all of these filings—disco biscuits, Andrea Constand's sexual orientation—on People.com. I also cite the original AP story in my Sources. The information about Dr. Amar came later, after reporters got the entire deposition. During Cosby's deposition Troiani asked him if he knew Andrea was gay. "No. I don't know," he responded. "The answer is I don't know if she's gay. What is gay? To me gay is a woman who is with women. But then again there are women who can be bisexual." The subject came up after Cosby gave his account of what he said happened between he and Andrea in January 2004, the night in question. He said he and Andrea had a phone conversation once, during which Andrea told him she was interested in a woman, "some sort of celebrity."

That night in mid-January 2004, he said, he told Andrea to "imagine that you are with her and that she is with you and just enjoy yourself. I am going upstairs." • Troiani is having a hard time grasping when this other conversation occurred, prompting Cosby to say, "One of the greatest storytellers in the world, and I'm failing." • He then gives a graphic description of what he said happened between them sexually that evening. Troiani also responded to the now-infamous "disco biscuits" filing by O'Connor with one of her own asking for the confidentiality agreement to be lifted. "Plaintiff sits quietly listening to descriptions fed to the media of celebrity parties and 'disco biscuits,' knowing that she never attended a celebrity party or requested to take a disco biscuit (or even heard of that term for that matter)," she wrote. Cosby retaliated by saying he wanted the settlement back if so. • The quote from Troiani is from my August 6, 2018, interview with her. I was so shocked about Andrea's sexual orientation finally being made public I didn't want to write about the filing until I confirmed with Troiani that it was OK, given the discussion we'd had in 2005. I knew it had to be, since it was a public document, but I wanted to be doubly sure given how sensitive the topic was. Troiani, of course, knew exactly what she was doing. • I did my own story for People.com about the investigation being opened on September 22, 2015, and had a copy of the open letter to Castor. I also included a screenshot of Castor's Facebook post.

CHAPTER 18

I covered this race for People.com, writing several stories about it. The quotes here are from those stories. • The Troiani quotes are from an October 26, 2015, interview I did with her for my People.com story about the defamation lawsuit. • I got that statement from Castor's campaign. • The quote from Troiani about Andrea being afraid is from an October 26, 2015, interview I did with her for an exclusive story I got about Andrea threatening to withdraw from the criminal investigation if Castor won. It posted on October 27, 2015. • The Joseph Cammarata quote about why he filed defamation lawsuits is from a July 12, 2018, interview with him. • Peggy Gibbon's story also ran in the *Intelligencer* in Bucks County. • Tamara's quotes are from an October 29, 2015, exclusive interview with her for People.com that posted that same day. By then the accuser total was actually past 60 so I amended Tamara's quote to reflect that figure. All of the women's accounts are in the defamation lawsuit, which I used to fact-check. The *Washington Post* story I reference is the one from November 23, 2014. • The Steele quote is from my November 4, 2015, People .com story. I used the quote from the November 4, 2015, *Inquirer* story. I got the Castor quote from his public Facebook page, where he posted it. • I wrote about Angela Leslie and Louisa Moritz joining the suit on November 13, 2015. I interviewed Kristina Ruehli on June 27, 2016, after she withdrew her lawsuit. • My former colleague at *People*, Chris Harris, wrote a story about the counter defamation lawsuits. • Beverly Johnson's statement was in a December 22, 2015, CNN story. • When Janice went public with her sexual assault story on November 18, 2015, Cosby's team released this statement: "Janice Dickinson's story accusing Bill Cosby of rape is a lie." • I've counted and recounted the number of accusers and came up with 63 as of December 2015. I included those who allowed their photo and at least their first name to be used and all of the original Jane Does, whether they had gone public yet or not.

CHAPTER 19

All the details about the case and the press conference are from my own notes and stories as well as the documents themselves. • In Cosby's deposition Troiani says Wiederlight told police in 2005 he had made similar travel arrangements for Cosby five to seven times in the past year. • I got the details about the arraignment and so forth from a *People* stringer, Diane Herbst, who covered it for us while I was writing another story about the arrest. • There is also plenty of video out there showing his arrival. We included Cosby's statement, which he also gave to CNN, in Diane's story. • The details about how Andrea was taking it come from her victim-impact statement from September 24, 2018. • My former colleague, Greg Hanlon, wrote about the motion on January 11, 2015. • I covered the two days of hearings about Castor on February 2 and 3, 2016. These quotes from Castor and Troiani are all from the testimony. • Ferman's letter to Castor saying she had no idea what he was talking about when he said the press release was an immunity agreement is an exhibit on the criminal case website for those hearings.

CHAPTER 20

The New Year's Eve 2015 People.com story was written by Christine Pelisek. • The ongoing dispute over Camille being deposed was covered by myself and Diane Herbst, a *People* stringer, stories I cite above. • I still have Andrew Wyatt's statement about race and Allred in September 2016. I wrote about it as well. • Stories about the Cosby accusers and the various statute of limitations extensions in Nevada, California, and Colorado are cited above. • The quote from Kristen Houser is from my September 3, 2018, interview with her. • The information about the Little Bill books being among the most banned can be found at "New Report Chronicles Library Community's Front Line Battles Against Fake News, Censorship, Bigotry," ALA, April 10, 2017, www.ala.org/news/press-releases/2017/04/new-report-chronicles-library-community-s-front-line-battles-against-fake. • The list didn't come out until April 2017. • You can still read Evin's statement on her father's Facebook page, dated April 26, 2017, at www.facebook.com/billcosby/posts/statement-from-evin-cosbyi-am-the-youngest-of-5-i-remember-our-family-trips-and-/10154900737544930/. • I wrote about her statement and Cosby's interview on People.com. AOL wrote about Ensa's statement. I was not at jury selection, so I cite a *Washington Post* story about the race issue. • My exclusive about the very special guest on the first day of trial is listed above.

CHAPTER 21

I was at this trial every day so anything I quote from this trial in this chapter and the next is from my own notes and what I describe is what I saw myself. You can also read the transcripts on the Bill Cosby criminal case website. I verified the courthouse history and the background on the portrait in the courtroom with court personnel. Anything happening outside the courtroom I didn't see myself is from news articles cited in my Sources or something I confirmed by looking at photos. You can read more about who the 13 women were that prosecutors wanted to testify and what Cosby's defense said about their allegations in the December 13, 2016, AP story I cite in my Sources list. Or the documents are on the Cosby criminal case website. • Pulliam's career details can be found at "Keshia Knight Pulliam," IMDb, www.imdb .com/name/nm0700443/. • Andrew Wyatt told me some of the men who showed up to support Cosby were comedians Cosby had mentored. A CNN story I cite explained more about who they are. • I didn't see a lot of things, like Cosby's tweet or his "Hey hey hey," until long after the trial was over because we couldn't be online while court was in session and the breaks were so short. NBC cameras captured his "Hey hey hey" moment: www.nbcnews.com/video/cosby-says-hey-hey-hey-to-spectators -while-leaving-court-961626179635?v=raila&. • You can still see Cosby's tweet about Pulliam on his Twitter feed, dated June 5, 2017, 1:25 PM, https://twitter.com/bill cosby/status/871779973350047744?lang=en. • I included the Gene Grabowski and former prosecutor interviews in this story at https://people.com/crime/bill-cosby- sexual-assault-trial-begins-monday-how-he-went-from-americas-dad-to-defendant/. • I got these details about McMonagle's past from the 2011 profile of him in the *Philadelphia Inquirer* article I cite, which also ran in the *Pittsburgh Post Gazette*. Mc- Moncale confirmed these details and others with me via email on January 2, 2019. • I wrote a story about McMonagle throwing the fundraiser for Castor, cited above. McMonagle also donated $2,500 to Castor's 2015 campaign. • The news stories and a press release for these various accolades and the Kodak and E. F. Hutton jobs are cited in my Sources section. • The *Wall Street Journal* reported he was trying to buy NBC with the investors, which got picked up everywhere. Nikki Finke did a big piece about it for *Vanity Fair*, which I cite above. • Cosby did an interview with *Newsweek* in 1993 in which he talked about the poor way TV writers and producers depicted blacks. That interview took place soon after his bid to buy NBC failed.

CHAPTER 22

Meloy coauthored the Icon Intimidation article on PsychologyToday.com with O'Toole. He sent me those comments via email on September 4, 2018. • Both of Kristen Houser's blog entries were emailed to me. Online it shows the author as Lauren Palumbo, but Houser wrote these she told me on November 8, 2018. • While Cosby did admit to giving "women" he wanted to have sex with Quaaludes in his deposition, he quickly amended it to make the word singular after his attorney interjected. The questions Anita Hill were asked are from a September 2018 CBS story I cite in my Sources. Cosby's defense team had even unsuccessfully tried to introduce evidence of Andrea's sexual orientation, something the prosecution re- acted to with outrage, calling it "victim shaming" and arguing it would violate the state's rape shield law. I include an NBC article about it in my Sources.

CHAPTER 23

That first quote from O'Neill comes from an article in the *Reporter Online* about his swearing in. • The drug court information comes from the 2017 *Montgomery News* article I cite. • NBC10 in Philadelphia did a story about the NOW demonstration. • You can watch Andrew Wyatt read Margo Jackson's statement at "Andrew Wyatt Reads Statement from Marguerite Jackson; A Witness Rejected from Bill Cosby Case," YouTube, June 13, 2017, www.youtube.com/watch?v=NWY5h5NCiMs. • You can watch his comments about the jury deadlock at "'Put an End to It Right Now': Cosby's Spox Andrew Wyatt," YouTube, June 15, 2017, www.youtube.com/watch?v=Xgv4DVsg9Mo&t=82s. • Diana Moskovitz wrote about Wyatt and Jewel Allison for *Jezebel*, which is where these details came from; the stories are cited in my Sources. Laura McCrystal also blogged about it on Philly.com. I then interviewed Jewel myself on December 21, 2018. • Troiani told me what Steele said to her in my August 6, 2018, interview with her. • Camille's statement was everywhere. Moskovitz posted it in her mistrial story. • Eli Segal sent me these quotes via email on September 5, 2018. • The interviews and quotes from the jurors are from the ABC, Philly.com/*Philadelphia Inquirer*, CNN, and Associated Press stories cited above. • You can watch Andrew Wyatt and Ebonee Benson's interview with *Good Morning Alabama* about the sexual assault tour at "Bill Cosby to Do Town Halls to Teach Men How to Avoid Sexual Assault Accusations," YouTube, June 22, 2017, www.youtube.com/watch?v=uxYn7EuM_LE. • Ebonee Benson and Andrew Wyatt defend the town halls, saying it's not a sexual assault tour, at "Bill Cosby's Publicists Defend Town Halls," CNN, June 25, 2017, www.cnn.com/videos/us/2017/06/25/cosbys-publicists-defend-town-halls.cnn. Cosby saying there would be no such tour is in a June 27, 2017, CNN story, cited above. It's from a statement issued by Wyatt. • I freelanced for *People* for more than a year before being put on staff in September 2006. • Alyssa Milano's #MeToo tweet was on October 15, 2017. • The AP and *Vox* ran a list of the men who have been accused; the AP lists how many accused them. Both are cited above.

CHAPTER 24

While I found these women in late 2017 and they agreed to do interviews then, I did not do formal interviews with them until later. • I interviewed Jane Doe Number Three on May 15, 2018, and again on September 4, 2018. She withdrew her participation in a September 6, 2018, email. • I interviewed Patte O'Connor on May 17, 2018. • I interviewed Virginia Bennett on May 14, 2018, and July 30, 2018. • I interviewed Denise Ferrari on May 22, 2018. • I interviewed Beth Ferrier about Ferrari on May 15, 2018. • I interviewed Tony Hogue on May 17, 2018. • I wrote a story about Jane Doe Number Eight that ran on June 11, 2005, and is listed in my Sources. The *Daily Beast* story about her, which doesn't mention her name, is also listed there.

CHAPTER 25

A copy of the video of Cosby's La Veranda dinner was sent to reporters, including me, which is where I got the details of the exchanges Cosby had with diners and reporters. • Laura McCrystal from the *Inquirer* only used part of the quote in her story. She told the rest of it on WHYY's podcast *Cosby Unraveled.* • I began covering the Cosby case for the *Daily Beast* in March 2018 and wrote an analysis/walk-up piece that posted on March 5, 2018. Grabowski's quote is from that piece. I was present at all of the hearings and for jury selection, the trial, sentencing, and so on, so this is all from my reporting, but the transcripts are all publicly available as well, which I used to double check my own reporting. You can find all the stories on my website. • I cite the *Daily Beast*'s Lynda Carter story in my Sources. • Moskovitz's stories are cited above. More recently Castor signed a sworn affidavit to help Cosby appeal his sentence and conviction. That document was first released to Stacy Brown of BlackPress USA for a story that posted on October 23, 2018 (cited in my Sources), then sent to the rest of the media that same day from Wyatt, Cosby's publicist. • Castor's defamation lawsuit against Andrea was dismissed on April 5, 2018. He later filed an appeal, then withdrew it in late October 2018. Andrea settled her defamation lawsuit against him in January 2019 with a confidentiality agreement. • I have the screenshot of Castor's Facebook rant against the media from late December 2015. I cite a story in Philadelphia's *Metro* about Castor's Facebook post. Laura McCrystal also cited it in her August 2016 profile of Castor. • Cosby put these videos on his Twitter page, dated January 21, 2018, 9:54 AM, https://twitter.com/billcosby/status/955091273203027968?fbclid=IwAR3ML1m9e2qmaU6cgFesbmcjBEzHjeKpiiT5aS8r8eZaByriPxH81CmrC78. Many outlets wrote about them as well. I mentioned them in my March 5, 2018, story for the *Daily Beast.* • Andrew Wyatt sent me Cosby's statement about Ensa's death. • Steele's memo with the RAINN statistics is on the Cosby criminal case website. • The February 12, 2016, AP story I cite in my Sources gives details of each of the allegations by the 19 women the prosecution wanted to testify and the defense team's response to them. The documents themselves are publicly available on the Cosby criminal case website. • The exact amount Andrea received in her settlement with Cosby became public for the first time on April 9, 2018, in Steele's opening argument. • Though the topless protester outside the courthouse occurred while I was inside the courtroom, we were told about it during our five-hour break as we waited for the trial to start and given a news release from the DA about how she was being charged. I included it in my wrap-up story that evening. • The quotes from her and from Wyatt come from the AP stories cited in my Sources.

CHAPTER 26

The 2012 Charles Thompson story explains the law change after Sandusky. • Lana Morelli wrote about the sexual assault expert from the first trial's Facebook post, a story I cite above. • You can read all of Dr. Ziv's testimony on the Cosby criminal case's website. • With Chelan I wove in some details of her story from our January 3, 2019, interview. • My former colleague, Jeff Truesdell, wrote about Cosby's Ennis tweet, a story I list in my Sources. • Cosby's FBI work was covered by the *LA Times* in 1985, while the Associated Press covered his testimony on behalf of the poor in 1982. His attempt to purchase the ABC station was covered by the *New York Times* in 1985. All articles are cited in my Sources section. • Cosby's friendship with Bill Harrah and his purchase of one of his Rolls Royces was in Whitaker's book. • I cite a story about The Cosby Show being number one five years in a row in my Sources.

CHAPTER 27

Andrew Wyatt's encounter with Allred can be seen at www.youtube.com/watch?v =kXoMDtZpbBw. • Others with he and Eonee Benson can be found on Bill Cosby's Facebook page, www.facebook.com/billcosby, and Bobby Allyn's Twitter feed in tweets dated April 11, 2018, 6:31 PM, https://twitter.com/BobbyAllyn/status /984197188640178176, and April 18, 2018, 5:26 PM, https://twitter.com/BobbyAllyn /status/986717551508979712. I asked Andrew Wyatt how he came to work for Cosby and if the stories about him I cite in my Sources were accurate and he emailed me this reply on October 10, 2018. "Nicole, Unfortunately, I can't participate due to my book that will include 'exclusive' interviews with the Cosbys, family members, friends and fellow entertainers. Kindest Regards."

CHAPTER 28

I interviewed Dianne Scelza on July 23, 2018. I interviewed Cheryl Carmel on July 29, 2018. • Stephanie Shaffer, another juror, did not want to do an actual interview but did send me comments via email on August 23, 2018. She concurred with what Scelza and Carmel said. She said she did not believe Margo Jackson because there were no travel records for her during the time she said she shared a room with Andrea, that they all found Andrea credible, that "she told the truth," that Cosby's own words convinced her he was guilty, and that the jury talked everything out and came to the verdict together. • You can watch Andrew Wyatt and Ebonee Benson's *Good Morning America* interview here: https://abcnews.go.com/GMA/ Culture/video/cosby-supporters-react-verdict-54775268. • The *New York Times* had a story on April 26 with the headline "Did the #MeToo Movement Sway the Cosby Jury?" which I cite in my Sources. • Camille Cosby's statement can be found on her husband's Facebook page, dated May 3, 2018, www.facebook.com/billcosby/ posts/official-statement-from-camille-o-cosbywe-the-people-are-the-first-three- words-o/10155902546254930/. • The exoneration statistics come from the March 2017 National Registry of Exonerations study. • The income information comes from the most recent statistics at "Income and Poverty in the United States 2017," US Census Bureau, www.census.gov/library/publications/2018/demo/p60-263.html, and the higher education statement is supported by data at "Completing College— National by Race and Ethnicity—2017," National Student Clearinghouse Research Center, https://nscresearchcenter.org/signaturereport12-supplement-2/. • The criminal justice statistics come from the NAACP's "Criminal Justice Fact Sheet, www .naacp.org/criminal-justice-fact-sheet/, and "Demographic Differences in Sentenc- ing," United States Sentencing Commission, www.ussc.gov/research/research- reports/demographic-differences-sentencing. • The statistics about how many rapes and attempted rapes end with convictions, incarceration, and so on come from "The Criminal Justice System: Statistics," RAINN, www.rainn.org/statistics/ criminal-justice-system, which are also included in a *Washington Post* story I cite in my Sources.

CHAPTER 29

The exact name for Cosby's diagnosis by Kristen Dudley is Other Specified Para- philic Disorder: Non-consenting women. You can read her full report on the Cosby criminal case website. • I did a follow-up interview with Tamara Green on September 27, 2018. • Stories about Camille's ethics board complaint are cited in my Sources. • I interviewed Stewart Ryan on October 1, 2018. • The additional quotes and details from Chelan are from my January 3, 2019, interview with her.

EPILOGUE

You can listen to Andrew Wyatt's comments at www.youtube.com/watch?v=1s9 naq6hsJs. • Ebonee Benson reads Camille Cosby's statement at www.youtube.com /watch?v=Gb3T951vB_U. • DL Hughley's posts are on his Facebook page, dated September 29, 2018, www.facebook.com/RealDLHughley/posts/proof-justice-is-for-justus-teamdl/2661582520550735/, and on his Instagram feed, dated September 25, 2018, www.instagram.com/p/BoKjdtOBdT7/?utm_source=ig_twitter_share &igshid=kjtgm9i5chy1. • Giorgis also references them in her column. • I was at the press conference with Sunni Welles, Stacey Pinkerton, Lili Bernard, and some of the other women. Stacey reached out to me three months later to tell me her full story, which she did on December 28, 2018. She also sent me the statement she gave law enforcement. She was one of the 13 Jane Doe witnesses prosecutors wanted to testify at the first trial and one of the 19 for the second trial. Those documents can be found on the Cosby criminal trial website. • A friend sent me the press release about the Television Critics Award being rescinded. • The Troiani quote is from my August 6, 2018, interview with her. • I confirmed all the information about Cosby's incarceration with the Pennsylvania Department of Corrections.